On Theology

EXPLORATIONS AND
CONTROVERSIES

On

Theology

EXPLORATIONS AND
CONTROVERSIES

On Theology

EXPLORATIONS AND
CONTROVERSIES

JOHN M. FRAME

LEXHAM PRESS

To Randy Greenwald

But one thing I do: forgetting what lies behind and straining forward to what lies ahead, I press on toward the goal for the prize of the upward call of God in Christ Jesus. Let those of us who are mature think this way, and if in anything you think otherwise, God will reveal that also to you. Only let us hold true to what we have attained. Brothers, join in imitating me, and keep your eyes on those who walk according to the example you have in us.

—Philippians 3:13b–17

Table of Contents

Preface xi

Abbreviations xiii

PART 1: THEOLOGICAL METHOD

1. Thirty Maxims for Theologians 3
2. Beginnings of Theological Papers. 9
3. Two Kinds of Theologians. 15
4. Three Theological Tasks. 19
5. *Theology in Three Dimensions*:
   A Summary by the Author 23
6. Theological Education (2 Timothy 2:1–2) 25
7. Review of Anthony Thiselton's *Systematic Theology* 35
8. Foreword to *Scripture and the People of God* 41
9. Preface to *Redeeming the Life of the Mind* 49
10. Traditionalism 57

PART 2: THE THOMIST CONTROVERSY

11. Letter to a Friend about the Thomist Challenge. 75
12. Calvinism, Arminianism, and Thomism 79
13. Why I Am Not a Thomist 81
14. Two Models of Transcendence: Pure Being vs. Divine Lordship. . 89
15. Scholasticism for Evangelicals: Thoughts on *All That Is in God*
    by James Dolezal. 101
16. Scholasticism and Biblical Personalism 119
17. Scholasticism and Creation 127
18. Scholasticism and the Gospel 131

PART 3: SYSTEMATIC THEOLOGY

19. Foreword to *What All Christians Believe and Why: A Contemporary Guide to the Historic Faith,* by H. David Schuringa 137
20. Scripture as a Divine Book 139
21. Is Scripture's Self-Attestation Sufficient? 141
22. Let God Be True 155
23. Canine Intelligence and the Incomprehensibility of God 177
24. The Gospel in an Image . . . . : 181
25. Resurrection Joy 183
26. Arminianism 187
27. Shepherd's View of Justification 191

PART 4: ESSAYS FROM *LEXHAM SURVEY OF THEOLOGY*

28. Unwritten Special Revelation 195
29. Revelation in Creation 199
30. Revelation in Conscience 203
31. The Bible 207
32. Inspiration 211
33. Authority 213
34. Truthfulness 215
35. Canon 219
36. Necessity 223
37. Sufficiency 227
38. Clarity 231
39. Interpretation 235
40. Translation 239
41. Prophecy 243

PART 5: ESSAYS FROM THE GOSPEL COALITION'S *CONCISE THEOLOGY*

42. Divine Revelation:
    God Making Himself Known 249
43. Divine Transcendence and Immanence 257
44. The Sovereignty of God 265
45. Divine Sovereignty and Human Freedom 269

46. Openness Theology and Divine Omniscience 277

47. God the Creator 285

48. Narrative Theology. 291

49. Analytic Theology. 297

PART 6: PHILOSOPHY AND APOLOGETICS

50. Apologetics. 305

51. Believing in Jesus in the First Century 309

52. Post-Truth and Chaos. 313

53. Presuppositionalism and Perspectivalism .317

54. Ten Problems with Presuppositionalism 335

55. Cornelius Van Til 341

56. Transcendental Argument 355

57. My Last Word on the Van Til Controversy. 357

58. Foreword to *Thinking through Creation*, by Chris Watkin 359

59. Interview with Dave Moore on
    History of Western Philosophy and Theology 363

60. Introduction to My Logos Courses. 367

61. Introduction to *History of Western Philosophy and Theology*
    (Korean translation) 369

62. Doubt, Skepticism, and Faith 371

63. Mystery 377

PART 7: ETHICS AND POLITICS

64. The First Commandment: Living for a Person 383

65. Foreword to Mike Milton, *Foundations of a Moral Government* . . 393

66. Review of *We Cannot Be Silent* by R. Albert Mohler, Jr. 397

67. When We Have No Recourse 401

68. Why I Signed the Nashville Statement. 407

69. Review of Douglas Groothuis's *Walking through Twilight:*
    A Wife's Illness—A Philosopher's Lament. 409

70. Diet, Theology, and Medicine. 411

71. The Priority of Medicine 415

72. Being on Jesus's Side 419

PART 8: PERSONAL REFLECTIONS

73. 1 Thessalonians 1 and Church Planting:
    Charge at Ross Meyer's Ordination 423
74. Blurbs... 427
75. Interview with *Theology for Life* Magazine.................... 431
76. Thoughts on My Friendship with Steve Hays................. 435

Permissions 441

Index of Subjects & Authors................................. 443

Index of Scripture 453

Preface

This is the fourth volume of my *Selected Shorter Writings*. Most of these have been written between 2015 and the present. The first three volumes were published by P&R Publishers.

I have dedicated this volume to Randy Greenwald, pastor of Covenant Presbyterian Church of Oviedo, who has been our family's pastor for most of the last decade. I am thankful to God for Randy's gentleness and kindness and for his thoughtful preaching ministry to us.

Abbreviations

ACC	*The Academic Captivity of Theology*
AGG	*Apologetics to the Glory of God*
CC	*Christianity Considered*
CVT	*Cornelius Van Til: An Analysis of His Thought*
CWM	*Contemporary Worship Music: A Biblical Defense*
DCL	*The Doctrine of the Christian Life*
DG	*The Doctrine of God*
DKG	*The Doctrine of the Knowledge of God*
DWG	*The Doctrine of the Word of God*
ER	*Evangelical Reunion: Denominations and the One Body of Christ*
ESV	English Standard Version
HWPT	*History of Western Philosophy and Theology*
KJV	King James Version
NCG	*Nature's Case for God*
NIV	New International Version
NOG	*No Other God*
NT	New Testament
OT	Old Testament
SBL	*Salvation Belongs to the Lord*
SSW1	*Selected Shorter Writings 1*
SSW2	*Selected Shorter Writings 2*
SSW3	*Selected Shorter Writings 3*
ST	*Systematic Theology*
TTD	*Theology in Three Dimensions*

WAAP	*We Are All Philosophers*
WCF	Westminster Confession of Faith
WLC	Westminster Larger Catechism
WSC	Westminster Shorter Catechism
WST	*Worship in Spirit and Truth*
WTJ	*Westminster Theological Journal*

PART 1

Theological Method

1

Thirty Maxims for Theologians

IN RESPONSE to the question, "What advice would you offer to theological students and young theologians as they face a lifetime of theological work?" I gave the following thirty-point answer:

1. Consider that you might not really be called to theological work. James 3:1 tells us that not many of us should become teachers and that teachers will be judged more strictly. To whom much (biblical knowledge) is given, of them shall much be required.

2. Value your relationship with Christ, your family, and the church above your career ambitions. You will influence more people by your life than by your theology. And deficiencies in your life will negate the influence of your ideas, even if those ideas are true.

3. Remember that the fundamental work of theology is to understand the Bible, God's word, and apply it to the needs of people. Everything else—historical and linguistic expertise, exegetical acuteness and subtlety, knowledge of contemporary culture, and philosophical sophistication—must be subordinated to that fundamental goal. If it is not, you may be acclaimed as a historian, linguist, philosopher, or critic of culture, but you will not be a theologian.

4. In doing the work of theology (the fundamental work, #3), you have an obligation to make a case for what you advocate. That should be obvious, but most theologians today haven't a clue as to how to do it. Theology is an argumentative discipline, and you need to know enough about logic and persuasion to construct arguments that are valid, sound, and persuasive. In theology, it's not enough to display knowledge of history, culture, or some other knowledge. Nor is it enough to quote people you agree with and reprobate people you don't agree with. You actually have to make a theological case for what you say.

5. Learn to write and speak clearly and cogently. The best theologians are able to take profound ideas and present them in simple language. Don't try to persuade people of your expertise by writing in opaque prose.

6. Cultivate an intense devotional life and ignore people who criticize this as pietistic. Pray without ceasing. Read the Bible, not just as an academic text. Treasure opportunities to worship in chapel services and prayer meetings, as well as on Sunday. Give attention to your "spiritual formation," however you understand that.

7. A theologian is essentially a preacher, though he typically deals with more arcane subjects than preachers do. But be a good preacher. Find some way to make your theology speak to the hearts of people. Find a way to present your teaching so that people hear God's voice in it.

8. Be generous with your resources. Spend time talking to students, prospective students, and inquirers. Give away books and articles. Don't be tightfisted when it comes to copyrighted materials; grant copy permission to anybody who asks for it. Ministry first, money second.

9. In criticizing other theologians, traditions, or movements, follow biblical ethics. Don't say that somebody is a heretic unless you have a very good case. Don't throw around terms like "another gospel." (People who teach another gospel are under God's curse.) Don't destroy people's reputations by misquoting them, quoting them out of context, or

taking their words in the worst possible sense. Be gentle and gracious unless you have irrefutable reasons for being harsh.

10. When there is a controversy, don't get on one side right away. Do some analytical work first, on both positions. Consider these possibilities: (a) that the two parties may be looking at the same issue from different perspectives, so they don't really contradict; (b) that both parties are overlooking something that could have brought them together; (c) that they are talking past one another because they use terms in different ways; (d) that there is a third alternative that is better than either of the opposing views and that might bring them together; (e) that their differences, though genuine, ought both to be tolerated in the church, like the differences between vegetarians and meat-eaters in Romans 14.

11. If you get a bright idea, don't expect everybody to get it right away. Don't immediately start a faction to promote it. Don't revile those who haven't come to appreciate your thinking. Reason gently with them, recognizing that you could be wrong and arrogant to boot.

12. Don't be reflexively critical of everything that comes out of a different tradition. Be humble enough to consider that other traditions may have something to teach you. Be teachable before you start teaching them. Take the beam out of your own eye.

13. Be willing to reexamine your own tradition with a critical eye. It is unreasonable to think that any single tradition has all the truth or is always right. And unless theologians develop critical perspectives on their own denominations and traditions, the reunion of the body of Christ will never take place. Don't be one of those theologians who are known mainly for trying to make Arminians become Calvinists (or vice versa).

14. See confessional documents in proper perspective. It is the work of theology, among other things, to rethink the doctrines of the confessions and to reform them, when necessary, by the word of God. Do not assume that everything in the confession is forever settled.

15. Don't let your polemics be governed by jealousy, as when a theologian feels bound to be entirely negative toward the success of a megachurch.

16. Don't become known as a theologian who constantly takes potshots at other theologians or other Christians. The enemy is Satan, the world, and the flesh.

17. Guard your sexual instincts. Stay away from internet pornography and illicit relationships. Theologians are not immune from the sins that plague others in the church.

18. Be active in a good church. Theologians need the means of grace as much as other believers. This is especially important when you are studying at a secular university or liberal seminary. You need the support of other believers to maintain proper theological perspective.

19. Get your basic training at a seminary that teaches the Bible as the word of God. Become well-grounded in the theology of Scripture before you go off (as you may, of course) to get firsthand exposure to nonbiblical thought.

20. Come to appreciate the wisdom, even theological wisdom, of relatively uneducated Christians. Don't be one of those theologians who always has something negative to say when a simple believer describes his walk with the Lord. Don't look down at people from what Helmut Thielicke called "the high horse of enlightenment." Often, simple believers know God better than you do, and you need to learn from them, as did Abraham Kuyper, for instance.

21. Don't be one of those theologians who get excited about every new trend in politics, culture, hermeneutics, and even theology, and who think we have to reconstruct our theology to go along with each trend. Don't think you have to be a feminist, e.g., just because everybody else is. Most of the theologies that try to be culturally savvy are unbiblical.

22. Be suspicious of all trendiness in theology. When everybody jumps on some theological bandwagon, whether narrative, feminism, redemptive history, natural law, liturgy, liberation, postmodernism, or whatever, that's the time to awaken your critical faculties. Don't jump on the bandwagon unless you have done your own study. When a theological trend comes along, ask reflexively, "What's wrong with that?" There is always something wrong. It simply is not the case that the newest is the truest. Indeed, many new movements turn out to be false steps entirely.

23. Our system of doctoral-level education requires "original thought," but that can be hard to do, given that the church has been studying Scripture for thousands of years. You'll be tempted to come up with something that sounds new (possibly by writing a thesis that isn't properly theological at all in the sense of #3 above). Well, do it; get it out of the way, and then come back to do some real theology.

24. At the same time, don't reject innovation simply because it is innovative. Even more, don't reject an idea merely because it doesn't sound like what you're used to. Learn to distinguish the sound-look-feel of an idea from what it actually means.

25. Be critical of arguments that turn on metaphors or extrabiblical technical terms. Don't assume that each one has a perfectly clear meaning. Usually they do not.

26. Learn to be skeptical of the skeptics. Unbelieving and liberal scholars are as prone to error as anybody—in fact, more so.

27. Respect your elders. Nothing is so ill-becoming as a young theologian who despises those who have been working in the field for decades. Disagreement is fine, as long as you acknowledge the maturity and the contributions of those you disagree with. Take 1 Timothy 5:1 to heart.

28. Young theologians often imagine themselves as the next Luther, just as little boys imagine themselves as the next Peyton Manning or LeBron James. When they're too old to play cowboys and Indians, they want to play Luther and the Pope. When the real Pope won't play with them, they pick on somebody else and say, "You're it." Look: most likely God has not chosen you to be the leader of a new Reformation. If he has, don't take the exalted title "Reformer" upon yourself. Let others decide if that is really what you are.

29. Decide early in your career (after some experimenting) what to focus on and what not to. When considering opportunities, it's just as important (perhaps more so) to know when to say no as to know when to say yes.

30. Don't lose your sense of humor. We should take God seriously, not ourselves, and certainly not theology. To lose your sense of humor is to lose your sense of proportion. And nothing is more important in theology than a sense of proportion.

2

Beginnings of Theological Papers

AS I MOVE TOWARD the end of my life, I don't expect to write any more major theological works. But there are some ideas in my head that in my view have not been sufficiently expressed, discussed, refuted, or affirmed. If I were to live another fifty years, and if during that time I were accepted as a participant in the theological dialogue, I would like to raise the following ideas for discussion. I would hope that in that case I could express these as questions, in a way that would not provoke certain people to attack them immediately. Theologians are far too inclined to form factions, attacking or supporting ideas, without anything like sufficient thought. Theology is the original "cancel culture." But I think the following points might be means toward unity—bridges between Calvinists and Arminians, philosophers and theologians, different Christian temperaments, political left and right.

1. In the doctrine of the Trinity, we confess that there is one God in three persons. But nobody has ever given a satisfactory definition of "person" from Scripture. Nor has anyone defined the singularity of God, his "substance" or "being," without palpable dependence on pagan Greek philosophy.

2. God is both transcendent and immanent in regard to the created universe. Keeping these in balance may be the key to reconciling Calvinism and Arminianism. The Calvinist describes God's transcendence, while conceding his immanence. The Arminian does the opposite. For the most part, each admits the points most important to the other. The Arminian admits that God is the creator, and that he has created the world with exhaustive knowledge of what those creatures will do through all of history. But he insists on "real choice," which cannot be satisfactorily defined. The Calvinist admits that we really do make choices and that those choices really affect the course of history. But he never talks about that choice without substantial reflection on the fact that God's plan is exhaustive and trans-historical.

3. We want to say that human beings can do many things, since they are made in God's image. They can even perform certain kinds of "civic" good. But in salvation, we emphasize (with Paul in Eph. 2) that they are dead and therefore can do nothing apart from grace. "Common grace" is an attempt to show that even "civic" goods are the product of a kind of grace, though they do not qualify one for salvation. Certainly, human beings can do nothing (even evil) without God in some sense allowing them to. So what is the difference between God allowing, in this sense, his bringing about a human action by common grace, and his bringing about a human act by special grace?

4. What does it mean for God to "act in history"? It evidently means that God can come into the temporal realm and enter into relationships with created persons and things. Those relationships are changing, hence the old theological formula that God is unchanging in his "being" but changing in his "relationships." Read the biblical narrative—it certainly seems that when God enters time, his own acts are part of a changing narrative. He does one thing on Monday, another thing on Tuesday. That is one kind of change. So how do we describe this in a theological formulation? (1) In history, God takes on attributes different from

his eternal attributes. (2) In history, God takes on a changing nature (similar to the incarnation), though "nature" needs to be defined. (3) In history, God only *appears* to change. This leaves it unclear as to what God is actually doing in history. (4) God doesn't actually come into history. When Scripture appears to say that he does, it is only talking figuratively. But God's entry into history is the heart of the gospel. If that is not literal, then what events does the gospel actually describe? (5) God really comes into history, and how this correlates with his eternal nature is beyond our understanding. This is the view that I find most cogent. History is his creation; surely he has the power and right to enter it. But we find it very difficult to understand, especially if we are trying to discuss it in a framework that presupposes Greek ideas of being and change.

5. First-century apologetics: What was it that persuaded people in first-century Palestine to become followers of Christ? (1) The Holy Spirit. Scripture teaches us that the choice to follow Christ is supernaturally motivated, as Jesus himself said to Nicodemus in John 3:5. (2) Jesus's miracles, healings, and supernatural knowledge. The chief miracle was the resurrection, and I've no doubt that the traditional "evidences for the resurrection" were powerfully convincing. (3) Certainly the mere *reports* of miracles influenced many to *investigate* Jesus, to pay more attention to him than they would have paid to other itinerant teachers. (4) Jesus's *goodness* to people, especially those on the lower rungs of society. (5) The opposition of this good man by the official Jewish leaders forced many to take sides. This intensified the loyalty of those who sided with Jesus, and their sense of antithesis with his opponents. (6) The ethical dimension of the controversy enhanced the analogy between Jesus's death and the sacrifice of animals in the OT. (7) That ethical dimension also must have led many to a reckoning with their own sin and a commitment to Jesus's death as God's means of salvation. (8) That ethical issue intensified the relationship between Jesus and his followers. (9) The written revelation given through Paul

and others formalized this interpretation of Jesus's person and work. I am convinced that the ethical dimension of apologetics deserves more emphasis in our own day (as in my *Christianity Considered*).

6. God and being: "Classical theology," which Wikipedia associates with Plato and Aristotle, affirmed God as part of its quest for pure being. Our world is impure, illusion, not fully real. Only the forms, pure forms, are "really real realities" (Gregory Vlastos). So God is what we truly are. As Plotinus saw, this amounts to pantheism and eliminates any real creator-creature distinction. On this account, I am not a classical theologian.

7. God and being II: Orthodox theologians distinguish between God's being and his attributes. But every attribute contains all of God's being (the doctrine of simplicity). Attributes are not parts of God, but rather aspects, or perspectives. But then why do we need to speak of God's being at all?

8. God's simplicity and the Trinity: I've never seen a credible account of how the doctrine of the Trinity is compatible with the doctrine of simplicity. Like the attributes, each person of the Trinity exhausts the nature of God. I am tempted here to explain this perspectivally, but that won't work in this case. The persons are not mere perspectives of ours; they are really different from each other, to the point where they enter into transactions with one another. I'm content to leave this relationship in mystery. At least I'd rather do that than pretend to reconcile this with a lot of metaphysical mumbo-jumbo.

9. Church government: In my view, the New Testament never presents a normative requirement for church government. It seems that different forms were possible in different places and cultures. When Paul tells Titus to appoint leaders, it seems that Titus is something like a bishop. But churches could be established and could choose leaders without bishops. And many churches were ruled by a plurality of elders.

10. Civil government: The first responsibility of civil government is to provide peace in its environment. That means prosecuting and punishing lawbreakers. Many governments today are not meeting this first responsibility. The rationales behind soft-on-crime policies are transparently wrong.

11. Worship: It seems from 1 Cor. 14 that the earliest Christian worship was informal. People offered suggestions as to what should be done. No evidence of a repeated liturgy, though such did occur in the synagogues, and one can't rule that out for churches. I assume that the elders had control of the proceedings, since they had control over everything. But I see nothing that would rule out exhortation/preaching by non-elders, under supervision of the elders.

12. Worship and Women: There are some passages, e.g., 1 Cor. 11, that suggest women sometimes led in worship. There are other passages (1 Cor. 14; 1 Tim. 2) that exclude women from teaching in some sense. The relevant question is, What are women excluded from? A quick reading of 1 Cor. 14 and 1 Tim. 2 would lead to the conclusion that they are excluded from teaching when men are present. But that would contradict 1 Cor. 11. I think what they are excluded from is the *eldership*: not teaching, but the teaching *office*. This interpretation implies that the elders have the right to appoint women to teach in any situation they deem appropriate.

13. Worship and Women II: But is it unfair that women participating in worship must be subject to male elders? (1) Actually, it is an advantage. Women have more important responsibilities than to serve as church administrators. (2) In creation, everyone is subject to an authority outside himself. And every authority is subject to the people he rules, for he must be a servant to them. (3) Is there a special problem when one *group* is subject to another, based on their immutable properties? No.

14. There are two views of knowledge. In the first, all of us have partial knowledge, and we work together to improve. I have my point of view, and you have yours. I correct you, you correct me, and in the end our knowledge is fuller, but not final. In the second view of knowledge, one person has the truth, and all the rest of us must get it from him. There is no discussion. Anyone who wants truth must get it from the supreme authority or be excluded from the discussion. Indeed, there is no real discussion, only warfare between those who accept the authority and those who do not. After all, the authority is the only one who has the complete and final truth, and there can be no dissent from that; there cannot even be discussion.

Now the second view is only appropriate when God is the authority. Only God is infallible and omniscient. But that view has often appeared in purely human contexts. When that happens, one human being is playing God, taking on the kind of authority appropriate only to God.

The first view of knowledge is what I was taught in high school and college. The second view has been more common today. It is the basis of cancel culture. The authority is Marx, or BLM, or Antifa. In this view, the "authority" is claiming a status appropriate only to God. The penalty for differing, cancelation, is in effect a religious excommunication.

3

Two Kinds of Theologians

SOME THEOLOGIANS are encouragers, others challengers. Of course, most theologians are combinations of the two, but usually their emphasis is one or the other.

A challenger is one who says to the church, "You've always thought this is right, but my research indicates that your view is wrong, and you have to change." The challenge may be in the area of exegesis, historical theology, systematics, or any other area of theology. It may also concern the practical applications of the church's doctrine.

An encourager says, "You know there are many who doubt your age-old belief. But I'm here to tell you that they are wrong and you are right. You can rest in confidence that your faith has not been misplaced."

We need both challenges and encouragements as we make our pilgrim journey. We need challenges because we get too attached to our ideas and our certainties are such that we often treat people too harshly who disagree with us. Sometimes we think wrongly that a person must agree with us on this or that idea in order to be faithful to Christ.

But we also need encouragements. Sometimes, especially these days, it seems that the whole world is against us. It is good to know that when people oppose the gospel, as we understand it, it is not necessarily because they have discovered new facts, but rather because they have adopted presuppositions[1] hostile to the truth. We need give no credence to arguments based on such presuppositions. In fact, the gospel obligates us to oppose them and any arguments based on them.

To state that fact, incidentally, can be an act of encouragement or an act of challenge, depending on the need of the hearer. Theology is often like that: a challenge to one group, an encouragement to another.

But some theologians emphasize one of these emphatically above the other. Systematic theologians like Herman Bavinck and Louis Berkhof are primarily encouragers. They tell their readers that the old Reformed faith of Calvin and Turretin is still viable after all these years. When they deal with skeptics or with contrary theological traditions, they show how these arguments fail to make the grade.

Challengers, within Christian orthodoxy, tend to be in the departments of biblical studies. I think of Meredith G. Kline, who taught Old Testament to me and my classmates at Westminster Seminary. He would often begin his classes by saying, "The traditional view is ... but I say to you ..." He developed a lot of theories that contradicted our Sunday school certainties. The "two tables of the Law" did not have five commandments on each tablet; nor did they have four on one tablet and six on the other. Rather, they were two copies of the Decalogue, and each tablet contained all ten. Noah's flood was local, not universal. Scripture is not just a long series of reflections by participants in the sacred story; it is an official document governing the covenant community, as the US Constitution governs the American people.

On the whole, I thought that Kline's new ideas were edifying. I have come to disagree with Kline on some matters, but on the whole I accept them as being within the bounds of orthodoxy. But for myself I have chosen a more "encouraging" stance, understanding that what encourages many believers will be challenging to others, especially to those who maintain the "challenger" mindset. That is more typical of the work of apologetics, which I have often pursued, and of systematic theology, which has constituted most of my written contributions.

---

1. Or attitudes, which are in my judgment the same thing.

In our time, I think, Christians are more in need of encouragement. They are under attack, not only by skeptics, but also by non-Christian religions, and especially by a culture that despises the Christian faith in the name of hedonism and political movements. My own study, and my own relation to God, have persuaded me that the rivals to the gospel have no intellectual or moral substance. My case for this bold assertion can be found in my larger writings.

But it is always useful, when you are reading theological works, to try to identify the writer's motivation. Is he trying to encourage believers that have been intimidated by the culture of our time? Or is he trying to challenge them to rethink things? Such questions provide context for evaluating the author's work.

4

Three Theological Tasks

LIKE SO MANY THINGS in life, it is convenient to divide theology into three parts. Theology has the responsibility (1) to define the content of biblical revelation, (2) to challenge Christians to reject ideas that are not biblical, and (3) to encourage Christians to hold their biblical beliefs with more assurance and confidence. In categories I have developed in other writings, I would describe (1) as normative, (2) as situational, and (3) as existential.

We are inclined to say that a theological work should be perfectly balanced among these emphases, but of course in actual theology such balance is rare. More common are theological works that can be characterized almost entirely by one of these emphases and neither of the others.

Normative theologies are often satisfied to set forth simply the teachings of Scripture as they understand these, with a minimum of opinion or passion. Often they present their teaching as a purely academic enterprise. But of course (and this is true of all academic writing) it is impossible to separate entirely the objective facts from one's opinions. When one tries to eliminate personal reactions entirely from a writing, the writing comes out expressing indifference to its subject matter.

Situational theology may be conservative or liberal. If conservative, it aims at refuting what the author considers heretical. If liberal, it aims at refuting traditional beliefs with the aid of recent scholarship. In either case, it may be charged with bias, a purpose

of distorting the facts to fit an agenda. In most colleges and universities and "mainline" seminaries, the teaching of theology is liberal
situational: the teacher tells the students to put aside what they
learned in family devotions or Sunday schools, in order to line up
their thinking with "serious" scholarship. In a few self-consciously
conservative institutions, the teaching is conservative situational: an
attempt to teach students how to stand firm in the face of Scripture-
twisting by fashionable thinkers.

Existential theology seeks, not to challenge, but to comfort and
reassure. It tells the students that what they have learned in the past is
basically right. They should be thankful for their heritage and take it
to heart. Of course, existential theology looks very different depending
on what heritage is in view.

These three perspectives overlap, of course. One cannot do a good
job with any of them, without doing at least some of the others. But the
world of academic theology has become somewhat unbalanced in favor
of a liberal situational approach.

In the Reformed world, theologians like Hodge, Warfield, Bavinck,
Vos, Van Til, and Berkhof aim at reassuring their readers that confessional Calvinism is biblical and therefore true. More recently that
emphasis can be found in the theologies of Wayne Grudem and Robert
Reymond. The liberal situational approach, however, can be found in
many more writers, including the whole of academic liberalism: Barth,
Brunner, Bultmann, Tillich, Moltmann, Pannenberg.

Evaluating theological proposals is thought to be a largely normative discipline: comparing those proposals with Scripture. But it is
instructive to remember that the lifeblood of a theological proposal,
or, more broadly, a theological movement, is often not a particular
interpretation of Scripture, but rather a desire to score points against
a rival movement that one has come to oppose for various reasons
other than biblical exegesis. That is what I have called a situational
motivation. And where there is a situational motivation, there is also
an existential one, an intention to reassure the audience that belongs
to one's own movement.

So theological battles have multiple dimensions.[1] If a theologian is to make a cogent case for his ideas, he must attend to the objective data of Scripture (normative), the present and past currents of theological ideas (situational), and the subjective openness of his likely readers (existential).

---

1. Like the dimensions of battles over scientific paradigms described in Thomas Kuhn's *Structure of Scientific Revolutions* (Chicago: University of Chicago Press, 1962).

5

Theology in Three Dimensions:
A Summary by the Author

MY BOOK EXPLAINS a theological method that I have been using for most of my 49-year teaching career. Some students and readers have expressed appreciation for it. So in *TTD* I seek to summarize the method briefly and make some applications of it.

Theologians today usually write with a primary focus either on church history or on the debates among modern theologians. Those kinds of theology are useful, but I have always felt that what people need most is a focus on the Bible itself. It is the Bible that is the supreme standard of truth for Christians, and the ideas of historical and contemporary thinkers must be secondary to it. But how can we focus on the Bible itself, without getting bogged down in historical and contemporary debates *about* the Bible, and without treading over and over again on very familiar ground?

What I have tried to do has been to emphasize a Trinitarian structure in the Bible's theology. God is Father, Son, and Spirit. That statement has profound depths to it, but it has some immediate applications that are often neglected. One of these is that there is a threefold structure to God's ways of working in the world. The Father devises the eternal plan by which everything happens. The Son accomplishes that plan in history. And the Spirit applies that plan to our hearts and to the depths of creation. God's lordship reflects that Threeness. To say that

God is lord is to say that he is our supreme authority (focusing on the
Father's eternal plan), the controller of history (focusing on the Son's
accomplishment) and the one who takes us in personal relationship to
himself, as his sons, daughters, friends (focusing on the Spirit's work
in our hearts). That concept of lordship is central to the biblical narrative: "God is Lord" summarizes the teaching of the Old Testament.
"Jesus Christ is Lord" summarizes the teaching of the New.

Looking at the Bible this way shows us a way to better balance.
Christian theology is a worldview (the Father), a history of redemption
(the Son), and a love letter from God to his people (the Spirit). We don't
need to choose one of these over the others, nor do we need to get into
constant debates about which we should "emphasize."

My students have described this way of reading the Bible as "tri-per-
spectival." I have expounded it in many books and articles, but in *TTD*
I focus on the fundamentals, both to justify the method and to teach
readers how to use it.

6

Theological Education (2 Timothy 2:1–2)

This is a message I presented in 2015 at The Expositors Seminary in Jupiter, FL. Part sermon, part lecture, it interacts directly with an important Scripture text on the training of people to carry out the Great Commission.

I THOUGHT it would be good for us to talk a bit from the word of God about theological education. I have been in that business since 1968, and of course you are involved in that same work here at Expositors Seminary.

It is interesting that there is no place in Scripture labeled "Rules for Theological Education." We might someday reflect on the "schools of the prophets" in the time of Elijah and Elisha—interesting communities, but possibly to think of them today would take us too far afield. In the NT, the Pastoral Letters and other passages comment on some things we ought to do and ought not to do in preparing students for ministry. But this is not presented distinctly and systematically, as is, for example, Paul's doctrine of justification in Romans and Galatians. But theological education, the preparation of ministers of the gospel, is, by the very logic of Scripture, an important topic. Our Lord's Great Commission presents the main purpose of the church, to preach the gospel of Jesus's saving grace to every nation. Those whom God calls to be sent out to the nations, surely, need to be qualified and trained. At least that seems to be common sense.

But how is this to be done? What is the biblical charter of the theological seminary? Or what we may call Great Commission Training Centers?

I think that in considering this question we sometimes make the mistake of looking for something special: an organization above and beyond the church itself. But we forget that the church itself is a training institution, besides being many other things. And it is a Great Commission training institution. For Jesus gave the Great Commission, not to a special group of Christians, but to all Christian believers. Not every Christian is called to travel a long distance to proclaim the gospel. Many are called to do it near home. But we all are called to do it: pastors, teachers, carpenters, farmers, cattle barons, civic officials, homemakers, soldiers, children in school. Jesus calls us all to proclaim by our words and lives that he has saved us by his grace and given us his Holy Spirit.

God teaches us how to do this in the church. Historically, the church has sometimes conducted special classes to train leaders. But much of that teaching takes place in the regular Sunday worship services. Every week when we meet to worship, some teaching happens. In 1 Cor. 14:26, Paul gives us a brief description of the earliest Christian worship services in Corinth:

> What then, brothers? When you come together, each one has a hymn, a lesson, a revelation, a tongue, or an interpretation. Let all things be done for building up. (1 Cor. 14:26)

We note that everyone contributes to this service. It may have seemed like a free-for-all. Paul evidently wants to make it a bit more orderly, to get it more under control, but he doesn't impose some rigid liturgy on the worshipers. But in the list of items, we have the term *lesson*, *didache* in Greek—a time for teaching. *Didache* is not necessarily a formal discourse. Paul doesn't say that worship must include a "sermon," as we conceive of it. The teaching may, so far as we can tell, take many forms, formal and informal. There may have been only one *didache*, or more than one. The *didache* teachers may have been elders, or perhaps others with the permission of the elders. But certainly there are some things about this teaching we can know with certainty. First it is teaching of God's word. And second it is Great Commission training. When it is done right, it equips the believers to take the gospel, by word and deed, into the places where God has called them. For the Great Commission is the distinctive task of the church. It is what the church is for. Jesus doesn't want the church just to hold together at its place of meeting, but to reach out, to spread out, to the whole world, and bring the gospel to every man, woman, and child.

So now we know one thing about theological education. It is not radically different from what goes on in church. In church meetings, both in worship services and in extensions of that in Sunday school, youth meetings, etc., Jesus prepares his people to speak and live in a way that testifies to the world, that lets others know that these people have "been with Jesus" (Acts 4:13 NIV).

Church history tells us that Christian teaching, *didache* (or, in other words, theology), eventually outgrew the boundaries of the local church. So it took place in academic exchange, as with Justin Martyr, Tertullian, and others. In time it became institutionalized, in monasteries, cathedrals, schools, and universities. But insofar as it was authentic *didache*, it remained what it was in the New Testament: Great Commission training. It taught the gospel of Jesus so that believers would be equipped to take that gospel to the ends of the earth.

One biblical description of this training is found at 2 Tim. 2:1–2, which reads as follows:

> ¹ You then, my child, be strengthened by the grace that is in Christ Jesus, ² and what you have heard from me in the presence of many witnesses entrust to faithful men who will be able to teach others also. ³ Share in suffering as a good soldier of Christ Jesus. ⁴ No soldier gets entangled in civilian pursuits, since his aim is to please the one who enlisted him. ⁵ An athlete is not crowned unless he competes according to the rules. ⁶ It is the hard-working farmer who ought to have the first share of the crops. ⁷ Think over what I say, for the Lord will give you understanding in everything. (2 Tim. 2:1–7)

This is a good text for ascertaining God's own vision of theological education, of Great Commission training, and I'd like to spend the rest of our time on it this morning.

The pattern here is that first, Paul is teaching his disciple Timothy, and secondly he charges Timothy to teach the same to others, and thirdly he wants these others, Timothy's disciples, to teach others also. First, Paul's own teaching to Timothy. He describes Timothy in three metaphors: Timothy is a soldier, an athlete, and a farmer. These metaphors pertain to each of us as we are trained for Great Commission labor. You should think of yourselves as soldiers, athletes, and farmers.

It is interesting that none of these three metaphors is particularly academic. Of course Paul is clear that we can't serve in these ways without knowledge: knowledge of Paul's teaching (v. 2), the rules of the athletic contest (v. 5), and the "thinking" and "understanding" that comes from the whole experience (v. 7).

But the predominant language about this experience is not of the student crouched over his books in the library. In verse 1, it is *strengthening*. Soldiers, athletes, and farmers often feel weak. You need to rest; you are tempted to do something else altogether. But Jesus knows you need strength. You need to be able to feel that you can stand up and bring the gospel to others. How does that happen? "By the grace that is in Christ Jesus." That same grace that brought you from darkness to light, that brought forgiveness of all your sins through Jesus's death on the cross, that raised you up into eternal fellowship with almighty God, that grace is able to empower you now, as you learn to be Jesus's soldier, his athlete, his farmer.

It is sometimes a strange kind of strengthening. For the soldier, it comes through suffering. The soldier gets separated from "civilian pursuits," the pursuits by which people in the world gain profits and enjoyment. The soldier will see his old friends gaining money and taking pleasant vacations, while he must stay in camp under the stern commands of his superior officer. He will be called to go to battle, to engage the enemy, perhaps to be wounded or even die. He may never be able to pursue civilian pursuits again for the rest of his life. What can motivate people to live that kind of life? Only the promise of God that says surely, surely your suffering will not go on forever. Surely you will win your battle. Satan will not be able to prevent you from taking the gospel to the ends of the earth. Surely you will defeat his kingdom. It is in that way that God's command and promise will strengthen you. In a biblical theological seminary, a Great Commission training center, you should learn to hear the word of God that way: constantly addressing you to carry on the work of a soldier.

It is similar with the metaphor of the athlete. In college or university, athletics is a bit of a nuisance. It can make all sorts of money for the school, and athletes often get the acclaim of being the big men or women on campus. But teachers often don't know what to do with athletes. If an athlete takes a course that you teach, is it OK to fail him if he doesn't do the work? But that might knock him off the football team, and that will get everybody mad at you. But if you pass a student who never comes to class and who writes a barely literate paper, you may be attacked for dumbing down your courses and destroying the school's academic standards. But in our passage, Paul takes a much more positive view of athletics. In one sense it is the central concern of the Great Commission training program.

Now remember, of course, that this is metaphor. I don't know how literally to deal with the problem of unqualified athletes in academic courses. But if your goal is to teach people how to take the gospel to the world, remember that these people are *like* athletes. And that is central to their training. Paul says that an athlete is not crowned unless he competes according to the rules. So you need to teach them the *rules* of the game. When people bring the gospel to their neighbors, or throughout the world, there are rules to follow. They can't just do it any old way. The rules are in the word of God. The word tells us what the gospel is, and it also tells us how we are to speak, with the same love and grace that the Lord Jesus Christ brought to earth. And the word tells us, as with the soldier, that like Jesus we may have to suffer in offering the gospel to people. So a Great Commission training program is a study of the word of God—not for academic comprehension, but as rules for our speech and living. Although it is not an academic exercise, it is something students will need to *think* about (v. 7), so that they may have "understanding in everything."

And then, finally, the Great Commission training center is for farm-ers. It is an agriculture program. (This seminary is "Expositors A&M; you are Aggies.") Beyond the metaphor, when we study the gospel, we are learning how to bring new life into the world. The New Testament often speaks of the gospel as something that grows and spreads, bring-ing with it new spiritual life. That life is first the salvation Jesus died to bring us, in which people become new creatures by the power of the Holy Spirit. That new birth brings change, renewal, and godly thoughts and behavior in all areas of life, where before there was rebellion, anger, hatred, and blasphemy. Scripture often presents the word of God as the source of this new life, without denying of course that this word of God is usually delivered by people—the farmers in our metaphor, the sowers in Jesus's parable. And Paul says that the hard-working farmer should have the first share of the crops. When you bring the gospel to people, and God brings new life, that new life will bring joy to you as it did to Paul. This new life brings you, as Jesus said, new fathers, moth-ers, brothers, sisters, friends, houses, and lands. So good it is to see new life flourish on your watch. A Great Commission training center should teach you how to do this.

If you've followed my paper trail, you may suspect that something is going on under the surface when I focus on three points, the soldier, the athlete, and the farmer. In many of my writings, I argue that God our Lord relates to us in three different ways. These ways reflect his Trinitarian existence as Father, Son, and Spirit. As our Lord, he gives us his word, his rules. I call that "normative." Second, he puts us into a dangerous situation, a war zone. I call that "situational." We need not be afraid of this situation, because our loving God has created that situation and directs it to his glory, bringing good out of all the horror. Thirdly, he attends to what is happening within us and within other people: the new life, replacing death. I call that "existential." The basic pattern of the Christian life and the Christian proclamation of the gospel is this: we apply the rules to the situation to bring existential new life. That is what a seminary, a Great Commission training center, ought to do.

It should teach the word of God, but not just as an intellectual object. It should teach the word of God as it applies to the situations we face in the warfare, and as it brings new life in ourselves and others. Teach the word of God, the rules for the Christian athlete. But remember that we live in a world that has rejected those rules, that has chosen to live on its own. And so it brings relentless warfare against the Lord God and his precious Son (Ps. 2). In our country, secularism has taken over society, setting the standards of intellectual discourse, philosophy, art, music, entertainment. The government sees no reason why it should not become bigger and bigger, more and more intrusive, and trample on the freedoms of religious people, for example, to resist abortion and to educate their children as they see fit. Overseas, Islam's opposition to Jesus Christ has never been angrier or more violent, nor has the opposition of the Communist government of China. But remember that effective resistance to all this never happens through merely human power.

So Paul tells us,

[10] Finally, be strong in the Lord and in the strength of his might. [11] Put on the whole armor of God, that you may be able to stand against the schemes of the devil. [12] For we do not wrestle against flesh and blood, but against the rulers, against the authorities, against the cosmic powers over this present darkness, against the spiritual forces of evil in the heavenly places. [13] Therefore take up the whole armor of God, that you may be able to withstand in the evil day, and having done all, to stand firm. [14] Stand therefore, having fastened on the belt of truth, and having put on the breastplate of righteousness, [15] and, as shoes for your feet, having put on the readiness given by the gospel of peace. [16] In all circumstances take up the shield of faith, with which you can extinguish all the flaming darts of the evil one; [17] and take the helmet of salvation, and the sword of the Spirit, which is the word of God, [18] praying at all times in the Spirit, with all prayer and supplication. To that end keep alert with all perseverance, making supplication for all the saints, [19] and also for me, that words may be given to me in opening my mouth boldly to proclaim the mystery of the gospel, [20] for which I am an ambassador in chains, that I may declare it boldly, as I ought to speak. (Eph. 6:10–20)

If human power were the issue, swords would be enough. If human wisdom were the issue, then Christian intellectual prowess would be enough. But Paul says that in this terrible situation of spiritual warfare, our weapons of war and our human intelligence is not enough, because we're fighting a war against demons, against devils. For this warfare, we need more than a strong shield; we need God's own righteousness in Jesus. We need more than a sword; we need the word of God, the sword of the Spirit. And above all, our ministry must be bathed in prayer, for we get nowhere unless we are constantly in touch with God, our only source of power.

Every seminary should ask itself regularly, How are we preparing our students to prosecute the Great Commission in conditions like these? How well are they learning to fight the spiritual warfare? How well are they learning to pray, to turn without ceasing to their heavenly Father?

And how are the students learning to expect new life, the existential, the power of the Spirit transforming themselves and others? For the spiritual warfare is not the end. Jesus has secured the beginning of victory, and we should see the fruits of his victory in ourselves and in others who have heard the gospel. There are some writers who seem to think that there are no rewards for believers this side of heaven. But Paul clearly says otherwise. There are fruits of the gospel, blessings of the gospel, in our own lives, and in the lives of those whom God touches through our ministry. How wonderful it is, when we see new creations, when we see lives transformed by the good news that Christ died for sinners, when we see the grace of God coming to dominate the lives of these new believers, turning them from selfishness to love, from immaturity to wisdom, from fear to hope. And how wonderful it is, when these people form a society, and that society affects other societies, bringing love in place of hate, justice in place of oppression, kindness in place of evil.

I hope your school, and mine, can be places where believers can find new strength to draw again and again on the grace of God. But of course a Great Commission training center cannot merely be a place where individuals refresh themselves. It must be a place where those individuals teach others, and then where those others learn to teach still others, so that the instruction has a multiplier effect: "You then, my child, be strengthened by the grace that is in Christ Jesus, and what you have heard from me in the presence of many witnesses entrust to faithful men who will be able to teach others also" (2 Tim. 2:1–2 NIV). As students, you should not only be learning the gospel; you must be learning how to teach others the gospel, and indeed to teach them to teach.

Now what I've described to you is very different from the typical academic theological schools of our time. Today, a theological school is mainly a place where people take courses, write papers, take exams, and receive grades, based on the criteria of the modern academic establishment, the Harvards and Cambridges of this world. I have written quite a bit on how that establishment has moved far from the gospel and in fact opposes the gospel.[1] It's not that we can never learn from them. But don't forget what Paul says in 1 Corinthians about the antithesis between the wisdom of the world and the wisdom of God. I have said that the work we are doing requires knowledge: knowledge of the rules of the game, and, more fully, what Paul calls "understanding in everything." To test your understanding, it may be a good idea for you to write some papers, to take some exams. But if that becomes the center, if that is the main factor in your learning experience, you are missing so very much.

Ask, rather, how am I learning to suffer, as a soldier of Christ? Am I learning the rules of the Christian athletic competition, so that I instinctively take the right step? And do I, the new Christian farmer, see delicious crops growing up in my life, sown by the Holy Spirit, and spreading from me to those around me? Think over those things. And the Lord will give you understanding in everything. That will be graduation day.

---

1. See especially *ACC*, *DKG*, and *HWPT*.

7

Review of Anthony Thiselton's
Systematic Theology

This review was published in WTJ 78:1 (Spring 2016): 196–99.
The book itself was published by Eerdmans in 2015.

THERE HAS BEEN NO SHORTAGE of systematic theologies published in recent years, so we should ask about the distinctive features in the volume under review. First, of course, is Thiselton's own thorough scholarship, well respected in the academic theological community. He is professor emeritus of Christian theology at the University of Nottingham, England, and the author of many acclaimed volumes.

But this book is also unique in that it goes far beyond theology in the usual sense. Thiselton says that it offers "as broad an interdisciplinary perspective as has been possible" (xii). That perspective includes not only doctrinal formulation and biblical exegesis, but also hermeneutics, history of doctrine, philosophical discussions, and many, many surveys of modern theologians and biblical scholars.

And Thiselton wants to do all of this in a concise format. He follows an invitation from his publisher "to write a systematic theology that would be 'affordable' for students and ministers, as well and others, and would easily fit into a single volume" (xi). He thinks, however, that the best systematics to date is the three-volume work of Wolfhart

Pannenberg. So, he says, "the compromise for me has been the requirement to write in less detail than I would have chosen" (xi). The result
of this compromise is 389 pages of text and with substantial indices
and bibliography.

Nevertheless, we can recognize in this book theology as it is done
today. Theology began as an attempt by believers to expound and
explain the biblical message. But after many centuries, theology has
itself become a large literature alongside the Bible. So to a large extent,
theology has itself become a substantial object of academic study, so
that theologies are less and less studies of the Bible and more and more
studies of theology itself. The present volume is in this tradition, a study
of theology as much as a study of the Bible. Hence the "multidisciplinary"
emphasis noted earlier. It is amazing to me how well Thiselton has done
with this project within the véry compact limits he has chosen.

But there are intrinsic limits to the summarization of these disciplines. Citing historical figures and modern theologians can illumine
the biblical message, but such citations are not the biblical message per
se. Sometimes they get in the way. The more concise the format, the
more difficult it is to harmonize the various emphases into a smooth
functioning narrative.

Further, the history of theology itself has not run smooth. There are
large differences between different theological traditions and between
liberal and conservative parties within each tradition. Thiselton is aware
of that, and he does offer criticisms of various theologians and theological schools. But for the most part he sees all theologians as a friendly
professional guild, working together to achieve common goals. He does
not describe theology as a spiritual warfare, what Van Til described
as "antithesis." Yet he often describes this or that writer as "careful,"
commending their arguments without, of course, having the space to
persuade those of us who remain skeptical. Even on serious doctrinal
issues, he tries to enlist our sympathy for a position on his own say-
so. Discussing conditional immortality, for example, he tells us that
"this view has always found a place in Christian theology and deserves
respect" (387). I would rather make up my own mind who to respect,
after a closer reading of the texts.

The result, I think, is an account of Scripture that, though usually orthodox, lacks sharp boundaries. Thiselton often tends to resolve problems with vague formulae that at best split the difference between rival positions. For example: Is God personal or impersonal? He is "suprapersonal," Thiselton tells us (30, 33, 267, elsewhere), and Thiselton seems to think that resolves the question. The term is appropriate, of course, because in every way including his personality God is superior to us. But when we debate the impersonal/personal question, we are asking more specific questions: Is God like a physical force—like gravity or electromagnetism (of course, a *supra*force)—or is he someone who plans, thinks, knows, loves, and speaks in some way analogously (but superior) to human beings? Here it seems to me that Scripture dictates an unambiguous vote in favor of personality that excludes Aristotle's Prime Mover. To split the difference by saying that he is "suprapersonal" is not enough.

Is God One? Scripture is pretty explicit on that matter, and it also clearly identifies three who equally deserve worship as God. But Thiselton credits the saying of Gregory of Nazianzus that " 'three' has nothing to do with numbers" (32). Then Thiselton expounds *circumincessio*, the doctrine that the persons of the Trinity are "in" one another. Fine; but "nothing to do with numbers"? Really? Does that mean that it doesn't matter whether you say that there are two persons, or three, or four? Is it not meaningful to ask how many beings have the same status as the Father, Son, and Spirit? There is much to be said here, I suppose. But Thiselton's compact format leaves no opportunity for a cogent discussion.

Similarly, Thiselton deals with the question of God's gender by saying that despite all the unmistakable masculine terminology for God in the Bible gender is "an inappropriate category" in which to refer to God (33). He is "beyond gender" (34). If Thiselton means only that God is incorporeal and therefore not physically masculine or feminine, we should have no problem here. But he doesn't think of gender as merely physical, and he seems to think it is wrapped up in a whole concept of "relationality" and "narrative" (34) and therefore carries metaphysical weight. Cf. also his discussion that God is "beyond time" (375) though "time is real for God." He thinks this is implied by "*post-Einsteinian phi-losophy of science*" (375–76, emphasis his), but I confess I don't find this particularly intelligible, let alone cogent or spiritually edifying.

Thiselton often gives great weight to the conceptual habits of modern theologians, without addressing significant problems. Often he takes pains to endorse the "dynamic" over the "static," for instance (40, 92, 374). But he has not persuaded me to reject what seems self-evident, that sometimes the static, the changeless, is good, and the dynamic (e.g., the instability of James 1:8) is bad. Perhaps Thiselton is willing to make common-sense disclaimers about this popular dichotomy, but his com-pressed format does not allow serious discussion of it. I would regard similarly his use of the very misleading and dangerous cliché, that God is "wholly other" (44), and the common admonition of modern schol-ars to focus on God's activity rather than his being (39).

Like many modern thinkers, Thiselton insists that God's almighty power in Scripture is for "enabling," not for "power over" (76). In my view, "enabling" and "having power over" are not inconsistent; indeed they are mutually reinforcing. And Scripture contains many examples of God's "power over" his creatures. But there is no space in the book for a serious discussion of these issues.

Thiselton is similarly concerned with clarifying the concept of God's wrath and human sin, though he lacks the space to do it adequately. "In popular thought today," he says, "people readily speak of 'wrongdoing,' but seldom, if ever, of sin or alienation" (148). What Thiselton dispar-ages as "popular thought" (and he is, in my view, all too ready to utter such disparagement) is an idea with a long history in Protestant con-fessions and arguably in Scripture (1 John 3:4, not to mention Gen. 3) that sin is violation of a divine command. No doubt, violating God's commands leads to alienation and breaking of relationships (both with God and with other people). I think it legitimate to define sin either as disobedience to God or as the violation of relationships: either leads to the other. (It is usually wrong in theology to insist that a term must be defined in only one way.) But Thiselton, like many modern theologians, thinks that an emphasis on obedience is somehow less biblical or less profound than an emphasis that focuses on relationships. (Thiselton also, in a very modern way, talks a lot about "emphasizing" this or that. But how can we quantify the exact proper emphasis between two things? Certainly there are many things that we may emphasize at different times or places.)

I have many more examples, but lest I transgress my own word-limit, I will sum up. I think this book can best be used as a reference text, to answer questions like "What are the theologians saying today about this or that issue?" But for clear, cogent, and profound analyses of biblical teaching, the reader is urged to look elsewhere. I don't know how much to blame Thiselton's understanding and how much to blame his over-compressed format for the deficiencies of the book, but it is plain that what we need in systematic theology is a sharper focus on what Scripture actually says and a better attempt to define terms clearly and argue positions cogently. That may make it necessary to draw a sharper line between systematic theology and the post-canonical history of theological thought, however much the two may illumine one another.

8

Foreword to *Scripture and the People of God*

The book is a Festschrift for Wayne Grudem, edited by John DelHoussaye (Wheaton, IL: Crossway, 2018).

I HAVE WRITTEN elsewhere[1] about the exciting period 1964–74, when Westminster Theological Seminary experienced a major theological transition. From 1961–64, I had studied under the "old faculty," the "boys" that J. Gresham Machen had brought with him when he left Princeton in 1929 to found Westminster. Those boys, John Murray, Cornelius Van Til, Ned Stonehouse, and Paul Woolley, joined later by several others including Edward J. Young, Meredith Kline, and Edmund P. Clowney, gave the school a formidable reputation for scholarship and consistent Reformed orthodoxy. But in the late sixties and early seventies, deaths, retirements, and other departures necessitated replacements. As a teacher I joined a group of new professors, including Jay Adams, C. John Miller, D. Clair Davis, Ray Dillard, and later Harvie Conn.

And God also brought to Westminster during this time a group of students with remarkable theological gifts, many of whom would

---

1. Frame, *Theology of My Life* (Eugene, OR: Cascade Books, 2017), 88–122; foreword to John Hughes, Wayne Grudem, and John Frame, ed., *Redeeming the Life of the Mind: Essays in Honor of Vern Poythress* (Wheaton: Crossway, 2017); "Backgrounds to My Thought" in John Hughes, ed., *Speaking the Truth in Love* (Phillipsburg, NJ: P&R Publishing, 2009), 9–30.

go on to write significant theological works and join the faculties of Westminster and other schools, becoming leaders in various fields of evangelical theology. In that group were William Edgar, James Hurley, David Clowney, Willem Van Gemeren, Moisés Silva, Alan Groves, Susan Foh, Dennis Johnson, Greg Bahnsen, Paul Wells, Tiina Allik, John Hughes, Vern Poythress, and Wayne Grudem, whom we honor in this volume.

Westminster had been known, not only for its high level of scholarship and of Reformed orthodoxy, but also for its creativity, creativity of course within the bounds of orthodoxy. The Westminster faculty was committed to the church's creeds and the Reformed confessions; but it had never been content with simply repeating and emphasizing those formulations. Rather, they had a strong motivation toward rethinking their tradition—both in order to apply it to new questions, and to verify its biblical basis. That was true of the Old Princeton tradition: one thinks, for example, of the development by the Hodges and Warfield of the church's doctrine of biblical authority and inerrancy. At Westminster, Murray's systematic theology, unlike many previous Reformed syntheses, was focused almost entirely on the exegesis of biblical texts, with minimal (though expert when necessary) interaction with the history of doctrine. Stonehouse, and Young, like Machen, dug deep into Scripture to respond in depth to the objections of modern critics of biblical teaching. Kline developed original responses to exegetical issues, such as the "framework hypothesis" in Gen. 1–2. Clowney built on the "redemptive historical" emphasis of Geerhardus Vos to develop a view of preaching that sought above all to preach Christ from all the Bible. Van Til rejected the dominant apologetic traditions of the church, seeking a more biblical way of defending the faith. Jay Adams, similarly, rejected the traditional accommodation of Christian counseling to secular psychology, developing a new system of "nouthetic" or "biblical" counseling. Harvie Conn insisted on the importance of "contextualization" in missions: presenting biblical truth in the language of those to whom the gospel comes. C. John Miller insisted on evangelism with a deep understanding of grace, overcoming the self-defensiveness of the church's "ingrown" traditions. And Vern Poythress and John Frame became known for something called "perspectivalism," the habit of looking at theological questions from many different angles. The pattern was this: at Old Princeton and Westminster there was a special passion to dig more deeply into what Scripture says, together with a creative independence from past historical formulations.

Of this group, Wayne Grudem may be the best known to the theological public, because of his wonderful 1993 *Systematic Theology*.[2] This best-selling, influential volume is often described as representative of the conservative Reformed tradition. But, like the other theologians I have mentioned, Grudem is far more than a mere representative. He too is an original thinker of the first order.

After his studies at Harvard and Westminster, Grudem earned his doctorate in New Testament at Cambridge University under C. F. D. Moule, writing a dissertation on the nature of prophecy in the New Testament, especially 1 Corinthians.[3] In his argument, he rejected the Reformed tradition of "cessationism," the view that God had removed the gift of prophecy from the church at the end of the apostolic age. But he nevertheless defended the Reformed understanding of the sufficiency of Scripture, by making a sharp distinction between the authority of Scriptural revelation and the authority of New Testament (and contemporary) prophecy. Prophecy in the Old Testament, he argued, was identical with God's own word and therefore of ultimate and permanent authority for the church. But prophecy in the New Testament consisted of less authoritative utterances, lacking the ultimacy and permanence of the biblical canon. Therefore in Grudem's view, as in traditional Reformed theology, Scripture alone is our final authority, inerrant and infallible, a suitable starting point for the development of Christian doctrine.

His *Systematic Theology*, then, incorporates his highly unusual view of prophecy, together with an emphasis on *sola Scriptura*, an intention (no less than John Murray's) to derive all doctrinal conclusions from biblical exegesis. His argument gives a certain level of support for the

---

2. Grand Rapids: Zondervan, 1995. Grudem has also published portions and abbreviations of this volume, with applications of its teaching to different topics.

3. For a revised version of his dissertation, see Grudem, *The Gift of Prophecy* (Wheaton: Crossway, 2000).

charismatic movement while insisting on a rigorous exegetical basis for all his theological positions. His view of prophecy is certainly creative, while his view of biblical sufficiency is deeply conservative.

At other points as well, Grudem differs from traditional Reformed thinking, while basing his ideas on a deep study of Scripture. He advocates believer's baptism and premillennialism—views never entirely absent from the Reformed tradition, but not typical of it.

But he has also put a huge effort into defending a very traditional Reformed and evangelical view: that the relation of men and women in the church is "complementarian" rather than "egalitarian." With John Piper, Grudem edited *Recovering Biblical Manhood and Womanhood: A Response to Evangelical Feminism.*[4] This book of essays argues comprehensively that although men and women are equal in dignity before God, the Scriptures do not prescribe for them identical roles in the family, society, and church. So he opposes the evangelical feminist movement to open the church's offices to women.

In the course of this debate, Grudem entered the controversy as to whether the term *kephale* (translated *head*), used to describe the relation of husband to wife in 1 Cor. 11:3 and Eph. 5:23, means "authority over" or "source." He argued the first alternative from a remarkably comprehensive examination of the term and the literature about it.[5]

So Grudem's concern with the theology of gender entailed a concern with Bible translations. His book with Vern Poythress, *The Gender-Neutral Bible Controversy: Muting the Masculinity of God's Words*[6] and their later *The TNIV and the Gender-Neutral Bible Controversy*[7] argued that some recent translations have distorted the biblical text to make it support egalitarianism. He and Poythress worked with the team of

---

4. Wheaton: Crossway, 1991. Cf. also his *Evangelical Feminism and Biblical Truth: An Analysis of Over 100 Disputed Questions* (Wheaton: Crossway, 2012). Grudem is also a co-founder of the Council on Biblical Manhood and Womanhood, which promotes the complementarian position.

5. Grudem, "Does *kephale* ('Head') mean 'Source' or 'Authority Over' in Greek Literature? A Survey of 2,336 Examples," *Trinity Journal* 10 (1985): 38–59. Grudem updated and supplemented his article in Grudem and John Piper, ed., *Recovering Biblical Manhood and Womanhood* (Wheaton: Crossway, 1991), Appendix I, 425–68.

6. Nashville: B&H Publishers, 2000.

7. Nashville: B&H Publishers, 2005.

translators that produced and edited the *English Standard Version*,[8] an "essentially literal" translation of Scripture that seeks to avoid theological, philosophical, and political bias, including gender ideology.

More recently, Grudem, who was an economics major at Harvard, has produced works in the economic, ethical, and political spheres: *Politics According to the Bible: A Comprehensive Resource for Understanding Modern Political Issues in Light of Scripture*,[9] *Christian Ethics: An Introduction to Biblical Moral Reasoning*,[10] and (with Barry Asmus) *The Poverty of Nations: A Sustainable Solution*.[11] These books do not mark any departure from Grudem's general theological emphasis or his direct engagement with the Bible. Indeed, these arguments for Christian ethical and political engagement reinforce his commitment to the Reformed tradition, as in Puritanism and in Dutch neo-Calvinism.[12] In the 2016 election, Grudem was a supporter of Donald Trump, with qualifications. (UPDATE, 2020: Grudem continues to support Trump, though continuing to recognize the truth of some criticisms of the President.)

There has been controversy between Grudem and some other writers about the doctrine of the Trinity.[13] The church confesses that there is one God in three persons, and that Scripture names those persons as Father, Son, and Holy Spirit. Scripture is clear both as to God's oneness and as to the deity of the three persons, but beyond those affirmations much is mysterious. It is not immediately obvious how God can be both one and three, or how a "person" of God is different from other persons or from the singular divine nature. Traditional theology confesses that

---

8. Wheaton: Crossway, 2001, and in many editions since. From 2005–2008, Grudem served as General Editor of the *ESV Study Bible*.

9. Grand Rapids: Zondervan, 2010.

10. Wheaton: Crossway, 2018.

11. Wheaton: Crossway, 2013.

12. There are some Reformed theologians who press Luther's "Two Kingdoms" distinction to argue that Scripture deals only with salvation from sin and not with politics or the general culture. Grudem, of course, is on the other side of this debate. His writings contain the best resolution of the controversy, showing how there are in Scripture solutions for specific social issues.

13. This controversy goes back to the formulations of Grudem's *Systematic Theology* and his controversy with evangelical feminism, but it was reignited at the 2016 Annual Meeting of the Evangelical Theological Society.

the three persons may be distinguished from one another by their "personal properties": the Father is unbegotten, eternally generates the Son, and eternally sends forth the Spirit; the Son is eternally begotten and eternally sends forth the Spirit; the Spirit eternally proceeds from the Father and the Son.[14] But it is unclear what these personal properties tell us about the persons beyond the names "Father," "Son," and "Spirit," and, if the properties are more than elaborations of these names, how their meanings can be established from Scripture.

Clearly there are differences among the three persons beyond those implied by their personal properties. It was the Son who became incarnate, not the Father or the Holy Spirit. And this fact was not an accident. In God's plan nothing is inappropriate, and so evidently there was a reason why only the Son became incarnate.[15] So the history of redemption reveals to us some truths about the eternal distinctions between the Trinitarian persons, however difficult it may be for us to understand them.

In Grudem's *Systematic Theology*, he maintains that although the three persons are equal in their being, deity, nature, power, and glory, there are some differences in "role" among them,[16] differences that exist through all eternity. Particularly, Grudem stresses that the Father has the distinctive role of being supreme authority, so that even the Son and the Spirit are eternally subordinate to the Father's eternal plan.

Other theologians, particularly evangelical feminists, have taken issue with Grudem here as elsewhere. Evangelical feminists have invoked the equality of the persons of the Trinity as a model for egalitarian marriage among human beings, and they have charged Grudem (wrongly, in my view) with holding to a subordinationism like that of the heretic Arius.[17] The 2016 annual meeting of the Evangelical Theological Society featured

---

14. Whether the Spirit proceeds from the Father AND the Son (*filioque*) or whether he proceeds only from the Father is disputed between the Eastern and the Western churches. My formulation of the personal properties reflects the Western understanding.

15. To cite a statement Einstein made in a different context, "God does not throw dice."

16. *Systematic Theology*, 248–52.

17. In my view, it was a mistake on Grudem's part to use the term "subordination" here, even in his highly qualified way ("functional," not "ontological" subordination), since theological critics often attend to words without paying due attention to their contexts and qualifications.

a number of lectures on the Trinity, and the views of Grudem and Bruce Ware (who holds essentially the same position) came up for scrutiny.

For the details of the controversy, consult the essay by Bruce Ware in this volume. For what it's worth, I would argue that (1) it is wrong for either side to use the classic doctrine of the Trinity as a model for human marriage. A biblical view of marriage ought to focus, not on the doctrine of the Trinity, difficult as that is to formulate, but on the passages of Scripture that address human marriage specifically, such as Gen. 1:24 and Eph. 5:22–33. (2) It is misleading to speak of "subordination" of the Son to the Father, since the Arian controversy gave that term a specific meaning that is hard to avoid and confusing to introduce into other contexts. And (3) that it is nevertheless quite legitimate for theologians to venture beyond the classic creedal statements, seeking better to understand the distinctions among the persons of the Trinity from the roles they play in the history of redemption.

In summary, I see Wayne Grudem as an excellent representative of the Westminster tradition in theology. He exhibits the Old Princeton/ Westminster passion to honor the authority and inerrancy of Scripture, and to bring all theological controversies directly to Scripture for their resolution.[18] At the same time, like many representatives of Old Princeton and Westminster, he is not bound by tradition, but applies the Bible creatively to many areas of human life.

Alongside my theological admiration of him, I would express thanks to God for Wayne Grudem's friendship over many years and the example of his Christian life. The essay in this volume by his son Elliott testifies to Wayne Grudem's love of worship and praise. And his love of God motivates him to be gracious to his colleagues as well. He has always been willing to support the work of other evangelical theologians.[19] He gladly acknowledged his debt to a number of us on the dedication page of his

---

18. Grudem is knowledgeable and appreciative of the creeds and catechisms of the church. But his son Elliott Grudem, in this volume, explains interestingly why his father had his son memorize Scripture rather than catechism questions.

19. He has been a very active member of the Evangelical Theological Society for many years and served as president of the organization in 1999.

Systematic Theology. Later, he wrote an article for my own Festschrift,[20] even though as it turned out we held different positions on the topic he chose to write on. When I published my own *Systematic Theology* in 2013[21] after many years of recommending Grudem's,[22] I would not have asked him to recommend mine; but P&R's editor did, and he was willing to give my book a gracious endorsement.

Though Grudem is now afflicted with Parkinson's disease, he maintains an active work schedule and continues to bless the church and the world with the riches of God's word. I hope that this Festschrift brings much further honor to his distinguished career and to the Lord Jesus whom he serves.

---

20. Grudem, "Why Is It Never Right to Lie: An Example of John Frame's Influence on My Approach to Ethics," in John J. Hughes, ed., *Speaking the Truth in Love* (Phillipsburg, NJ: P&R, 2009), 778–801. When Grudem began the article, he had the impression that his position on lying was the same as mine. After reading my *Doctrine of the Christian Life* (Phillipsburg: P&R, 2008), he realized that I had changed my position and we were in different camps! To Grudem's credit, however, he stuck by his guns and presented at great length and depth what he believed the Scriptures taught. I still disagree with him on this matter, but I deeply respect his allegiance to Scripture as he understands it.

21. Phillipsburg, NJ: P&R Publishers.

22. In fact, I still recommend it. The two books have some different features and serve different purposes. Grudem's is more complete than mine in many areas, and I love the study materials he places after each chapter. The hymns and memory passages and points of personal application he cites are immensely valuable.

9

Preface to *Redeeming the Life of the Mind*

I was one of the editors of this book, the Festschrift for Vern S. Poythress (Wheaton: Crossway, 2017). Vern was a student of mine and has become a good friend and close collaborator. We share many seminal theological ideas. This is my preface to the volume.

WESTMINSTER THEOLOGICAL SEMINARY has played a major role in the history of orthodox Reformed theology in America. Founded in 1929, its original faculty affirmed that the seminary would continue the historic position of "old Princeton Seminary." Princeton had for many decades represented the theology of Calvin and the Westminster Confession of Faith, as opposed to the liberal theology taught after 1929 by many professors at "new Princeton." But Westminster was not merely a clone of the older school. Although committed to the Reformed doctrinal standards, it quickly displayed a pattern of creative thought within the bounds of Reformed orthodoxy. Westminster professors produced many books and articles on threats to the orthodoxy that was distinctive to the modern period. The chief founder of Westminster, J. Gresham Machen, brought his great expertise in modern European theology and biblical criticism to the new faculty, as can be seen in his books *The Virgin Birth of*

Christ,[1] *The Origin of Paul's Religion*,[2] and *Christianity and Liberalism*.[3] Cornelius Van Til, professor of apologetics, also attacked liberal theology, but from a new biblical epistemology that became known as *presuppositionalism*. Many Westminster professors also advocated the "biblical theology" of Geerhardus Vos, a Princeton professor who was too much neglected during his years at Princeton. John Murray in systematics focused like a laser on the basis of Reformed doctrines in the biblical texts themselves. So at Westminster, there was a strong defense of the old doctrines by some strikingly new methods.

The 1960s marked significant changes at Westminster. The "boys" that Machen brought with him from Princeton began to retire and go to glory. I studied, largely with this old faculty, from 1961–64, earning my B.D. degree, which is now called the M.Div. My time at Westminster was a great blessing as I grew in my understanding of the word of God. But it was also an intellectual treat, and when I went on for graduate work at Yale, I felt well prepared, for Westminster taught me not only to embrace Reformed orthodoxy but also to think carefully and creatively about theology and Scripture. When I returned to Westminster in a teaching capacity in 1968, I was determined to continue for my students both the oldness and the newness that had characterized Westminster's heritage. In time that led me to examine American language analysis philosophy, just as Van Til and Knudsen had studied European philosophy and theology. And it led me to develop a theological method called *triperspectivalism*, about which there will be more references in this book.

In the late 1960s and early 1970s, there was an atmosphere of transition, as new faculty were added and new thoughts entered our corporate discussion: Jay Adams' "nouthetic counseling," Jack Miller's views of how to outgrow the ingrown church, and D. Clair Davis's Jesus-centered understanding of church history. Discussions in my classes

---

1. New York: Harper, 1930.
2. New York: Macmillan, 1921.
3. New York: Macmillan, 1923.

often felt like "passing the torch," as I taught and learned from many students who turned out to be notable thinkers in their own right, bringing forth in the Westminster tradition ideas old and new. Among those students were Wayne Grudem, later author of a wonderful systematic theology and co-editor of this volume; Greg Bahnsen, who defended theonomy and Van Til's apologetics with rigor; Dennis Johnson, now a professor at Westminster in California; John Hughes, who taught at Westmont College and is co-editor of this volume; Bill Edgar, who now teaches at Westminster; Jim Hurley, who founded the Marriage and Family Therapy program at Reformed Theological Seminary in Jackson, Mississippi; Dick Keyes, who for many years has directed the L'Abri program in Southborough, Massachusetts; and Tiina Allik, who doctored at Yale and taught for some years at Loyola University in New Orleans. Others, too, who attended Westminster at that time later entered the theological profession. Willem Van Gemeren taught OT for many years at Reformed and Trinity seminaries. Moisés Silva was a professor of biblical studies at Westmont College and Gordon-Conwell Seminary. Andrew Lincoln served as Portland Professor of New Testament at the University of Gloucestershire from 1999 to 2013. And Susan Foh later wrote *Women and the Word of God*.[4] There was also a group of academically sharp students who followed and sought to apply the teachings of Herman Dooyeweerd. When I think of having many of these students in the same classroom, I wonder how I managed to survive those years. Yet I remember them as a group that loved Jesus and who sought to dig deeply into the word of God, following its teaching wherever it led.

Vern S. Poythress fit right in with this group. I remember well the faculty meeting in which President Edmund P. Clowney told us that we needed to have something new, an "experimental honors program." Clowney had often spoken to students at Harvard, and he had met Vern there, concluding that the present Westminster program would not be sufficiently challenging for Vern. Vern had a Ph.D. in mathematics from Harvard. He had also studied theology extensively and wanted to earn

---

4. Phillipsburg, NJ: Presbyterian and Reformed, 1978.

a theology degree. So our faculty voted to establish a program in which especially gifted students would not have to attend regularly scheduled classes (though they could attend any lectures they desired), but would take comprehensive exams and write papers in major areas of theology.

As it turned out, many of the lectures that Vern chose to attend were in my courses, so he joined the group to which the torch was being passed. In fear and trembling, I presented my triperspectival method in these classes with Vern and the others listening carefully and, somewhat to my surprise, Vern found this approach fascinating and consonant with his own thinking. He had studied linguistics with Dr. Kenneth Pike, the inventor of "tagmemics," the theory of linguistics that governed the Bible translation work of Wycliffe Bible Translators. Vern found that my triperspectival triad of normative, situational, and existential perspectives was congruent with Pike's distinction between particle, field, and wave, as well as the other concepts of Pike's linguistic theory. Then in 1976 Vern wrote a book called *Philosophy, Science, and the Sovereignty of God*[5] in which he correlated these triads and many others, developing doctrines of ontology, methodology, and axiology. Throughout the 1970s, he worked with Wycliffe Bible Translators and earned a D.Th. degree in biblical studies at the University of Stellenbosch in South Africa. From 1976 to the present, he has been a professor of New Testament at Westminster.

Throughout his career, Vern's work has illumined many fields of study, as the bibliography in this volume will attest—from biblical theology and mathematics, to sociology, philosophy, logic, theory of chance and determinism, hermeneutics, and biblical authority. Many of us will testify that his character is equally inspiring. Vern believes that the work of the scholar must be done, not only from God's word and in God's name, but also in the *presence* of God.[6] He is God-centered in the workplace and in his family. Many of us have been moved by the way that he has taught his two sons Ransom and Justin. Both boys attended public school, but Vern and his wife, Diane, understood that a secular education was not enough. Students from Christian families needed to be untaught a

---

5. Phillipsburg, NJ: Presbyterian and Reformed, 1976.
6. See especially his *Reading the Word of God in the Presence of God* (Wheaton: Crossway, 2016).

great many things to make sure that their own thinking would reflect biblical presuppositions. So Vern and Diane taught Ransom and Justin intensively in biblical content and theology. They prepared both boys for what they called "Bar Yeshua" ceremonies. These were similar to the "Bar Mitzvah" ceremonies of the Jewish people, but full of gospel content. You will learn some of the results of this from the Poythress sons themselves in the first section of this book, "Sons of Yeshua." And in those essays you can find some beautiful testimonies of Vern's godly character.

In this volume we also seek to honor Vern by presenting to him essays from his fellow scholars on topics with which he has been concerned through the years of his ministry. Following the "Sons of Yeshua" section, part one of our book, we present groups of essays on biblical exegesis, the doctrine of the Trinity, worldview, history, and ethics.

In part two, on biblical exegesis, Greg Beale, Vern's Westminster colleague, presents in chapter 3, "The New Testament Background of ἐκκλησία Revisited Yet Again," a study of the term *ecclesia* in Scripture. He argues that the main background of this term is to be found in the Septuagint translation of the OT, not in secular Roman usage. He concludes that the church of the OT and the church of the NT are the same church.

In Whan Kim contributes in chapter 4 his essay "Standard of the Divine Choice between the Offerings of Cain and Abel in Gen. 4:1–16," arguing that what differentiates the offerings of the two brothers is not something in the offerings themselves, but the attitudes of the brothers' hearts: Abel sought above all to please God and Cain did not.

Brandon Crowe, another of Vern's colleagues, in his essay "Reading the Lord's Prayer Christologically" (chapter 5), teaches us how to do what the title of his essay communicates. Like his colleagues, Vern has always taught that Christ is the center of the Scriptures, both OT and NT. Crowe shows how a Christological focus sheds light on all the petitions of the Lord's Prayer.

Then Robert J. Cara, vice president in charge of academic affairs at Reformed Theological Seminary, who has studied with Vern, continues the Christological theme, considering in chapter 6 "Psalms Applied to Both Christ and Christians," some Psalms that the NT applies both to

Christ and to Christians. As in Vern's teaching, Christological exegesis gives us not only facts about Christ, but applies Scripture to our own lives in the most helpful way.

Next, Iain Duguid, who teaches OT at Westminster, in his contribution "What Kind of Prophecy Continues? Defining the Differences Between the Continuationism and Cessationism" (chapter 7), takes up "cessationism," the question of whether and in what form the charismatic gifts of the NT (tongues, prophecy, healing) continue today. He follows Vern's own treatments of this controversial and difficult issue, with a careful, nuanced discussion. He believes that we should give more consideration to the variations in the biblical concepts. This carefulness will lead to the conclusion that the cessationist Richard Gaffin and the continuationist Wayne Grudem (who both have essays in this volume) are not as far apart (or as far from Vern) as they might initially appear.

Lane Tipton, who teaches NT at Westminster, addresses in "Christocentrism *and* Christotelism: The Spirit, Redemptive History, and the Gospel" (our chapter 8) a recent controversy within the seminary faculty. He helpfully brings to bear on the problem Vos's distinction between symbol and type, yielding two ways in which Christ is the theme of the OT: the symbols point to Christ as the substance of Israel's present life, and the types point to him as the future consummation of Israel's hope. Neither of these requires an explanation in terms of "Second Temple hermeneutics."

Richard B. Gaffin is a longtime (and recently retired) colleague of Vern at Westminster. His essay, "What 'Symphony of Sighs'? Some Reflections on the Eschatological Future of the Creation," is our chapter 9. In this essay, Gaffin draws on his recent work of translating the *Reformed Dogmatics* of Geerhardus Vos and develops cogent reasons for seeing the new heavens and new earth as a purification of the old, rather than as an annihilation of the old and replacement with something totally different.

Part three of our book is dedicated to the doctrine of the Trinity, one of the major areas of theological discussion in evangelicalism today. Vern has taken a great interest in this doctrine. In the context of his triperspectivalism, he sees the Trinity as the root of all the unity and diversity of the creation. Camden Bucey begins this discussion in chapter 10 with his contribution "The Trinity and Monotheism: Christianity and Islam in the Theology of Cornelius Van Til."

Combining in chapter 11 Vern's concern with the Trinity and his interests in language and linguistics, Pierce Taylor Hibbs writes on "Language and the Trinity: A Meeting Place for the Global Church."

In chapter 12, Jeffrey C. Waddington contributes his "Jonathan Edwards and God's Involvement in Creation: An Examination of Miscellanies 1263." There has long been controversy over Edwards's "occasionalism." Some have suspected Edwards of pantheism or panentheism, since for him everything in nature immediately depends on God, making Edwards an advocate of "continuous creation." At the end of his essay, Waddington makes comparisons between Edwards's views and Vern's essay, "Why Scientists *Must* Believe in God," the remarkable apologetic that begins his book *Redeeming Science*.

Part four of our collection deals with worldview, a central concern of Vern's writings, inherited from Cornelius Van Til. In chapter 13, Peter A. Lillback, president of Westminster, presents his thoughts on "Redeeming the Seminary by Redeeming Its Worldview." My essay in chapter 12, "Presuppositionalism and Perspectivalism," discusses two matters of central concern to Vern and me. I try there to show how presuppositionalism, an apologetic focused on worldview (developed by Cornelius Van Til), is quite compatible with triperspectivalism and indeed inseparable from it. Chapter 14 is the deeply stimulating essay "The Death of Tragedy: Reflections upon a Tragic Aspect of This Present Age" by the Westminster church historian Carl Trueman. In chapter 15 of our book, Brian Courtney Wood brings this part to an inspiring conclusion in his "Beholding the Mind-Renewing and Life-Transforming Glory of Jesus Christ the Lord: How a Christ-Centered Perspective Restores in Us the Beauty and Glory of God's Image." Here the emphasis on Christian worldview combines with the emphasis on Christ-centered exegesis, reminding us that Christ-centered exegesis of Scripture *is* the Christian worldview.

Part five deals with history, a somewhat neglected area of Christian philosophy. The essay by Luke Lu in chapter 16 is "Christian Missions in

China: A Reformed Perspective." Vern's wife, Diane, has long had a special concern with China. She speaks fluent Mandarin, and she and Vern have had a special ministry to Chinese students on the Westminster campus, as well as to other international students. Diane herself brings her missions interests to bear on the philosophy of history in her essay, chapter 17, on "Historiography: Redeeming History." Diane is herself a working historian, and in this essay she adds to her husband's "Redeeming" books, adding another important realm to the discussion of Christ's lordship over all realms of life. She shows that in the Christian worldview, God is in control of time as well as space. So there can be no religious neutrality in the way we interpret history.

Part six concludes our volume with the question Francis Schaeffer asked, "How Then Should We Live?" Two of the book's co-editors (and good friends of Vern) here contribute essays on biblical ethics. In chapter 18, Wayne Grudem presents "Christians Will Never Have to Choose the 'Lesser Sin.'" And in chapter 19, John Hughes presents a triperspectival analysis of some ethical terms in Paul's Letter to the Romans: "Perspectives on the Kingdom of God in Romans 14:17."

We trust God that this collection will honor Vern and, above all, as Vern certainly wishes, honor the Lord Jesus Christ. May it promote Vern's vision among God's people, a vision to glorify Christ's lordship over all areas of human life, redeeming all areas of human thought.

10

Traditionalism

ONE OF THE LARGEST PROBLEMS today in evangelical and Reformed theology is the tendency toward traditionalism. I hope in this paper to take some steps toward analyzing this danger and commending its antidote, the Reformation doctrine of *sola Scriptura*.[1]

TRADITIONALISM AND *SOLA SCRIPTURA*

Traditionalism is hard to define. It is right and proper to revere tradition, since God has raised up many teachers for his church over the years who, through their writings, continue to speak to us. A teacher in the church does not lose his authority after he dies. So God does intend for us to learn from teachers of the past, or, in other words, from tradition. On the other hand, the Protestant doctrine of *sola Scriptura* teaches us to emulate the Reformers in testing every human tradition, even the teachings of the church's most respected teachers, by the word of God.

"Traditionalism" exists where *sola Scriptura* is violated, either by adding to or subtracting from God's word (Deut. 4:2). To subtract from the word is to contradict or neglect its teaching. To add to it is to give

---

1. I have previously addressed these issues in my books *Evangelical Reunion* (Grand Rapids: Baker, 1991) and *Contemporary Worship Music* (Phillipsburg: P&R, 1997), in "In Defense of Something Close to Biblicism," published in longer form in *Westminster Theological Journal* 59:2 (Fall 1997): 269–318, with responses by Richard Muller and David Wells. I also participated in an e-mail debate on this and other subjects with Darryl Hart in early 1998, also available at www.frame-poythress.org.

to human teaching the kind of authority that belongs to God's word alone (Isa. 29:13–14; Matt. 15:8–9). Too great a reverence for tradition can lead to both errors.

In this article, I will focus on one way in which evangelical and Reformed theologians are tempted to add to the word of God: by seeking to resolve substantive theological issues by reference to historical traditions, without searching the Scriptures.

This error in theological method has, of course, been characteristic of Roman Catholic theology since long before the Reformation, and it was one of the Reformers' chief complaints against the Roman magisterium. It has also been characteristic of the liberal theology of the last several centuries. For liberal theology is, almost by definition, the attempt to present the Christian message on some basis other than that of the infallible authority of Scripture.[2] Liberals use Scripture in their theological work, to be sure. But they reserve the right to disagree with it. So in the final analysis they are on their own, basing their thought on human wisdom, human tradition.

How do liberals reach theological conclusions without appealing to the ultimate authority of Scripture? It isn't easy. But essentially, the liberal appeals to Christian tradition. With some exceptions, liberals do not like to present their work as mere speculation. They want to be recognized as Christian teachers, as members of the historic theological community. So they seek to position themselves within the church's theological tradition. I shall mention three ways in which they do this, using my own nomenclature:

1. *Identification:* choosing a historical or contemporary movement and endorsing it, allowing it to set standards of truth.

2. *Antithesis:* choosing a historical movement and opposing it, making it into a paradigm case of error. (Thus the

---

2. By "liberal" I refer to the whole tradition from Enlightenment rationalism to the present which currently dominates mainstream theological discussion and ministerial training in the large denominations. It includes not only the "older liberalism" of Ritschl and Harnack, but also neo-orthodoxy, existential theology, secular theology, liberation theology, post-liberalism, and other movements.

mainstream of liberal theology has typically demonized
especially modern "fundamentalism" and the post-Reformation Protestant theologians.)

3. *Triangulation:* Identifying two or more historical movements thought to be of some value, identifying weaknesses
in these movements, and defining a new position which
supposedly overcomes these weaknesses.[3]

When I studied at Yale in the mid-1960s, the courses labeled "systematic
theology" were actually courses in the history of liberal theology since
Schleiermacher. (Theology before Schleiermacher was called "history of
doctrine.") Whatever movement the professor espoused (process theology, narrative theology, Kierkegaardian individualism, etc.) provided
the "identification." Fundamentalism or Protestant orthodoxy provided
the "antithesis." Triangulation was the method urged upon the students
for developing their own theological perspectives. Barth had too much
transcendence, Bultmann too much immanence; so the students were
encouraged to go "beyond" both, to a position that did justice to the
insights of Barth and Bultmann, without going to such indefensible
extremes. Doing their own triangulating, some professors pointed us
to the "futuristic" theologies of Moltmann, Gutierrez, and Pannenberg,
in which the future provides transcendence and the concrete movement of history provides immanence. But more importantly, students
were urged to go their own way, triangulating on whatever movements
inspired them, to develop their own distinctive brands of theology.

EVANGELICAL TRADITIONALISM

Evangelical scholars often study in liberal institutions, and so it is not
surprising that the methods of identification, antithesis, and triangulation have also entered evangelical theology, sometimes alongside a
genuine concern for *sola Scriptura*. There is, of course, nothing wrong
with the three methods themselves as long as Scripture supplies the

---

3. These three methods form a Hegelian triad of sorts.

norms for evaluation. But using them without biblical norms (as in the examples of my Yale experience) amounts to theological autonomy and the loss of *sola Scriptura*.

Most theologians in the evangelical tradition do confess *sola Scriptura*. But alongside that confession has arisen an increasing emphasis on tradition.

Thirty years ago, the best-known evangelical scholars were apologists, biblical scholars, and systematic theologians (Clark, Henry, Carnell, Van Til, Bruce, Packer[4]). Today, evangelical academic leaders are largely in the field of historical theology, or they are systematic theologians who greatly emphasize church history: Armstrong, Bloesch, Godfrey, Grenz, Hart, Horton, Marsden, McGrath, Muller, Noll, Oden, Thiselton, Wells, et al.[5]

In addition, we should note (1) the movement toward a renewed confessionalism led by the Association of Confessing Evangelicals, and (2) recent "conversions" of people of evangelical background to communions giving more stress to the historic traditions of the church: Anglicanism, Roman Catholicism, Eastern Orthodoxy.

What lies behind these trends? An adequate answer to that question would probably require historians of the caliber of the men listed above. But here are a few suggestions that make some sense to me.[6]

I. EVANGELICAL EXPOSURE TO LIBERAL
THEOLOGICAL METHODS

The academic stars of evangelicalism are chosen, to a great extent, by the secularist-liberal academic establishment. Those whose scholarship is most admired among evangelicals are those who have earned degrees and/or obtained appointments at outstanding secular universities. The secular academic establishment does not, of course, reward theologians

---

4. Bruce and Packer were, of course, historians too. But during the 1960s they were better known for biblical scholarship and systematic theology, respectively.

5. Let me make clear my profound respect for these men and the quality of scholarship they have maintained. My criticisms of evangelical historicism, which may in part apply to some of these brothers, is not intended in the least to dishonor them or to belittle their achievements.

6. For those familiar with my "perspectives," the following three suggestions can be classified as situational, normative, and existential, respectively.

who derive their conclusions from the divine, infallible authority of Scripture. But gifted evangelicals can do well in the secular environment if they write their dissertations and phrase their conclusions in *historical* terms. One could not, for example, expect Oxford University to grant a Ph.D. to a dissertation defending biblical inerrancy. But it is not too hard to imagine such a degree being given for a thesis on the *history* of the doctrine of inerrancy, in which the writer's own evaluations are couched in the modes of identification,[7] antithesis, and triangulation.

If an evangelical doctoral candidate has a bias in favor of sixteenth-century theology instead of nineteenth or twentieth, the secular establishment will not normally consider that attitude any sort of challenge, as long as in other respects the candidate respects the methods and standards approved by the establishment. Indeed, the candidate's advisors and readers may regard his bias as a quaint sort of antiquarianism, a charming affectation appropriate to the academic vocation.

So it has been natural for evangelicals to focus on historical studies and methods, even when seeking to give some normative support to evangelical distinctives.

That is not wrong in my estimation. It does not necessarily entail compromise. One does what one can do in such a situation. It has been going on a long time. I recall that when the Reformed scholar John H. Gerstner taught at the liberal Pittsburgh Theological Seminary, he held the title Professor of Church History, though in my estimation most of his interests were better classified as systematic theology and apologetics. Holding his conservative beliefs, he was not invited to teach systematic theology, but he regularly taught courses in the "history of" various doctrines: biblical authority, justification, and so on. Gerstner had a tremendous influence. R. C. Sproul attributes his Ligonier Ministries to Gerstner's theological inspiration.

Though the emphasis on history can certainly be justified by the inherent value of historical studies and by the pragmatics of evangelicalism's marginal position in the academic world, there is a downside.

---

7. Of course, in such a context one must identify with a movement that has the approval of the liberal establishment.

Scholars can[8] get into the habit of using the methods of identification, antithesis, and triangulation, without taking adequate care to find biblical standards of evaluation.[9]

a) *Identification:* They may sometimes attach themselves to some movement in the past or present that they come to regard virtually as a standard of truth.[10] In Reformed circles, this tendency leads to a fervent traditionalism, in which, not only the Confessions, but also the extra-confessional practices of the Reformed tradition, in areas such as worship, evangelism, and pastoral care, are placed beyond question. In an atmosphere of such traditionalism, it is not possible to consider further reform, beyond that accomplished in the Reformation period itself. There is no continuing reformation of the church's standards and practices by comparing them with Scripture. Thus there is no way in which new practices, addressing needs of the present time, can be considered or evaluated theologically. This is ironic, because one of the most basic convictions of the Reformed tradition itself is *sola Scriptura* which mandates continuing reformation, *semper reformanda*. At this point, Reformed traditionalism is profoundly anti-traditional.

In other circles influenced by evangelicalism, there is an identification with evangelical feminism. Paul K. Jewett's *The Ordination of Women*[11] is so strongly governed by feminist assumptions that even the authority of the apostle Paul comes under question.

---

8. I am not saying, of course, that study in liberal institutions leads *necessarily* to these distortions. Some students have resisted these influences successfully, J. Gresham Machen being a conspicuous example. But fallen human nature being what it is, it is not surprising that some have succumbed to these temptations.

9. I have used the example of David Wells in my "In Defense of Something Close to Biblicism," cited above. See also comments on Hart, Marva Dawn, and others in my *Contemporary Worship Music.*

10. Hart, in the debate cited earlier, describes Reformed tradition as a kind of "presupposition," in the Van Tillian sense of that term. Elsewhere in the debate, he does claim belief in *sola Scriptura,* but not very credibly in view of his enormous reverence for tradition. He expresses terror of ever departing from Reformed tradition in any respect, comparing that to the terror Luther experienced at the prospect of breaking fellowship with the Roman Church.

11. Grand Rapids: Eerdmans, 1980. His later systematic theological work, *God, Creation, and Revelation* (Grand Rapids: Eerdmans, 1991) also affirms the feminist movement and adopts sexual egalitarianism as one of its main structural motives. See pp. 13–14, 322–25, and the sermons included in the book of the Rev. Dr. Marguerite Schuster.

b) *Antithesis:* Such scholars tend also to focus on other movements which serve as paradigms of error. In Reformed circles, these
movements usually include Roman Catholicism, Arminianism, the
charismatic movement, dispensationalism, and such contemporary
movements as liberalism, Marxism, feminism, and "pop culture." I am
not an advocate of any of these movements, and I see them as deeply
flawed. But I think it is wrong to make them *paradigms* of error, so that
nothing true or good can ever be found in any of them. Our world
is fallen, but it is also the object of God's common and special grace.
Therefore, both good and bad are to be found in all people and social
institutions.[12]

But one sometimes gets the impression in reading evangelical theology that it is wrong to find any good in such movements, or even to
formulate our own positions in ways that "blunt our testimony" against
these movements. It is almost as though a theology cannot be genuinely Reformed unless it is "set over against" these other movements
in the sharpest way.

At its worst, this method becomes a *via negativa:* we attempt to
define the truth by looking at a movement we don't like and defining
our own position to be the opposite of that. Thus, ironically, the false
movement becomes, by logical inversion, a standard of Christian truth.
Antithesis becomes a perverse form of natural theology. But surely this
is wrong. We should define the Christian message positively, from the
clear revelation of God's word. I consider the *via negativa* to be fatal to
the doctrine of *sola Scriptura.*

c) *Triangulation:* Or, evangelical scholars trained in the methods of
liberal theology may seek to develop new and fresh forms of evangelicalism by the method of triangulation. I see some evidence of this in
Stanley Grenz and Roger Olson, *Twentieth-Century Theology,*[13] in which

---

12. I do hold a Van Tillian view of antithesis between the church and the world, between
truth and error. But Van Til himself recognized the importance of common grace, and he spoke
of a "mixture of truth and error" in the thought of unbelievers. He also recognized that antithesis
in the proper biblical sense requires definition on biblical standards, not on the basis of our
autonomous evaluations of historical movements. See my *Cornelius Van Til* (Phillipsburg: P&R,
1995), especially chapter 15.

13. Downers Grove: Inter-Varsity Press, 1992.

everything turns on the concepts of transcendence and immanence and the challenge to evangelicals is to seek a "balance" that Kant, Barth, Tillich, and others have failed to achieve. My response: don't seek to balance the profoundly false notions of transcendence and immanence found in liberal theology, but go back to the Bible.

I also believe that the "open theism" of Pinnock, Rice, Basinger, and others is essentially a triangulation between traditional Arminianism and process theology. Arminianism doesn't adequately safeguard its own concept of free will, because of its affirmation of divine foreknowledge. Process theology overcomes this problem by denying foreknowledge; but its god is so immanent that it is not clearly distinct from the world. Ergo, open theism: God is transcendent, but does not have complete knowledge of the future. It would have been better, in my view, for Pinnock and the others to look harder at Scripture.[14] A more careful look at the Bible would have led them to question the heart of their system: the libertarian view of human free will.

2. EVANGELICAL WEARINESS OVER THE INERRANCY DEBATE

The "battle for the Bible" has virtually defined American Evangelicalism from the time of B. B. Warfield until very recently. In the early days of that period, the battle was against the liberals, who defined themselves in effect as being opposed to biblical inerrancy. In the mid-1960s, however, it became evident that some within the evangelical tradition also found it difficult to affirm biblical inerrancy, and the battle raged within the evangelical movement as well as with those outside. The International Council on Biblical Inerrancy held conferences and published a great many writings on the subject, before it disbanded. It remains to be seen where this discussion has led the evangelical movement.

Since inerrancy was often mentioned as the doctrine that defined evangelicalism over against its Protestant liberal rivals, the questioning of inerrancy within evangelicalism led to a profound identity crisis. The

---

14. I realize that their writings do include exegetical arguments, but I find these quite implausible. Ironically, it seems to me that their exegesis falls into the error that they regularly attribute to Calvinists: their exegetical conclusions are governed by their dogmatics.

"limited" or "partial" inerrantists were not liberals; they were supernaturalists who held to the traditional "fundamentals" (virgin birth, miracles, blood atonement, physical resurrection, second coming) *except for* biblical inerrancy. But with such a deep rift on a central matter, how was the evangelical family to stay together?

There were different answers to this question among evangelicals. Some inerrantists simply read their opponents out of the movement. Others tried to recognize the remaining common ground, along with the differences. Questions of inerrancy sometimes, at least, resolved into questions of interpretation (e.g., the question of whether Genesis 1 teaches a temporal sequence of divine creation in 24-hour days), and increasing realization of that fact led some on either side to see the issue as something other than black-and-white. And there was a *rapprochement* from the far side as well: scholars from the liberal tradition were taking the Bible more seriously and coming to more conservative conclusions on historical and dogmatic questions. Thus the gap between evangelicals and liberals narrowed, appearing in some cases to be a continuum rather than an antithesis.

With these developments came a weariness with the inerrancy debate. Today there is far less interest, even among those committed to a strong view of inerrancy, in proving the Bible right about every matter of history, geography, and science, than there was twenty years ago. Further, some have sensed a need for a common-ground methodology that will enable inerrantists, limited-inerrancy evangelicals, and liberals to work together without constantly arguing the detailed accuracy of the biblical texts.

That methodology is essentially the methodology of historical scholarship. When Wolfhart Pannenberg, coming from the liberal tradition, declared the necessity of verifying all theological statements by (religiously neutral) historical scholarship, many evangelicals applauded.[15] They perceived this dictum as vindicating their evidential apol-

---

15. For reasons *not* to applaud religious neutrality in apologetics, history, and theology, see my *Apologetics to the Glory of God* (Phillipsburg: P&R, 1994) and *Cornelius Van Til*, cited above. See also the abovementioned articles, "Muller on Theology" and "In Defense of Something Close

ogetic. And in effect many evangelicals of different convictions about inerrancy, and many liberals of different stripes, are now working together to develop theology on this model.

But a theology based on religiously neutral historical scholarship must find its standards of truth elsewhere than Scripture. And so the methods of this kind of theology tend to be the methods of identity, antithesis, and triangulation discussed earlier in this paper, rather than any direct and detailed appeal to biblical texts.

3. EVANGELICAL SHAME OVER PAST PAROCHIALISM

Evangelicals have in this century often been called to re-examine themselves. Carl Henry's *The Uneasy Conscience of American Fundamentalism*[16] chastised Evangelicals for their poor scholarship and their withdrawal from issues of social justice. The "new" evangelicalism of the postwar period tried to reconstruct fundamentalism along the lines suggested by Henry and others. In the debate over inerrancy from around 1967–1990, again the very nature of evangelicalism was up for discussion.

Meanwhile, other evangelicals found their tradition wanting in its lack of any sense of the great traditions of the church. Evangelicalism, it seemed, was not well-connected to the roots of Christendom: the church fathers, Augustine, the Fathers of the Eastern church, the great liturgical traditions of Catholicism and Protestantism. This was connected with the feeling that evangelicalism was liturgically inadequate: too simplistic, without a sense of transcendence or depth, aesthetically inane, culturally parochial. Some evangelicals studied carefully the traditions of the broader church, and some of them defected to church bodies that are not generally considered evangelical: Anglicanism, Roman Catholicism, Eastern Orthodoxy.

Others have remained within evangelical churches, but have urged upon their denominations a greater respect for broader Christian traditions. I applaud this development as a symptom of a reawakening of

---

to Biblicism." By "religiously neutral" I mean scholarship in which the ultimate standards of truth are found somewhere other than Scripture.

16. Grand Rapids: Eerdmans, 1947.

biblical ecumenism.[17] But insofar as this movement represents a weakening of the *sola Scriptura* principle, I fear that its ultimate thrust will be anti-ecumenical, for it will forfeit the only firm basis for a reunion of the church.

These developments have come, of course, through historical study, and they have both presupposed and confirmed a higher evaluation of the importance of tradition than has been common in evangelicalism. Indeed, conversations with former evangelicals who have crossed the wall into these other movements often turn on the subject of *sola Scriptura*. Converts from evangelicalism often report that their turning point came with a radical questioning of *sola Scriptura*, leading to an identification of tradition (of course *including* Scripture) as the fundamental source of revelation.

THE RESULTS OF TRADITIONALISM

As one committed heart and soul to the principle *sola Scriptura*, I find the trend toward traditionalism most unfortunate. It has, in my view, weakened the evangelical witness in our time. Note the following:

1. It has bound the consciences of Christians in areas where Scripture gives freedom. Traditionalists have often insisted, for example, that popular music is entirely and always unfit for use in Christian worship. But where does Scripture say this? What biblical principle implies it? How does this scruple stand up against Paul's willingness to "become all things to all people so that by all possible means I might save some" (1 Cor. 9:22 NIV)? The argument against the use of "contemporary worship music" is based largely on a historical argument about the genesis of the genre and its incompatibility with certain traditions.[18]

2. It has thus led to unnecessary divisions and partisanship among churches and denominations. That displeases our Lord (John 17; 1 Cor. 1–3).

---

17. See my *Evangelical Reunion*.

18. There are also biblical arguments, but rather shallow ones, based on the assumption that contemporary worship music does not honor, e.g., the transcendence of God. In my view, emphasis on divine transcendence (holiness, majesty, and power) is one of the strengths of this music. See my *Contemporary Worship Music*.

3. Traditionalism has weakened the rational basis of Christian theology insofar as it has replaced exegetical arguments with historical-traditional ones. In Christianity, only Scripture is ultimately authoritative. Arguments based only, or largely, on traditions (either evangelical or non-evangelical) will not be persuasive to Christian hearts.

4. Many traditionalist arguments should be classified as genetic fallacies. For example, we sometimes hear the argument that something is good (e.g., Reformed liturgy) because it comes out of Reformed tradition.[19] That assumes that everything historically connected with the Reformed tradition is good. So either the Reformed tradition itself is ultimately normative, or the argument is a fallacy. Or, negatively, we sometimes hear that a song comes from the tradition of pop culture and is therefore unsuitable to Christian worship. This is an antithetical argument, as the former was an argument from identification. It is valid only on the assumption that there is nothing at all that is good in pop culture, an assumption impossible to prove and unlikely on a biblical view of common grace. It is hard for me to avoid the impression that traditionalism accounts for much of the poor quality of thought and argumentation one finds in evangelical writings today.[20]

5. The traditionalist-historicist argument that the church must be completely separate from modern culture is hard to square with the Great Commission of Matt. 28:18–20. The biblical stance of Christians is not to hide from the world, but to go forth and win the world for Christ. We are not to be "of" the world, but we are to be "in" it. And, to carry out the evangelistic mandate, we are to become like the world, like the prevailing culture, in some ways: Paul says, "I have become all

---

19. This sort of thing is even worse, of course, when an idea is adopted because it "sounds" Reformed and another is rejected because it "sounds" Arminian. I have often encountered this kind of sloppy thinking among theological students.

20. I speak, to be sure, as one who has been burned by reviewers who have attacked my writings without any meaningful argument, merely because I disagreed with traditions with which the reviewers identified. See, for example, the exchange between Mark Karlberg and myself concerning my *Cornelius Van Til* in *Mid-America Journal of Theology* 9:2 (Fall 1993): 279–308.

things to all people so that by all possible means I might save some" (1 Cor. 9:22 NIV).[21]

This raises the issue of communication, for as Christ's ambassadors, we must proclaim the gospel in the languages of the world. The movement toward contemporary worship music is essentially an attempt to speak the musical language that many people are speaking today. The traditionalist would forbid this and require us to use antiquarian music. But has he considered adequately Paul's emphasis on intelligible communication in worship (1 Cor. 14)?

6. There are distressing signs that some are seeking to *define* the evangelical and Reformed movements in traditionalist ways. I have called attention to this danger in the "Cambridge Declaration" of the Association of Confessing Evangelicals.[22] I have also heard recently of a conference sponsored by that organization in which one speaker made a scathing attack on contemporary forms of worship and worship music. These issues, to be sure, are complex, and I certainly do not insist that all evangelicals agree with me. I have explored this issue in a book-length discussion,[23] and I freely admit that there is far more to be said. I am happy to see these matters freely and vigorously discussed. However, I wish that ACE would see the value of presenting more than one view of these matters when, after all, they are not actually resolved by the confessions themselves.

This is a time of definition for evangelicals, especially those who, like myself, genuinely wish to be known as "confessional." And I fear that the message people are hearing in the ACE writings and conferences is that those who are motivated by the Great Commission to speak in God's praise the languages of our time are not fit to bear the name of evangelical. That suggestion, I think, is unhistorical, divisive, and untrue.

---

21. The argument that we must avoid any contamination of contemporary culture in our means of proclaiming the gospel seems to me also to be at odds with the exhortation of Abraham Kuyper to bring all of culture under the dominion of Christ (cf. Paul in 2 Cor. 10:5). Some aspects of culture—e.g., its immorality and selfishness—should be avoided. Scripture tells us what to avoid. But for the most part Scripture calls us to conquer, not to hide.

22. In my "Biblicism" paper, cited above.

23. *Contemporary Worship Music.*

THE ANTIDOTE: *SOLA SCRIPTURA*

In this situation, the Reformation (traditional!!) principle of *sola Scriptura*, the sufficiency of Scripture, needs to be heard anew. Scripture itself proclaims it:

> Do not add to what I command you, and do not subtract from it, but keep the commandments of the Lord your God that I give you. (Deut. 4:2 NIV; cf. 12:32; Josh. 1:7; Prov. 30:6; Rev. 22:18–19)

> This people draw near with their mouth and honor me with their lips, while their hearts are far from me, and their fear of me is a commandment taught by men. (Isa. 29:13 ESV); Jesus quotes this passage against Pharisaic traditionalists in Matt. 15:8–9)

> All Scripture is God-breathed and is useful for teaching, rebuking, correcting and training in righteousness, so that the man of God may be thoroughly equipped for every good work. (2 Tim. 3:16–17 NIV)

Scripture does not, of course, tell us everything we need to know about everything. We must look outside Scripture if we want specific directions on how to fix a sink or repair a car. But Scripture tells us everything that God wants us to know "concerning all things necessary for His own glory, man's salvation, faith and life" (*Westminster Confession of Faith*, 1.6). Scripture doesn't tell us how to repair a car, but it tells us how to glorify God in repairing a car, namely by doing whatever we do "in the name of the Lord Jesus, giving thanks to God the Father through him" (Col. 3:17), and by working at it with all our hearts "as working for the Lord, not for human masters" (v. 23 NIV).

Even in worship there are some things that cannot be derived from Scripture, "some circumstances concerning the worship of God, and government of the church, common to human actions and societies, which are to be ordered by the light of nature, and Christian prudence, according to the general rules of the Word, which are always to be obeyed" (*Westminster Confession*, 1.6). So there is room for tradition. But Scripture and Scripture alone has the final word. Nothing outside

Scripture may be imposed as law on God's people. No mere historical argument, no critique of culture, no human tradition, not even a church confession, can be ultimate law in God's church.

Some would argue that the church preceded Scripture. In one sense this is true. From Adam to Moses, there is no clear record of any written revelation. But when God gives his written word to Israel, that word stands as his written covenant with them, the written constitution of the people of God. That covenant document is to be the highest authority for God's people, the word of the living God himself. Thus the people are not to add or subtract; they are not to turn to the right or to the left. Open any page in Deuteronomy at random, and you are likely to find admonitions to obey all the commands, statutes, testimonies, words, judgments, etc. in God's law, the written law.

The New Covenant in Jesus is also subject to God's written word (2 Tim. 2:16–17, again). No human wisdom must be allowed to take precedence over Scripture, either to allow what Scripture forbids, or to forbid what Scripture allows.

So when questions arise concerning worship, we must ask first of all, What does Scripture command? What are the things Scripture requires? What are the areas in which Scripture gives us freedom to make decisions within the bounds of its general principles?

Where we have freedom to make our own choices (as, I believe, concerning music style), we still have to evaluate the possibilities. Are there contemporary styles of music that are incompatible with biblical norms for worship? I think there are. But if someone wants to argue that a particular style is incompatible with Scripture, he will need to show that he has carefully understood what the biblical principles are, and not just rely on genetic-fallacy historical arguments or arguments which assume that tradition should never be changed. And he will need to do justice to *all* the relevant biblical principles: not just the transcendence and holiness of God, but also the Great Commission and the importance of edifying worshipers.[24]

---

24. And of course he will need also to show that he understands the style of music under discussion.

Sola Scriptura, therefore, forbids us to absolutize tradition or to put the conclusions of historical scholarship on the same level as Scripture. As such, it is a charter of freedom for the Christian, though, to be sure, Scripture restricts our freedom in a number of ways. Jesus's yoke is easy, and as we take that yoke upon us, we lose the tyrannical yokes of those who would impose their traditions as law. May God enable us to understand and celebrate his gentle bonds and his wonderful liberty.

PART 2

The Thomist Controversy

11

Letter to a Friend about
the Thomist Challenge

Since around 2014, the evangelical theological world has been subjected to controversy originating from a group of writers including James Dolezal who have claimed that many American Evangelicals hold defective doctrines of the Trinity, God's simplicity, his eternity, and his changelessness. The argument of these writers is that the evangelicals in question (myself among them) fail to conform to the definitions, arguments, and conclusions of Thomas Aquinas. In effect, the Dolezal group has charged these evangelicals with heterodoxy for their failure to agree with Aquinas.

In defending myself and others against these charges, I wrote a few short letters, journal entries, and essays, which I include below. I am not interested in pursuing the controversy further, but these pieces indicate the gist of my thinking about these matters. These essays were not written in a particular sequence, to be read in a particular order. There is overlap among them, which I have not attempted to smooth out.

DEAR _____,

You know, there's this line in *The Godfather*, part 3, where Michael Corleone, played by Al Pacino, tears his hair and says something like, "Just when I think I've gotten out, they pull me back in!" He was talking about the Mafia, but I have similar feelings about academic theology. I retired to get away from all that. Then several times since, I've been assaulted with stuff about Dolezal and Helm (not to mention Swain and Allen!) about the Trinity, divine timelessness, and all.

No way am I going to analyze all the titles you've linked below. But in general I think that Scott Oliphint has the better argument.

What has happened is, I think, something like this: When I was in seminary, Van Til taught us to be skeptical of medieval and post-reformation scholasticism. Aquinas was a bad guy, for the most part. We were encouraged to be BIBLICAL, like the Reformers. Vos and Clowney picked it up from there: everything we do in theology must have an exegetical basis, and the chief theological categories are REDEMPTIVE-HISTORICAL, not logical, philosophical, or even ethical.

I emerged from this liking Aquinas and the scholastics a bit more than Van Til did, with an overall orientation closer to Edmund Clowney, but with more emphasis than Clowney on "application." I called it "Something Close to Biblicism."[1] I found I could defend such things as simplicity, eternal generation, and divine timelessness from my biblical model. But I could not stop there. Scripture is given to us, not so that we can produce an abstract metaphysical account of everything, but for doctrine, correction, reproof, and instruction in righteousness that we may be complete and thoroughly furnished unto good works.

The Trinitarian metaphysic of Scripture is a background to its main gospel message, that the Son of God came to be WITH US, to die in our place, and to rise again.

And to me it is as "plain as a pikestaff," as CVT used to say, that though God transcends time, he is completely able to enter the temporal world he has created and to reveal himself there unambiguously. He has done this, and we owe our salvation to that fact (John 1:14). He is "outside the box," but he is also "inside the box," for the box is his creation, and he is everywhere in the world he has made. Really present (Ps. 139). Outside time, but also inside time.

---

1. See SSW3, 27–65.

What has happened lately is that a lot of confessional/historically oriented people have failed to appreciate Van Til or to appreciate the Vos/Clowney model. They have gone back to an essentially scholastic position and have called it "classical theism." Even worse, they have claimed, evidently, that when Scripture speaks of "God with us," it is speaking non-literally, anthropomorphically, etc. What is literal in their view is that God is outside history, outside time, etc., and when it says God is in history, that is somehow bracketed.

I think that's biblically wrong. I think I can defend the proposition that the biblical God is outside time (and I defended that years ago against the process thinkers and open theists). But it is just as plain from Scripture—plainer in fact—that God comes INTO time and becomes an actor in history. That is, in fact, the heart of the gospel. Terms like "non-literal" and "anthropomorphic" have their uses. I think whatever we say about God transcends our literal understanding in some measure. But if it is in some way "anthropomorphic" to say that God became flesh, it is at least as anthropomorphic to say that "God transcends time." But it is not right to put brackets around "God became flesh" and to suggest that it is much more adequate to say that "God transcends time." Where does Scripture justify that kind of relative judgment? If the former expression reflects the weakness of our understanding, certainly the latter expression does too, at least as much. Or are we back to the Clark controversy where we must debate the meaning of "incomprehensibility"?

There is more analysis, more thinking to be done. But there is something deeply wrong with accommodating the God of the Bible to the Prime Mover of Aristotle and Aquinas.

12

Calvinism, Arminianism, and Thomism

This is a letter to myself, from my journal of Sunday, December 27, 2020.

I'M THINKING that a lot of theological controversies arise out of confusion over the distinction between God's transcendence and his immanence. As CVT pointed out, neo-orthodoxy made a terrible mistake in these categories, which I illustrated by the Frame square. I've also argued that recent Reformed Thomism neglects divine immanence, relegating it to "figurative" status, even though it is the heart of the gospel message. But I'm now inclined to think this distinction also illumines the historic difference between Calvinism and Arminianism. The difference between these is essentially this: Calvinism is impressed with God's transcendence and doesn't think much about his immanence. Arminianism does the reverse.

Some Calvinists get upset when you say that human beings must "choose" Christ. Yes, God's choice precedes theirs. But he does not choose them without decreeing that they will choose him. "Choose you this day ..." Human choice is vitally important.

Arminians, on the other hand, seem to deny Eph. 1:11, that God works *everything* according to his eternal plan (cf. Rom. 8:28).

Reformed Thomists don't like the idea that God "responds" to events in the creation. But what about prayer?

A more comprehensive view of the truth is: (1) God brings everything to pass by an eternal decree. (2) Part of that decree is that God himself will play a role in history itself. (3) In his immanent role, he decrees to interact with finite events, so that he does one thing on Monday, something else on Tuesday. (4) His attitudes toward creation and parts of it respond to events (which of course are among the events decreed), so that when one thing happens, he responds in grace, e.g., and, when another thing happens, he responds in judgment. (5) It probably is not prudent, in the current theological situation, to say that God "changes" in his immanent relations. But it is not prudent to deny it either. We await a better vocabulary, and a more collegial theological society.

13

Why I Am Not a Thomist

THOMAS AQUINAS (1225–1274) was an enormously influential scholar, a philosopher, theologian, and canon lawyer, and eventually declared a saint and a "doctor" of the Roman Catholic Church. He is one of the most influential thinkers of all time, possibly the most influential among Christian thinkers. But none of this entails that he was always right.

Over the years of my own theological study, I have taken a serious interest in Aquinas. I studied him as part of my college philosophy major. Then at Westminster Theological Seminary I took a course from Cornelius Van Til in medieval philosophy (focused on Aquinas's *Summa Theologica* and Thomist scholar Etienne Gilson's *The Spirit of Medieval Philosophy*[1]). At Yale University I had a course taught by George Lindbeck on "The Natural Theology of Thomas Aquinas," and we read much of Aquinas's *Summa Theologica*. When I returned as a teacher to Westminster, I continued to read Aquinas and to share my conclusions with the students. One of the first elective courses I taught at Westminster was "The Aseity of God," in which I explored much of Aquinas's thought on this subject and compared him with others like Van Til. More recently I published my own *History of Western Philosophy and Theology*,[2] which

---

1. Notre Dame, IN: University of Notre Dame Press, 1991.

2. Phillipsburg, NJ: P&R Publishing, 2015. Van Til's *Christianity in Conflict* (Phillipsburg, NJ: privately printed, 1962), his history of apologetics, is also significant, though it is currently out of print.

contained a ten-page analysis of Aquinas as part of a chapter which dealt with the whole medieval period and compared Aquinas with a number of other thinkers.

Like most scholars who have studied Aquinas, I have gained a great admiration for the academic quality of his work. Though he lived less than fifty years, he produced large amounts of tightly reasoned books and articles that have deeply influenced later thinkers. He exegeted the Bible, commented on previous theologians and philosophers, and produced original ideas of high quality. His arguments are intricate and elaborate. One of his special concerns was to integrate ideas of Aristotle (critically) into his theology and philosophy, as previous thinkers had incorporated Plato and other Greek thinkers. Roman Catholic writers never forget that Aquinas is an official doctor of their church, and they differ with him only with expressions of deference and respect.

Protestant scholars are less bound by the *authority* of Aquinas, but they also view his work with great respect. Although Aquinas does not have the privileged official status among Protestants that he has among Roman Catholics, he has nonetheless had significant influence on Protestant theological formulations, including their creeds and confessions. Although Luther and Calvin showed little deference to the medieval thinkers, later Protestant writers like John Owen have used a number of Aquinas's terms, concepts, and arguments.

Some Protestants, however, have taken a strongly negative stance toward Aquinas. Cornelius Van Til, like other Dutch neo-Calvinists, thought that Aquinas was a major source of the thinking that made the Reformation necessary.[3] Herman Dooyeweerd thought that Aquinas's thought presupposed the "form-matter scheme" of Greek philosophy, by which the natural world could be understood by the autonomous human mind, though Aquinas supplemented (and sometimes vetoed) this conception by reference to Scripture and tradition. According to Dooyeweerd, Aquinas represented the relationship between Scripture

---

3. See Van Til, *The Defense of the Faith*, ed. K. Scott Oliphint (Phillipsburg, NJ: P&R Publishing, 2008); Herman Dooyeweerd, *Reformation and Scholasticism in Philosophy* (Grand Rapids: Paideia Press, 2012).

and autonomous human thought by the "nature-grace scheme," in which autonomous human thinking (about "nature") was supplemented by Scripture (the revelation of "grace").

More recently some Protestant scholars have taken a far more favorable position toward Aquinas than did the earlier neo-Calvinists. Some of these scholars have focused on echoes of Aquinas's concepts in the Protestant Confessions, and in major post-Reformation theologians like John Owen (1616–1683). Writers like Richard Muller, Paul Helm, Kelly Kapic, Carl Trueman, and Christopher Cleveland have argued that the Thomistic themes in Owen and other post-reformation Protestants deserve more respect than they were given by Van Til and Dooyeweerd.[4] An especially influential recent defense of Aquinas's doctrine of God is James Dolezal, *All There is In God*.[5]

I have not been completely convinced by either evaluation of Aquinas. I am more favorable to him than were Van Til and Dooyeweerd, less favorable than Muller. It does, however, seem obvious to me as it did to the neo-Calvinists that Aquinas made much use of Aristotle's philosophy and that in some respects Aquinas was influenced by Aristotle's argument for God as the Prime Mover. It does not seem to me that the contemporary scholars have taken into sufficient account the influence of Aristotle's formulation on Aquinas and the compatibility of this formulation with Scripture.

Often the more contemporary approach to Aquinas seems to me to amount to an appeal to authority. These writers seem to claim that Protestant theologians ought to follow the Aristotle-Aquinas approach because it is somehow the definition of Christian orthodoxy.[6] Dolezal says often that the approach he recommends is found in all the Christian theological traditions before and after Aquinas and among Protestant theologians until the nineteenth century. (He thinks that Isaak Dorner [1809–1894] was a major figure in the breakdown of the Thomist

---

4. For a summary of this discussion, see http://themelios.thegospelcoalition.org/review/thomism-in-john-owen.

5. Grand Rapids: Reformation Heritage Books, 2017.

6. Muller says that those who differ from Dolezal's formulation are at odds with "traditional Christian orthodoxy." See his foreword to Dolezal, *All There Is in God*, xi.

consensus.) So in the view of Dolezal, Muller, and others, Protestants have an *obligation* to follow Aquinas.

It is at this point that my dissent is most strong. In my view, Protestants have no *obligation* to follow Aquinas, or for that matter any other theologian of past tradition. The Protestant principle is *sola Scriptura*, which means that Scripture alone serves as our ultimate standard of faith and life. That does not mean that we should disrespect tradition or theological genius in any general way. But neither tradition (including confessions and creeds) nor theologians like Owen command unconditional acceptance in Protestant theology. Rather, tradition must commend itself by showing that it has a foundation in Scripture.

The Reformation began with an insight into the justification of sinners which contradicted the teaching of the medieval church. There are legitimate debates about theological precedents for this insight. But Luther and Calvin were never moved by the sheer authority of the papacy and the defenders of its theology. Nor did they adopt the principle of justification by faith alone on the basis of a contrary tradition within the history of doctrine. They did not, of course, reject tradition in some general way. But they insisted that traditional theological views defend themselves by comparison with Scripture.

Many of us have concluded that just as the medieval notions of justification needed to be corrected on the basis of Scripture, so does the Thomistic-Aristotelian consensus about the doctrine of God. In both cases, these doctrines have been corrupted by the influence of Greek philosophy and the lack of a serious exegesis of Scripture. And I have come to the conclusion that the defects in the medieval concept of justification are related to its inadequately personalistic doctrine of God.

It should be obvious that the biblical doctrine of God is highly personalistic. The God of the Bible is a metaphysical absolute, to be sure: "a Spirit infinite, eternal, unchangeable in his being," but also in his "wisdom, power, holiness, justice, goodness, and truth."[7] I have

---

7. *Westminster Shorter Catechism*, answer 4.

described him elsewhere as "a personal absolute."[8] His infinity, eternality, and unchangeability establish his metaphysical absoluteness; his other attributes (including the fact that he is a Spirit) establish that he is a personal, not an impersonal, being.

This balance between absoluteness and personality is a unique feature of the biblical worldview. In nonbiblical worldviews, it is common enough to find metaphysical absolutes (Aristotle's Prime Mover is a significant example) that have no personal qualities, and it is equally common to find personal gods without infinity, eternality, or unchangeability (for example in pagan polytheisms). Only in the worldview of Scripture (and of course of religions significantly *influenced* by Scripture[9]) is God both metaphysically absolute and fully personal. This fact is theologically and apologetically significant. A God without metaphysical absoluteness is not clearly distinct from finite beings. But a God without personal qualities is unable to communicate to his creatures: to command, to promise, to express love, to befriend, to administer justice.

The attempt of Aquinas and more recent thinkers to model the biblical God after Aristotle's Prime Mover risks turning the biblical God into a metaphysical absolute without personal qualities. Aristotle's god is one, eternal, infinite and unchangeable, so it is understandable that scholars compare him (or it) to the God of the Bible. Aristotle's cosmological argument for the existence of this being also naturally tempts Christian philosophers to apply it to the Christian god. But the comparison fails at points that are of central importance for Christianity. Aristotle's Prime Mover does not speak to human beings. It does not make promises. It does not know or love the world. Nor is it even the creator of the world in the biblical sense, though it is called the Prime Mover. For Aristotle, the world is eternal. The Prime Mover did not originate the world out of nothing. Rather, it accounts for the world by existing eternally alongside the world, somehow accounting for the

---

8. Frame, *Systematic Theology* (Phillipsburg, NJ: P&R Publishers, 2013), 36–52; Frame, *A History of Western Philosophy and Theology* (Phillipsburg, NJ: P&R Publishers, 2015), 14–19.

9. As Judaism, Islam, and cults like Mormonism.

world's motions through all time. The world and the Prime Mover are two correlative aspects of Being in general, not, as in Scripture, distinct beings related as creator and creature.[10]

Now we know something of Luther's story, his passion to be right with God. He sought justification through the sacraments of confession and communion, but nothing in these rites would cleanse his conscience. He sought to win God's approval through good works, which was likewise fruitless. It had seemed to many at the time that grace was something mechanical and automatic—a substance that flowed from God to the believer by way of the church hierarchy and the sacraments. But Luther had no peace until he dealt with his need in a fully *personal* way. He came to see sin as a personal transaction, a disobedience, rebellion, and betrayal. So salvation, justification, must likewise be personal. Nothing mechanical would suffice. The sinner's only hope was to personally confess his sin, repent, and receive God's promise through the atonement of Christ. To receive that promise was faith alone, *sola fide*, which became the great watchword of the Reformation. Saving faith was, therefore, an entirely *personal* relation between the sinner and the living God.

So, however much the successors of Luther appreciated Aquinas and Aristotle, they could not worship a God who was *only* a Prime Mover. They came to God as a gracious Father, who sent his Son to die for us, bringing us salvation as a free gift to be received by faith alone. That God was a God who knew and loved us before the foundation of the world, who proclaimed good news, who made and kept promises, who was always present to keep us from danger. The Heidelberg Catechism begins,

1. Q. What is your only comfort in life and death?

A. That I am not my own, but belong with body and soul, both in life and in death, to my faithful Saviour Jesus Christ. He has fully paid for all my sins with His precious blood, and has set me free from all the power of the devil. He also preserves me in such a way that without the will of my heavenly Father not a hair can fall from

---

10. Thomists like Etienne Gilson and Jacques Maritain have revised Aristotle in the name of Aquinas by stressing that God is the cause, not only of motion, but also of *being* (*esse*).

my head; indeed, all things must work together for my salvation. Therefore, by His Holy Spirit He also assures me of eternal life and makes me heartily willing and ready from now on to live for Him.

Protestant Christians, therefore, could never accept Aristotle's argument that God could not know or love the world because that would mean the world could change him in some way. For Aristotle, the governing presupposition was that God could not be changed, affected, moved, or caused by anything other than himself. Otherwise, God could not be truly the "first" cause; the Prime Mover could not be truly prime. For Aristotle, that implied that the Prime Mover was essentially an impersonal principle. He could not be a gracious Father to anyone in the world, nor could he enter into any other truly personal relationship. The Prime Mover proclaimed no gospel; he did not so love the world that he gave his only Son.

In fairness, Aquinas also had to break with Aristotle at many points. He contradicted Aristotle's view of the eternity of the world. And he certainly proclaimed the biblical truths that God was, not only the first cause, but also wise, powerful, holy, just, good, and true. Whatever differences there were between the followers of Aquinas and those of Luther, the two theologians agreed with the Nicene Creed that Jesus was fully God, and with the formula of Chalcedon that Jesus had two distinct natures, fully divine and fully human. Contrary to Aristotle, God knew, loved, and entered into covenants with human beings. He revealed himself to mankind in words as well as in nature. So Aquinas as well as Luther believed that where Aristotle contradicted Scripture the church must reject him and accept the teachings of the Bible.

But this story has injected considerable complication into the work of theology. It has not been easy for theologians to bring together the ideas of Aristotle, Aquinas, and Luther, not to mention others such as Plato, Augustine, Calvin, and Owen, to balance one idea with another, and sometimes to choose one and reject another. And this difficult task itself obscures another task which is equally difficult but far more important: the task of stating, teaching, and applying what lies behind and stands far above all these theological conceptions: what Scripture actually says.

Historical figures with great gifts have joined us to aid the church in this higher task, but they have often made it more difficult. For the historical figures have forced us to study, not only Scripture, but also their own work. Their writing has produced a large secondary literature, and later theologians must study that secondary literature as well as the Bible itself. To some extent, we come to understand Scripture by asking which historical figure is most nearly right about Scripture. But sometimes it is necessary for us to look away from all these figures, having learned what we can from them, and to look as best we can at the Bible itself.

So whenever we study a theological issue, we must ask the relation between biblical exegesis and historical theology. I should mention that I have criticized Richard Muller, a historian of doctrine greatly revered in Reformed circles (rightly so) as someone who thinks that theology is to be *defined* as the history of doctrine.[11] As I indicated earlier in this essay, Muller supplied a foreword to Dolezal's *All That Is in God* and in that foreword criticized those who differ with Dolezal as deviants from "traditional Christian orthodoxy." It never occurs to Muller that after all has been said and done about historical theology the chief task of theology remains: to ascertain what Scripture says, over and above all the competing historical figures. But that is the definitive task of theology; that is what, in the end, theology is. For Scripture is canon, the supreme authority for the church. If it is helpful for us to study the creeds and confessions of the church, to say nothing of the historical theological traditions, it is helpful because it brings us closer to Scripture, closer to what God expects us to believe.

So what shall we do with Aquinas, Aristotle, and the Prime Mover? In further essays, I will consider the argument of Dolezal in the volume referenced earlier. Dolezal is a fervent disciple of Aquinas, and he is convinced that those who differ from Aquinas (including the present writer) have departed from orthodox Christianity. Indeed, he believes that such writers may as well not believe in God at all.

---

11. See my "Muller on Theology," in Frame, *Selected Shorter Writings* 3 (Phillipsburg, NJ: P&R Publishing, 2016), 3–26. The several essays following this one in SSW3 are also relevant to the present discussion. See also the essay "Traditionalism" in the present volume.

14

Two Models of Transcendence:
Pure Being vs. Divine Lordship

GOD'S TRANSCENDENCE is beyond our power to imagine it. But even to make that statement we must have in our minds some idea of what the term *transcendence* means and how it might apply to God. Further, Scripture tells us that God is "high and lifted up." Theologians and preachers have an obligation to expound this description of God along with all others. Indeed, it appears to be part of the meaning of the very word *God* that he transcends our existence and our thoughts. One can hardly claim to believe in God, much less to be a theologian, if he does not affirm in some sense divine transcendence.

In this paper, I will discuss two ways of understanding God's transcendence that have been common in our theological history. I will argue against the first, in favor of the second.

PURE BEING

The first model of transcendence is the model of "pure being." This means that of all the beings in the world, God is the one most entitled to be called "Being." He is not the only being, of course. But other beings are not *pure* being. In some measure they are metaphysically defective, so that they to some extent lack the fullness and perfection of being that only God has. To that extent, beings other than God are not completely real; they do not fully exist. Since God's being is perfect and complete, it is *pure*, and in that sense God's being is higher than the being of other beings. It is in that sense transcendent.

The idea of "degrees" of being, implying levels of higher and lower being, comes from Greek philosophy. The Greeks were not biblical theists, but they cared much about relations between being and nonbeing in the world. That was, indeed, their philosophical project: to understand the universe as being, being in some sort of relation to nonbeing.

It was a promising project, because it would seem that if anything can be said about the universe in general it is that the universe has being, that it is real. No thing, quality, or relation other than being is truly universal. So it would seem that if we could understand being we could understand everything.

But the project ran into some immediate roadblocks. For it quickly became evident that "being" could not be defined or described in any persuasive or helpful way. For to define "being" it was necessary at the very least to distinguish it from nonbeing. But if being is a truly universal predicate, if everything is being of some sort, then there is no nonbeing. Any time we try to define nonbeing (e.g., as "an absence of all qualities"), then that definition designates something in our world—i.e., a form of being. An absence of all qualities is, after all, something. It is something we can discuss and analyze in various ways. So nonbeing, so defined, is a form of being. But that means that there is no nonbeing, or that nonbeing (however defined) is a form of being.

But if there is no such thing as nonbeing, then there is not possible to contrast being with its opposite. It has no opposite. That implies that it is impossible to define being, or to form a concept of being. To define war, we must be able to contrast it with peace. To define "automobile," we must be able to distinguish between automobiles and non-automobiles.

The lack of any possible contrast between being and an opposite created problems for the Greek philosophers. Parmenides (born around 500 BC) tried to develop a philosophy, a view of the world, in which there was being but no nonbeing. He was convinced that "nonbeing" was a bogus concept, a meaningless expression. For him, the world is entirely being, not anything other than being. But the world of Parmenides's philosophy came out looking very different from the

world of our ordinary experience. In Parmenides's philosophy, nothing changes, because change is always a change from being to nonbeing or the reverse. Parmenides also denied that there was plurality in
the world: there was only one thing, namely being. For if there is more
than one object, one of them is *not* the other, and the difference between
them is a form of nonbeing.[1] Similarly, Parmenides denied that there was
any kind of generation (change from nonbeing to being) or destruction
(change from being to nonbeing).

Parmenides's attempts to rid his worldview of negative elements pro-
vokes amusement. Pure being, he wants to say, excludes negation. But
viewed objectively, his system is full of negation: no change, no generation, no destruction, no plurality. What can these negatives be, other than
elements of nonbeing in a system that is supposed to exclude nonbeing?

So in the end Parmenides's system proved unsatisfactory to his successors. And there were more difficult problems with the whole project of analyzing the universe as a form of static being. For Heraclitus
(540–480) had argued (with a bit more confidence in sense experience than Parmenides had) that change is not only real, but universal:
everything changes (the opposite of what Parmenides taught). So it
seemed that a radically new approach was needed.

Plato (429–327 BC) tried to combine the philosophies of Parmenides
and Heraclitus into one: a view of the world that was like Parmenides's
world in one portion, like Heraclitus's in the other. He distinguished
between a "world of Forms" and a "world of change." The latter is the
world of our experience, in which, as Heraclitus said, everything is constantly changing. But how is knowledge possible, if everything is changing into something else? Plato's answer is that we can know the world
of our experience because it is related to a higher world, the world of
Forms. This higher world contains unchanging standards which serve
to define objects in the world of change. We can identify a tree in our
experience, because although it is constantly changing it measures up
to a standard, an ideal tree in the world of Forms. Same for animals,
humans, and abstract concepts like virtue, truth, beauty, and goodness.

---

1. This point is related to later theological discussions of divine simplicity.

For Plato, then, the concept of being was more complex than in previous philosophy. For him, there are "degrees of being," rather than the binary division between being and nonbeing found in earlier philosophy. The Form of Manhood, for example, has more reality, more being, than any actual man; for, as the very definition of manhood, it is more "mannish" than any instance of manhood in the changing world. And the Form of Goodness, Plato's highest Form, is more perfectly good than any instance of goodness in our experience. It is the very definition of goodness, and nothing in our world can perfectly measure up to it. But there is somehow a continuum between the Form goodness and goodness in our experience, so that the latter can be understood as in some sense the same thing as the former, and the former can be understood as the reality of which the latter is an appearance.

Parmenides would have complained that Plato's system did not resolve the original problem, the problem of defining "being" as opposed to "nonbeing." For what are "degrees of being" if they are not degrees of mixture between being and nonbeing? If the Form "man" is more real, has more being, than any man in the changing world, what can that mean except that men in the changing world have an admixture of nonbeing? And Parmenides would want to know, what is that? How can there be any such thing as nonbeing, in any kind or quantity? As in Parmenides's philosophy, the nonbeing in Plato's system is undefinable, for any definition makes it into being.

Plato was not a Christian, or even a theist in any way comparable to the biblical worldview. But the church fathers, like Justin Martyr and Athenagoras, studied Plato and asked whether the transcendence of the biblical God could be understood in terms of Plato's degrees of being. Might it be possible to see God as the supreme Being on Plato's scale? They appealed to some Scripture in this connection, particularly Ex. 3:14. In this passage, Moses at the burning bush asks God his name, and

> God said to Moses, "I AM WHO I AM." And he [God] said, "Say this to the people of Israel, 'I AM has sent me to you.' " (ESV)

Is it possible that in this verse God is identifying himself as pure being, the highest degree of being in Plato's philosophy? For the church fathers, and to many later theologians, the temptation to read "I AM" as meta-physical being was great.

More recent scholars, however, have argued that this identification is a mistake. For one thing, the Exodus text is centuries older than the lifetime of Plato, and there is no reason to think that Moses had any interest in anything like Greek philosophy. In my own analysis, the "I am" of Ex. 3:14 is presented as the basis for the name *Yahweh* in verse 15, and that name (typically translated *LORD* in English Bibles) refers primarily to God's covenant relation to human beings, including his special covenants with Israel and with NT believers.[2]

Nevertheless, many thinkers from the first century on sought to understand the biblical God in terms of Plato's philosophy of being. Plotinus, the father of Neoplatonism, was a further influence on Christian thought at the time. Rather than divide the world into two realms as Plato had, Plotinus identified a single perfect being as the "One" and taught that that One emanated lesser forms of being into what we know as the world of experience, then received those lesser forms back into his (its) own being. Neoplatonism was a major influence on such thinkers as Pseudo-Dionysius and John Scotus Erigena.

The use of Plato in Christian theology faced three major problems: (1) Plato's forms were impersonal, and therefore were unfit to represent the God of Scripture. (2) In the systems of Plato and Plotinus, there is no clear distinction between creator and creature. The Forms of Plato and the One of Plotinus were not clearly distinct from the world of our experience. The difference between these levels of being is a difference in degree. (3) As I mentioned earlier, it is impossible, in Greek philosophy, to define or even describe being, since it cannot be intelligibly distinguished from nonbeing. Being in this context is not a coherent concept.

In these three respects, Platonistic Christian theology differed sharply from the theology of Scripture. In Scripture, God is personal; there is a clear distinction between him and creatures, and he is capable of revealing himself intelligibly to human beings, though not without some residuum of mystery.

---

2. See Frame, *The Doctrine of God* (Phillipsburg, NJ: P&R Publishing), especially 37–46.

But there is more to be said. Plato's greatest student was Aristotle (384–322 BC), and Aristotle taught a somewhat revised form of Platonism that was also influential among Christian theologians. For Aristotle, the terms *form* and *matter* do not distinguish two different realms, as in Plato. Rather, there is only one world, and form and matter are aspects of it. Everything (except the Prime Mover, which I shall discuss shortly) has both form and matter. A book is made of matter (papyrus, parchment, ink, etc.), and also form (the shape into which the matter is made to accomplish the purpose of the object). A human being is similarly made of matter (various chemicals, food, water, etc.), and form (his body and mind).

But above the world of "form" and "matter" stands a being who is pure form, without any matter at all. Aristotle invokes this being (which he calls the Prime Mover, but whom he also addresses as divine) primarily to explain change. This being is the ultimate explanation of all change in the world, but it never itself undergoes change. When you pursue a chain of causation (A causes B, B causes C, etc.) that chain never goes on indefinitely. It comes to an end, and that end is the Prime Mover, the First Cause, the ultimate source of all motion. If the Prime Mover itself were subject to change, then there would be no first cause and therefore there would be no ultimate explanation for change in the universe.

The Prime Mover, therefore, is much like Parmenides's Being: in him there is no change, no generation, no destruction, no plurality. Because he cannot be changed, he cannot be the effect of any cause. Therefore, he cannot be influenced by anything outside himself. He cannot *know* the world, because then the world would be causing changes in his thought life. For Aristotle, the Prime Mover did think, but he thought only about himself. In fact he thought only about his own *thoughts*: "thought thinking thought." Similarly, the Prime Mover cannot *love* the world as does the God of Scripture. For Aristotle thought that if the Prime Mover loved the world that love can only be an effect upon him by the world, something outside himself. If the Prime Mover could be changed in any way by lesser beings, he would not be the first cause, and therefore he could not be a pure or perfect being. Lesser beings are affected by beings outside themselves. The fact that they can be changed shows that they are not themselves perfect beings. Only the Prime Mover is a truly perfect being.

Like the earlier Greek thinkers, Aristotle understood the supreme principle of the universe to be a perfect being. But he understood perfection somewhat (though not entirely) differently from Plato and Parmenides. For Plato and Parmenides, perfection was largely understood as the absence of negatives: no change, no plurality, no generation, no destruction. But for Aristotle, perfection was to be understood especially as *aseity*, the capacity fully to exist without dependence on anything outside the self. These two Greek approaches were not entirely different from one another. One could argue that each is implicit in the other. But there is a difference of emphasis.

Like Plato and Plotinus, Aristotle was well known to Christian theologians through the medieval period. They made use of his writings in logic and science. But it wasn't until later in this development that Christian theologians made full use of Aristotle's metaphysical works, particularly the doctrine of the Prime Mover. When these writings were rediscovered in the West, in part through Arabic translations, the church at first did not know what to do. In a number of obvious respects, Aristotle's teachings contradicted the teaching of the church. Aristotle believed, for example, that the world was eternal, that it did not begin in a moment of time as Genesis describes.

Thomas Aquinas (1225–1274) faced this problem squarely, and his solution to it prevailed. He distinguished sharply between the realm of philosophy and the realm of "sacred doctrine." Both these disciplines deal with theological concepts like the doctrine of God, but philosophy focuses more on the deliverances of "natural reason," while sacred doctrine focuses more on revelation (i.e., Scripture and the tradition of the church). Natural reason is able to apprehend truth on its own, for the most part, but we need sacred doctrine if we are to attain salvation. And if natural reason ever conflicts with sacred doctrine (as when Aristotle claims that the world is eternal), sacred doctrine must prevail. Nevertheless, Aquinas said, we should not condemn the work of the Greeks, particularly Aristotle. We can learn much from them, as long as we allow to Scripture a kind of veto-power over what they say.

Aquinas was knowledgeable in all phases of Greek philosophy, including the Platonic tradition. But in his view, Aristotle was the master of "natural reason." Aquinas often calls him, simply, "the Philosopher." And Aquinas made most use of his work in the doctrine of God. Central to Aquinas's thought was the "cosmological argument," similar to the argument by which Aristotle proved the existence of his Prime Mover. Any chain of efficient causes, he argued, must end in a being who is the first cause, the uncaused cause, the unmoved mover, the wholly non-contingent being. The First Cause is a perfect Being, who is in no sense dependent on anything other than himself. As in Aristotle, therefore, the chief mark of a perfect being is its aseity.

His aseity implies that he is pure actuality, with no admixture of potentiality. That means that there is nothing in him that needs to be further developed. He has eternally attained perfection. As with Parmenides, a perfect being can never change into something more perfect or less perfect.

That implies that he cannot be a physical being, because bodies are subject to change. And he cannot be composed of matter and form (as finite beings are, according to Aristotle) since matter embodies poten-tiality, which leads to change. By similar arguments, Aquinas concludes that God, the Prime Mover, is absolutely "simple," without any kind of complexity. Everything in God is identical to God himself.

So Aquinas's doctrine of God is a connected argument, beginning with the cosmological argument and inferring consequences concerning God's being and attributes. Aquinas concludes that God is good, omni-present, immutable, eternal, and one. Occasionally he quotes Scripture, but the nuances of these theological concepts grow out of the meta-physical argument rather than biblical exegesis. His main point is that we must construe the nature of God so that God will never be depen-dent on anything other than himself. He is "pure being," "pure actuality," devoid of any change.

In Aristotle, this kind of argumentation led to a conception of God as unable to know or love the world. Aquinas avoids those conclusions by saying that God knows the world by knowing his own thoughts and actions, and that he loves the world by loving his own plans, actions, and intentions for the world. But those answers to Aristotle would seem to compromise Aquinas's doctrine of the absolute simplicity of God. For it appears in this analysis that in God there is an interaction between complex elements: his knowledge, his plans, his thoughts, his actions, his intentions. Once God decides to create beings different from himself, he enters into relations with those beings by the mediation of his own mind. But those beings are still different from himself, and in knowing and loving them he is still being affected by them. Aquinas does not seem to have maintained consistently his central doctrine of the divine aseity.

In addition, there are problems with Aquinas's formulation that hearken back to the larger problems with Greek philosophy that I identified in Parmenides and Plato. (1) The perfect beings of Parmenides, Plato, and Aristotle were impersonal, unlike the God of Scripture. It is not clear how Aquinas establishes the personal character of the God of Scripture, since he begins his argument with the notion of a first cause, a pure being. Where does the God of Abraham, Isaac, and Jacob enter this argument? Aquinas argues that God has knowledge because he is immaterial (*ST* I, XIV.1), but I have never understood that inference. Similarly for God's love and will. Aquinas, since as a Christian he believes the Scriptures, tries very hard to treat God as personal. But his Aristotelian argument does not lead to this Christian conclusion.

(2) Aquinas, like Plato and Aristotle, fails to make a clear distinction between creator and creature. His God, like Aristotle's, is pure being, and created beings are in some way impure. If they were not impure, they would not be creatures but would themselves be God. So evidently the pure being faces the dilemma of creating imperfect products or creating gods. It is not clear to me how Aquinas resolves this question.

(3) To put it differently, it is theologically important to distinguish God and the world by making a clear distinction between the pure being of God and some degree of lesser being that belongs to the creation. Aquinas, like Parmenides, Plato, and Aristotle, places considerable weight on the contrast between being and nonbeing. But how has Aquinas managed to do what Parmenides and the others were unable to do, to give being and nonbeing coherent definitions?

A God who differs from the creation only as a higher degree of being is not clearly transcendent, certainly not transcendent in the ways presented in Scripture.

DIVINE LORDSHIP

I propose a different way to understand God's transcendence.[3] It emerges out of the recovery of the gospel by the Protestant Reformation.

The Reformation, among many other things, recovered the personal character of our relationship to God. In the medieval period, salvation was often conceived formally and somewhat mechanically, as the dispensing of grace on sinners through the Roman hierarchy and the sacraments. What Luther recovered was the personal dimension: as an individual, I myself have sinned against God, and I need his forgiveness. As the sinner comes before God, all he can do is to fall on his knees in repentance and faith, receiving God's free gift of salvation through Jesus Christ alone. God be merciful to ME, a sinner.

When the sinner comes before God, he approaches God, not as pure being, not as a being with a greater degree of being, but as lord and judge, as savior and shepherd, as father and friend.

When Scripture speaks of God, it speaks of him *primarily* in these terms. I do not discount the occasional passages that can be employed in service of a being-metaphysic. But personalism is the *primary* way in which Scripture presents God to us. It is important to respect that presentation, especially for Protestants who embrace the principle *sola Scriptura*, the principle that Scripture alone is the ultimate authority for human thought.

We saw that Ex. 3:14, so important to Aquinas and others, does not identify God with pure being, but as the LORD, the one who rules and redeems his covenant people. Nevertheless, God's personal lordship can be seen as a metaphysical principle. Indeed, the personal lordship model can be seen as the basis for all of God's attributes. God is simple, because he thinks and acts as a whole, not as a combination of potentially conflicting thoughts, impulses, and qualities.

---

3. For a fuller treatment, see Frame, *The Doctrine of God* (Phillipsburg, NJ: P&R Publishing, 2002), 21–115.

He is eternal, because he is Lord of time. He has created time, and he stands above it, seeing with equal vividness the past, present, and future, and ruling the events in all temporal realms. Nevertheless, again because he is the creator of time, he is able to enter into it and play a role, indeed the major role, in Providence and Redemption.

He is immutable in his attributes, his promises, his sovereignty.

Similarly, God is the Lord of space, for space is his creation. He is immense, beyond all spatial dimensions; yet he is also omnipresent, located in all the spaces of the world he has made.

He is impassible, for as the sovereign Lord he cannot be harmed by any of his creatures; nevertheless, he understands the suffering of others as it really is, and understands it from the heart.

God is the highest being, for he is the sovereign Lord. If we seek to develop a philosophy of the universe, that is where we must start. This is a personal world, not a world made of abstract, impersonal forms of "being." He is "above us," transcendent, not because he has a higher degree of being, but because he is the Lord, the ruler of all.

Advocates of pure being theology admit that the biblical description of God and our relation to him is very different from that of Aristotle or Aquinas. James Dolezal speaks of the biblical picture as "mutabilist."[4] But this mutabilist language, he says, is "anthropomorphic" or an "accommodation" to finite minds. What God *really* is, is "pure being," as Aquinas conceived it. I grant that biblical representations of God are accommodated to finite minds, but I think that is true, not only of the mutabilist language, but also of passages like "For I the LORD do not change" (Mal. 3:6). We are not put in a position of having to say that metaphysical descriptions of God are literally true, while passages describing God's interaction with history are literally false. Indeed, God's interaction with history is what Scripture is all about: creation, fall, and all the events of redemption including Jesus's incarnation, earthly ministry, atoning death, and resurrection. In the church, we confess that these events really happened, that they are not mere symbolic descriptions of metaphysical principles.

---

4. Dolezal, *All That Is in God* (Grand Rapids: Reformation Heritage, 2017), 19.

There is something ridiculous about saying that the predominant message of Scripture, God coming to redeem his fallen world, is somehow untrue, and that what is true is that God is pure being. As a Protestant I must put redemption before philosophy, and I must allow redemption to govern my philosophy.

Thomas Aquinas was a godly Christian man, very brilliant, who put his mind in the service of Christ. Much of the time, he referred to God in a deeply personal way. But many times he mixed the biblical teaching up with ideas of the Greek philosophers in a way that distorted the biblical gospel, and for that he must be held accountable.

God is not the pure being of Aristotle; he is the sovereign Lord of heaven and earth. The Prime Mover of Aristotle is not the God of the Bible.

15

Scholasticism for Evangelicals: Thoughts on *All That Is in God* by James Dolezal[1]

I retired in June 2017, weary of academic theology in general and eager, especially, to avoid involvement in theological controversies. I especially sought to avoid intra-Reformed controversies, which I had thought to be typically confused and unedifying. But then I was blindsided by the news that James Dolezal had attacked me as a heretic, for my doctrine of God of all things. Of course, I had published DG in 2002, which dealt in detail with the Bible's teaching about God, and which, incidentally, won a gold medal from the Evangelical Christian Publishers Association. My book championed the traditional doctrines of God's immutability, eternity, simplicity, and Trinity, over against the challenges of process thought and open theism. I did not, however, follow a line consistent with Thomist scholasticism, and Dolezal thought that my failure to do so separated me from the tradition of "classic theology" and made me a "theistic mutualist." He thought similarly of 11–12 other Reformed and evangelical theologians. The fact that my colleague (and new president of Reformed Theological Seminary where I had taught for 17 years) Scott Swain gave an ebullient, full-throated endorsement to Dolezal's book was a further disappointment, and an indication that I would be expected to say something in reply. I published the essays below, first on www.frame-poythress.org, and now here.

---

1. Grand Rapids: Reformation Heritage Books, 2017.

Scholasticism names a type of theology that matured in the thought of Thomas Aquinas. In the post-Reformation period, both Protestant and Roman Catholic thinkers adopted many of the methods and conclusions of scholasticism, and some of these are even reflected in the Protestant confessions. In the Enlightenment of the late seventeenth and eighteenth centuries, many philosophers and theologians reacted strongly against scholasticism, so that in the nineteenth century scholastic and anti-scholastic agendas contended for supremacy in the theological academies.

I studied with Cornelius Van Til, who was in turn influenced by but critical of the Dutch neo-Calvinists such as Kuyper and Dooyeweerd. They accepted some doctrines characteristic of scholasticism—divine simplicity, aseity, supratemporal eternity—but in general they treated scholasticism as a theological blind alley. They were highly critical of Aquinas and saw him as a "synthesis" thinker who tried to combine Christianity with Aristotelian and Neoplatonic philosophy. When a neo-Calvinist referred to someone as "scholastic," that was a term of reproach. The general consensus was that those who do theology in the scholastic way were on a slippery slope that could end only in Roman Catholicism.

Besides extensive study in church history and the history of doctrine, I studied Aquinas in some depth in a course with Van Til, later in a course with George Lindbeck at Yale Graduate School, and after that in my own research and writing. In the end, I emerged with great respect for Aquinas, one of the most brilliant and penetrating thinkers I have ever encountered, and certainly an impressive Christian man. But I also saw some truth in the neo-Calvinist critique of him. I trust that experience has given me something of an open mind when confronting scholasticisms of various kinds, such as that of Dolezal.

Dolezal's book is a defense of some aspects of the doctrine of God that were stressed in the scholastic tradition. Among these, divine unchangeability, simplicity, eternity, and Trinity. He believes that the general rejection of scholastic method among evangelicals has led them to compromise these doctrines or to deny them altogether. As he sees it, the only remedy is to return to scholasticism, even to those aspects of scholasticism that make the least sense to modern thinkers.[2]

The most common evangelical alternative to scholastic metaphysics is what Dolezal calls "theistic mutualism" (1).

"Mutualism," as I am using the term, denotes a symbiotic relationship in which both parties derive something from each other. In such a relation, it is requisite that each party be capable of being ontologically moved or acted upon and thus determined by the other.[3]

Dolezal thinks that "theistic mutualism" (TM)[4] is very common among evangelical writers today and in the recent past. He cites as examples Donald MacLeod (21), James Oliver Buswell (23), Ronald Nash (23), Donald Carson (24), Bruce Ware (24), James I. Packer (31), Alvin Plantinga (68), John Feinberg, J. P. Moreland, William Lane Craig (69), Kevin Vanhoozer (72), Rob Lister (92), Scott Oliphint (93), and, yes, John Frame (71–73, 92–95). Wayne Grudem joins the group later for his adherence to "eternal functional subordination" in the Trinity (132–33). This group brings together many of the most important thinkers in evangelicalism today, and I am honored to be included in it, though I do not agree with all of them on everything. Dolezal, I think, should be more respectful of this group than he is. Is it not even a little bit daunting to stand against such a consensus?

---

2. If you enter Dolezal's conceptual universe, you must be prepared to navigate some terminology that is fairly abstruse to many modern readers. Often he says that God is "pure actuality" (xiii, 7). The language of Scripture, he says, tells us something true about God, but not "under a form of modality proper to him" (20, cf. 72). Dolezal throws around terms like "ontological" (26), "real" (25), "essence," "quiddity," and "substantial form" (41), assuming that the reader is well enough versed in scholastic philosophy to immediately perceive that Dolezal is using these terms in something other than a conventional modern sense. Often he makes no attempt to explain or justify his distinctive scholastic vocabulary.

3. 1, note 1.

4. This term is quite offensive to me and to the other evangelicals on this list. If anybody had called Van Til a "theistic mutualist," Van Til would have thrown chalk at him. The central doctrine of Van Til's doctrine of God is the creator/creature distinction, the doctrine that God is not relative to anything in the world he has made. The doctrine Van Til opposed, he called "correlativism," a fair synonym for Dolezal's ugly phrase. Correlativism is the view that God and the world are mutually dependent. Van Til, John Frame, and all the others on Dolezal's list quite abhor the notion of correlativity between God and the world. But we don't believe that abhorrence requires us to adopt all the details of the Thomist system.

Dolezal thinks that TM is a departure from "traditional Christian orthodoxy."[5] He agrees with E. L. Mascall that if we accept TM "we may as well be content to do without a God at all" (6), and with Herbert McCabe that TM presents a "false and idolatrous picture of God" (6). David Bentley Hart also charges TM with idolatry. Plainly, on Dolezal's view, TM is vile heresy.

Now, if Dolezal really thinks that all the men in the above list are heretics, he will need to spend quite a bit of time bringing charges against them in ecclesiastical courts. For my part, I shall defend only my own orthodoxy in this paper, for what difference that may make.[6]

Nevertheless, there are a number of points on which I agree with Dolezal and would even contend with him against some prevailing theological trends. When I began teaching theology at Westminster Seminary in 1968, my first elective course was "The Aseity of God." Van Til, despite his disdain for scholasticism in general, was a strong advocate of divine aseity, what he called "the self-contained God."[7] In my course, I drew on Van Til, Bavinck, and the Reformed tradition. But I noted that despite the fact that many Reformed theologians considered divine aseity to be a central doctrine, few of them had developed any credible biblical basis for it. Given *sola Scriptura*, this seemed to me to be a serious lack, and so I spend much of the course trying to develop the doctrine from explicit biblical teaching. So I was pleased that Dolezal referred in his defense of aseity to 1 Kings 8:27, Acts 17:23–28, and Rom. 11:35–36, passages I also stressed in my elective course. Like Van Til, I emphasized the creator/creature distinction and opposed any

---

5. This phrase comes from Richard Muller's foreword, xi. Dolezal does not say anything precisely equivalent, but it is fair to assume that Dolezal agrees with Muller. Incidentally I have disagreed with Muller before. See Frame, "Muller on Theology," in Frame, *Selected Shorter Writings* 3 (Phillipsburg: P&R Publishers, 2016), 1–26. Although I respect Muller's great achievements as a historian of doctrine, I strongly reject his assertion that systematic theology is essentially based on the work of church history. Rather, I insist, *sola Scriptura* obligates us to judge all historical theology (and everything else) by the teaching of Scripture.

6. For my history of theological skirmishes, see my memoir, *Theology of My Life* (Eugene, OR: Cascade Books, 2017). I defend my thesis that the Reformed community wastes a lot of time in fruitless controversies in "Machen's Warrior Children," in Frame, *Selected Shorter Writings* 3 (Phillipsburg: P&R Publishers, 2016), 86–121.

7. He also understood divine simplicity, eternity, and the Trinity, in a more-or-less scholastic manner, following Bavinck.

tendency toward "correlativism," the notion that God and the universe (or something in the universe) are dependent on one another. I thought that issue had implications for epistemology as well as for metaphysics: God made human beings to think his thoughts *after* him, implying that all human thinking should be subordinate to divine revelation. That is the view called "presuppositionalism." You can imagine how I recoil when someone accuses me of "theistic mutualism." "Mutualism" seems to be the same as Van Til's "correlativism," and I've been fighting against that all my life.

When I wrote my *Doctrine of God*, mostly in the 1990s, my chief opponents were process theists and their evangelical cousins, the open theists. When I sent P&R the completed manuscript of *Doctrine of God*, I suggested to them that I could take some of the material from that book, add to it some specific references to open theist writings, and thereby develop a critique of that movement. They responded favorably, and in 2001 they published *No Other God*. They thought it best to release this smaller book a year ahead of the complete *Doctrine of God*, and I respected their judgment. Clearly it seemed to me that the process and openness thinkers were guilty of correlativism, and I opposed those notions from Scripture. In *The Doctrine of God* I defended the doctrines that Dolezal stresses in his current volume: divine aseity, simplicity, unchangeability, timeless eternity. I did not always use the scholastic arguments and definitions, and I used some arguments Dolezal doesn't use.[8] But many of my arguments were the same as Dolezal's.

Nevertheless, it did seem to me that the process and open theists had gotten hold of something in the biblical text—something orthodox theologians would have to deal with, without taking the path of correlativism. That something was that in Scripture God does enter into genuinely personal relationships with human beings. Indeed, Scripture *emphasizes* these relationships. Among them are *covenants*, which of course are central to biblical redemption. And the principal promise

---

8. It still seems to me that the best argument for divine simplicity is that the biblical God is *personal*, and like human persons he acts and thinks as a whole being. It is the *person* who thinks, for example, not his intellect or his wisdom.

of the covenants between God and believers is "I will be *with* you," the "Immanuel principle," fulfilled in the coming of Christ. Christ came to be with us in space and time, to take to himself our sins, and to bring us new life *in him*. He came to be our covenant *Lord*. This is the gospel, and I determined not to accept any metaphysical premise that compromised this covenantal relation between God and man.

God's theophanies, as in the burning bush, the fire and cloud, and in the holiest place in the temple, prefigure the incarnation. And through the biblical story, God walks and talks with human beings that he chooses to be his covenant mediators. He is not a temporal being, but most certainly Scripture presents him as coming *into* time. He is the creator of time and space, and there is no principle that can keep him out. He is not a changeable being, but he really enters the changing world. In that world, he participates in the drama of redemption. On Monday he judges; on Tuesday he blesses. I have called that a kind of change, understanding the problems that creates with our general doctrine of God. Should we call that merely the *appearance* of change? That is a possible formulation we should consider, and it seems to be what Dolezal wants to say. But if we say that God only *appears* to change in these contexts, must we also say that God only *appears* to enter time, that the Son of God only *appeared* to become man (that is the textbook definition of Docetism), that he only *appeared* to die on the cross and rise again? I don't know how any of these expressions can avoid the implication that God's entry into time is somehow unreal, fictional, untrue. Appearance and reality are contrasted. If God's self-revelations are *merely* appearance, then we cannot simultaneously regard them as real.

Dolezal understands that there is a problem here for those who advocate a changeless God. He admits that much biblical language is "mutabilist" (19). And he thinks the problem is adequately solved by saying that this language is nonliteral, accommodationist, anthropomorphic. He cites Bavinck's statement that "Scripture does not contain a few scattered anthropomorphisms but is anthropomorphic through and through" (20). These convey "something true about God, though not under a form of modality proper to him" (20). The modality *proper* to God asserts that God does *not* change, even in the ways the accommodated biblical language suggests that he does. This doctrine actually contradicts the meaning of the accommodated language.

But Dolezal never seems to understand the consequences of this distinction. It implies that Jesus did not "literally" become man, suffer, and die for us. He was not literally born of a virgin. He did not work literal miracles. Of course Dolezal confesses that there is "something true" about these doctrines of the faith, but every heretic in the history of Christianity has been willing to say that much.

Another difficulty is that the problem he raises recurs on to his own view. Dolezal wants his readers to believe that the changelessness of God (and the other doctrines he defends) is derived from Scripture. But if Scripture is "anthropomorphic through and through," why is it not anthropomorphic when it speaks of God's changelessness? Why should we believe literally that God is changeless, but not that God literally became flesh in Jesus? Is it not possible that when God says "I change not" he is speaking nonliterally, anthropomorphically? That text may well be saying "something true about God," but why should we take it as literal truth, while relegating "the Word became flesh" to a figure?

In fact, texts like "I change not" which yield metaphysical truth about God are fairly rare in Scripture. Most of the statements about God in Scripture are "mutabilist." One can argue that the metaphysical statements should take second place to the mutabilist ones in a legitimate hermeneutic. Why should we not say "the Word became flesh" is literal, and "I change not" is figurative? Of course, frequency does not equal primacy. But shouldn't there be some argument at least that the metaphysical statements are so fundamental that they reduce mutabilist statements to a lesser status? So far as I can tell, Dolezal does not supply us with such an argument.

I think what has happened here is that Dolezal is dead-on sure that Aquinas and the scholastic tradition is right. He is so sure of this that he wants to make it a lens through which to interpret Scripture. Following Paul Helm, he maintains that "classical Christian theism" (i.e., the scholastic approach) is "a set of rules, a 'grammatical template' by which we are enabled to coherently hold together the diversity of biblical statements about God" (37). So when there appears to be an inconsistency between the "classical" statements and the "mutabilist language of Scripture," the former must necessarily trump the latter. But there are many of us who do not have such a high opinion of scholastic theology. It is by no means certain that "I change not" must trump "the Word became flesh." Indeed, if we must choose between these, many of us, certainly I among them, would choose the latter. But most of us would rather not make such a choice. What we really want is to combine these two ways of thinking into one, to make them "perspectives" on a larger reality. We want to develop a theology that allows us to confess both truths firmly and loudly. Dolezal, unfortunately, wants us simply to give up the mutabilist narrative of Scripture in the interest of consistency with a theology of changelessness that emerges from the scholastic tradition.

In my *Doctrine of God* I attempted to develop a theology that does equal justice to the metaphysics of Scripture and to its mutabilist language. I wanted to say, with full confidence, that God is unchangeable, while also asserting, with equal confidence, that the Word became flesh.

Was this task impossible? Some might say that I should have taken more seriously the alternative of mystery. There is a lot of truth in that suggestion.[9] God is mysterious, incomprehensible, ineffable. And often when we reach a seemingly impossible problem in theology, like the problem of evil, like divine sovereignty and human responsibility, we should consider the possibility that we have reached the brick wall of divine mystery. There are no contradictions, of course, in God's mind or in God's revelation. If we run up against something that looks like a contradiction, and we can make no progress toward resolving it, we are often wise to set it aside, trusting that God has an answer even if we don't. Perhaps the wall we have run into is simply the infinite depth of God's mind.

Dolezal appeals to mystery (38), showing that he understands that the relation between mutabilist language and scholastic metaphysics is not easy to resolve. And predictably he adds that the TMs are the ones who don't understand mystery. But in the end, he insists that the

---

9. See my essay, "Mystery," later in this volume.

metaphysics must prevail over the mutabilism. We cannot have both, he thinks. They are not two perspectives. It is the metaphysics that is literally true, and the mutabilism is only anthropomorphism. So the mystery, however Dolezal understands it, devolves finally into a certainty about Thomist metaphysics.

In my book, I tried to explore other options. Theologians have sometimes said that God is "unchangeable in his essence, but changeable in his relations to changing things." That should not be difficult for readers to understand. To say that God is unchangeable in his essence is to say that he always remains God, and he always remains the same God. He always has the same attributes and the same three persons. But he has also decided to create a world, something different from him. And he is, of course, related to that world. The phrase "creator of" itself designates a relation. And if God is "creator of" the world, he is also creator of everything in the world. That means that God is significantly related to indefinitely many things and persons outside himself. He is the creator of the sun and of the moon. He is the creator of the angel Gabriel, of the earth, the sky and the water around it, of the birds, fish, and animals, of Adam and Eve, of King David, of George Washington, of Herbert Hoover, and, and ... And his plan for the world and all the things in it is incredibly complex. God is unchangeable, but he has indefinite numbers of relations to changing things.

When the changing things change, those relationships change. When Adam obeys, then disobeys God, his relation to God changes. When Jonah tries to escape from God by taking a ship to Tarshish, God knows about that and the relationship changes. Indeed, you can't escape from God, for God is everywhere (Ps. 139). I don't know what Dolezal does with the divine attribute of omnipresence, but he clearly wants to avoid saying that God "experiences" anything in the changing world,[10] let alone that God actually enters that world.[11] So it doesn't seem to me to be

---

10. He says, "As an aside, I find the whole notion that God has 'experiences' to be wrong-headed" (31n49).

11. Even God's attribute of omniscience would seem to be problematic for Dolezal, for how can a God who has no significant relations to changing things know what is going on in the changing world?

an abuse of language to say that God *becomes* creator when he creates, though of course that becoming is based on qualities of his unchanging nature. And it is not wrong for us to speak of attributes (an attribute is nothing more than a description or designation[12]) of God that correspond to his creative acts and the relationships he has with the created world. He is not only "creator of" the world in general, but also creator of the sun and moon, of the tree of life, of Adam and Eve, etc. These are attributes of God, qualities he has by virtue of his relationships with creation. Dolezal thinks that such language is really "inventing new attributes,"[13] but certainly this language has at least as much biblical justification as the attributes of changelessness, simplicity, and eternity.

Dolezal, of course, wants to insist with the scholastic tradition that all of God's attributes are identical with his essence and therefore identical with one another (42). Is "creator of the world" identical with divine changelessness or simplicity? I don't understand how that can be, for that would mean that the act of creating our world is a necessary attribute of God, and that would eliminate the creator-creature distinction. Perhaps the question can be relegated to mystery. In any case, the answer does not seem to be that we cannot speak of divine attributes based on his actions in the world.

Such is Dolezal's account of divine immutability, set forth in chapter two of his book. In chapters three and four, he takes up the question of simplicity directly, to which we have alluded. Like Dolezal, I have argued the case for divine simplicity, using, indeed, some of the same arguments Dolezal refers to. But I have qualified that case by saying that God is not only simple, but in his own way, highly complex, as I have argued above. Dolezal criticizes this view, which he finds in Kevin Vanhoozer's work and my own. He thinks that divine complexity is inconsistent with his simplicity, and he denies that language denoting the complexity of God's attributes literally applies to his actual being:

---

12. Perhaps there is some technical definition of "attribute" in scholastic theology that I am missing, but if so I don't think that Dolezal has supplied that definition.

13. Muller (ix, x) and Dolezal (65) charge TM evangelicals with "inventing new attributes" of God based on his relation to creation.

Frame means not only that the truth of our propositions cor-
responds to the reality of God's nature, but that the *form* of our
propositions mirrors the *form* or *manner* of God's intrinsic act
of being. (72)

As before, he thinks that any statements we make about the complexity
of God's nature are "accommodations," not literally true. I'm not sure
what he precisely means here by the italicized words or by the phrase
"intrinsic act of being." But I would like to know whether he considers
his denial of such mirroring to be literally true. If he is making a literal
statement, that would seem to contradict his claim. If he is not, then
the whole discussion vanishes into the air. My concern is simply that
Scripture does represent God as a complex being. He performs innumerable acts for innumerable reasons. He has innumerable thoughts
and plans. His love has innumerable objects. And he is three-in-one.[14]
Are we supposed to deny all of these biblical teachings for the sake of
the simplicity doctrine? I don't doubt that God's actual nature is beyond
our ability to understand or describe it. But God has given us a book,
and we ought to be able to trust its statements about God without fear-
ing the wrath of the scholastics.

Chapter five deals with the eternity of God, affirming the timelessness of God's existence. I too have defended the doctrine of timeless
eternity over against process thought and open theism. Dolezal presents the following definition:

God does not experience successive states of being and thus has
no future and no past. (82)

He concedes that Scripture sometimes speaks of God as a mutable
being, using temporalist language (85), just as he earlier admitted
that Scripture sometimes uses mutabilist language to refer to the
simple God. But the temporalist language, like the mutabilist language, is non-literal, accommodation. Dolezal criticizes a number of

---

14. I shall take up the doctrine of the Trinity later in this essay. I know that Thomists have
a way or reconciling simplicity and Trinity, but I don't find their formulation persuasive or even
coherent.

TM theologians who hold different views of God's eternity. Here is what he says about me:

> The key to Frame's doctrine is his apparent belief that God's existence extends beyond his atemporality. As Creator and providential Lord of time, Frame believes that God also exists as a changing being within history itself. He can say this because he believes that "there are two modes of existence in God." Frame does not agree that biblical talk about change in God is merely anthropomorphic, as the classical view explained it. Rather, if God acts in time, then he really exists temporally. (93)

I have no serious quarrel here with Dolezal's paraphrase of my position, though "extends beyond" is a spatial metaphor that I do not use and do not consider useful. But the overall position I hold is the same principle I stated earlier in this paper: that according to Scripture God really enters the temporal world. That seems to me to be obvious from biblical accounts of God's involvement with human history, with providence, and especially with redemption. Certainly these biblical accounts are anthropomorphic, in that they are in human language, and doubtless they are describing realities that human ears cannot entirely understand. But these accounts are in God's authoritative book, and that book authorizes us to speak as it speaks about God, both in the area of metaphysics and in the area of history. And the central message of Scripture is not that God is changeless or simple or timeless but that he came to save us from our sins. The Word became flesh and was crucified for us. How can a changeless God enter time? The metaphysics may well elude us to some extent. But the ultimate reason is that God is the creator of time and therefore the Lord of time. He can do with time what he wants. He can enter it or not, as he chooses.

I have gone out on a limb, slightly, saying that because God comes into time he has a temporal existence. That simply means that he exists in time as well as outside time. He can fully enter relationships with temporal beings, becoming an actor in the historical drama. He answers their prayers, punishes their sins, forgives them on the basis of Jesus's

work, speaks to them, and governs all the forces of nature and history to fulfill his purposes. In that temporal existence, God does not
sit somewhere as a static block of wood. He is dynamic. He responds
to people. He does one thing on Monday, and another, different thing
on Tuesday. That existence seems to me to be very different from the
existence of the Trinitarian persons "before" the creation of the world.
But I will be the first to concede that we don't know how precisely to
describe these two kinds of divine existence. Maybe Dolezal can find
a better way; but you won't find it in this book. Rather, what he does is
to *deny* God's "temporal existence." And to deny that, I believe, entails
denial of the biblical gospel, that

> in Christ God was reconciling the world to himself, not counting
> their trespasses against them, and entrusting to us the message
> of reconciliation. (2 Cor. 5:19)

Great is the mystery of reconciliation. But I cannot clarify that mystery
by denying that God really was in Christ, reconciling the world to himself. If I must choose between this confession and the scholastic account
of divine eternity, I will unhesitatingly choose the former.

The last chapter, chapter 6, deals with the doctrine of the Trinity.
Rightly, Dolezal begins this discussion by reiterating what he said earlier about the unity and simplicity of God. God's Threeness cannot
be understood outside the context of his Oneness. But what are these
three that the church has historically called "persons"? Dolezal quotes
G. L. Prestige:

> If Christianity is true, the same stuff or substance of deity in the
> concrete has three distinct presentations—not just three mutually
> defective aspects presented from separate points of view ... but
> three complete presentations of the whole and identical object,
> namely God, which are nevertheless objectively distinct from
> one another. (118)

Each is fully God, for each possesses the whole divine essence. Dolezal
goes on:

Yet the three persons are really distinct. How so? Classical
Christian theists generally locate this distinction in personal relations or, in slightly more imprecise language, "several peculiar
relative properties." Specifically, it is in relations that we locate
the real distinctions of paternity (unique to the Father), filiation
or begottenness (unique to the Son), and spirated procession
(unique to the Spirit). (119)

So, like Aquinas, Dolezal's view of the Trinity is that there is one God,
with three "subsistent relations."

Now it is possible that Dolezal is working with an unconventional
definition of "relation." If he is, he has not told us, and I confess that in
all my study of scholasticism over sixty years I have never found a definition of "relation" that could sustain this kind of talk. Some philosophers
have distinguished four elements of a fact: things, properties, actions (or
states), and relations. So "the yellow cat is on the mat" can be analyzed
as two things (the cat and the mat), a property (yellow), a state (is),
and a relation (on). One can imagine a scholastic philosopher trying
to determine by process of elimination how to describe the persons of
the Trinity: well, they are not things (substances), for God is only one
substance. They are not properties (attributes). They are not actions or
states. So they must be relations. But what can it possibly mean to say
that persons are relations? Well, they are not ordinary relations (like "on"
in our example) but *substantive* relations. But what could that be? What
would it mean to regard "on" as a substantive (or any other relation, like
"behind," "taller than," "nephew of," "to the right of," etc.)?

Here, Dolezal identifies the relations as Christians have often done,
by reiterations of the names of the persons. For "paternity," "filiation,"
and "spirated procession" are of course reiterations of the names "Father,"
"Son," and "Spirit." I do believe there is some additional biblical evidence
for "eternal generation" and "eternal procession;" these are not *merely*
extrapolations from their personal names, though I think that these concepts are basically grounded in the nomenclature. But in this discussion
it is easy to forget the question I posed earlier: what is a substantive
relation, and why is this concept sufficient to identify the three persons?

When we speak of the eternal generation of the Son from the Father, what are we talking about? It appears that we are talking about two persons, the Father and the Son. But how can there be two persons within a being who is supremely simple? It is no answer to say that we should somehow focus, not on the persons, but on the relations between them. There are two persons (and another, making three), and that fact creates a problem for people who try to attribute simplicity to God.

But the difficulty is worse than that. For to Dolezal, the "persons" are not the beings who are *related by* eternal generation. Rather, the persons are the relations themselves, the "substantive relations." In this case, the persons are not the Father and the Son; rather the persons are paternity and eternal generation (and similarly for eternal procession). The "persons" are abstractions,[15] not what we normally call persons, and not even something reasonably analogous to those we normally call persons. And even if we can defend the concepts of eternal generation and procession from Scripture, Scripture never comes near to asserting that these abstractions are what the Father, Son, and Spirit really are.

So I think the analysis of the Trinity into substantive relations is a failure. To say this is not to reject the whole scholastic doctrine of simplicity, which both Dolezal and I defend, with some differences. I cannot supply an analysis that overcomes all the problems. Rather, I throw up my hands in the face of the greatest mystery in God's revelation. For all of Dolezal's talk about analogy and anthropomorphism, I wish he had acknowledged that here. I fear that Dolezal is one of many theologians who are fond of speaking about mystery in general terms, but who demand absolute conformity to the conclusions of their own specialized study. They think God is mysterious, but that their own conceptual formulations are utterly without mystery, so that theologians who question them should be defrocked.

But until a better way appears (perhaps in the new heavens and new earth) I intend to follow the biblical depictions of the Father, Son,

---

15. Keep in mind, of course, that Dolezal affirms Aquinas's statement that "the abstract and the concrete are the same in God" (121). But we should always remember that the reason for invoking "relation" in this context is its abstract character. Three concrete beings in the Trinity would not sustain the simplicity of the Godhead.

and Spirit as a holy family, both in heaven and on earth, analogous to (though certainly not identical with) our earthly families, with a unity far beyond what any society of human beings is capable of.

I am grateful to God for giving to James Dolezal substantial gifts of theological knowledge and intelligence. But insofar as he desires to convict most of his colleagues of heresy, I cannot join him on the side of the prosecution.

Rather, I am hoping that in time Dolezal will develop a more mature way of responding to his colleagues. What he has done has been to adopt scholasticism, one philosophical model of the relation of God to the world, and demand that his colleagues agree with this model in detail, if they are to maintain their claims to orthodoxy. But there are all sorts of things wrong with this approach:

1. Dolezal seems to think that Aquinas and his scholastic successors were infallible. There is not the slightest hint in this book that Aquinas was, or may have been, wrong about anything. He has accused his colleagues of idolatry, but it doesn't seem difficult to charge him with the same thing.

2. Like Muller, then, he tries to make systematic theology totally subordinate to historical theology. But this is to put the cart before the horse. We can learn much from the theologians who have preceded us in history, but *sola Scriptura* requires us to test everything they say by the direct study of Scripture.

3. As we can learn much from our predecessors like Aquinas, we can also learn from our colleagues, especially those who have labored longer than we in seeking the meaning of Scripture. None of our colleagues is infallible any more than historical figures are; but we should criticize our colleagues with a level of humility and respect, especially those who are older than we ("Do not rebuke an older man but encourage him as you would a father" [1 Tim. 5:1]). We might even be able to learn from colleagues who take

positions opposite to our own, if we carry out friendly conversations, rather than swooping down on them and laying down the law. I do not sense that humility in Dolezal's book. Rather, his manner feels like a steamroller, ready to crush anyone who takes issue with any of his jots or tittles.

4. Dolezal's book shows no sense of proportion. He wants us to confess without doubt the traditional metaphysical doctrines, but his method creates many problems for the biblical gospel of salvation, and he does not seem to sense any need to work those problems through.

5. I repeat what I have said elsewhere, that traditionalism is not a biblical virtue. And total alignment with a historical tradition leads to spiritual shipwreck.

16

Scholasticism and Biblical Personalism

I AM IN THE MIDST of some discussions about the role of scholastic methods in Reformed theology, centered around James Dolezal's *All That Is in God*. My first response to Dolezal is available in the previous essay in this book. I continue to stand by my argument of that article. But the ensuing discussion has suggested to me that the discussion needs to go deeper. There are facts about Greek philosophy and its relation to theology that I have taken for granted for many years, of which many younger theologians seem unaware. Some, therefore, will find the present article to be superfluous, but others may find it to be informative.

Mostly it is a condensation of arguments in my *History of Western Philosophy and Theology*, and, behind that, the work of Cornelius Van Til. In the recent discussion, one Facebook antagonist chided me for my lack of historical knowledge. *HWPT* is 867 pages. I hope the Facebook writer didn't bet any money on that proposition. But of course the issue before us is not *quantity* of historical knowledge, but the *use* of historical knowledge in resolving theological issues. I will maintain again that in Reformed theology our rule is *sola Scriptura*. That is to say, although historical theology may bring vital information to us, all the views of human theologians and philosophers must be tested by the word of God.

Scripture tells us quite a bit about how we should make use of unbelieving thought. Rom. 1:18–32 is a key text. In that passage, Paul tells us that God's nature and attributes have been "clearly seen" (v. 20) by

119

all human beings, including the pagans whom he discusses later in the chapter. So we can expect that non-Christian thinkers have gained some true insights from their exposure to God's revelation in creation. But Paul also says that these pagans "by their unrighteousness suppress the truth" (v. 18). So when we study pagan philosophy we encounter a paradoxical mixture of truth and falsity: truth from divine revelation, falsity from sinful suppression. We must be aware of both elements of pagan thought, and of their interactions.

Western philosophy is generally thought to have begun with the Greeks around 600 BC. The earliest Greek philosophers sought to understand the world in general. But to do that, they put aside their traditional religions and myths and sought to understand the world by reason alone, that is, as Van Til put it, "autonomously." Parmenides believed that our normal ways of understanding the world were deeply flawed, because they were not sufficiently rational. To most of us it appears that the world is changing. But, Parmenides said, change is rationally impossible. If the world is changing, then things become what they are not. But "nonbeing," he thought, was not a rationally coherent concept. When we try to define nonbeing, the definition turns it into a form of being. So nonbeing is rationally meaningless, and so change is rationally meaningless. Similarly, Parmenides said, plurality is an irrational notion; for a plurality appears to be a collection of at least two objects, one of which is *not* the other. But Parmenides has shown, he thinks, that plurality is impossible. So Parmenides believes that despite appearances, the world is really changeless, without any pluralities, without generation, without destruction. He understood, I think, that we could not really live in the world while conceiving of it in this way. But he stuck by the authority of his own reason.

Parmenides does not argue that simplicity and changelessness are attributes of God, as scholastic theologians later argued. Rather, he believes that simplicity and changelessness characterize *all* reality, and we would know that, if we were willing to use our autonomous reason as consistently as Parmenides did. To Parmenides there is no creator/ creature distinction. If there is God, then we are all God.

And if there is a God, that God is an impersonal Being. It is an "it," not a "he." Indeed, since we all are divine, we are all impersonal, and we can know that by the consistent use of our autonomous reason.

But not all the Greeks were willing to follow Parmenides. In fact, some Greeks gave up on reason entirely. If Parmenides was a textbook rationalist, the Sophists, such as Protagoras, were textbook irrationalists. They did not call themselves that. Like all Greek thinkers, they thought they were living according to reason. But what shall we make of their assertion that there is no such thing as universal truth? The Sophists said, very much like recent postmodernists, that what is true for you may be false for me and vice versa. How do you reason with somebody like that? But they claimed to be following their autonomous reason just as surely as Parmenides did.

Plato, one of the greatest of the Greek thinkers, tried to bring together the two extremes. In his view, Parmenides was right about one aspect of the world, the Sophists right about another. Plato divided the world into form and matter. Matter is the stuff of which our experienced world is made. Form is that rational structure that determines what things are. But these two factors constitute different worlds. The world of matter, or ordinary experience, is a world of confusion, error, ignorance. In this world there is constant change; nothing can be understood or defined. To live in this world is like living in a cave, when one views objects in very dim light or in no light at all. This dark world is irrational, unknowable.

But the world of form is entirely opposite. The forms are changeless and totally knowable, like Parmenides's Being. They serve as criteria for the realities in the darker world. The perfect triangle in the world of forms serves as the criterion by which we should assess the imperfect triangles of the darker world. Same for perfect manhood, perfect virtue, perfect wisdom, and, the highest of all, perfect Goodness.

Later philosophers, however, thought that Plato needed some way of connecting the two realms to one another. How did the realm of forms produce the realm of matter? (Plato treated that question, but answered it by a rare lapse into mythology.) How can the forms govern change, themselves being changeless? How can the forms account for evil, when they themselves are nothing but good?

The later Platonist Plotinus thought these issues can be dealt with by means of a continuum. The highest point of the continuum (like Plato's Good) was Plotinus's One. But unlike Plato's Good, the One is ineffable. It cannot be described, or even intelligibly spoken of. So the questions addressed to Plato are resolved in mystery. And the continuum, like Parmenides's Being, erases all distinction between creator and creature, so that we all participate equally in the ineffable mystery.

Plato's pupil Aristotle also distinguished form and matter, but he denied that the two realities occupy separate worlds. Rather, to him, form and matter are aspects of everything we experience in this world. Everything has matter, the stuff of which it is made, and everything has form, the qualities that make it what it is. But Aristotle did not entirely neglect the transcendent. His investigation of causality led him to a First Cause, a cause behind other causes, which he called the Prime Mover. Like Parmenides's Being, Aristotle's Prime Mover later had a large influence on Christian theology. But the Prime Mover was very different from the God of the Bible. Since it was First Cause, it could not be influenced by anything outside itself. In Aristotle's view, this implied that the Mover could not know the world, or love the world. He could know and love only himself (actually, he could know only his own thoughts—"thought thinking thought"—which reduces his thinking to tautology). This being, of course, is certainly one that we must call "impersonal," an "it" rather than a "he," although Aristotle did for some reason attach religious predicates to this being. And that being could have no personal relationships with human beings.

Aquinas was a great Christian thinker, perhaps the greatest in terms of his sheer intellectual depth and accomplishment. But he set himself the task of combining his biblical faith with the chief philosophical movements of his past: Platonism and Neoplatonism (Plotinus) and Aristotle. In addressing the relationship between sacred doctrine and philosophy, he said that both of these were legitimate means of knowing, even of knowing God, but that in philosophy reason plays a leading role, and in sacred doctrine faith and revelation. He did qualify this distinction by saying that if a conclusion of reason contradicted a truth of faith, the truth of faith would have to prevail. For example, Aristotle believed that the world existed eternally, but Aquinas could not accept that view given Gen. 1:1 and other passages on the doctrine of creation. But I know of no place in Aquinas's massive literary output in which he grants the truth of Rom. 1:18 that nonbelievers "suppress" the truth.

These distinctions gave Aquinas a rationale for bringing a great deal of Greek philosophy into his Christian system, even into his theology. He made considerable use of Aristotle's first-cause argument for the existence of God. Once he had proved the existence of God, he proceeded to discourse on the simplicity of God. Since God is the first cause, he cannot be made of parts, since then he would be influenced ("caused") by something, namely the parts. So God is identical with his attributes, and they are identical with each other. His *esse* ("that he is") is identical to his existence ("what he is"). And so on. The notion of God that emerges is similar to that of Aristotle, who also emphasized that God could not be influenced by anything within or outside himself. And it is like Parmenides, for whom any change or complexity is irrational.

Aquinas defined what we call the "scholastic" tradition in Christian theology. Although Protestants often criticized Aquinas and other scholastics in detail, they were often under the influence of this tradition. Post-Reformation Protestant theology is often described as a variety of scholasticism. It should also be admitted that the Protestant confessions generally affirm God's simplicity and unchangeability, but without the philosophical explanations, arguments, and elaborations noted above.

It is plain to me, however, that Protestant theology on the whole operates according to a principle very different from the rational autonomy of the Greeks and the two-disciplines view of Aquinas. That principle is *sola Scriptura*, the principle that only Scripture has ultimate authority. That doesn't mean that there is no truth in pagan philosophy. It means only that such truth claims must be tested by the higher authority of God's word. This authority binds all spheres of life, philosophical, theological, scientific, psychological, economic, and whatever other spheres there be.

When we ask about the worldview, the metaphysics, of Scripture itself, a picture emerges that is very different from that of the Greek philosophers, though similar in some details. Certainly God is the first cause; the Bible's affirmation of creation establishes that. But he is cause of all, not as an impersonal principle, but as a personal (actually tri-personal) being who utters commands to things and persons and they obey. I believe too that God is simple. But that is not because plurality is an irrational notion as Parmenides thought. It is because God is a personal being who is Lord of himself and of everything he makes; and whatever he does, he does as a whole, with no inner conflict.

The most prevalent biblical description of God in the Bible is LORD. Hebrew and Greek words designating his lordship are found over 7,000 times in the Scriptures. Lord is a *personal* name. God's relations to the world and to himself are the sorts of relations persons have. He is not an impersonal object or force. In biblical metaphysics, the personal is prior to the impersonal. That is true also of human knowledge. God's word governs all our thought and behavior. There is no place for autonomous reasoning.

So the main content of Scripture is not that God is simple or changeless (though I think these concepts can be derived from Scripture), but that God has dealt with his creation through history, particularly with human beings, in a thrilling historical drama. His relations with us are not merely causal, but are relations of knowledge, wrath, and mercy. The central message of Scripture is that God came to earth to live among us as a man and to die the death we deserved. As a philosopher, I can argue that this narrative presupposes that God is above time, simple, eternal, and unchangeable. But the main biblical narrative is one of divine-human personal interaction.

If someone says that this interaction implies that God is changeable, so we must regard the narrative as figurative or anthropomorphic, I cry foul. The narrative is true, indeed the highest truth, the truth by which all other truth should be measured. Paul said,

> The saying is trustworthy and deserving of full acceptance, that
> Christ Jesus came into the world to save sinners, of whom I am
> the foremost. (1 Tim. 1:15)

Doubtless there are parts of the biblical narrative that are figurative rather than literal, as when John says that Jesus is the Lamb of God. But to claim that the whole narrative is figurative, in contrast to philosophical propositions about changelessness and simplicity that are literal, seems to me to be entirely wrongheaded. It comes dangerously close to Parmenides, who thought that our whole changing world is an illusion and that the real world is changeless. And of course Parmenides also dismissed any thought of distinction between a personal creator and the world he made. The notion that the changing world is something other than the domain of God assumes a Platonic metaphysic. And when someone says that God cannot "experience" changing reality, that is Aristotle talking, not the Bible.

If someone asks how this lordship narrative can be consistent with divine unchangeability and simplicity, I would direct him to my discussions in *Doctrine of God*. I think these concepts can be shown consistent. But if my arguments are insufficient, the answer is not to deny the lordship narrative or to regard it in toto as a figure. Rather the answer is to take the lordship narrative as our ultimate presupposition and to find an interpretation of unchangeability and simplicity that is consistent with it.

The Bible's personalistic worldview opens up to us a great and wonderful cosmic drama. God is not impersonal, and his personality is not a concession to our anthropomorphic language. God really is Father, Lord, and Savior. He really speaks to us, authoritatively and personally, in Scripture. The Son of God really was born of a virgin, worked miracles in time and space, died for our sins, and rose for our justification.

17

Scholasticism and Creation

This is the third of my discussions of issues relating to
James Dolezal's All That Is in God.

IN "SCHOLASTICISM FOR EVANGELICALS," I focused on Dolezal's book. In "Biblical Personalism," I discussed some of the philosophical issues surrounding these topics. In the present essay, I will focus on some of the central conceptual issues as I understand them. These cluster around the doctrine of creation.

Dolezal says, "God's glory is not actually increased when we glorify Him" (14). He explains,

> Human actions are simply the occasions for the unfolding of God's *ad extra* display of these unchanging and unacquired virtues. ... God simply is that act of existence by which He is. This means that even His relation to the world as its Creator and Sustainer does not produce any new actuality in Him. (15)

I do not disagree with these statements, but I do think they raise a problem that Dolezal does not discuss: What is the status of God's "relation to the world as its Creator and Sustainer?" Is that relation within him? One might argue that it is, because it certainly is a fact about God that he is related to the world. But on Dolezal's view, if this relation is within God, then it is identical with his essence. That implies that God would not be God unless he were related to the world. And on that basis, the world itself is God's essence. But to say that the world is God's essence is pantheism.

That would not have been a problem for Parmenides, for whom all relations exist as aspects of a distinctionless "Being." Parmenides was a consistent pantheist, as were his Greek philosophical predecessors. But in a Christian theology, pantheism destroys the creator-creature distinction, which of course is quite central to the biblical worldview.

But consider this alternative: Perhaps the relation between God and the world is not his essence, but something entirely outside him. To assert that would allow us to renounce pantheism. And since on any plausible analysis this relation is a changing one, it could not be, on Dolezal's account, identified with God's essence. But for Dolezal, God cannot be present in a changing environment. He says, "God does not experience successive states of being" (82). Elsewhere, he elaborates:

> As an aside, I find the whole notion that God has "experiences" to be wrongheaded. An experiencer must be acted upon and so receive a determination of being from another. Experience requires that something "happens to" the individual going through the experience. But nothing "happens to" or befalls God since he is pure act. (31n49)

So God does not experience the world of change. He exists somehow above it, beyond it. Scripture does, of course, teach (for example in Ps. 139) that God is wherever we are, and that he knows our changing plans. But Dolezal regards that language as nonliteral, as anthropomorphism, as I indicated in my earlier paper. In my earlier discussion I remarked at how bold this argument was, for the whole Bible is about God's involvement with the temporal world and with human beings. For Dolezal to say that all of this is nonliteral is somewhat jaw-dropping. It is as if the whole biblical story were just an image of a metaphysical scheme. It is as if we have to abandon everything Scripture says, in the interest of scholastic metaphysics. And if the earlier alternative I discussed amounts to pantheism, this one amounts to deism. On this view, God is not really "with us."

The pantheistic alternative comes from Parmenides, the deist alternative from Aristotle, who excluded from his Prime Mover meaningful relationships between the god and the creation. Greek philosophy was never able to affirm the biblical relationship between creator and creature, because they didn't conceive of God in a truly personal way. To them, God was either part of a vague, impersonal Being (Parmenides), or he/it was an impersonal cause of a world it was indifferent to (Aristotle). In either case, he/it was an impersonal principle.

In an earlier paper, I suggested an alternative which I called biblical personalism. In Scripture, God is not an impersonal Being who either includes within himself (Parmenides) or excludes from his knowledge (Aristotle) other kinds of being. Rather, he is a person called the Lord. Lordship includes his rule over the world he has made, but it also enables him to enter the changing world and to become part of the historical narrative. He is both transcendent and immanent.

What shall we say, then, about the divine attributes Dolezal discusses, namely immutability, simplicity, eternity, and triunity? Dolezal is right to say that these are the common property of the church and are enshrined in the church's confessions, Protestant, Catholic, and ecumenical. But there are different ways of understanding these attributes, and the scholastic is only one. Here is how I affirm them, as a believer in biblical personalism:

God is immutable in that his nature, eternal purpose, and promises never change. But in my judgment Scripture never says that his immutability is imperiled by engaging in relationships with changing people in history. That it is imperiled is an Aristotelian assumption, not a biblical one. In Scripture, God really enters the historical process, and, as Berkouwer said against Barth, there is real "transition from wrath to grace in history." His lordship means that he cannot be threatened by changes in the world.

God is simple in that everything he does, he does as a whole being, not by the influence of independent parts or constituents within him. But he is also complex: he has in his mind a vast amount of knowledge. Ps. 139:17 says, "How precious to me are your thoughts, O God! How vast is the sum of them!" His works and words are manifold.

God as eternal transcends time. He is the creator of time, and he rules time as its Lord. His knows every moment of creation's history with equal vividness. And as the Lord of time, he is able to enter time and participate in the ongoing temporal drama. The Bible has no Aristotelian squeamishness about the danger that the temporal world might bring to God. Because of God's lordship, nothing can keep him out of the world he has made. The world has no power to change his nature or to threaten his sovereignty. And indeed he is everywhere—in and outside the world.

And God is Triune. I don't have a very good understanding of how that can be, and I don't think the church in general understands it very well either. Both Testaments insist that God is One, but they also teach that three persons are equally God. The church has determined some terminology to express this: God is one "substance," "essence," "being," and he is three "persons." But nobody has definitively analyzed what the difference is between being a substance and being a person. Dolezal and the scholastic tradition have tried to analyze "person" into "subsistent relation," but as I indicated in my first paper that analysis makes no sense to me. Better to regard this doctrine as a mystery (as Dolezal advises in other contexts) and worship the one God in three persons. It is significant that the doctrine of the Trinity underscores what I have called biblical personalism. God is not only personal, he is tri-personal. He is not only the model of individual personal existence, but also of social personal existence. As such, we are his image, and redemption restores us in that image, in Christ.

1. I can't help recalling that this was what Hegel thought the Bible was. And of course for him the metaphysical scheme in question was his own philosophy.

2. I would be curious to know how Dolezal deals with the doctrine of humanity in the image of God, which seems to me now to propose some challenges to his system.

18

Scholasticism and the Gospel

This is the fourth of my short essays on scholasticism. I keep promising that each will be my last. Perhaps if I do not make such a promise this time, I'll be able to stop. So this time I do not promise to quit.

EACH ESSAY has been more elementary, more basic, more simple, than the last. The reason is that as I continue to meditate on these issues, it seems to me that certain points that I learned at the beginning of my theological studies (fifty years ago!), things that I took to be common wisdom back then, have become largely forgotten today, if not actively opposed.

So in this essay I will consider the basic gospel. How does God save us from sin and all its effects?[1]

All the religions and philosophies of the world agree that something is wrong with us. We are beset by pain and suffering, weakness, poverty, moral weakness, and wickedness. But among those philosophies and religions, there are two opposite diagnoses of our problem, and two different and opposite remedies. As Cornelius Van Til

---

1. It's appropriate to note that the week before I wrote this essay, R. C. Sproul passed into glory. R. C. was a bit more Thomistic than I would have preferred. But he was a strong advocate of the Reformation doctrine of salvation and an uncompromising opponent of Roman Catholicism. He insisted that the "gospel" should always be central. I believe that he would have been less favorable to Aquinas if he understood how much Thomistic metaphysics undermined the gospel.

put it, one diagnosis/remedy is metaphysical, the other ethical. Two different gospels.

The metaphysical diagnosis blames our plight on our metaphysical nature. On this view, the evils of life exist because we are finite. And the only way to escape from the suffering is to gain a new metaphysical status. We must transcend our finitude to become infinite, according to the Gnostics and the Greeks. According to the Buddhists we must escape from being itself and enter Nirvana, which is a form of nonbeing. The Gnostics prescribed various exercises, including knowledge and good works, which eventually would lead us to a union with the ultimate. Various brands of mysticism presented meditation as a cure, a way of transcending this existence and becoming one with the infinite.

The ethical diagnosis is very different. In the ethical understanding, the sufferings of this world have their origin in our personal rebellion. The personal being who made the world and ourselves commanded us to obey him, and we refused. The sadnesses of this life are in part punishment, in part motivation toward repentance, in part reminders that God rules the world and not ourselves. But that personal God sent his Son as a sacrifice, so that those who trust in him might walk with him in joy through this life, and live with him in a renewed heaven and earth through all eternity. The problem, then, is not finitude, but sin. And the remedy is not for us to climb by our own efforts to a higher metaphysical status. The remedy is for us to be reconciled to God and accept his restructuring of our personal relationship, through the sacrifice of his Son and the resurrected life of his Son dwelling in us by his Spirit.

Metaphysical salvation is impersonal; ethical salvation is utterly personal.

Greek philosophy advocated various forms of metaphysical salvation. Parmenides urged us to rethink everything, so that we could accept the sufferings of this world as illusion. Plato acknowledged that the world of suffering had a kind of shadowy being, but compared to the world of Forms it was unreal, and we need to enter that higher world somehow. Plotinus turned Plato's dichotomy into a continuum, and he taught that salvation came through mystical union with the One, a being that cannot be described in human language.

The Bible rejects any such scheme. Its message is thoroughly personal: repent from sin and trust in Christ. But some of the early church theologians felt that they needed to combine this gospel with the metaphysical form of salvation. They were emphatically committed to the personal gospel of the Bible. But they thought it important to make common cause with the most respected of the ancient thinkers. So Justin Martyr, who loved Jesus to the point of dying for his faith, sometimes spoke of God as "Being," in impersonal terms. Using a dubious interpretation of Ex. 3:14, many theologians started thinking of God as Aristotle did, as the "pure act of being," without understanding how much they were conceding to an impersonalist worldview. Aquinas worked out a very impressive intellectual system that sought to do justice both to biblical personalism and to Greek impersonalism.

But the Reformers wouldn't have it. One way of understanding Luther and Calvin is by noticing how personalist their preaching was. There was little if anything in their theology that recalled the scholastic doctrine of God. Rather, they saw God as a personal—tri-personal—ruler of heaven and earth, the sovereign LORD of Scripture. While medieval Catholicism tended to see God's grace as a kind of substance, dripping from God to the Pope and bishops, through the sacraments, to the individual believer, the Reformers saw themselves personally standing before God's throne, in his presence, *coram deo*. Like the tax collector in Jesus's parable, they prayed, "Lord, be merciful to me, a sinner"; and they were justified, forgiven, and sent into the world to bring others.[2]

In our current dispute within evangelicalism over Thomism/scholasticism, this is the issue. Are we saved by transcending our finitude and accepting an existence within the divine essence? Or are we saved

---

2. Some of the successors of Luther and Calvin followed Aquinas somewhat, as they sought to transform the Reformation gospel into a form fit for academic discussion. They are sometimes called "Protestant Scholastics," though that title overestimates their agreement with Thomistic thought. Some today tell us that because concepts like divine simplicity and immutability are found in the Protestant confessions, people subscribing to those confessions are obligated to accept all the arguments made by the sixteenth- and seventeenth-century theologians. I reject that principle. Subscribing to the Westminster Confession's statement that God is simple means only acknowledging that God is simple. It does not require subscribers to accept all the Thomistic argumentation used in the theological tradition.

by maintaining our individuality and personality and coming before the living personal God begging for his mercy in Christ?

The Bible does teach that God is simple, immutable, eternal, and triune. But it ascribes these qualities to a personal God who interacts with human beings in a history of redemption. This is a metaphysic of what I have called "biblical personalism." And our salvation comes not through changing our metaphysical status (as if our sin were part of our nature), but by entering a personal covenant with the Lord God in Jesus Christ.

WED., FEB. 6: I read another chapter in Allen's "Pro-Nicene" book, an article by Fred Sanders. Like the others, he goes on about ineffability, then shifts gears to affirm Trinitarian revelation. I've noticed that a lot of theologians do this. Karl Barth talks about God as "Wholly Other," but he considers historical criticism perfectly OK when it belittles Scripture, and he bellows curses on anybody who questions Barthian dogma. If God is really "wholly other," how can Barth be so sure? Indeed, how can he be sure of anything?

THURS., FEB. 7: Today I read another chapter in *Pro-Nicene Theology*, this one by Stephen Duby on simplicity. Not one persuasive paragraph in the article. By the second paragraph he is imposing Thomistic terminology on us: essence, existence, "three personal modes of subsisting," pure act, unrealized potency, being, participate, subsisting being itself (which he helpfully explains by the Latin phrase *ipsum esse subsistens*). He seems to have no idea that any of these expressions might need further explanation to some of us non-Thomist dunces. In the next paragraph he says that there are no "real" distinctions in God, or any distinction between one "thing" (in case you don't know the word, he gives in parentheses its Latin equivalent *res*) and another. But there are, he says, "modal" and "relative" distinctions in God. This is not modalism, of course, for the three are distinct only as "modal subsistences." (Ah, yes! Modal *subsistences*! Why didn't I think of that??) The persons of the Trinity are not "serial *ad extra* limitations of one immanent mode of subsisting but are in fact three immanently, eternally distinct pesometimes necessary, but it always throws up caution lights.

PART 3

Systematic Theology

19

Foreword to *What All Christians Believe and Why: A Contemporary Guide to the Historic Faith*, by H. David Schuringa[1]

EVERY THEOLOGIAN is really two theologians. First, he represents the faith of his own background and tradition. No theologian can avoid doing this. We are all finite and therefore "people of our time," examples of our culture, family, congregation, and denomination. Trying to deny this is both foolish and disrespectful. Our historical connectedness is both a limitation and a blessing. For these connections are family, whom God has used to help us grow.

But second, every theologian represents Christ, who transcends all cultures, families, cultures, and denominations. If Christ is Lord, then he governs all areas of our life, including our thought, including our theology. When conflict arises, and it often does, between our historical attachments and the mandates of Jesus's kingdom, the latter must prevail, even if that gets the theologian into trouble with his historical family. So every theologian must be an ecumenical theologian, as well as a member of his tradition.

David Schuringa is a longtime friend of mine, a student at Westminster Seminary in Philadelphia, and a colleague at Westminster in California, after earning his doctorate at the Theological University at

---

1. North Star Ministry Consultants, 2018.

Kampen in the Netherlands. He left Westminster in 1989 and has served in a number of pastoral and academic positions. In 1999 he accepted an appointment to head the Crossroad Bible Institute, a worldwide discipleship ministry to 40,000 prison inmates and their children. In these situations, he has worked as a faithful minister of the Christian Reformed Church but has also taught people new to the Christian faith and some from a wide range of denominations and traditions. These experiences have encouraged him in many ways to minister both to those of his own tradition and to the church universal.

What All Christians Believe would seem to be a bold title for a theology book, even one that focuses on the basics. Surely some readers will find fault with this or that statement, and others would suggest that the book omits something important. For what it's worth, however, I think that David succeeds here in describing the first steps of understanding the gospel message. The book is "Reformed," as David and I both seek to be. But it also sets forth what is precious to every Christian.

I also love the emphasis that the gospel here is good news for all of life, not just for a narrowly defined "religious" area. So this book serves admirably to lead an inquirer from the basics of belief in God to a full embrace of the kingdom of Christ. David's illustrations and vivid language contribute to this excellent pedagogy. I do pray that God will give this book a wide, enthusiastic reception.

20

Scripture as a Divine Book

This brief essay was previously published as "Let the Church Read Scripture as the Very Word of God," in Aaron B. Hebbard, 95 Theses for a New Reformation (Eugene, OR: Resource Publications/Wipf and Stock), 11–12.

LET THE CHURCH READ SCRIPTURE as the very voice of God.

Every great reformation in church history of the church has been a new recognition of divinity. God has been leading the church, over and over, to a deeper recognition of himself. In the fourth century, the church came to a clearer understanding that the Son of God, Jesus Christ, was nothing less than God himself, the second person of the Trinity. In the sixteenth century, God showed the church that salvation was a *divine* work, pure grace received by faith alone, not a combined effort of God and man. As God's Son is God, so salvation is God saving us. A divine Son, a divine work.

A twenty-first century reformation, I believe, will also be a recognition of divinity, focusing on the Scriptures. As Jesus is God's Son and salvation is God's work, so Scripture is God speaking. In a sense, this has always been the conviction of the church, but the church has sometimes compromised this understanding. In the early centuries, Christian philosophers and theologians have sometimes compromised the authority of Scripture. They sometimes tried to make Scripture conform to pagan philosophies and have sometimes made it subordinate to supposedly rational schemes.

But Scripture itself rejects such compromise. According to 2 Tim. 3:15–17, Scripture is the very breath of God, that is, God's actual speaking to us. God told Joshua, therefore, that he should do according to *all* that is written in the law (Josh. 1:8). The Gospel of John (1:1) identifies Jesus as the Word of God and the Word of God with God himself: "In the beginning was the Word, and the Word was with God, and the Word was God." So it is impossible to separate God's word, wherever it is found, from God himself. To encounter the word is to encounter God. And when you despise the word, you despise God as well.

But the church has often made the mistake of giving little honor to the written word, while trying to give much honor to God. Many have said that Scripture is only the word of human authors (perhaps with some vague kind of divine influence) and that their writing is full of errors. That has led to movements that have denied the authority of Scripture entirely and therefore have greatly distorted the doctrines of the faith. If this error continues unopposed, little of the gospel will remain. For the gospel is nothing if it is not the promise of God himself. It is itself the word of God, God coming to us to tell us our need and the wonderful work of Christ to supply that need. If the gospel is only a human theory, it is of little worth, and there is no reason for us to embrace it.

But if there is a reformation in the doctrine of Scripture, people will again receive the good news of Christ with assurance and joy. If the gospel is just human thoughts, it is dispensable. But if it is really God speaking to us, then it is momentous, a matter of life and death.

A twenty-first century reformation should seek to teach, through the pulpit, the Sunday schools, theologies, and seminaries that the Scriptures are nothing less than God himself speaking to us. As the fourth century learned afresh that Jesus is fully God, and the sixteenth that the work of salvation is fully a divine work, so we today must learn that the Bible is fully God's word: not only a collection of human words, not only a collection of human words that happen to be true, but God's own speech to us.

21

Is Scripture's Self-Attestation Sufficient?

This essay has been published in Scripture and the People of God, *the Festschrift for my friend and colleague Wayne Grudem.*

WAYNE GRUDEM, a former student of mine and for many years a respected friend, is one of few recent theologians who has defended, without apology. the full authority of Scripture, along with its inerrancy. My contribution to his Festschrift will carry forward this shared conviction and deal with some issues of importance to both of us.

Reformed Christians (and some other Christians) have often referred to Scripture as *self-attesting*. But understandably some have asked how any book can authenticate itself. As John Murray once posed the question,

> It might seem analogous to the case of a judge who accepts the witness of the accused in his own defense rather than the evidence derived from all the relevant facts in the case.[1]

Initially, at least, to say that a book is self-attesting would seem to mean that its content is a sufficient basis for affirming its truth, that

---

1. Murray, "The Attestation of Scripture," in Ned B. Stonehouse and Paul Woolley, ed., *The Infallible Word* (Grand Rapids: Eerdmans, 1946), 5.

its authority is not based on anything beyond its own words, and that its own words are a sufficient reason for affirming its authority. But such claims seem to be inherently problematic. Who would argue that a book of mathematics, or physics, or history, is true, just because it claims to be?

But there is more to be said. In this article, I hope to deal with some theological confusions over the concept *self-attestation* applied to Scripture,[2] and over the claim that Scripture does indeed authenticate its own content. This discussion will lead to considerations relevant to general epistemology and apologetics, as well as theology.

I will focus on the following statements from Chapter 1 of the *Westminster Confession of Faith*, generally understood as an authoritative summary of the Reformed doctrine of Scripture's self-attestation:

> IV. The authority of the Holy Scripture, for which it ought to be believed, and obeyed, depends not upon the testimony of any man, or Church; but wholly upon God (who is truth itself) the author thereof: and therefore it is to be received, because it is the Word of God.

> V. We may be moved and induced by the testimony of the Church to an high and reverent esteem of the Holy Scripture. And the heavenliness of the matter, the efficacy of the doctrine, the majesty of the style, the consent of all the parts, the scope of the whole (which is, to give all glory to God), the full discovery it makes of the only way of man's salvation, the many other incomparable excellencies, and the entire perfection thereof, are arguments whereby it does abundantly evidence itself to be the Word of God: yet notwithstanding, our full persuasion and assurance of the infallible truth and divine authority thereof, is from the inward work of the Holy Spirit bearing witness by and with the Word in our hearts.

---

2. For my purposes, I will use *self-attestation* interchangeably with such terms as *self-authentication*, *self-witness*, and *autopistia*.

VI. The whole counsel of God concerning all things necessary for His own glory, man's salvation, faith and life, is either expressly set down in Scripture, or by good and necessary consequence may be deduced from Scripture: unto which nothing at any time is to be added, whether by new revelations of the Spirit, or traditions of men. Nevertheless, we acknowledge the inward illumination of the Spirit of God to be necessary for the saving understanding of such things as are revealed in the Word: and that there are some circumstances concerning the worship of God, and government of the Church, common to human actions and societies, which are to be ordered by the light of nature, and Christian prudence, according to the general rules of the Word, which are always to be observed.

1. THE SOURCE OF SCRIPTURE'S AUTHORITY

The first quoted paragraph, IV, says God is the source of Scripture's authority, and we are to believe Scripture *because* God is its author and therefore because Scripture is his word. First, we should note that God is not only the source of Scripture's authority, but of all authority. It is he who grants authority to human beings over the rest of creation, to civil rulers, to heads of households, to husbands in the home, and so on. None of these forms of authority depend on the testimony of man alone, but on God, who grants that authority. In this respect, the authority of Scripture is no different from that of any other legitimate authority.

But there are other considerations. In some ways, the authority of Scripture is different from other authorities. Particularly, not all forms of authority confer infallibility and inerrancy. A civil ruler, for example, has genuine authority, given by God, and he should be obeyed because of that divine authority. But that authority is not absolute: the ruler is not the lord of all things in heaven and earth, as God is. He can violate the law and therefore be sanctioned by a higher authority. And he is not, because of his authority, infallible in his beliefs or statements.

What, then, is the difference between the authority of Scripture and the authority of civil rulers? In the case of Scripture, God (who is truth itself) is the *author* thereof, according to the Confession: and therefore "it is to be received, because it is the Word of God." Scripture is not distinctive in having authority from God; rather, it is distinctive because God is its "author."

Scripture describes this "authorship" in different ways. When Israel met God at Mt. Sinai, God gave to them the Ten Commandments:

> And he gave to Moses, when he had finished speaking with him on Mount Sinai, the two tablets of the testimony, tablets of stone, written with the finger of God. (Ex. 31:18)

In this passage, we learn that God spoke these specific words to his people and wrote them down as well—directly, with his own "finger." Similarly, the apostle Paul says,

> All Scripture is breathed out by God and profitable for teaching, for reproof, for correction, and for training in righteousness, that the man of God may be complete, equipped for every good work. (2 Tim. 3:16–17)

The divine "breathing" here is his *speaking*. And since the divine speech here results in written words ("Scripture") it is equivalent to the writing of the divine finger in Ex. 31:18.

Authorship is not synonymous with publication. A publisher may or may not agree with the content of a book he produces and sells. But the author of that book necessarily agrees with that content. It is the author's own writing, his own speech, his own viewpoint. So to agree with the book is to agree with the author, and to disagree with it is to disagree with the author. So to say that God is the "author" of Scripture implies that if one disagrees with the content of Scripture he disagrees with God.

Here already we are moved to confess the *sufficiency* of Scripture, or *sola Scriptura*. The point is not that Scripture is the only authority over our lives. It is not. But it is the only written language of which God is the author, the only language that is "the Word of God."

So paragraph IV concludes by saying that we are to receive Scripture "because it is the Word of God." That is what cannot be said of any other kind of authoritative speech. The speech or writing of a civil official ought in most cases to be obeyed; but God is not its author, and it is not the word of God in the Confession's sense. If the Confession, here based on passages like Ex. 31:18 and 2 Tim. 3:16–17, is right, then Scripture is the *only* written document in this category.

That is the meaning of *sola Scriptura*. The *sola* simply means that alongside all the other authorities God has given us, this is the only written document that has the authority of God himself. Therefore it is the only *ultimate* authority, the only authority that takes precedence over all other authorities.

Does this doctrine of Scripture's authority imply that Scripture is self-attesting? To "attest" in this context means to give reasons for believing something. We have seen that one thing Scripture does is to give reasons why we should believe it, as in Ex. 31:18 and 2 Tim. 3:16–17. Those reasons are God's reasons. They are God bearing witness to the truth of his own word. Certainly they are sufficient: we may not demand any higher reasons than God's own reasons. We may not demand that God's reasons be validated by reasons of a higher authority, for there are no reasons with a higher authority. To demand higher evidence is in effect to tell God that we are unsatisfied with his own evidence, and we demand evidence from a source higher than him. But to even consider that there might be such a source is to violate the First Commandment. There is only one God, one Lord, and he is above all other sources of truth.

This is to say that God's attestation of his word is sufficient. And therefore Scripture's attestation of its own authority is sufficient reason for us to accept it.

2. WHY WE SHOULD BELIEVE IN SCRIPTURE'S AUTHORITY

But we need to pursue our question farther. For even granting that Scripture's own self-testimony is the word of God, we need to ask how we can best appropriate that self-testimony in our thinking and living. How does one come to believe that Scripture attests itself? With that question in view, let us look at the Confession again, this time paragraph V of chapter 1.

First, paragraph V recommends that we consider the "testimony of the church" so that we can gain a "high and reverent esteem of the Holy Scripture." Since the earliest days of the church, it has appealed to Scripture (i.e., the books of Scripture extant at each period) as its supreme doctrinal authority. The church as a body has never been critical of Scripture, and it has accepted as true Scripture's accounts of the history of redemption.

But the Confession does not see the testimony of the church as itself self-attesting. The testimony of the church is, for all its value, a *human* testimony. Human testimony, even at its best, is not infallible; it can be wrong. We should remember too that the Westminster Confession emerges out of the Protestant Reformation, in which the authority of the church in its official hierarchy, particularly the authority of the Pope, came under severe critique. One of the main themes of the Confession is that the Roman Catholic tradition and teaching ministerium is deeply flawed.

So the testimony of the church is persuasive, but not the absolute basis of faith in Scripture. Of course it could not be, even if it were without flaws. For only Scripture itself is self-attesting.

So paragraph 5 moves on to consider the *evidences* of Scripture's authority:

> the heavenliness of the matter, the efficacy of the doctrine, the majesty of the style, the consent of all the parts, the scope of the whole (which is, to give all glory to God), the full discovery it makes of the only way of man's salvation, the many other incomparable excellencies, and the entire perfection thereof...

Much can be said about these evidences, but the main thrust of this discussion seems to be this: that reading Scripture brings you into a different world. It is a "heavenly" place, where God is executing his eternal plan of redemption. He participates in a context of spiritual warfare, but carries out his will in overwhelming power, love, and grace. Although much of this story takes place on the earth, we normally have a very clouded view of what is happening. But when we read Scripture (directly and through accurate expositors) we are overwhelmed by the glory of it all.[3] Scripture's account of this story is immediately persuasive.

The individual evidences in the Confession's list contribute to this "heavenly vision," set forth specifically in the first evidence. The second, the "efficacy of the doctrine," alludes to the *power* of the biblical content, stressed for example in Heb. 4:12, its power to convict of sin and to arouse faith. The third, the "majesty of the style" raises questions: Parts of Scripture are in a common style, not a high literary style, as that is understood by linguists. But the Confession sees this "majesty" as a spiritual quality, not primarily as a literary one. A high form of literary style would not be impressive to one who is seeking God. But when one looks at Scripture with illumined eyes (see later), it seems to the writers of the Confession that even the common words open our eyes to reveal something of the greatness of God himself.

The fourth evidence is the "consent of all the parts." This consent includes logical consistency, but it is a broader concept. It is the reader's amazement that this book, written by scores of authors over thousands of years, tells a single story: that something written in 60 AD can furnish a resolution of tensions created in 723 BC.

The fifth evidence is the "scope of the whole," defined as giving all glory to God. The Scriptures, as we shall see in paragraph VI, are not limited to a narrow subject-matter. Rather, they stretch over all reality and find God's glory in every aspect of creation and redemption. Then, sixthly, "the full discovery it makes of the only way of man's salvation." Without this full discovery, we would perish at Scripture's revelation of the glory of God. But instead of condemnation, Scripture provides for everything we need to live and flourish in the presence of a glorious God. Scripture sets for all our needs: for righteousness (justification), for a divine family (adoption), for holiness (sanctification), for final perfection (glorification).

---

3. I have great admiration for John Piper's recent book, *A Peculiar Glory: How the Christian Scriptures Reveal Their Complete Truthfulness* (Wheaton: Crossway, 2016), which sets forth this point most eloquently.

Perhaps we have left something out. So the Confession speaks also of "the many other incomparable excellencies." And, lest we worry that God gives us too little of these excellencies, the Confession finds in Scripture "the entire perfection thereof ..."

The Confession here presents the evidences in a highly positive way. It does not say only that the evidences are probable, or even highly probable. Many apologists are content with that sort of modest claim. But the Confession itself says that the evidences are "arguments whereby (Scripture) does abundantly evidence itself to be the Word of God." It is not that the evidences are 85% or 90% credible. They are 100% cogent. Of course, the Confession makes this claim for the evidences themselves, not for every writing or speech by a human apologist. Many apologetic presentations of the evidence are less credible than the evidence itself, and those presentations should legitimately be made in modest terms. But the content of Scripture itself "abundantly evidences" that it is the word of God, so that once that evidence is presented the case should be settled.

Evidently, the logic of the Confession's apologetic is rather different from the usual modern way of assessing the evidences for Scripture's truth. The evidences listed in the Confession are not easily assessed by the methods of empirical science. The "heavenliness of the matter," for example, is not a quality capable of scientific measurement. How does one compare the relative heavenliness of two documents, say, the Bible and the Qur'an? The Confession assumes that readers have some ability to measure these qualities and to derive the right conclusion from them. But this ability is not simply the ability to make use of sense experience and logic. In an argument over the relative heavenliness of two books, it is not clear what considerations would resolve it. The same is true of the other excellences listed in paragraph V. There is evidently something intuitive about the process of reasoning. But the Confession says that the evidence is abundant and immediately certain.

Yet, of course, for many people it is not. Many have read through the Bible many times and remain indifferent to its message. They entertain doubts.

In epistemology it is important to remember that a good argument has three features: logic (validity), evidence (soundness), and persuasion. An argument with good logic is an argument from which the conclusion validly follows from the premises. An argument with good evidence is an argument in which the premises are true and therefore (given the good logic) the conclusion is true. But many arguments are both valid and sound, but they are not persuasive, at least to some hearers. For example,

Premise: Scripture is God's word.

Premise: Scripture teaches that Jesus worked miracles.

Conclusion: Jesus worked miracles.

I believe both premises, and so I regard the conclusion as certain. But some doubt the two premises and therefore doubt the conclusion. For them the argument lacks *persuasiveness*.[4]

In the Confession, this problem is based on the fact that some lack spiritual perception; they lack ears to hear (Jer. 25:4; Matt. 11:15; Rom. 11:8). Our fall into sin affected our thinking, so that people "by their unrighteousness suppress the truth" (Rom. 1:18). Fallen people "exchanged the truth about God for a lie" (v. 25). They "did not see fit to acknowledge God" (v. 28). The problem is not any defect in the evidence, or in the logical argument from the evidences to the truth of Scripture. Rather, the problem is that in the fact of perfect evidence and good logic, sinful people refuse to acknowledge Scripture's conclusions.

The remedy, according to paragraph V: "Our full persuasion and assurance of the infallible truth and divine authority thereof, is from the inward work of the Holy Spirit bearing witness by and with the Word in our hearts." Persuasion comes, not from additional evidence or more powerful logic, but from a personal encounter with God, the Holy Spirit. As such it is a subjective event. We need no more objective evidence; rather something needs to happen inside us. As Jesus said, "Unless one is born again he cannot see the kingdom of God" (John 3:3).

---

4. Of course, their doubt of the conclusion presupposes doubt of the premises and perhaps of the validity of the logic as well. In my understanding, the three elements validity, soundness, and persuasiveness are "perspectivally related," so that the lack of one imperils the others. See my *DKG* and *AGG*.

The Spirit must give us a desire to believe. The desire to believe is not a sufficient reason for believing. Wanting to believe something doesn't make it true. Wanting to believe something doesn't make it worthy of belief. But though this desire is not a sufficient condition for belief, it is a necessary condition.

This event is a moral and spiritual event. It is part of redemption, in which the Spirit takes away the veil Satan has laid over our eyes.

The Confession says that the Spirit's testimony works by his "bearing witness by and with the Word in our hearts." It is significant that although the Spirit's testimony is different from the testimony of the church and of the evidences, it does not abandon the word itself. It is, first, "by" the word. That is, the Spirit draws upon the inherent power (Heb. 4:12) and glorious truth (see above) to break through the unbelieving heart. Second, it is "with" the word in our hearts. Since the Spirit's work is subjective and not merely objective, the Spirit adds something to the content of Scripture. But in this subjective work, he is *with the word*; the word is never out of the picture. It is this word that enters our heart, that we can no longer resist.

3. HOW TO FIND GOD'S WILL

This discussion brings us to paragraph VI, which tells us how to find "the whole counsel of God" (Acts 20:27). I take it that here "the whole counsel of God" refers to everything God wants us to know, everything we have come to call "divine revelation." Paragraph VI subdivides this content into "all things necessary for His own glory, man's salvation, faith and life." We should note that these categories are very broad. Theologians have sometimes tried to limit the scope of divine revelation to "man's salvation," so as to justify human autonomous reasoning outside the sphere of salvation. (So theologians have claimed that Scripture contains errors in areas supposedly outside this sphere.) But the Confession clearly will not allow this limitation. Some have also appealed to "faith and life" as a way to limit the scope of revelation. But there is no reason to think the Confession should be read in this way. Faith is what we believe, and life is what we do.

And even if it were possible to limit "man's salvation" and/or "faith and life" to some narrow sphere of human knowledge, certainly there cannot be any such limit on the phrase "all things necessary for His own glory." For absolutely everything has the purpose of glorifying God. Question and answer 1 of the Westminster Shorter Catechism describes glorifying God as the "chief end of man," the very purpose for which God made human beings. Indeed, we saw in paragraph V that one of the significant evidences for Scripture's truth is precisely this breadth, "the scope of the whole (which is, to give all glory to God)." Clearly paragraph V is saying that the scope (the subject matter of Scripture) is the glory of God which it brings to everything in creation. In Scripture, *everything* brings glory to God, and everything has the purpose of bringing glory to God. Scripture shows us how everything brings glory to God, and how we should be seeking to bring glory to God in everything we do.

From paragraphs IV and V, we might be led to suppose that divine revelation is a combination of Scripture itself and something in addition to Scripture brought to us by the Holy Spirit. But perhaps to our surprise, the Confession again stresses that Scripture itself is all we need. According to paragraph VI, the whole counsel of God is either "expressly set down in Scripture, or by good and necessary consequence may be deduced from Scripture." This is the familiar distinction between what Scripture explicitly teaches and what it implicitly teaches. The implicit teachings of Scripture are derived from the explicit teachings by logical deduction. For example, "All men are sinners; David is a man; therefore David is a sinner." Scripture does not say in so many words "David is (was) a sinner," but that statement follows from "All men are sinners" (Rom. 3:23) by good and necessary consequence.[5]

So according to paragraph VI, the whole counsel of God is limited to the explicit and implicit contact of Scripture. The paragraph adds two violations of this limitation: "new revelations" and "traditions of men." I mentioned earlier that the Confession was written in the context

---

5. "Good" here refers to logical validity and "necessary" to the certainty of the conclusion generated by the argument.

of Reformation controversy. Often the Confession opposes the attempt by Roman Catholics to place tradition over the Bible, and it does that again here. The other regular opponent of the Protestant Reformers was the "sectarian" or "Anabaptist" theology which sometimes argued that the Spirit gives to the church "new revelations" beyond the biblical canon. So paragraph VI rules out both of these proposed additions to the canonical source of the whole counsel of God.

But as we saw earlier, the Confession never minimizes the work of the Holy Spirit, despite the sectarians' distortions of his role. We saw earlier that it is the Spirit who opens our sinful eyes to receive the truth of Scripture. Now in paragraph VI, we see that the Spirit, having opened our eyes, gives us an "inward illumination" so that we can understand what is revealed in the word.

The whole counsel of God, of course, does not include our mistakes and misinterpretations. It is an objective reality, the content of Scripture which we are responsible to see, but sometimes fail to see, because of our finitude and remaining sin. So the inward illumination of the Spirit is revelatory in that it uncovers the true meaning of Scripture underneath our distortions of its content. Illumination does not add additional content to the biblical canon, but it enables us to see that canon as it is.

Have we then completely identified the revelation of God's will? So far, we would have to describe that revelation as (1) Scripture's explicit teaching, (2) Scripture's implicit teaching, and (3) the Spirit's influence to properly understand (1) and (2). And yet this list of factors would seem to be incomplete. There are many things God evidently wants us to know that cannot be found either explicitly or implicitly in Scripture. That would include, for example, scientific knowledge which we need to "be fruitful and multiply and fill the earth and subdue it, and have dominion over the fish of the sea and over the birds of the heavens and over every living thing that moves on the earth" (Gen 1:28). Scripture itself does not contain directions for catching fish, except for Jesus's command before the disciples' miraculous catch (Luke 5:4), and there does not seem to be a way for us to obtain such directions by logical deduction from the biblical text.

So it would seem that God does reveal to us some facts beyond the explicit and implicit content of Scripture. Not only Scripture, but also the created world reveals God. This is the common theological doctrine of "general revelation," set forth in passages like Ps. 19:1 and Rom. 1:19–21. Through the world God has made, and apart from Scripture, human beings know God, even apart from the internal testimony of the Holy Spirit.

It is obvious that we must resort to general revelation often in daily life. Through general revelation we learn what time it is, whether it is raining, how far we must drive to our next destination, and billions of other facts. But paragraph VI of the Confession tells us that the knowledge of general revelation is also important in the church. It indicates "some circumstances concerning the worship of God, and government of the church, common to human actions and societies, which are to be ordered by the light of nature ..." I presume that these circumstances include the time of worship, the arrangement of seats, the number of hymns to be sung, etc.[6] These "are to be ordered by the light of nature, and Christian prudence."

But even these are not to be ordered without the Scriptures. These circumstances must be arranged "according to the general rules of the Word, which are always to be observed." That is, when, for example, we decide how to arrange the seats in the worship area, our decision must be consistent with biblical principles of worship. For example, it would not be best to put the seats on top of one another.

A problem arises here. If the precepts of Scripture, even in worship, must be supplemented by precepts from outside of Scripture (that is from general revelation), how is Scripture sufficient? The answer, I think, is that Scripture itself authorizes us to make such use of general revelation. Scripture teaches us what general revelation is (Ps. 19:1; Rom. 1:19–21), and it regularly authorizes us to make use of it. It tells us, for example, to count the cost before we build a tower (Luke 14:28).

---

6. I have elsewhere explored more fully the scope of these circumstances, as distinguished from "elements," "expressions," "forms," and so on. See my "A Fresh Look at the Regulative Principle" in Frame, SSW 3 (Phillipsburg: P&R, 2016). See also the discussion of the Second Commandment in DCL.

Counting the cost will mean assessing our financial situation, which we will not be able to find in the Bible alone. And it will mean researching the cost of tower-building materials in the current economy.

Scripture tells us not only to obey God's explicit commandments, but also to employ "wisdom" (as Proverbs, Ecclesiastes, 1 Cor. 1–3), the "prudence" prescribed in paragraph VI.

So the right use of general revelation is not a violation of *sola Scriptura*. It is simply an application of Scripture, in effect an implicit content of Scripture. When we act wisely based on general revelation, we are doing what Scripture tells us to.

In this sense, biblical revelation is the only revelation there is, for it encompasses and includes general revelation. The only general revelation there is, is a general revelation defined and directed by Scripture. So the word of God that directs our decisions consists entirely of Scripture, *sola Scriptura*.

CONCLUSIONS ON SELF-ATTESTATION

I began this paper by asking questions about the concept of "self-attesting Scripture." Initially, that concept raises the question: How can any piece of writing attest itself? To deal with this question, I explored the concept of self-attestation in chapter 1, paragraphs IV–VI of the Westminster Confession of Faith. The answer to our question, from paragraph IV, is that Scripture is the word of God, and only God can attest the word of God. There is no higher authority sufficient to attest God's own authority. But if Scripture is his word, the same may be said of Scripture. There is no authority high enough to attest Scripture, to prove that it has authority.

Paragraph V indicated that Scripture's self-attestation does not rule out evidence from the history of the church, from the evidences in Scripture itself, and from the inner testimony of the Holy Spirit. Indeed, when they are rightly understood, they are part of Scripture's own self witness. For these evidences do nothing more than to set forth the glory that is inherent in the word itself. The same is true from the doctrine of general revelation in paragraph VI: properly used, general revelation is itself a form of Scripture's self-witness. As such when God reveals himself, he attests himself.

22

Let God Be True

PREFACE

THIS PAPER is my edited version of the Reformation Lectures I presented at Covenant College on Oct. 24–25, 2011. I was asked to present them to the student body following my publication of *The Doctrine of the Word of God*,[1] and though these lectures include some formulations different from DWG, they may fairly be described as a summary of the larger volume. I am thankful to the faculty, administration, and students of Covenant for their invitation, their kind hospitality, and their gracious reception of the lectures.

The first and third lectures were given as chapel talks. The second was presented in a classroom and was intended to be more academic in content. For me, however, the distinction is not great. The purpose of theology in all its forms is edification.[2] In the edited version, I have tried to keep the style conversational, without diluting the content of the argument.

I had thought about turning this material into a small book; but it would have been too small indeed. So I publish it here, with some "book" features: a table of contents, and a dedication, to Dr. James I. Packer.

---

1. Phillipsburg: P&R, 2010.
2. See my book *The Academic Captivity of Theology* (Lakeland, FL: Whitefield Publishers, 2012).

A word about the dedication to James I. Packer. Dr. Packer's book *"Fundamentalism" and the Word of God* was the first book I read that dealt with the issues I am considering here. I was a college student at the time, and I was delighted to read such a strong argument undergirding Christian faith in God's word. For many years I have received much guidance from Dr. Packer's work, and I was greatly humbled when he agreed to write a foreword to DWG. His kind commendations there are much appreciated, and I pray that God will continue to bless his teaching ministry to the minds and hearts of his people.

Let God Be True, from Rom. 3:4, was a title we considered for the book we eventually called *No Other God.*[3] *No Other God*, from the First of the Ten Commandments, seemed more appropriate for my critique of open theism in the earlier book, which was concerned with the nature of God and the divine attributes. But the choice between the two titles was difficult. The issue of God's truthfulness was one of the specific problems raised by open theism, and indeed it is one of the main issues in modern theology generally. Further, Rom. 3:4 has always been one of my favorite texts. I'm delighted that I can use it as a title for the present volume. It is eminently appropriate here, and I hope that it will motivate readers to meditate on Paul's argument in Rom. 3:1–4:

> Then what advantage has the Jew? Or what is the value of circumcision? Much in every way. To begin with, the Jews were entrusted with the oracles of God. What if some were unfaithful? Does their faithlessness nullify the faithfulness of God? By no means! Let God be true though every one were a liar, as it is written, "That you may be justified in your words, and prevail when you are judged."

1. GOD'S PERSONAL WORDS:
GOD SPEAKS AT YOUR BEDSIDE

I am thankful to faculty and administration of Covenant College for the opportunity to present these lectures here. These talks are part of your observance of the Protestant Reformation, which I happily honor.

---

3. Phillipsburg: P&R, 2001.

These will not, however, be typical "Reformation Lectures." I will not be speaking about the history of the Reformation, or about specific figures like Luther and Calvin.

Rather, I will seek to honor the Reformation by doing what Luther and Calvin did. Although they were scholarly historians, they did not as a rule produce studies of their predecessors. Rather, they took the historic doctrines of the church and reworked them in the light of Scripture to meet the needs of the church of their own day. I will be seeking to do that with you, employing one of the main themes of the Reformation itself, *sola Scriptura*, the doctrine that Scripture alone has the final word in the Christian's thought and life.

Albert Einstein taught us the value of "thought experiments." Allow me to propose one to you today.

Imagine you wake up in the night, and there is God standing at your bedside, talking to you. Perhaps your Mom has done this in the past; but now it's God.

He tells you he loves you, with an infinite love.

And he tells you some wonderful news—that in ten years you'll have all the money you need.

And he asks you to do something: Change your major from history to experimental psychology.

Could it be a dream? But you know it's not. How do you know? You just know, just as you know right now that you're not sleeping.

What is your response? If you *know* it's God, you respond to his love, you rejoice at the promise of money, and you change your major.

What do you NOT do? You don't argue. You don't doubt. You don't criticize what he says. This is like the experiences of Noah, Abraham, Moses, and David. This is what revelation is like all through the Bible.

God came to Abraham in Gen. 12 (then called Abram), told him to leave his country, go to a place I'll tell you later.

Abraham got up and left.

Later, God told him he would have a son by his wife Sarah. But he and Sarah were too old. Sarah laughed.

Abraham wavered a bit—the Hagar story—but basically he believed. Eventually he came around. Paul says that's what was so great about Abraham. In Rom. 4:19–21:

> He did not weaken in faith when he considered his own body, which was as good as dead (since he was about a hundred years old), or when he considered the barrenness of Sarah's womb. No distrust made him waver concerning the promise of God, but he grew strong in his faith as he gave glory to God, fully convinced that God was able to do what he had promised.

And so he believed God again, and God gave him and Sarah a son, despite their old age.

But one day, God came to him again and asked him to take his son Isaac, the son God promised and delivered to him, up on a mountain to make him a human sacrifice.

That would have been the end of it for me. I would have said, that can't be God, because God would never tell me to do something as horrible as that.

But I have to remember here: Abraham could not have made that kind of response.

Because he *knew* it was God.

So even though God said something horrible, Abraham had to say "Yes, Lord."

He couldn't say "No, Lord"; that's an oxymoron in any case.

So he said "Yes, Lord." Of course, that doesn't mean he couldn't do some conceptual juggling. Thinking through some creative possibilities: Hey, maybe I will indeed kill Isaac and God will *raise the dead* (Heb. 11:19). But "No, Lord" was out of the question. With God, you don't criticize. You don't find fault. You don't say no. Occasionally you argue.

Remember when God said he was going to condemn Sodom for its sins, and Abraham realized that was where his nephew Lot was living. So Abraham *argued, pled* for Sodom, really for Lot:

> Then Abraham drew near and said, "Will you indeed sweep away the righteous with the wicked? Suppose there are fifty righteous

within the city. Will you then sweep away the place and not spare it for the fifty righteous who are in it? Far be it from you to do such a thing, to put the righteous to death with the wicked, so that the righteous fare as the wicked! Far be that from you! Shall not the Judge of all the earth do what is just?" And the LORD said, "If I find at Sodom fifty righteous in the city, I will spare the whole place for their sake." Abraham answered and said, "Behold, I have undertaken to speak to the Lord, I who am but dust and ashes. Suppose five of the fifty righteous are lacking. Will you destroy the whole city for lack of five?" And he said, "I will not destroy it if I find forty-five there." Again he spoke to him and said, "Suppose forty are found there." He answered, "For the sake of forty I will not do it." Then he said, "Oh let not the Lord be angry, and I will speak. Suppose thirty are found there." He answered, "I will not do it, if I find thirty there." He said, "Behold, I have undertaken to speak to the Lord. Suppose twenty are found there." He answered, "For the sake of twenty I will not destroy it." Then he said, "Oh let not the Lord be angry, and I will speak again but this once. Suppose ten are found there." He answered, "For the sake of ten I will not destroy it." And the LORD went his way, when he had finished speaking to Abraham, and Abraham returned to his place. (Gen. 18:23–33)

Fifty, forty-five, forty, thirty, twenty, ten.

Sounds like an argument—but notice two things: one, Abraham never questions God's word. God said he would judge Sodom. Abraham doesn't criticize that; he only argues about what God hasn't said, namely *how* God will judge Sodom.

And two, verse 25 is the key: Shall not the Judge of all the earth do what is just?

Abraham doesn't say God is unjust. He knows better. His assumption is that God will do justly. 50, 45, 40, 30, 20, 10 … What if there are only 9 people? Then, by the terms of their agreement, God is entitled to destroy the whole city. That would, however, be contrary to the spirit of the discussion, which seems to lead to the conclusion that God will not destroy the city if even one righteous person is found there. But Abraham keeps his promise to speak no more. He knows that the judge of all the earth will do right.

That's the way it is with God. Even when you argue with him, you have to keep reminding yourself, and him, that he judges you, not the other way around.

Now if anybody wants to know what the word of God is, what revelation is, that's it. It's God speaking personally with persons.

Some of his speech is within himself: a conversation within the Trinity. The Father says to the Son, go down on planet earth; bring wisdom and life; and the Son says, behold, I come (Ps. 40:7; Heb. 10:5–10).

Sometimes God talks to human beings, as with Abraham. Sometimes he talks to many human beings at once, as on Mt. Sinai (Ex. 19–24).

Just think how frightening that must have been to the Israelites camped around the mountain: fire, thunders, trumpet blasts, and this person talking. The Lord said, Don't touch the mountain. This was hardly a place where you could argue with God.

The people couldn't take it.

And you (Israel) said, "Behold, the LORD our God has shown us his glory and greatness, and we have heard his voice out of the midst of the fire. This day we have seen God speak with man, and man still live. Now therefore why should we die? For this great fire will consume us. If we hear the voice of the LORD our God any more, we shall die. For who is there of all flesh, that has heard the voice of the living God speaking out of the midst of fire as we have, and has still lived? (Deut. 5:24–26)

The people said no; don't let this happen. You know, sometimes people say, "If God wants to speak with me, let him come down and have a personal conversation with me. Why does he stay up in heaven? I'm not interested in reading the Bible, but I will be happy to have an individual conversation with God." When people talk like that, they don't know what they're saying. The Israelites at Mt. Sinai literally thought they were going to die. The voice of the Lord can be terribly frightening, because, after all, as the Bible says, we do deserve to die at his hand, apart from Jesus. Remember how Adam and Eve must have felt, when they had sinned against God, and then heard God coming to talk to them.

But fortunately there was an alternative. They didn't have to talk to God directly. Moses was there, and he had a special relationship with God. So the people said to Moses,

> Go near and hear all that the LORD our God will say, and speak to us all that the LORD our God will speak to you, and we will hear and do it. (Deut. 5:27)

And that became the general pattern. God spoke to prophets and apostles, and they brought his words to the rest of the people.

But don't mess with the Prophet. In Deut. 18:15–19, Moses says,

> The LORD your God will raise up for you a prophet like me from among you, from your brothers—it is to him you shall listen— just as you desired of the LORD your God at Horeb on the day of the assembly, when you said, "Let me not hear again the voice of the LORD my God or see this great fire any more, lest I die." And the LORD said to me, "They are right in what they have spoken. I will raise up for them a prophet like you from among their brothers. And I will put my words in his mouth, and he shall speak to them all that I command him. And whoever will not listen to my words that he shall speak in my name, I myself will require it of him."

You see, disobeying the words of the prophet is as bad as disobeying God.

Remember—no criticizing God? No criticizing the prophet either. Don't say, well, he's just a man ... wait a minute; that's the word of God on his lips. In that prophet, God is talking to you, you personally.

And then, God sent his Son.

His Son is more than a prophet. He is the Word of God:

> In the beginning was the Word, and the Word was with God, and the Word was God. (John 1:1)

Now, we know why he came—to die for our sins and rise again. But he also came to *speak*.

> For he whom God has sent utters the words of God, for he gives the Spirit without measure. (John 3:34)

> Truly, truly, I say to you, whoever hears my word and believes him who sent me has eternal life. (John 5:24)

> It is the Spirit who gives life; the flesh is no help at all. The words that I have spoken to you are spirit and life. (John 6:63)

> Simon Peter answered him, "Lord, to whom shall we go? You have the words of eternal life ..." (John 6:68)

> So Jesus said to the Jews who had believed in him, "If you abide in my word, you are truly my disciples ..." (John 8:31)

> The one who rejects me and does not receive my words has a judge; the word that I have spoken will judge him on the last day. (John 12:48)

> (To Pilate) For this purpose I was born and for this purpose I have come into the world—to bear witness to the truth. Everyone who is of the truth listens to my voice. (John 18:37)

Those are words you don't mess with. You don't mess with the word from Mt. Sinai, or at your bedside, or through a prophet, or through the Son of God.

These are words that will judge you.

And you desperately need to have the words of Jesus, as Peter did, when he said, "Lord, to whom shall we go? You have the words of eternal life."

Where are those words? Jesus didn't write any books.

That's where the Bible comes in. Jesus appointed his disciples, his apostles, to remember his words, and to speak more words God was going to give them.

And you don't mess with those. Listen to the apostle Paul:

If anyone thinks that he is a prophet, or spiritual, he should acknowledge that the things I am writing to you are a command of the Lord. (1 Cor. 14:37)

So there is a written word. But don't let the looks of it deceive you.

The Bible doesn't *look* like God, any more than Moses or Isaiah did. But it talks like him. You don't mess with it.

... and how from childhood you have been acquainted with the *sacred* writings, which are able to make you wise for salvation through faith in Christ Jesus. All Scripture is breathed out by God and profitable for teaching, for reproof, for correction, and for training in righteousness, that the man of God may be competent, equipped for every good work. (2 Tim. 3:15–17, emphasis added)

You don't argue with it. You don't criticize it, though many do. You don't disagree.

You may ask questions, as some of the biblical prophets themselves did. When you read something perplexing, ask why. With the Psalm writers, ask "how long" it will be until God straightens out this world forever (Pss. 4:2; 6:3; 13:1–2; 35:17; 62:3; many more). And with Abraham, argue when you need to. Tell God, "OK, but please do it this way." "Lord, don't destroy our country; there are a lot of godly people here."

But always remember who you're arguing with.

Read it as God talking to you, because when Paul says that all Scripture is "God-breathed" (2 Tim. 3:16–17), that's what "God-breathed" means.

So revelation, the word of God, is simply God talking. His personal conversation with other persons. His personal words to you.

So easy to forget that. Consider passages like these:

Adam, Seth, Enosh; Kenan, Mahalalel, Jared; Enoch, Methuselah, Lamech; Noah, Shem, Ham, and Japheth. The sons of Japheth: Gomer, Magog, Madai, Javan, Tubal, Meshech, and Tiras. The sons of Gomer: Ashkenaz, Riphath, and Togarmah. The sons of Javan: Elishah, Tarshish, Kittim, and Rodanim. (1 Chron. 1:1–7)

> If his offering is a burnt offering from the herd, he shall offer a
> male without blemish. He shall bring it to the entrance of the
> tent of meeting, that he may be accepted before the LORD. He
> shall lay his hand on the head of the burnt offering, and it shall
> be accepted for him to make atonement for him. Then he shall
> kill the bull before the LORD, and Aaron's sons the priests shall
> bring the blood and throw the blood against the sides of the altar
> that is at the entrance of the tent of meeting. Then he shall flay
> the burnt offering and cut it into pieces, and the sons of Aaron
> the priest shall put fire on the altar and arrange wood on the fire.
> And Aaron's sons the priests shall arrange the pieces, the head,
> and the fat, on the wood that is on the fire on the altar. (Lev. 1:3–8)

Passages like these can be a "hard slog," in Donald Rumsfeld's phrase. But sometimes God says things like this:

> The LORD is my shepherd; I shall not want. He makes me lie
> down in green pastures. He leads me beside still waters. He
> restores my soul. He leads me in paths of righteousness for his
> name's sake. Even though I walk through the valley of the shadow
> of death, I will fear no evil, for you are with me; your rod and
> your staff, they comfort me. You prepare a table before me in
> the presence of my enemies; you anoint my head with oil; my
> cup overflows. Surely goodness and mercy shall follow me all
> the days of my life, and I shall dwell in the house of the LORD
> forever. (Ps. 23:1–6)

and

> For God so loved the world, that he gave his only Son, that
> whoever believes in him should not perish but have eternal life.
> (John 3:16)

Don't you wish that that God would say this directly to you? He has. He really has. In fact, he just did.

How do you know it's really God? More on that in the next lecture. But if you trust Jesus as your lord and savior, you do know.

When you trusted Christ as your lord, you trusted him as lord of
everything in your life—1 Cor. 10:31.

That includes your reasoning. Prov. 3:5–6,

> Trust in the LORD with all your heart, and do not lean on your
> own understanding. In all your ways acknowledge him, and he
> will make straight your paths. (Prov. 3:5–6)

You trusted Christ on the basis of the gospel, which is the message of
Scripture.

So you said, "Lord, I'm going to believe that gospel as the most certain thing in my life, as your very word to me." So yes, you know that
this book is the word of God. All you need to do is get your life consistent with it.

You know why this is so important? Two reasons.

1. It's true. That's really what the word of God is.

2. If God hasn't spoken to us this way, our faith is a delusion.

Think a bit more about that second point. Because many people today
think that faith is precisely a delusion, and we have to be ready to deal
with them.

For us, it's wonderful to believe that God has made everything, and
us in his image.

It's great to believe that sin and evil are not part of our nature, but
come from a historical event in the distant past that can be reversed.

It's wonderful to believe that God sent his Son into the world, born
of a virgin, worker of miracles, teacher like no other, who died for our
sins and rose from the dead, ascended to heaven, and is coming again.

But I want you to feel this morning how strange this teaching is—
how ridiculous it sounds to modern people. Blood atonement? Salvation
by human sacrifice?

Of course it sounded ridiculous in the ancient world too: the wisdom
of God, says Paul, is foolishness to the world.

But it's ridiculous today too, when people assume as a matter of course that everything happens by natural causes, without any supernatural interference.

Many of you were raised in Christian homes, and here you are at a Christian college, where the Bible stories are taken for granted.

But if and when you work or study in the secular world, you'll find that people think you're crazy if you believe such things. If you believe, for example, that a wife should submit to her husband (Eph. 5:33), then they will say (as they said to Michele Bachmann) that you are not fit to hold political office.

But now: if these stories don't come from God, we have no reason to believe them.

If they come from ancient tribes who got the idea of blood atonement from who knows where, they are not worth believing.

If they come from some philosopher's speculation, the same. Philosophers can be pretty smart, but I'm not going to trust any of them with my life for this life and eternity.

Only if it comes from God do I have any basis for believing it.

That's why it's important to believe that the Bible is like God talking to you, at your bedside.

2. SCRIPTURE AND CERTAINTY: ESCAPING AND EMBRACING GOD'S VOICE

As I said, it's important to believe that God has spoken to you, just like your Mom or Dad at your bedside. But sometimes that's hard to believe.

We don't seem to be in the same position as Abraham—hearing God's voice and at the same time automatically knowing that it's God.

So let me ask now: If God talks to you—at your bedside, in the voice of a prophet, in writing—how do you know it's God?

That's the "epistemological" question: How do we know, how are we certain?

Perplexing question, and one that we sometimes use to escape God's voice.

EPISTEMOLOGY AND ETHICS

Philosophy includes three disciplines: metaphysics (What is?), epistemology (How can we know what is?), ethics or value theory (How ought we to live?).

Some people make a sharp distinction between these, but it seems to me these are inseparable.

How can you know what is, if you don't know anything about how to know what is?

How can you know what it is to know, if you have no idea what the world is like? (At least there must be something that can be known.)

How can you know without any ethical values at all?

More on that last point. I'm happy that in the last few years many have addressed the relationship between ethics and epistemology. Indeed, many philosophers have written about the ethics of epistemology.[4]

Knowing requires some ethical values: truth, diligence, honesty, trust, humility, discipline.

In Scripture, even more.

If anyone's will is to do God's will, he will know whether the teaching is from God or whether I am speaking on my own authority. (John 7:17)

Here, knowing the authority of Jesus's teaching presupposes a willingness to do God's will.

---

4. A much-discussed essay on this subject is W. K. Clifford, "The Ethics of Belief," originally published in *Contemporary Review*, 1877, presently in print in Clifford, *The Ethics of Belief and Other Essays* (Amherst, NY: Prometheus Books, 1999), and available at http://www.infidels .org/library/historical/w_k_clifford/ethics_of_belief.html. Clifford argues the thesis of David Hume that it is unethical to hold a belief without adequate evidence. But other writers have challenged Clifford's thesis, arguing that in some situations it is ethical to believe something without being able to cite evidence for it, and arguing that there are other ethical considerations that enter into the justification of beliefs. See, for example, W. Jay Wood, *Epistemology: Becoming Intellectually Virtuous* (Downers Grove: InterVarsity Press, 1998); Esther Lightcap Meek, *Longing to Know: The Philosophy of Knowledge for Ordinary People* (Grand Rapids: Brazos Press, 2003); Meek, *Loving to Know: Introducing Covenant Epistemology* (Eugene, OR: Cascade Books, 2011). I would mention also John Frame, *Doctrine of the Knowledge of God* (Phillipsburg: P&R, 1987) and *Doctrine of the Word of God* (Phillipsburg: P&R, 2010).

> Now concerning food offered to idols: we know that "all of us possess knowledge." This "knowledge" puffs up, but love builds up. If anyone imagines that he knows something, he does not yet know as he ought to know. But if anyone loves God, he is known by God. (1 Cor. 8:1)

There are lots of complicated conceptual relationships in this passage, between true knowledge, false knowledge, love, God knowing us, knowing as we ought to know, but at any rate it is clear that we can't know rightly without love.

Here's a familiar passage:

> Trust in the LORD with all your heart, and do not lean on your own understanding. In all your ways acknowledge him, and he will make straight your paths. (Prov. 3:5–6)

So, in Rom. 1:18–21:

> For the wrath of God is revealed from heaven against all ungodliness and unrighteousness of men, who by their unrighteousness suppress the truth. For what can be known about God is plain to them, because God has shown it to them. For his invisible attributes, namely, his eternal power and divine nature, have been clearly perceived, ever since the creation of the world, in the things that have been made. So they are without excuse. For although they knew God, they did not honor him as God or give thanks to him, but they became futile in their thinking, and their foolish hearts were darkened. (Rom. 1:18–21)

Here, Paul speaks of knowledge suppressed by ethical rebellion.

So in Scripture, there is a close relationship between knowledge and obedience.

> Who is wise and understanding among you? By his good conduct let him show his works in the meekness of wisdom. But if you have bitter jealousy and selfish ambition in your hearts, do not boast and be false to the truth. This is not the wisdom that comes down from above, but is earthly, unspiritual, demonic.

For where jealousy and selfish ambition exist, there will be disorder and every vile practice. But the wisdom from above is first pure, then peaceable, gentle, open to reason, full of mercy and good fruits, impartial and sincere. And a harvest of righteousness is sown in peace by those who make peace. (James 3:13–18)

By nature, we are sinners, which means, among other things, that we don't want to hear God's voice. What is the remedy? Only saving grace, brought into our hearts and minds by the Holy Spirit.

But for believers, this means that we still try to find ways of escaping God's voice. Even though we believe in Christ, we still sin. And some of that sin is epistemological. The problem is not that God's voice is faint, or unclear, but that we try to escape from his voice.

So the best cure for uncertainty is obedience, being willing to do God's will.

People sometimes complain that God hasn't spoken to them, but they haven't asked whether they would obey if God did speak to them. Scripture sometimes equates knowledge and obedience:

For I desire steadfast love and not sacrifice, the knowledge of God rather than burnt offerings. (Hos. 6:6)

He judged the cause of the poor and needy; then it was well. Is not this to know me? declares the LORD. (Jer. 22:16)

And we learn how to obey by his word.

I appeal to you therefore, brothers, by the mercies of God, to present your bodies as a living sacrifice, holy and acceptable to God, which is your spiritual worship. Do not be conformed to this world, but be transformed by the renewal of your mind, that by testing you may discern what is the will of God, what is good and acceptable and perfect. (Rom. 12:1–2; cf. Phil. 1:9; Eph. 5:8; Heb. 5:11–14)

ASSURANCE

But now, how does *that* work?

It doesn't *seem* that obedience, an obedient heart, gives us assurance as to when God is speaking.

So let me ask, is it possible, by obedient knowledge, servant knowledge, to be certain of what God says?

Scripture says that eternal life is to *know* God (John 17:3). In that verse and many others, knowledge of God is not a conjecture or speculation, or even a probable maybe; it's real knowledge.

Luke says to Theophilus that he has written his Gospel so "that you may have certainty concerning the things you have been taught" (Luke 1:4). Whatever people may say today, certainty is a good thing.

Doubt, in Scripture, the absence of certainty, is usually something bad. Jesus says to his disciples, "O you of little faith, why did you doubt?" (Matt. 14:31).

Talking about food controversies in the church, Paul says, "But whoever has doubts is condemned if he eats, because the eating is not from faith. For whatever does not proceed from faith is sin" (Rom. 14:23).

Now this doesn't mean that doubt is always sinful and we should always be certain about everything. Where we are ignorant, we ought to be honest and admit that. Deut. 29:29; Rom. 11:33–34; Job 38–42.

But the Christian always has certainty as his starting point: Jesus. "I know whom I have believed," 2 Tim. 1:12.

Here is a fundamental point: the Christian has a different *definition* of certainty from people who don't know Christ. That definition is Jesus himself. We know *whom* we have believed.

Jesus is our definition of certainty—and not just any Jesus. Jesus, the Son of God, crucified for our sins, risen again. Jesus our Lord and Savior.

These are truths that define our lives, the starting point for our thinking. Foundations for living, and thinking too, because thinking is part of life. If Jesus is the foundation of our lives, he is the foundation of our thinking as well.

If Jesus is Lord, he's Lord of the mind—as he said, you are to love the Lord with all your mind (Matt. 22:37).

If you love him with your mind, you'll reject anything that conflicts with these fundamental truths. So those truths are certain, not because you've measured them by some other standard, but because they are the standard.

Of course, I'm talking here about the fundamental truths of the gospel. Theoretically, all the teachings of the Scriptures should be fundamental to us, because the Scriptures are the word of God. But of course there are some truths in Scripture that we don't understand and some problems in Scripture that we don't have answers to. That ignorance is partly due to our sin, partly due to our finitude (the human mind just cannot encompass all of God's truth).

When I speak of "fundamental truths of the gospel," I mean truths like these: God exists. Jesus is the Son of God. Jesus is Lord. Jesus died for our sins and rose again. If you don't believe those, you really cannot call yourself a Christian. If you do believe those, then they constitute the basis of your thinking, and you hold them for certain, because they are the very definition of certainty.

When I speak of truths in Scripture that we cannot understand, cannot be sure of, each believer has a different list. I am pretty sure that Scripture warrants the baptism of babies. But I'm not as sure of that as I am of the resurrection of Jesus. And I'm not at all sure of what Rev. 20 is talking about when it speaks of a millennium of peace.

My friend Richard Pratt speaks of a "cone of certainty," narrow at one end, broad at the other. At the narrow end are a few truths that determine the Christian's certainty. At the broad end are truths about which there is room for conscientious differences among Christians. Between the two ends are truths that can move through our lives from positions of uncertainty to certainty and back again, like infant baptism and the millennium.

But I'm so thankful for the narrow end, for the truths that serve as our fundamental certainties. From those truths we can derive others. They can guide our search through life for greater and greater levels of assurance. In time most Christians develop a group of *settled* beliefs, beliefs that govern all our other beliefs.

Doubts come and go. Things we were once sure of can become uncertain, and vice versa.

But the goal is to be certain about Christ, about his word, building on the foundation (Matt. 4:4).

Our settled beliefs about Scripture teaching take precedence over any ideas derived from a different source.

That is the objective way to certainty. The way to truth.

But there is also the subjective side. We know that psychologically our certainty has ups and downs. It's not enough to say, as above, that the truth is out there, in the Bible and in the world. It is also important to think about the mind. How does the Spirit work to deal with the sin in the mind, so that the mind seeks out the truth we have been speaking about? According to Paul in Rom. 1, the sinful mind suppresses the truth in unrighteousness, rather than embracing it (v. 18). How does the Spirit work to stop that suppression?

Here's another way to look at that question. When someone asks me, "Why do you believe in God?" I can offer reasons: biblical texts, rational arguments. Or I can comment on the condition of my mind: I was trained to think this way. So I can answer the question "why" either by offering a rational ground, or by presenting a subjective cause. The "ground" of belief is, in a sense, objective; the "cause" is subjective. We have talked about the objective ground of our certainty. Now we must consider the subjective cause of our certainty, the work of the Holy Spirit:

> ... our gospel came to you not only in word, but also in power and
> in the Holy Spirit and with full conviction. You know what kind
> of men we proved to be among you for your sake. (1 Thess. 1:5)

3. GOD'S WORD ON OUR HEART

We've talked about God's word as personal discourse: God speaking to people.

The main problem with this is, How can a human being know that God is talking to him or to her?

We discussed that in the second lecture: Christians have a unique definition of certainty that is part of our Christian commitment. And we become able to use that definition of certainty subjectively by the work of the Holy Spirit in our hearts. He enables us to actually *feel* certain, to use our new definition of certainty in every inquiry.

But God wants more for us even than this. When he speaks to us, he wants us to be certain about truth; but that's not all. The word is not just for the mind, but for the heart. The heart is the inner core of our being, the basic direction of our lives. Jesus taught,

> The good person out of the good treasure of his heart produces good, and the evil person out of his evil treasure produces evil, for out of the abundance of the heart his mouth speaks. (Luke 6:45)

To say that God sees the heart, then, is to say that he sees you as you really are, beneath the masks you wear. He knows if you are basically evil, repressing the truth as Paul says, or whether you are born again, regenerated to a good life, created in Christ Jesus for good works (Eph. 2:10).

If the Spirit has changed your heart, you have been through a radical change. All things have become new (2 Cor. 5:17). Your new way of thinking and living is full of surprises—for you and for other people.

Have you ever known somebody—maybe your Mom or Dad—who almost always, automatically it seems—does the right thing? A kind of instinct?

He or she acts in biblical ways, loves to study the Bible, but typically does the right thing without even looking it up?

That's a person with the word written on the heart.

A life surrounded, saturated by God's words.

That's the way God always wanted us to live. When he gave his law to Israel, he told them that these statutes should absolutely saturate their lives:

> You shall teach them diligently to your children, and shall talk of them when you sit in your house, and when you walk by the way, and when you lie down, and when you rise. You shall bind them as a sign on your hand, and they shall be as frontlets between your eyes. You shall write them on the doorposts of your house and on your gates. (Deut. 6:7–9)

So the psalmist says,

> I have stored up your word in my heart, that I might not sin
> against you. (Ps. 119:11)

And,

> Let not steadfast love and faithfulness forsake you; bind them
> around your neck; write them on the tablet of your heart. (Prov.
> 3:3)

Not all Israel had God's word in their heart, but some did.

> Listen to me, you who know righteousness, the people in whose
> heart is my law; fear not the reproach of man, nor be dismayed
> at their revilings. (Isa. 51:7)

These are the remnant of Isaiah's day, the few that remain faithful to
the Lord. But God looks forward to a time when all his people will
have new heart.

> Behold, the days are coming, declares the LORD, when I will
> make a new covenant with the house of Israel and the house of
> Judah, not like the covenant that I made with their fathers on the
> day when I took them by the hand to bring them out of the land
> of Egypt, my covenant that they broke, though I was their hus-
> band, declares the LORD. But this is the covenant that I will make
> with the house of Israel after those days, declares the LORD: I will
> put my law within them, and I will write it on their hearts. And
> I will be their God, and they shall be my people. And no longer
> shall each one teach his neighbor and each his brother, saying,
> "Know the LORD," for they shall all know me, from the least of
> them to the greatest, declares the LORD. For I will forgive their
> iniquity, and I will remember their sin no more. (Jer. 31:31–34)

We hear about this new covenant again in the book of Hebrews of the New
Testament, chapters 8–10. There we learn that the new covenant was established by the atonement of Jesus, making the old covenant "obsolete" (8:13).

What, then, should we say about the believers of the Old Testament? Were they not able to have the word written on their heart?

What Scripture says is that they are saved by Christ retrospectively: by looking forward to God's provision.

They heard the prophecies of the Messiah, and they saw in the animal offerings pictures of Jesus, the lamb of God, who takes away the sins of the world.

They were saved by looking ahead to the cross, we by looking back to it.

Did their salvation include writing on the heart? Yes, I believe it did.

But here we are *now*, looking back on the complete work of Christ. And his word is on our heart.

The amazing fact is that if you are a believer in Jesus Christ, your deepest inclination is to follow Jesus. So we become God's letter to the world:

> You yourselves are our letter of recommendation, written on our hearts, to be known and read by all. And you show that you are a letter from Christ delivered by us, written not with ink but with the Spirit of the living God, not on tablets of stone but on tablets of human hearts. (2 Cor. 3:2)

It's not just that you have received revelation; you *are* revelation. You are God's letter to the world. Since the word is on your heart, it is what you *are*. When people see you, they hear God speaking. Oh, yes, they also hear your sinful distortions of God's speech. That will continue until the end of life. But often, in a provisional and fragmentary way, you will see people changed from listening to God's word in your life.

You are God's word, because you have received God's word in the deepest possible way.

Think of it this way: When you really communicate with someone, even on the human level, there is a word in your mind that comes through your mouth, goes through the air, vibrates the eardrums of another person, goes to his brain, and heart.

That doesn't always happen; sometimes it gets lost.

But when there's real communication, that's what happens. When you hear, it goes into your mind and heart and changes your life. You don't forget it. It affects your mind, words, deeds. Your habits.

And that's what God's word does.

Our hearts, then, are the destination of God's revelation. In us, the process of communication reaches its terminus.

In our hearts we receive God's personal words to us in such a profound way that they become the foundation of all our thinking and living. (So of course we are certain about them.)

It's a process. We all have to grow into it, and we never get it perfect in this life. But some do better than others.

That should be our goal, our purpose.

The point is not that we need to be reading the Bible all the time, though reading it is a good thing and most of us need to read it a lot more. But the point is getting to know the Bible so well that we obey it without looking things up. So that obedience becomes our second nature.

We look forward to the consummation of this knowledge in the last day, when God will tear away from us all our sinful inclinations to disobey and devalue this wonderful word.

God has accompanied his word through all the vicissitudes of history, the problems of Scripture, and the spiritual battles of our lives, so that we might receive it with joy. And he will continue to accompany it until he receives us into glory.

23

Canine Intelligence and
the Incomprehensibility of God

I HAVE OWNED THREE WELSH CORGIS during my lifetime, and my parents owned four before me. Our dogs were always the smartest. Under the influence of a show at the San Diego Wild Animal Park, I taught my pet at that time, not only to sit, stand, and shake, but also to "turn to the left," "turn to the right," "lie down," and "relax" (with chin on the ground). She could even "kiss" and "cuddle" on command. The corgi I had before her learned to recognize dogs and cats on the TV screen, making me wish I had never taught her that particular skill. Another performed the most incredible feats of athleticism, risking her life to pick a rubber ball out of the air. But (certainly for lack of a better trainer) my dogs never learned the finest forms of canine intelligence, like detecting drugs, attacking villains, locating game, guiding the blind, assisting the wounded, and comforting the sick. Still, somehow I knew my dogs had all those skills deep down somewhere. I knew that in a post-apocalyptic scenario my dogs could find food for me far more efficiently than I could find food for them.

Sometimes friends of mine have despaired of their human intelligence. But I have usually consoled them with the thought that with humans as with dogs there are many different kinds of intelligence. There is the kind of intelligence measured by IQ tests, the kind measured by football scouts as they evaluate quarterbacks, the kind described by music critics, the shrewdness of politicians, the practical skills of problem-solvers in all fields. Those who excel in one of these often look stupid when they move outside their sphere of competence and get compared to intelligent people in a different field.

So, just as "everything is beautiful in its own way," most everyone is intelligent in one way or another. Yet there are some tasks that are completely alien to all sorts of created intellect. To return to my dog illustration, there are some tasks completely beyond even the smartest. I showed one corgi my first book, *The Doctrine of the Knowledge of God*. She sniffed at it with moderate interest. It was and is a foundational volume to my general theological method. If any dog were to begin a program of theological study, this book was certainly the place to begin. But after the initial sniff, detecting no culinary aroma, she passed it by. She literally had no idea what was in it. She had no appreciation for its conceptual content, although I had spent nearly twenty years researching and writing it.

I often imagine how my corgi felt when I approach the deeper things of God. God himself says,

> For my thoughts are not your thoughts, neither are your ways my ways, declares the LORD. For as the heavens are higher than the earth, so are my ways higher than your ways and my thoughts than your thoughts. (Isa. 55:8–9)

This text refers in context to our difficulties in reconciling ourselves to God's revealed will, including our difficulty in believing that grace is possible for sinners. But it certainly applies all the more obviously to our more general attempts to comprehend God's mind intellectually. I've made an honest try in my writings to understand such issues as the relation between God's sovereignty and man's responsibility, and the problem of evil. But I haven't been able to remove all the difficulties in these doctrines, even my own. And when I get my nose up against these questions, I feel very much like my corgis must have felt sniffing out my *Doctrine of the Knowledge of God*. There's no food there for me, and there's nothing, otherwise, that even begins to engage my analysis.

It's not just that these questions are too difficult for me to comprehend. It's that I do not know how even to begin trying to comprehend
them. They don't speak a language that is meaningful to me. I cannot
even begin the quest. God has told me quite a lot in Scripture. Beyond
that, I have no hope of gaining enlightenment.

My disability here is profound. I can't imagine doing what some
theologians do. Many of them drop the biblical doctrine of election
because they think it ought to be transparent to them, to be easily reconciled to our intuition of freedom. And because they cannot reconcile their view of freedom to the biblical teaching they emerge with a
new conceptuality. To me the new conceptualities (I'm now thinking
of "Open Theism") are always worse. They compromise something
important in the Bible.

Others try to see beyond the veil what it is that makes God a Trinity,
and precisely how the Trinity is like and unlike various triads in our
experience. Often they present these theories with great assurance. I
scratch and sniff, occasionally bark. But for the most part, in these academic attempts to improve on the church's theology there is nothing for
me, and I suspect nothing for anyone else either. Often they seem to be
trying to make something out of nothing. God does give us a glimpse
of the Trinity in the Bible—but not a treatise.

I am happy to say the obvious things and to bypass the topics that
many consider to be more profound. Increasingly I am feeling on this
account more and more estranged from the theological profession.
Perhaps that is a good thing. At 77, I am slouching toward retirement.

24

The Gospel in an Image

I SAW THE NEW *STAR WARS* film recently.[5] The last scene (slight spoiler warning) is a wordless image that summarizes the goal of all the action of the film and points ahead to the plots of the sequels. Many films are like that: after all the fights, misunderstandings, reconciliations, evil deeds, narrow escapes, heroism, foolishness, and wisdom, there is a quiet ending that sums it all up, often without words. I have always felt that the Lord's Supper is like that.

In our worship service, the Supper comes at the end, before the benediction. We use some words to explain the sacrament, but for the most part the sacrament is an image. The bread is broken and distributed to those who have received Jesus by faith. We eat together. Then we drink the cup as well.

When I introduce the sacrament I usually connect it with the sermon. Our sermons, of course, range over the whole of Scripture. But it is never difficult to connect them to the Lord's Supper, because the Lord's Supper summarizes the whole Bible. In the Lord's Supper, God gives us gifts of his good creation, which nourish our bodies, but broken they represent the death of the Son of God, the result of man's fall into sin. But the image is not only death, but death as redemption—Jesus

---

5. *The Force Awakens.* Since I wrote this essay, the Star Wars saga has continued beyond this point.

enduring death for sinners, for us who killed him. And in the Supper we also look to the future: as Paul says, we "proclaim the Lord's death until he comes" (1 Cor. 11:26).

This redemption is the whole meaning of the Bible. Whatever the preacher preaches on, if he's preaching rightly, he's preaching Christ (Luke 24:27). If he preaches God's moral law, he's preaching how the fall has injured us, why we need to turn to Christ in faith, and how the Lord wants his redeemed people to live. If the preacher speaks about Israel's history, he's telling us how God prepared the earth for the coming of Jesus and for his sacrifice for sin. When he preaches from the book of Acts, he is telling us how God made his word to grow throughout the world, as believers set out to proclaim the Lord's death "until he comes."

What is true of the sermon is also true of the hymns and prayers in our worship service: they too drive into our hearts the gospel of God's wonderful grace. God, who is perfectly holy, showed his amazing grace by sending his dear Son to give his life for us. We confess our sins, acknowledging that we have no hope of having eternal fellowship with God and one another, apart from what Jesus did for us. In our church we "greet one another" after the confession of sin, confessing that the gospel is the very basis of our friendship and brotherhood. If someone is baptized, he or she is baptized into Christ, symbolizing our cleansing from sin through Jesus's work.

The Bible does not specify a single liturgy or order of events in worship that all churches must follow. My point, though, is that however we arrange the specifics, the service is all about Jesus and all about his sacrifice for us.

So at the end we sum it all up with one humble, but glorious image: the bread and the cup, proclaiming the Lord's death until he comes.

25

Resurrection Joy

THE RECENT FILM *RISEN* excited my interest more than most films about the events surrounding Christ. The narrative centers around Clavius, a Roman tribune played by Joseph Fiennes. It therefore seeks to present the story from the viewpoint of people who are initially nonbelievers and to appeal to people in the viewing audience who think similarly today. The film has been described as "faith-based," however, and its view of the story is certainly affirmative. Clavius becomes a convert, which implies his rejection of the Roman ethos.

The film takes a very negative view of that Roman culture, for all the glory that later ages have ascribed to it. That culture achieved its accomplishments by killing people of other nations and by destroying anyone or anything within the empire that opposed its intentions. That led to jealousy and suspicions among the leaders of the military and the political establishment.

But what to do when rumors of a resurrection begin to fly in the Jerusalem community? Since the rumors detract from the glory of Rome, the authorities need to disprove the rumors and to destroy the movement that is spreading them. Clavius receives the commission to trace the story down and to stop the rumor in its tracks. For a while he takes on the role of a detective. But in time it is evident that those with first-hand information, Jesus's disciples, are living largely in the open. Clavius interviews one named Bartholomew, and, far from terror in the presence of the great Roman authority, Bartholomew appears (as at least two reviewers have put it) *giddy*. He laughs, he dances around, he utters strange sayings. Eventually, Clavius finds the same attitude in Jesus himself. As Katie Walsh said in her *Los Angeles Times*[6] review, "This is the case when Clavius meets Yeshua himself—a beatific and groovy Cliff Curtis, and his tribe of merry men."

An ordinary "biblical epic" would have made the disciples deadly serious, preaching the word and casting out Satan. One doesn't expect much humor or delight in such drama. But this movie makes us ask in a serious way how we would feel in such a situation. Jesus had predicted his resurrection, but it was hard for the disciples to believe that he would die, let alone be raised up. And the biblical narrative seemed to grow darker and darker as the band of disciples came to Jerusalem for that last, terrifying week. When Jesus was beaten brutally and died on the cross, it seemed that hope was gone. The Roman worldview, in which meaning comes through might, prevailed again.

But then imagine being there when people began reporting the resurrection. And imagine the transformation of your own spirit when you actually meet the risen Christ. The resurrection of Christ means that his people are saved from their sins and are eternally united with the eternal God. And that resurrection is the final refutation of the Roman worldview. Everything is different now, not because of an army's brute strength and cruelty, but because God loved the world and because his beloved Son was willing to die.

That means that world history is most fundamentally a comedy rather than a tragedy. God sat in the heavens (Ps. 2) and laughed at the silly claims of the Roman emperor and the other bullies of the world. In the resurrection, the wisdom of the world became foolishness to our God, and foolishness as well to us his people (1 Cor. 1–2).

It is only in biblical religion—Christianity and Judaism—that humor has an honored place. Because the ruler of the world is personal, rather than a horrible, dark force, we can laugh at all the foolishness around

---

6. May 30, 2016. My friend Andrew Sandlin also picked up on this theme in his review. See https://docsandlin.com/2016/02/20/risen-a-cinematic-and-theological-triumph/.

us. It's fine, even necessary, to take seriously what should be taken seriously—the honor of God, the horrible destiny of those who hate him. But our lives in Christ are in the end full of joy.

I have always been most attracted to those forms of Christianity that take the joy seriously. There are denominations, congregations, and traditions that seem to have more in common with the Roman arrogance than with the Christian joy. They seem always to be afraid that someone might find them to be wrong about something. They seem more eager to take vengeance against those who disagree than to seek common ground. But I came to believe in Christ in a youth fellowship where jokes and good feelings abounded. The goal was not to punish the bad kids but to draw them into a happy friendship, a group of merry men. Christ was the center of everything, but he was the Christ I later recognized in *Risen*, not the Christ of the theological warriors. As Sandlin put it,

> It's not quite the attitude of Jesus as we view him 2000 years later through the media of traditional interpretations of his immediate post-resurrection activities—a Jesus of solemnity and austerity and the full weight of eternity on his shoulders. Rather, it is Jesus spending time with his closest friends in an upper room and on a seashore and having (dare I say it?) *fun*. The giddiness of the apostles, led by a loud and ebullient Peter, as they snag a drag-net-breaking school of fish on the suggestion of a Galilean that they tardily realize as none other than their friend Yeshua, is worth the admission price of the movie. This Jesus usually isn't the Jesus of our theology, but it is the Jesus of the Bible.

This is what the church should be like. And this is the kind of fellowship the church can offer to the world: not a mere self-centered hedonism, not a place for angry people to say nasty things about their enemies, but a place of joy and friendship.

This is also a model of the heavenly society, and a model for how we should seek to live together here in this world. It has been said that there are two political theories: One is that a good society consists in a government strong enough to force everyone to accept its ideology. This was the philosophy of Rome, and we can see it today in extreme forms in Communism, Fascism, and Islam. The other is that a good society is one in which we seek to love one another and extent our agreements through friendly discussion. When we speak of America as an "exceptional" nation, what we mean is that it is (to a large extent) informed by the Spirit of Jesus. When we speak of America's enemies, our best critique of them is that they are informed by a spirit like that of Rome, the foolishness of those that try to impose their will by brute strength. Of course, no earthly government perfectly reflects either of these philosophies. But there are practical ways in which the two spirits can be distinguished. One is that people want to come to America, and people often make strong exertions to escape from other nations.

26

Arminianism

AFTER I'VE TAUGHT FIFTY YEARS as a self-proclaimed Calvinist, readers would certainly be entitled to assume that I understand the basic differences between Calvinists and Arminians. This distinction would seem to be Lesson One, since this opposition in effect defines the two parties. Surely, one cannot claim to be a Calvinist unless he understands this opposition and comes down unambiguously on the Calvinist side. But I confess that in my declining years the distinction has been harder for me to make.

The conflict between these two positions centers around two issues: predestination and free will. Let us consider these in order:

PREDESTINATION

Calvinists confess, on the basis of Bible passages like Eph. 1:11, that God devises, determines, and controls the whole course of nature and history. God makes everything happen that happens.

Arminians deny this, at least verbally. But traditional Arminians affirm that God's foreknowledge is exhaustive. It includes knowledge of the future as well as of the past. But that view raises a problem: If God made the world, knowing in advance everything that would happen in the course of nature and history, how is this view different from Calvinism? In both views, the act by which God created the heavens and the earth is the beginning of history. It is the first event, that sets all other events in motion. And we have seen that in both views God knows precisely what will happen as the sequel to this creative act. I wonder, therefore, if the supposed difference between these parties over predestination is a distinction without a difference.

FREE WILL

Both Calvinists and Arminians profess the existence of human freedom, but they define that freedom differently. Calvinists define it as "compatibilism." Compatibilism means that we are free to follow our desires, to do what we want to do. On this view it is not relevant to ask whether our choices are somehow "caused." Whether caused or not, our actions are free if they are what we want to do. The name "compatibilism" means that our freedom is consistent with causation, either by our own desires, by our own nature, by the natural causal order, or by God. It is "compatible" with predestination.

Arminians claim that compatibilist freedom is not free enough. They argue in favor of "libertarian" or "incompatibilist" freedom. That means that a truly free act has no cause. Of course, when we choose freely we may be influenced by various factors—by our desires, our natures, the natural causal order, or God. But for the libertarian, none of these factors constrain; none of them make us do what we do.

There are many problems with libertarianism. Elsewhere I have listed fifteen or so arguments against the concept.[7] The Bible contradicts it by saying that sin is a kind of bondage that we can escape only by God's saving grace in Christ (John 8:34–36; Rom. 6:16–20; Titus 3:3; 2 Pet. 2:19). And I have already pointed out that even in Arminianism God foreknows the events of history (including human choices) exhaustively. Exhaustive divine foreknowledge is inconsistent with libertarian freedom. For God's foreknowledge necessarily constrains what it knows. If God foreknows that something will happen, that event cannot turn out differently.

So exhaustive divine foreknowledge implies universal predestination, and it rules out any kind of "free will" that is inconsistent with this predestination. Since both Calvinists and Arminians affirm universal

---

7. See my DG, 138–45.

divine foreknowledge, they both implicitly affirm Calvinist predestination and reject libertarian freedom.

GOD'S PLAN AND THE GOSPEL

But more may be said. In God's eternal plan, which he knows by his exhaustive foreknowledge, he envisages a world of causes and effects. When he plans that event A will take place, he may choose that A will happen in various different ways. It may happen as the result of a human choice, a natural event, an angelic intervention, or simply as a divine act, with no other cause. This means that although there is a divine cause behind every event, that cause may employ any number of secondary causes. Perhaps God wills for a certain tree to be brought down. He may will for that to be accomplished by a man wielding an axe, or by a man wielding a power saw. In some cases he may accomplish that result through a very strong man pushing the tree over. Or he may accomplish it through a severe storm. Or he may choose to bring about the result "miraculously," as we say—just by reaching into history and doing it himself.

So there are some events in nature and history that do not happen without secondary causes. These events may require human effort or tools of various kinds. Or they may require no human cause at all, only God's direct intervention.

Some of these events have obvious spiritual significance. Human salvation, for example, requires faith. So the gospel calls people to repent of sin and believe in Christ. God's own plan has ordained this causal structure. People will be saved if they believe; they will not be saved if they don't believe. So it is important when we preach the gospel to urge people to believe. This human decision is necessary. People will not be saved without making this decision.

So predestination (God's exhaustive foreknowledge and control) does not imply that human choices are unnecessary. Often a human choice is an essential cause within God's plan. Without that choice, the result doesn't come. God has designed it that way. It is part of his plan. So there is no competition between God's predestination and man's (compatibilist free) choice.

27

Shepherd's View of Justification

A friend asked why I didn't try very often to clarify the debate at Westminster (1974–82) about Norman Shepherd's view of justification by faith alone. I replied:

DURING THE SHEPHERD DISCUSSIONS, we had a faculty meeting in which even us younger guys were asked to speak and give our opinions. Well, I went to the board and gave what I thought was a pretty careful analysis of all the terminology on either side. I hoped to move the discussion forward, not just reiterate points made in the past, to raise the discussion to a higher level. That was a huge disappointment. Nobody was even a little bit interested. Shepherd (for whom I had enormous respect and still do) acted as though my comments were completely worthless and that I had missed the whole point. Similar, everybody else. So I just dropped the whole issue. To me it was sufficient to say, as I had always heard from John Gerstner, that "it's faith alone that saves, but the faith that saves is never alone." It wasn't necessary to go any deeper than that.

PART 4

Essays from *Lexham Survey of Theology*

28

Unwritten Special Revelation

Scripture and Revelation > Special Revelation > Unwritten Special Revelation

DEFINITION

IN SPECIAL REVELATION, God discloses his plan to renew the cosmos and human lives following the fall and its repercussions. This special revelation comes both in written and in unwritten forms.

DESCRIPTION

Unwritten special revelation, according to Scripture, occurs in *tradition, dreams, prophecy, theophanies,* and *visions.* Many of these are eventually described in written form, though their original occurrence is in a form other than writing. These original occurrences take place in a person's subjectivity (*dreams, visions*), in experienced events (*theophanies*), in God's direct utterances from heaven, in inspired oral proclamation (*prophecy*), and in the church's reflection and application of previous revelation (*tradition*).

It is also helpful to summarize the forms of revelation under the three categories *events, words,* and *persons. Events* are the works of God in creation, providence, and redemption. The history of redemption is the subject matter of special revelation. In that revelation, God's people discern his hand, delivering his people from slavery in Egypt, establishing his kingdom in the promised land, and sending Jesus to redeem his people from sin through his death and resurrection. In theophany, God himself appears as a participant in this historical drama. Eventually God inspired chosen men to describe this history in writing; but the events themselves precede their written descriptions.

The category of *words* includes this process of writing, but it also includes the inspired oral preaching of *prophets*, selected by God to proclaim his promises and judgments to people. Sometimes prophecy begins in *dreams* and *visions*, though these experiences are to some extent independent of prophecy. *Tradition* includes both words and practices in which the church interprets and applies revelation.

The category of *persons* is a reminder that God himself is personal rather than impersonal and that his revelation is often closely connected to his personal presence. As noted above, this is the case with *theophany*. Most significantly, though, God reveals himself in Jesus, the Word made flesh. As God's personal Word, to see him is to see the Father. His very being is the supreme revelation of God.

In the history of the church, people have often claimed to be the recipients of unwritten special revelation, especially through dreams, visions, and prophecy. As noted above, God does sometimes reveal himself in these ways. But in Reformation theology the supremely authoritative word of God is found only in Scripture (*sola Scriptura*). So claims of unwritten special revelation must not be accepted immediately as God's supreme word; rather they must be tested by that word.

KEY PASSAGES

- Ex. 7:5, 14:18 (knowing God through his mighty acts of redemption)

- Pss. 135, 136

- John 2:11 (Jesus's "signs" [miracles] as revelation)

- Acts 15:12

- Ex. 20:19 (prophecy)

- Deut. 18:18–19

- Jer. 1:4–12

- Ex. 16:6–10 (theophany)

- John 14:9 (Jesus as theophany)

- 1 John 1:1–3 (Jesus's person as God's revelation)

- Acts 2:17 (dreams and visions)

- 2 Thess. 2:15 (traditions)

RESOURCES

- *The Doctrine of the Word of God* (Frame), 71–84, 280–88, 304–15

- *Reformed Dogmatics* (Bavinck), 1:323–85

- "The Biblical Idea of Revelation" (Warfield, in *Revelation and Inspiration*), 3–48

- *Theophany* (Poythress)

29

Revelation in Creation

Christian Theology > Scripture and Revelation > General Revelation > Revelation in Creation

DEFINITION

REVELATION IN CREATION describes how God makes himself known in and through the world he has created.

DESCRIPTION

Scripture teaches that God makes himself known in the world he has made, that is through nature and history. These are not God's actual speech, but they are media through which God communicates himself to us.

Human beings are well-acquainted with him through this revelation. It not only reveals to them facts about God; it confronts them with God himself. Therefore, when people claim that they don't know God, they "suppress the truth." That suppression takes the form of idolatry, in which unbelievers misrepresent God's nature through false images or through false teaching. Such distortions of God's revelation inevitably lead to sin. So revelation in creation, in itself, does not redeem; it doesn't bring sinners to embrace Christ as savior.

Nevertheless, when the apostle Paul preached Christ he did refer to revelation in creation. In Athens he perceived that the people were "very religious" because of their idolatry, and he told them about the God they did not know, one who could not be represented by idols, but who made himself known in the creation and governance of the world. The true God did indeed reveal himself in creation, and that revelation should have shown the people that their idolatry was sin. Paul then told them that they could escape divine judgment only by repenting of sin and turning to Jesus Christ, appointed by God to administer the final judgment. God has certified Jesus by raising him from the dead.

So although God's revelation in creation does not save sinners, it plays an important role in our preaching of the gospel. It sets forth clearly the basis on which God will judge our sin, and it tells us why we need a Savior.

In the history of the church, many theologians have advocated "natural theology," that is theology based on nature alone, apart from Scripture. Others have argued that natural theology in this sense is impossible and wrong, since Scripture alone (*Scriptura sola*) is our sufficient source for the knowledge of God. But as we have seen Scripture itself teaches that the knowledge of God is available in the natural world, even to people who (contrary to that revelation) suppress the truth. The right approach to natural revelation will incorporate *Scriptura sola* into its method: it will proceed by asking Scripture what it is that God has revealed in the creation, what human beings ought to do with it, and how people should go about finding it.

KEY PASSAGES

- Rom. 1:18–32

- Acts 17:22–34

- Acts 14:15–17

- Ps. 19:1

- Ps. 104:1–35

RESOURCES

- *Salvation Belongs to the Lord* (Frame), 50–53

- *Christianity Considered* (Frame), 47–55

- *Nature's Case for God* (Frame)

- *The Doctrine of the Word of God* (Frame), 3–84

- *Reformed Dogmatics* (Bavinck), I, 283–386

30

Revelation in Conscience

Scripture and Revelation > General Revelation > Revelation in Conscience

DEFINITION

CONSCIENCE, an aspect of human nature in God's image, is a gift from God which, when working properly, tells people their obligation to God, accusing them when they do wrong and excusing them when they wrongly feel guilty.

DESCRIPTION

Conscience is a person's inner sense of right and wrong, given by God. Because human beings are made in God's image, they reflect his moral standards. Nevertheless, conscience is not infallible. Conscience, like all elements of human nature, has fallen into sin. Therefore its promptings are sometimes distorted, and even when they are accurate people sometimes repress them in unrighteousness.

Scripture speaks of various conditions, various ways and degrees in which the fall has affected the conscience. Paul ascribes to the most hardened sinners a *seared* conscience: a conscience utterly insensitive to God's standards of right and wrong. But even in such hardened sinners, conscience is not entirely destroyed. Speaking of pagan unbelievers, Paul says that their conscience *accuses* and *excuses* them. But God's saving grace enables the conscience to function at still a higher level. Regeneration transforms the conscience as it transforms the whole personality to reflect God's revelation accurately and to honor it in our behavior. So Paul speaks of the *awakened* or *purified* conscience. This awakening leads to a spiritually mature conscience, what Paul sometimes calls a *good* or *clear* conscience. When someone has a good conscience, he knows that nobody can bring a just accusation against his actions.

In the history of the church, many theologians have written about "cases of conscience," trying to resolve ethical issues that people find perplexing. This project has led to a large body of tradition setting forth ethical teachings of various churches. The Roman Catholic Church has accumulated a large body of "Catholic social teaching," and among Protestants the Puritans, especially, have been known for their "casuistry," that is, the application of divine revelation to questions raised by conscience.

KEY PASSAGES

- 1 Tim. 4:1–2 (the *seared* conscience)
- Titus 1:15
- Gen. 6:5
- Rom. 3:10–12
- Rom. 2:14–15 (the *accusing* conscience)
- Rom. 2:1–5
- 2 Cor. 4:6 (the *awakened* conscience)
- Rom. 12:2
- Heb. 5:14
- 1 Pet. 3:16 (the *good* conscience)
- Acts 23:1
- 2 Cor. 1:12

RESOURCES

- *Nature's Case for God* (Frame)

- *Conscience with the Power and Cases Thereof* (William Ames)

- *The Revenge of Conscience: Politics and the Fall of Man* (J. Budziszewski)

- *What We Can't Not Know: A Guide* (Budziszewski)

- *The Nature of True Virtue* (Jonathan Edwards), in Paul Ramsey, ed., *Ethical Writings, in Works of Jonathan Edwards*, vol. 8

- *Doctrine of the Christian Life* (Frame), 361–82, esp. 362–64

31

The Bible

Scripture and Revelation > Special Revelation > The Bible

DEFINITION

THE BIBLE is the written word of God, and therefore the supreme constitution of his covenant people.

DESCRIPTION

God's special revelation, the revelation of his saving purpose, takes many forms, some of them unwritten. But God also intends to give his revelation in permanent form. According to Genesis, the patriarchs erected memorials so that later generations could visit the places where God revealed himself to their ancestors. And in the book of Exodus, when God consecrated Israel to be his special covenant people, he produced two stone tablets on which were Ten Commandments, written by the very "finger of God." Note that God was not only the author of these commandments (the commandments were his words, expressed in the first person), but the publisher as well, since he inscribed the commands by his own finger. The tablets then were placed in the holiest location in Israel, the inner court of the tabernacle and later the temple, underscoring the fact that as his very word, these documents partook of God's very holiness. This procedure was similar to those in other nations when a mighty emperor would make a treaty with a lesser king, putting it into writing and preserving it in a holy sanctuary.

God gave more holy words through Israel's history. Words of God's inspired prophets were written down and added to the holy document. In the NT we learn that Jesus and the apostles reverenced this document as God's word, and therefore a document with ultimate authority. Further, Jesus appointed and equipped his apostles to speak with the same authority, an authority sometimes delegated by the apostles to others of their company, like Luke, James, and Jude. This authority extended to their writing. Today all branches of the Christian church accept the OT covenant document together with the NT words of Jesus and the apostles as "the Bible," indeed the *holy* Bible, the written word of God.

As God's own word, the Bible is the supreme authority for all areas of human life. In both Testaments, God urges his people to reverence his holy written word as their ultimate criterion of truth.

KEY PASSAGES

- Gen. 12:7, 13:18, 28:18, 35:14 (Patriarchs' memorials)

- Ex. 24:12, 31:18, 34:1, 27–28 (Ten Commandments, written by God's finger)

- Deut. 32:46–47, Josh. 1:7–8 (God's written words as Israel's "very life")

- Matt. 5:17–19, John 5:45–47, 10:34–36 (Jesus's reverence for the OT as God's word)

- Acts 24:14, Rom. 15:4, James 4:11–12, 2 Tim. 2:15–17, 2 Pet. 1:16–21 (the apostles' regard for the OT)

- 1 Cor. 14:37–38, Col. 4:16, 2 Thess. 3:14–15 (writings of the apostles as holy Scripture)

RESOURCES

- *Salvation Belongs to the Lord* (Frame), 42–71

- *The Doctrine of the Word of God* (Frame), esp. 71–252

- *Revelation and Inspiration* (Warfield)

- *Thy Word Is Still Truth* (ed. Lillback and Gaffin)

- *The Structure of Biblical Authority* (Meredith Kline) (parallels between the Bible and extra-biblical suzerainty treaties)

32

Inspiration

Scripture and Revelation > Special Revelation > The Bible > Inspiration

DEFINITION

INSPIRATION is a divine action that creates an identity between a human word and a divine word.

DESCRIPTION

The term *inspired* is found only once in the English Bible, in 2 Tim. 3:16. In that passage it translates the Greek term *theopneustos*, "breathed out by God." The idea would probably be better expressed as "expired" rather than "inspired." To breathe out words is to speak them. So to say that a prophecy or a book (as in 2 Tim. 3:16) is inspired means that it is God's very speech, that the words in question are the word of God.

Although the Bible does not use the terms *inspired* or *inspiration* very often, it refers in other language to many words, given to human speakers and writers by God, which function as divine utterances. Scripture refers in this way to the original document of the Ten Commandments, to the words of true prophets, to the speech of Jesus, and to the preaching and writing of the apostles.

In modern language, we often use *inspired* to refer to something far less. Today, we use the term to refer to any kind of poetic or elevated language, or to any kind of felicitous expression. Unfortunately, some have used this diminished meaning of inspiration to define the concept of prophetic and biblical inspiration. Such a weakened notion of biblical inspiration inevitably reduces also the nature of biblical authority and of Scripture's truth. But if we accept the Bible as an inspired text in the sense of 2 Tim. 3:16, we must infer that it is always truthful and has ultimate authority over all aspects of our lives.

KEY PASSAGES

- 2 Tim. 3:15–17, 2 Pet. 1:19–21

- Deut. 18:18–19, Jer. 1:4–12 (prophecy)

- John 5:45–47 (Moses)

- Matt. 24:35, Mark 8:38, Luke 1:20, John 1:1–14, 5:24, 6:63, 68 (Jesus)

- Matt. 10:19–20, John 14:26, 15:26–27, 16:13 (the apostles)

- Col. 4:16, 2 Thess. 3:14–15, 1 Cor. 14:37–38 (the apostles' writings)

RESOURCES

- *Salvation Belongs to the Lord* (Frame), 42–71

- *Revelation and Inspiration* (Warfield)

- *The Doctrine of the Word of God* (Frame)

- *Thy Word Is Still Truth* (ed. Lillback and Gaffin)

33

Authority

DEFINITION

AUTHORITATIVE WORDS are words that impose obligations on the lives of their readers and hearers. To say that the Bible is authoritative is to say that it governs all areas of human life.

DESCRIPTION

God is by nature the supreme authority in the universe, governing the lives of all his creatures. When he speaks, creatures must obey, or bear the consequences of disobedience. The Bible is his word, and therefore human beings must obey all aspects of it in every area of their lives. The *Westminster Confession of Faith*, 14.2, says that by saving faith "a Christian believeth to be true whatever is revealed in the Word, for the authority of God himself speaking therein; and acteth differently upon that which every particular passage thereof containeth; yielding obedience to the commands, trembling at the threatenings, and embracing the promises of God for this life, and that which is to come."

This is not to say that the content of Scripture measures up to our standards of what is right and wrong, true and false. Rather, Scripture is itself the very standard, the ultimate criterion of what is true and right. Nor should we restrict the authority of Scripture to some narrow sphere of human life, such as religion or worship. Scripture governs the religious life, but before God all of life is religion in the sense that we are to do everything to the glory of God. Scripture is the supreme guide as to how to glorify God in all of life. So however difficult it may be in a social environment, the Christian must be bold to obey the Bible, not only in church, but in the workplace, in intellectual life, in science, philosophy, law, politics, the arts, culture, commerce, and entertainment. Believers must, of course, respect the fact that Scripture focuses on redemption rather than general culture. But that redemption itself is cosmic, the removal from all creation of the curse of the fall, and the reconciliation of all things to God.

KEY PASSAGES

- Deut. 4:1-8, 6:1-9, 6:24-25, 7:11, 8:11, Josh. 23:6, Ps. 19:7-11

- 2 Tim. 3:15-17

- 1 Cor. 10:31

- Gen. 3:17-19 (effects of the fall on all creation)

- Rom. 8:18-22, Col. 1:19-20, Rev. 1:21-27 (effects of redemption on all creation)

RESOURCES

- *Salvation Belongs to the Lord* (Frame), esp. 58-71

- *The Doctrine of the Word of God* (Frame), 47-219

- *Reformed Dogmatics* (Bavinck), 1:323-496

- *Lectures on Calvinism* (Abraham Kuyper)

34

Truthfulness

DEFINITION

BECAUSE THE BIBLE is the word of an absolutely truthful God, all of its teaching is truthful.

DESCRIPTION

Truth is an attribute of God in Scripture and pertains to all his speech. Jesus even identifies himself with truth when he claims to be "the way, the truth, and the life." Given that Scripture is the written word of God, it is therefore entirely true. That means that Scripture will never mislead its readers in what it asserts or commands. It does sometimes record lies or mistakes by beings other than God, but in all its text it represents God's point of view (alongside the views of its human authors). Therefore, its message as a whole is normative for all its readers.

The truthfulness of Scripture is sometimes expressed in other terms. Theologians have often spoken of Scripture as *inerrant*, which simply means that it contains no errors. This term, therefore, is an equivalent of *truthfulness*, though negatively expressed. There is also the term *infallible*. This is a stronger term than *inerrant*, though theologians have sometimes construed it as weaker. To say that Scripture is infallible means not only that it contains no errors (inerrant) but that it *cannot possibly* contain error. The fact that the Bible is God's word excludes even the possibility of error, because God cannot lie or be mistaken.

Many have claimed, nonetheless, that there are errors in the Bible, based on apparent contradictions, apparent discrepancies with science, history, philosophy, and other learned opinions. Many of these claims can be refuted by looking more carefully at the biblical texts under discussion, or by a closer examination of the facts that supposedly conflict with Scripture. Such refutations have generated a very large apologetic literature. What must be remembered, however, is that Christians do not confess the Bible's truthfulness because they have decisively answered every criticism of Scripture. Rather, they believe in Scripture's truth because God himself, Jesus Christ, and the apostles have taught them that Scripture is the word of God. That is, finally, the same basis Christians have for believing the gospel of salvation: divine testimony. There is no higher authority by which that testimony can be verified.

So believing in Scripture requires faith, just as believing in the gospel of Christ requires faith. In fact, Scripture and the gospel are a single package. You cannot believe one and reject the other. "Faith" in this context does not mean believing contrary to evidence; it means trusting God as the criterion of evidence. Christians believe that even when we do not have definitive answers to Bible problems, God does. And since he has the answers, we do not need to know them unless he chooses to reveal them.

KEY PASSAGES

- Deut. 18:22

- Pss. 18:30, 19:9, 119:142

- Prov. 30:5

- John 8:26

- John 10:35

- John 17:17

- 2 Tim. 3:15–17

- 2 Pet. 1:19–21

RESOURCES

- *The Doctrine of the Word of God* (Frame), esp. 167–200

- *Thy Word is Still Truth* (ed. Lillback and Gaffin)

- *Inerrancy and Worldview* (Vern Poythress)

- *Inerrancy and the Gospels* (Vern Poythress)

35

———

Canon

Scripture and Revelation > Special Revelation > The Bible > Canon

DEFINITION

THE CANON is the divinely authorized collection of books that God has given to govern his people.

DESCRIPTION

By inspiration God identifies human books with his own, so that they are the word of God. But he also acts to gather such books together so that some of them form a larger document, a canon, which serves to rule the people of God. The canon is like a written constitution in a nation, its highest law. It governs all activity within God's covenant community. In nations outside Israel, a Great King would often produce a written treaty by which he governed a conquered nation. That document would be kept in the temple of the Great King and in the temple of the conquered nation. Similarly, the document of God's covenant with Israel was stored in the tabernacle, and later the temple, of Israel. That document governed all aspects of the relationship between Israel and its Lord.

In the NT, Jesus and the apostles, agreeing with the Jewish understanding, refer to the OT covenant document as an authoritative collection, the "Holy Scriptures." That is what we call the canon of the OT. But there was more to come. Jesus commissioned his apostles to write additional documents, describing his words and deeds, and dealing with issues in the church following his resurrection and ascension. They wrote books and letters, which we regard today as the "New Testament."

But there is much discussion as to how the *canon* of the NT was identified, since the inspired books were not put in a single place as in the OT. First, we should note that these writings became canonical immediately when God inspired them to be his word. Contrary to some scholars, there was no long period of many centuries during which these books "became canonical." Second, God intended from the beginning that his people would be ruled by a written document, a canon, as in the OT. So when he inspired these books he did it for that purpose. Given that intention, we should assume that God would arrange for his people to recognize the canonical collection. It would be wrong to assume that there was a great mystery about where these books were to be found. Scholars need to give more attention to this divine purpose as they interpret and evaluate the history of the canon in the first four centuries.

But there was, of course, a period of several centuries during which the church came to *recognize* which books God had made canonical. Most of the NT books we currently accept as canon were recognized as Scripture by Irenaeus, who died around 202 AD. Others, such as 2 Peter, 2–3 John, and Revelation continued to be disputed for various reasons. But the Easter Letter of Athanasius, Bishop of Alexandria, in 367 AD contained a list of inspired documents identical to that we recognize today, and after that there was no further dispute in the church about the contents of the canon.

The resolution of disputes from the first NT documents to 367 AD is an interesting story. Various factors entered into the recognition of different books as God's word. Apostolic authorship, association of an author with an apostle (e.g., Mark with Peter, Luke with Paul), and the association of James with Jesus as his half-brother were important factors in the acceptance of these books. Controversies over content also needed to be resolved. But this process was remarkably peaceful, compared with other controversies in the early church (even controversies over such central doctrines as the deity and humanity of Christ). We cannot rule out a supernatural factor in the recognition of the canon. As Jesus said, "My sheep hear my voice." Heart-reception of God's word always involves the illumination and empowering of the Holy Spirit.

KEY PASSAGES

- Deut. 31:24–29 (the OT books put in the holiest place)

- John 10:35

- Rom. 15:4

- 2 Tim. 3:15

- John 10:27 (Jesus's sheep hear his voice)

- 1 Thess. 1:5 (the Spirit empowering the word)

- 2 Tim. 1:14 (the Spirit enabling us to guard the deposit of revelation)

RESOURCES

- *The Doctrine of the Word of God* (Frame), 133–39

- *Canon Revisited* (Michael J. Kruger)

- *The Question of Canon* (Michael J. Kruger)

- *Who Chose the Gospels?* (Charles E. Hill)

- *The Structure of Biblical Authority* (Meredith Kline) (canon as "covenant document")

36

Necessity

Scripture and Revelation > Special Revelation > The Bible > Necessity

DEFINITION

GOD'S WRITTEN WORD in Scripture is an indispensable element of the believer's covenant relation to Christ.

DESCRIPTION

In the OT period, when a Great King entered into covenant with a lesser king or "vassal," he often produced a written document, called a treaty or covenant, to serve as the highest law for the relationship. Indeed, the treaty *was* the covenant (Deut. 4:13). If the vassal were to reject the law of this covenant, he would be at war with the Great King. God's covenant with Israel followed this pattern. The Ten Commandments were "written by the finger of God" and put in the holiest part of Israel's tabernacle (later the temple). These commandments, and later ones that were added to them, served as the supreme law governing Israel's relationship to her Great King, the Lord.

So the written constitution was *necessary* to the relationship. No treaty, no covenant. No treaty, no Lord. To obey God, Israel must obey his word. To love God, Israel must love his word.

In the NT, Jesus himself is Word, so that the necessity of the word is the same as the necessity of Jesus. If one loves Jesus, he will keep his commandments. And the biblical word is also the word of the gospel, God's message of salvation. Without that word, there is no salvation.

It is true, of course, that people can be saved without actually reading the biblical text. Many, perhaps most believers, have heard the gospel from oral proclamation and witness rather than from actually reading it. But the oral proclamation and witness is itself a retelling of the message that comes from the Bible. Without the Bible, there could be no gospel. So without the Bible, there is no salvation.

The work of Christ is not something that human wisdom could have devised. The atonement comes out of the wisdom of God's eternal plan, and its definitive meaning could be given only in divine words. It is God's promise that if one believes he will be saved. A mere human promise to that effect could be dismissed as wishful thinking. So just as salvation is not by human works, it is not by human wisdom. In the message of the cross, God destroys the wisdom of the wise (1 Cor. 1:19) and makes it foolish (v. 20).

Historically, revivals of the church have been connected to the rediscovery of Scripture as the living and active word of God, speaking in areas where its teaching had been neglected. The church lives, not by bread alone, but by everything that comes from the mouth of God.

In this skeptical age, one often hears people say that their allegiance is to Christ, not to a holy book. But the holy book itself is indispensable to the salvation Jesus accomplished. One may not be a disciple of Christ without obeying his written word.

KEY PASSAGES

- Deut. 4:13
- Deut. 8:3, Matt. 4:4
- Ps. 119
- Prov. 1:7

- John 14:15, 21, 15:10

- 1 Cor. 1:19–20, 2:6–13

RESOURCES

- *The Doctrine of the Word of God* (Frame), 210–15

- *Reformed Dogmatics* (Bavinck), 1:465–74

- *Systematic Theology* (Grudem), 116–26

- *The Structure of Biblical Authority* (Meredith Kline) (Scripture as a covenant treaty)

37

Sufficiency

Scripture and Revelation > Special Revelation > The Bible > Sufficiency

DEFINITION

THE SUFFICIENCY OF SCRIPTURE means that it contains all the divine words necessary for human decisions.

DESCRIPTION

The *Westminster Confession of Faith* says (1.6),

> The whole counsel of God concerning all things necessary for His own glory, man's salvation, faith and life, is either expressly set down in Scripture, or by good and necessary consequence may be deduced from Scripture: unto which nothing at any time is to be added, whether by new revelations of the Spirit, or traditions of men.

Here the Confession contrasts the sufficiency of Scripture with the views of its two main opponents, the Anabaptists (who sometimes advocated "new revelations of the Spirit") and the Roman Catholics (whom the Protestants accused of absolutizing "traditions of men").

We should note that in this view the sufficiency of Scripture is quite general: Scripture is sufficient for all things necessary for God's glory.

Some have sought to limit this sufficiency to matters of salvation or worship. The Confession does refer specifically to "salvation." But insofar
as every human decision is a decision to glorify God (1 Cor. 10:31), the
Confession's view of the sufficiency of Scripture must pertain to *every*
human decision.

Scripture itself warns against living by human wisdom rather than
God's. The Pharisees adhered to their own traditions so rigidly that
they rejected the commandments of God. So Paul, in his famous statement about the inspiration of Scripture, also speaks of its sufficiency:
through Scripture, "the man of God may be competent, equipped for
every good work."

Some will object that this does not seem reasonable. There are many
human activities in which we need information from outside the Bible.
The Bible does not teach how to make bran muffins. It doesn't teach
plumbing, or auto repair, or how to play the violin. Even in theology
scholars often need more than the Bible itself. For the work of theology
requires them to *apply* the Bible to areas of life that were not envisaged
by the biblical writers. The theologian, moreover, needs to go beyond
the Bible to learn such things as Hebrew grammar, the geography of
Israel, the cultural influences on biblical concepts, the uses of various
doctrines in post-biblical church history, and so on.

But that objection misses the point. Scripture is sufficient, not to
provide all manner of information, but to provide God's authoritative
words. It is right that people gain information from many sources (of
course, God is the provider of these sources too, in "general revelation"). But words of ultimate authority are found in only one place, in
the holy Scriptures. The Bible is sufficient to give us words of this kind,
the very words of God.

The sufficiency of Scripture stands against the present temptation
of the church to assign more and more weight to church historical traditions in theology and worship. The church's task today, as always, is
to adhere more closely to the word of God, in opposition to human
intellectual fashions, and even when God's word is opposed to traditions within the church itself.

KEY PASSAGES

- Isa. 29:13–14 (God's wisdom, vs. wisdom taught by men)

- Mark 7:8 (the Pharisees reject the commandment of God for the traditions of men)

- 2 Thess. 2:2

- 1 Cor. 10:31 (do all to the glory of God)

- 2 Tim. 3:16–17 (Scripture sufficient for "every" good work)

RESOURCES

- *The Doctrine of the Word of God* (Frame), 220–38

- *Reformed Dogmatics* (Bavinck), 1:481–94

- *Systematic Theology* (Grudem), 127–38

38

Clarity

Scripture and Revelation > Special Revelation > The Bible > Clarity

DEFINITION

SCRIPTURE IS SUFFICIENTLY CLEAR to leave people no excuse for disobedience to their present duties.

DESCRIPTION

In one sense nothing is ever revealed unless it is revealed clearly. Unclarities mask content and deter communication. But revelation is a form of communication; it cannot exist when unclarities defeat its purpose. But God's revelation is always successful. It accomplishes his purpose; so it must have enough clarity to reach God's intended audience. Special revelation, therefore, surely has as much clarity (sometimes called "perspicuity") as Paul attributes to general revelation in Rom. 1:18–21.

But we all know that it is not always easy to understand the Bible. Not only is its content often twisted by unbelief, but there is much in Scripture that many believers cannot understand. As an obvious example, it is obvious that most three-year-old children, however much their genuine childlike faith, will not be able to distinguish the various offerings in Leviticus. So we will need to make some distinctions to determine more precisely *how* Scripture is clear.

First, to say that Scripture is clear is to honor God in revelation, to praise him that his sovereign power succeeds in his purpose to reveal his truth to those he means to address. Without clarity, he has not really revealed what he wants his readers to know.

But second, we honor his right to distinguish between hearers of his revelation. We should not assume, for example, that the offerings in Leviticus are revealed to everybody, so that God intends everyone to immediately understand them equally. Rather, God directs his words to people whom he has providentially prepared to understand them. Those who are called to teach these passages to the church have adequate resources to understand them. (Among those resources may be other gifted teachers whom one may and should consult.) The text is clear enough for them, with those resources, to carry out their present duty to teach that material. It is not clear enough for a three-year-old child to understand immediately; but the child does not need to understand it immediately. He has no present duty to understand it. Perhaps if he is called in later life to expound Leviticus, he will then have such a duty. All of us can understand Scripture to the extent that we have a present duty, a divine calling, to understand it.

And third, by saying the Bible is clear we affirm the presence of God with the readers as they seek to understand the text. In Deut. 30:11–14, God tells Israel that his word is clear: it is not up in heaven or down in the depths, but it is near them, "in your mouth and in your heart, so that you can do it." Paul quotes this passage and applies it to the nearness of Christ (Rom. 10:5–10): the word is clear, because it brings Christ near to us, that we may believe in him. As we read the Bible in faith, we encounter the living God, who will certainly bring his best blessings on us.

The Protestant Reformers appealed to this principle to show that believers are not bound to the clergy in studying the Scripture, but that they are qualified to read the Bible for themselves. The clarity of Scripture does not mean that we need no teachers; Scripture say that God provides teachers to the church, as part of his clear communication of the biblical content. But the doctrine of clarity calls on everybody to hear God's word, of whatever age, social status, and education level.

KEY PASSAGES

- Deut. 30:11–14, Rom. 10:5–10

- Rom. 1:18–21

- 1 Cor. 12:28–29, Gal. 6:6, Eph. 4:11, 1 Tim. 4:13 (God provides teachers)

RESOURCES

- *The Doctrine of the Word of God* (Frame), 201–9

- *Reformed Dogmatics* (Bavinck), 1:475–81

- *Systematic Theology* (Grudem), 105–15

39

Interpretation

Scripture and Revelation > Special Revelation >
The Bible > Interpretation

DEFINITION

INTERPRETATION is the attempt to help readers and hearers of Scripture to understand and apply the biblical text.

DESCRIPTION

Some philosophers like Heidegger and Gadamer have treated interpretation as a comprehensive epistemology, as a way of understanding all reality, not just verbal documents. These writers have preferred the term *hermeneutics* to the term *interpretation*; but their program depends on an analogy between the interpretation of texts and human knowledge in general: the world is like a "text" that our knowledge seeks to interpret. But in the context of the doctrine of Scripture, interpretation usually has a more literal meaning: it is the attempt to help students of Scripture to understand and apply biblical passages. "Passages" here includes biblical language of all levels: words, sentences, paragraphs, sections, books, testaments, and the Bible as a whole.

It is wrong to think of "the" interpretation as a unified layer of meaning submerged beneath the actual text, which people can reach if they dig very deep. It is better to think of interpretations in the plural: responses to readers' perplexities about the meaning of the words. Interpretations are attempts to answer someone's complaint that "I cannot understand this." Note: the problem that necessitates interpretation is not a deficiency in Scripture; it is a deficiency in the reader or hearer.

Misunderstandings are of many types. One kind is when an English speaker, for example, confronts the Greek text and says that he doesn't understand Greek. In response to this complaint, one might translate the text into English. In that case the interpretation is the translation. Another type of misunderstanding occurs when a reader misconstrues the grammar of a sentence. To remedy that, an interpreter might offer a paraphrase, or give a lesson in grammar. In other cases, interpretations might describe the historical background of the problem text, or the logical relations between the text and other texts, or the systematic theological concepts joining the problem text to others, or the worldview presuppositions of the biblical author.

Sometimes interpretations can be very practical. A reader asks, "What does this text mean *to me*?" In response to this kind of question, the interpreter might cite various practical situations of human life in which the text could make a difference. We can see that the task of interpreting Scripture is very nearly identical with the work of teaching.

But though interpretations are responses to human perplexities, it is wrong to suggest that all meaning is in the eye of the beholder, rather than being objectively present in the text. Problems of interpretation may not be resolved simply by reporting the reader's response. Rather, there must be engagement to find out what the text itself, as God's own word, requires the reader to think and to do.

In the history of the church, there have been controversies over how literally or how figuratively we should interpret the Bible. Some, as in the Alexandrian tradition, have sought to find multiple meanings in every passage: (1) the literal, (2) the "allegorical" (using the passage as a figure of something far removed from the original context), (3) the "tropological" (using the text to teach moral lessons that may or may not be based in the original context), and (4) the "anagogical" (the fulfillment of the passage in the consummation of history, the new heavens and new earth). Others, as in the Antiochene tradition, have sought to make interpretations as literal as possible, so as to avoid importing meaning that is not in the text.

The rule, of course, is that the interpretation must be true to the original, to the possibilities of understanding and application warranted by the text in question. Interpretations should not all seek maximum literality, since some texts clearly warrant nonliteral interpretations (for example, the allegory of Hagar and Sarah in Gal. 4:21–31). The intentions of the divine and human authors and the actual context of the passage must be our guide in such questions. And when a study of a "problem passage" cannot be solved from the original context, often a resolution can be found in other passages of Scripture that take up the same subject matter. Hence the Reformation slogan *Scriptura Ipsius Interpres*, "Scripture is its own interpreter."

Thus, interpretation, as a form of teaching, must be *sound* (*hygiainos*, healthy), true to God's revelation and therefore able to communicate spiritual health to its hearers.

KEY PASSAGES

- Luke 24:27
- Acts 8:21–39
- Rom. 12:7
- 1 Cor. 12:28–29
- Gal. 4:21–31
- 1 Tim. 1:10, 4:13, 16, 6:2–3
- 2 Tim. 1:13, 2:2, 3:16, 4:3
- Titus 1:9, 13
- Titus 2:1–2

RESOURCES

- *The Doctrine of the Word of God* (Frame), 292–96

- *God-Centered Biblical Interpretation* (Vern Poythress).

- *In the Beginning Was the Word: Language: A God-Centered Approach* (Vern Poythress)

- *Reading the Word of God in the Presence of God: A Handbook for Biblical Interpretation* (Vern Poythress)

- *Dictionary for Theological Interpretation of the Bible* (Kevin Vanhoozer)

- *Is There a Meaning in This Text?* (Kevin Vanhoozer)

40

Translation

DEFINITION

TO TRANSLATE is to restate the meaning of words in one language with words of another. Translation of Scripture is part of the work of interpreting and communicating it.

DESCRIPTION

The Bible was originally written in Hebrew, Aramaic, and Greek. But its message was intended to bless all nations, indeed to be proclaimed throughout the world as the only way of salvation. So the translation of Scripture into all the languages of the world is an important part of Jesus's Great Commission, to teach the gospel to every nation.

Scripture itself assumes that its message can be translated, contrary to Islam, which teaches that translation necessarily distorts the meaning of its holy book. The Greek text of the NT freely quotes the OT text (originally in Hebrew or Aramaic), without any fear that translation from one language to another corrupts the meaning of the text. Sometimes God brings about a supernatural translation of the gospel, as in Acts 2, when Peter preaches to people of many languages on the Day of Pentecost, or when believers are given the gift of tongues. These events indicate that God himself is concerned with the translation of his message into the languages of the peoples. This is part of the supernatural element which always exists when the word is proclaimed in the power of the Holy Spirit.

To translate a text is to restate its meaning in a different language. *Meaning* is the range of applications for which a piece of language may legitimately be used. In a good translation, one may use the translation, to a large extent, in the same ways and for the same purposes in which he may use the text of the original language. "The window is open" is an adequate translation of *"la fenêtre est ouverte,"* because the second sentence can be substituted for the first in a great many contexts, when the target audience is French. The two sentences share many common purposes for which they can be used among their target audiences.

Although many translations are good in this sense, translations are rarely if ever perfect. In translating, there is almost always some loss of meaning. For this reason it is important for believing scholars to keep going back to the original languages of Scripture, so as to improve our translations from time to time. Nevertheless, the loss of meaning in translation should not make us skeptical about the content of our translated Bibles, for these reasons: (1) Scripture is redundant in a good sense: what readers do not understand in one passage is often stated more clearly in another passage. So the overall content of Scripture is typically repeated many times, increasing our confidence that God in Scripture has clearly communicated with us. (2) The work of the Holy Spirit who empowered Peter to be heard in many languages (reversing the curse of Babel) continues to bless the communication of his word even in translation. (3) God has provided preachers and teachers in the church to clarify his word for the edification of people. Those teachers give God's people a greater insight into the original meaning of the inspired words.

So Bible translation is often the first step in the fulfillment of Jesus's Great Commission, to teach the gospel all over the world. It is itself a form of teaching. Like all teaching, it has great potential for the edification of people. And as in all teaching there are dangers in translation to be avoided. Translators must be reminded that it is their work to reproduce, as much as possible, the authentic word of God, and not to corrupt that word by their own mistakes, by adding to the meaning, subtracting from it, or otherwise distorting it. Despite such dangers, it is encouraging to remember God's promise, that the preaching and teaching of the gospel, of which translation is a part, will by God's grace succeed in bringing people of all tongues and tribes to Jesus, to the glory of God.

KEY TEXTS

- Gen. 11:1–9

- Gen. 12:3

- Matt. 28:18–20

- Acts 2:5–12

- 1 Thess. 1:5 (the Spirit's power in the proclamation of the word)

- Rev. 7:9 (the great multitude of saved people from all tribes and languages)

RESOURCES

- *The Doctrine of the Word of God* (Frame), 253–57

- *God-Centered Biblical Interpretation* (Vern Poythress)

- *In the Beginning Was the Word: Language: A God-Centered Approach* (Vern Poythress)

- *Reading the Word of God in the Presence of God: A Handbook for Biblical Interpretation* (Vern Poythress)

- *Authorized: The Use and Misuse of the King James Bible* (Mark Ward)

- *The Gender-Neutral Bible Controversy: Muting the Masculinity of God's Words* (Vern Poythress, Wayne Grudem)

41

Prophecy

Scripture and Revelation > Special Revelation > Unwritten Special Revelation > Prophecy

DEFINITION

PROPHECY is a divine gift by which a human being is enabled to speak words of divine authority.

DESCRIPTION

Often in Scripture, we read of human beings whom God has appointed and empowered to speak his very words. In the book of Genesis, Noah and Jacob evidently spoke words that could have come only from God. But the paradigm of prophecy is Moses in the book of Exodus, who led Israel out of bondage in Egypt. God tells Moses that he and successive prophets will speak the words of God himself. After Moses, there is a tradition of prophets who receive divine revelation and communicate it to God's people: Samuel, Elijah, Elisha, Isaiah, Jeremiah, and so on. King David also spoke as a prophet, and many of his psalms reflect that gift. In the NT, the prophet John the Baptist preaches to Israel God's demand for repentance. But John points forward to Jesus who is prophet *par excellence*, the very Word of God. Jesus is the Messiah, the redeemer, and therefore the chief theme of prophecy in the OT.

After Jesus's resurrection and ascension, there were prophets in the early church. There is some difference of opinion among scholars as to whether these NT prophets had the same level of authority as prophets in the OT: Did they, like the OT prophets, utter the very word of God, or was their speech a supernaturally assisted human reflection? In any case, it is clear that the apostles, the group directly appointed by Jesus to lead the church, spoke with plenary divine authority, the same authority given to Moses and the other prophets of the OT. The apostle Paul claimed the right to judge among prophets, and he insisted that his own writings should be the standard by which prophecy is judged. There were false prophets among God's people, individuals who claimed to be speaking God's word, but in fact spoke only their own words.

There was some controversy in the early church about the relative place of prophecy and tongues. The meaning of the gift of "tongues" is disputed, but evidently it was a divine gift by which a speaker could utter words of a language unknown to those around him. If those words were translated into a familiar language by someone who had the "gift of interpretation," the speech in tongues would have been equivalent to prophecy. Since the meaning of prophecy was easier to discern than the meaning of utterances in tongues, Paul urges the church in Corinth to have a higher regard for prophecy than for tongues, even though he himself claims that he often speaks in tongues.

Today there are some Christian churches and denominations ("Pentecostal" or "charismatic") that encourage prophecy and/or tongues in their worship services and as private devotional practices. Others ("cessationists") believe that prophecy and tongues ceased at the end of the apostolic age, since God intended them to be employed only in the foundation period of the church's existence.

Many words of the prophets were eventually written down, and some of these form part of *written* special revelation. But the words of true prophets and apostles are authoritative even before they are written down.

The content of prophecy is both "forthtelling" and "foretelling." In forthtelling, the prophet, in God's name, demands repentance from sin. In foretelling, he or she promises curses and blessings yet to come.

Theologians have expended much energy trying to describe the future events set forth in biblical prophecy, but most of these attempts are uncertain. Scripture is clear that Jesus will return in the future and that when he does he will judge the righteous and the wicked. That is the "blessed hope" of the church. But we do not know the day or the hour when Jesus will return. And about the details of these events there is much uncertainty.

KEY PASSAGES

- Ex. 20:19 (the need for a prophet)

- Deut. 18:18–19 (definition of a prophet)

- Jer. 1:4–12

- Acts 11:27–28, 21:9–14 (NT prophecy)

- Rom. 12:6, 1 Cor. 12:10, 12:28–29 (the gift of prophecy in the church)

- 1 Cor. 11:4–5 (women prophesying in church)

- 1 Cor. 14:1–40 (prophecy and tongues)

- 2 Pet. 2:1 (false prophets)

RESOURCES

- *The Doctrine of the Word of God* (Frame), 87–100

- *Systematic Theology* (Wayne Grudem), 1049–88

- *The Christ of the Prophets* (O. Palmer Robertson)

- *The Prophet and His Message* (Michael J. Williams)

- *My Servants the Prophets* (Edward J. Young)

PART 5

Essays from The Gospel Coalition's *Concise Theology*

42

Divine Revelation:
God Making Himself Known

THE GOD OF THE BIBLE is a personal being, in contrast with the gods of many other religions and philosophies who are abstract or impersonal forces. The doctrine of the Trinity underscores this fact, for the biblical God is not only personal, but a society of persons, existing eternally in mutual love and deference (John 17).

So whatever God does he makes known. The persons of the Trinity know one another exhaustively and each understands the thoughts and actions of the others. In human beings, there are hidden depths in our nature so that we cannot fully understand our own actions and motives. But God is fully known to himself. Much about God is mysterious to us, but not to him.

One way Scripture describes God's exhaustive self-knowledge is by saying that he is a *speaking* God or, simply, that he is *Word*:

In the beginning was the Word, and the Word was with God, and the Word was God. (John 1:1)

God is not only eternal, holy, all-powerful, and so on, but he expresses and shares those qualities through something like human speech. In his eternal nature he has the power to speak (the "word"), and that power to speak is who he is: his word is eternally with him, and his word is his very nature. John identifies this word with Jesus Christ in

1:14. In Jesus the Word became flesh. So the existence of the word did not begin with Jesus's incarnation. There are hundreds of references to the divine word in Scripture, both Testaments, as the means by which God reveals himself.

So God reveals himself to himself, each Trinitarian person to the other two. But his revelation extends beyond his own being. It comes also to the world he has created, and especially to the intelligent creatures of that world: angels and human beings. Because self-revelation is his nature, he wants all his creatures to know him.

The creatures of the world cannot know God exhaustively. One cannot know God exhaustively unless one IS God. But creatures receive great benefits from knowing God; indeed, they cannot live without knowing him, for he is the author of life. This is true both of our natural lives and our spiritual lives. Adam came alive when God breathed into his nostrils the breath of life (Gen. 2:7). And Jesus says that the great benefit of eternal life, his salvation from sin, is the benefit of knowing God:

> And this is eternal life, that they know you the only true God, and Jesus Christ whom you have sent. (John 17:3)

In one sense, all human beings, even the wicked, know God:

> For what can be known about God is plain to them, because God has shown it to them. For his invisible attributes, namely, his eternal power and divine nature, have been clearly perceived, ever since the creation of the world, in the things that have been made. (Rom. 1:18–20)

But many reject this revelation, people who, Paul says, "by their unrighteousness suppress the truth" (Rom 1:18). Though God is clearly revealed to all, fallen people prefer to deny that they know him, as Adam hid from God in the garden (Gen. 3:8). When people say they do not know God, it is not because God has failed to reveal himself, or that God's revelation is not clear enough. Rather, their ignorance of God is something they have done to themselves. They are lying to themselves, trying to convince themselves that God does not exist or that he is obscure, while all the time God is staring them in the face.

GOD REVEALS HIMSELF AS THE LORD

God's personal name is *Lord*, which translates the mysterious name *I AM* which God revealed to Moses in Ex. 3:14–16. His lordship connotes particularly his *control*, *authority*, and *presence* in relation to the world he has made.[1] Everything he does reflects his lordship in these ways, including his revelation. So Scripture describes God's word-revelation in terms of his *control* as a powerful force:

> Is not my word like fire, declares the Lord, and like a hammer that breaks the rock in pieces? (Jer. 23:29)

> For the word of God is living and active, sharper than any two-edged sword, piercing to the division of soul and of spirit, of joints and of marrow, and discerning the thoughts and intentions of the heart. (Heb. 4:12)

It also makes clear that God's word of revelation has supreme *authority*:

> The one who rejects me and does not receive my words has a judge; the word that I have spoken will judge him on the last day. (John 12:48)

> All Scripture is breathed out by God and profitable for teaching, for reproof, for correction, and for training in righteousness, that the man of God may be complete, equipped for every good work. (2 Tim. 3:16–17)

And God's word, his revelation, is also his *presence*, the place where he meets with his people. God's nearness to Israel is the nearness of his word (Deut. 4:7–8, 30:11–14). And God comes to be "with us," *Immanuel*, in the person of his Son Jesus Christ, his living word to us (John 1:1–14).

---

1. In a number of my books I discuss this understanding of divine lordship at length. See *The Doctrine of God* (Phillipsburg, NJ: P&R Publishing, 2002), 21–240; *The Doctrine of the Word of God* (Phillipsburg, NJ: P&R Publishing, 2010), 3–14, 47–68.

> And the Word became flesh and dwelt among us, and we have
> seen his glory, glory as of the only Son from the Father, full of
> grace and truth. (John 1:14)

I mentioned earlier that the biblical God is *personal,* not an abstract force
like the gods of the nations. His revelation is particularly a personal
encounter between him and his people. When we hear revelation, we
hear God himself. Our response to it should be a response appropriate to supreme power, to ultimate authority, and to an intimate Father.

GENERAL AND SPECIAL REVELATION

Theologians make various distinctions among types of revelation. The
most common is between *general* and *special* revelation. General revelation is revelation of God given to everybody. It is the kind of revelation
described in Rom. 1, which I discussed above. It tells us that God exists,
what kind of God he is, and his moral standards. In revealing God's standards, it shows us that we have not measured up to them. So Paul says
of general revelation that it reveals God's wrath on sinners (Rom. 1:18).

General revelation comes to us through the natural world (what is
called *natural* revelation) and through our own nature. For we ourselves
are revelation. the image of God according to Gen. 1:26–27.

Special revelation is revelation God gives to selected messengers,
charging them to bring the message to others. Those messengers may be
angels, prophets, or apostles. The message may be presented orally or
may be consigned to writing, as when the apostles wrote authoritative
letters to the churches (see 1 Cor. 14:37–38). The Bible as a whole is a
special revelation of God in written form (2 Tim. 3:15–17). The messages
of special revelation typically contain one or both of two different kinds
of contents: threats of judgment and promises of grace. The *gospel* is a
special revelation of grace, a message of supremely good news:

> For God so loved the world, that he gave his only Son, that
> whoever believes in him should not perish but have eternal life.
> (John 3:16)

MEDIA OF REVELATION

Another way to distinguish between types of revelation is to distinguish the different ways in which revelation comes to us, the *media* of revelation. There are basically three types of media: *events*, *words*, and *persons*. These three categories correspond roughly to our earlier distinction between control, authority, and presence. But both these threefold distinctions are perspectives on the whole of revelation. The events of revelation not only manifest God's control, but also his authority and presence; similarly the words and persons.

EVENTS

God reveals himself in the events of nature and history. We learn of him from the changing seasons, from the power of nature, from the sun, moon, and stars. We also learn of him through history, the particular events that shape the fortunes of human beings. He is the one who gave to all the nations their boundaries (Acts 17:26) and brought Israel out of slavery in Egypt to possess the land of promise. So in his plan general history becomes *redemptive history*, the events by which God arranges to redeem his people from sin by the coming of Jesus.

WORDS[2]

But God does not leave us to figure out for ourselves what he is doing in history. He enters our experience and *speaks* to us in human words. So the words of the prophets are the very words of God himself. God defines *prophet* to Moses in this way:

> "I will raise up for them a prophet like you from among their brothers. And I will put my words in his mouth, and he shall speak to them all that I command him. And whoever will not listen to my words that he shall speak in my name, I myself will require it of him. But the prophet who presumes to speak a word in my name that I have not commanded him to speak, or

---

2. In one sense, all of God's revelation is word revelation, because it proceeds from God's own speech, the word of John 1:1–14. But sometimes God gives us word-revelation in a further sense: revelation in which the media are human words.

who speaks in the name of other gods, that same prophet shall die." And if you say in your heart, "How may we know the word that the LORD has not spoken?"—when a prophet speaks in the name of the LORD, if the word does not come to pass or come true, that is a word that the LORD has not spoken; the prophet has spoken it presumptuously. You need not be afraid of him. (Deut. 18:18–22)

When a prophet or apostle writes down God's words, the document is holy Scripture, a document to be received as the Lord's power, authority, and presence (2 Tim. 3:15–17, 2 Pet. 1:19–21).

PERSONS

Since God is a personal, indeed a tri-personal being, his revelation is particularly vivid when it takes the form of persons. So God made Adam and Eve in his image, to be revelations of him (Gen. 1:26–27). And it should not surprise us that the highest, deepest divine revelation is the incarnate Lord Jesus Christ, God in person. Jesus displays his Father's control over all things (Mark 4:41), speaks his Father's words (John 3:34), and appears as the Father's glorified presence with his people (Matt. 17:1–8).

CONCLUSION

If we are to know God, it is important for us to seek knowledge in God's own way. Many have tried to gain knowledge of God through their unaided reason, or through some kind of subjective intuition. But the God of the Bible has told us not only who he is but also how we should seek knowledge of him. That knowledge comes as we attend to his created world, not repressing the truth in unrighteousness, but accepting his own guidance, his special revelation in Scripture and in Jesus. Only through these appointed means can we come to know him as Lord and as our Savior from sin.

BIBLIOGRAPHY

Frame, John M. *The Doctrine of the Word of God*. Phillipsburg, NJ: P&R Publishers, 2010. Discusses the topics of the present essay in greater depth.

Kuyper, Abraham. *Principles of Sacred Theology*. Grand Rapids: Eerdmans, 1965. Discusses revelation in the broader senses, in relation to the sciences and philosophy.

Lillback, Peter, and Gaffin, Richard, ed. *Thy Word is Still Truth*. Phillipsburg, NJ: P&R Publishers, 2013. Contains a great many classic articles on this subject since the Protestant Reformation.

Machen, J. Gresham. *Christianity and Liberalism*. Grand Rapids: Eerdmans, 2009. This is Machen's classic critique of Protestant liberalism, from 1924. It shows powerfully what happens when people try to separate Christianity from its historic doctrine of revelation and Scripture.

Stonehouse, Ned, and Woolley, Paul. *The Infallible Word*. Philadelphia: Presbyterian and Reformed, 1946. Important essays on biblical authority.

Van Til, Cornelius. *The Defense of the Faith*, ed. K. Scott Oliphint. Phillipsburg, NJ: P&R Publishing, 2008. Discusses Scripture as part of a general Christian theory of knowledge.

——. *The Protestant Doctrine of Scripture*. Den Dulk Christian Foundation, 1967.

Warfield, Benjamin B. *Revelation and Inspiration*. Grand Rapids: Baker Book House, 2000. This is a classic text on the doctrine of revelation. Many of these essays are also included in another collection, Warfield's *The Inspiration and Authority of the Bible* (Benediction Classics, 2017).

43

Divine Transcendence and Immanence

THE TERMS "TRANSCENDENCE" AND "IMMANENCE" are not found in most versions of the Bible, but they are common in the theological literature to designate two kinds of relationships that God sustains to created beings. In general, to say that God is transcendent is to say that he is exalted, above, beyond us. To say that God is immanent is to say that he is present in time and space, that he is near us. There is no biblical term that captures all of what theologians want to say about God's transcendence, but the idea of immanence is helpfully summarized in the term *Immanuel,* God with us (Isa. 7:14; 8:8; Matt. 1:23).

But let us look first at the ways in which God is *transcendent.* For though the term *transcendent* is not itself biblical, it is a convenient way of grouping together certain biblical ideas. Scripture often speaks of God as "exalted" (Pss. 57:5; 97:9). He dwells "in heaven above" (Deut. 4:39; cf. Eccl. 5:2), even "above the heavens" (Pss. 8:1; 57:5). He is "enthroned on high" (Ps. 113:5); indeed he is himself the "most high" (Ps. 97:9). So *transcendence* is a convenient term to summarize these ways in which God is "above us."

Some ancient and modern writers, however, have taken God's transcendence to mean something else:

... that God is so far above us, so very different from anything on earth, that we can say nothing, at least nothing positive, about him. He transcends our language, so anything we say about him is utterly inadequate. In modern theology, this concept leads to a skepticism about the adequacy of Scripture itself as a revelation of God and about the ability of human beings to say anything about God with real assurance.[1]

But Scripture itself never connects God's transcendence with human uncertainty about God, let alone skepticism. While affirming God's transcendence, Scripture speaks in clear and certain language about his nature and actions. Indeed, when God reveals himself "from heaven," he reveals himself clearly, so that those who reject him have only themselves to blame.

> For the wrath of God is revealed from heaven against all ungodliness and unrighteousness of men, who by their unrighteousness suppress the truth. For what can be known about God is plain to them, because God has shown it to them. For his invisible attributes, namely, his eternal power and divine nature, have been clearly perceived, ever since the creation of the world, in the things that have been made. So they are without excuse. For although they knew God, they did not honor him as God or give thanks to him, but they became futile in their thinking, and their foolish hearts were darkened. (Rom 1:18–22)

Clearly, then, it is wrong to think of God's transcendence as a kind of cloud hiding God from the human mind. To be sure, there are passages in Scripture that emphasize God's incomprehensibility, his mystery, such as Rom. 11:33–36:

> Oh, the depth of the riches and wisdom and knowledge of God! How unsearchable are his judgments and how inscrutable his ways! "For who has known the mind of the Lord, or who has been his counselor?" "Or who has given a gift to him that he

---

1. John Frame, *The Doctrine of God* (Phillipsburg: P&R Publishing, 2002), 110. Compare preceding references to Herman Bavinck's discussion. He traces this doctrine of transcendence from the church fathers to medieval and modern theologians.

might be repaid?" For from him and through him and to him
are all things. To him be glory forever. Amen. (Rom 11:33–36)

However (1) this passage does not speak of God's transcendent existence "on high," but about God's "ways" in history as described in Rom.
1–11:32. What is mysterious in this passage is his "immanence," not his
"transcendence." (2) As we saw earlier, Paul has spoken in Romans about
the clarity of God's revelation from "heaven" (1:18–21). (3) Granting the
mysteriousness of God's actions in history, Paul is still able to speak of
the mystery in clear human language. He tells the Roman church what
it is that they do not know, and why they do not know it. The unknowns
are "known unknowns." And the mystery is always a mystery about a
God who otherwise is "clearly" known.

How, then, should we define God's transcendence, if it is not
a barrier to our knowledge of God and our clear speaking about
him? The biblical language of God "on high" or "in heaven" refers
uniformly to God's royal dignity. He is "high" in the sense that the
king's throne is high above his subjects. "Heaven" is a way to refer
to God's throne (Isa. 66:1). Of course God transcends space as he
transcends time. He does not literally dwell on a material throne, as
Solomon observes at the consecration of the Jerusalem Temple (1
Kings 8:27). But there are certain places in the creation where God
has ordained that we will sense his presence with particular intensity,
like the burning bush in Ex. 3, the inner court of the temple, indeed
the person of Jesus Christ, God's temple incarnate (Matt. 12:6; John
2:19–22). Heaven is one of those places, a literal dwelling place of
God far up in the sky, to which Jesus ascended when his earthly work
was done (Acts 1:11).

But to say that God is "high" is not primarily to speak of his presence
in any of those places. It is to speak of why he has the right to dwell in
such places. They are his thrones, and he sits on them because he is
the King. So if we choose to use the term *transcendence* to refer to God,
we should use it to refer to his lordship, to his powers and rights as the
king of everything he has made.

In other writings,[2] I have analyzed these lordship rights and powers as his *control* and his *authority*. First, his control: Because he is lord, he is omnipotent; he has the power to do anything. That is, he has full control over the world he has made. Many of the psalms, for example, celebrate his kingship by praising the strength by which he controls his domain (Pss. 2; 47; 93:1; 96:10–13; 97:1; 99:1).

His *authority* may be understood as his control over the moral sphere; but it would also be possible to understand God's control as his authority over everything that happens. Still, in our usual philosophical discourse we generally see control in terms of physical causation and authority as an imposition of moral obligation: control represents might and authority represents right. As God's control, so his authority is, in the Bible, an implication of his lordship:

> I am the LORD your God, who brought you out of the land of Egypt, out of the house of slavery. You shall have no other gods before me. (Ex. 20:1–3)

> And the LORD spoke to Moses, saying, "Speak to all the congregation of the people of Israel and say to them, You shall be holy, for I the LORD your God am holy. Every one of you shall revere his mother and his father, and you shall keep my Sabbaths: I am the LORD your God. Do not turn to idols or make for yourselves any gods of cast metal: I am the LORD your God." (Lev 19:1–4)

Through the Leviticus text, the refrain "I am the LORD your God" is repeated 15 times to reinforce the truth that Israel's law is based on the authority of God's lordship over them.

So I would propose that we define *transcendence* as God's *lordship* over his world with particular reference to his royal prerogatives of *control* and *authority*. So understood, God's transcendence does not imply that he is hidden from people; quite the contrary. Indeed, since his transcendence governs all the events of creation, and his authority

---

2. Frame, *Doctrine of God*, 21–115; Frame, *The Doctrine of the Knowledge of God* (Phillipsburg, NJ: P&R Publishing Co,. 1987), 11–75.

governs all his creatures, he is certainly the most visible being in the universe. As Paul says, his revelation is clear (Rom. 1:20).

So God's control and authority are such that he is present, immanent in all of his creation. So it is appropriate that we now consider God's *immanence*. We know already that God's immanence is not some kind of opposite to God's transcendence, some paradoxical negation of transcendence. Rather it is a necessary implication of his transcendence.

We have seen that God's transcendence is a way of referring to his *lordship* over the world. But as we have already seen, lordship does not confine God to a sphere beyond our knowledge. Indeed, it often refers to the way he rules the world of our history and experience. He controls the events of nature and history, including the course of our salvation from sin. And he expresses his authority by proclaiming to us his commands.

Indeed, God's lordship is his *covenant* relation to the world he has made, particularly to the persons in it. So it is not just a relationship of control and authority, but also of *presence* with his covenant partners. The heart of the covenant is a relationship of intimacy. The chief promise of the covenant is the Lord's word, "I will be with you" (Gen. 21:22; 26:28; 28:15; 28:20; 31:3; 31:5; 39:3–4; Ex. 3:11–12; Isa. 7:14; Matt. 1:23). God's promise to Israel prior to the Exodus was,

> I will take you to be my people, and I will be your God, and you shall know that I am the LORD your God, who has brought you out from under the burdens of the Egyptians. (Ex. 6:7)

This intimate relationship, the heart of the covenant, resounds through Scripture. See Deut. 4:7, 4:20, 7:6, 14:7, 26:18, 2 Sam. 7:24, 2 Cor. 6:18, and Rev. 21:7. Because he is our God and we are his people he will be "with us" for all eternity. Immanuel!

I cannot stress enough the important truth of this divine-human intimacy. It is the heart of our relationship to God in Christ. We should especially avoid two errors in this connection: (1) Mysticism or pantheism, the notion that this immanence eliminates the distinction between creator and creature so that we become God, or he becomes indistinguishable from us. Our relation with God is always *personal*—a relation between the divine person and ourselves as human persons. (2) Deism, or the notion that since God is transcendent his nearness to us is only a figure of speech, an "anthropomorphism." No; God is really and truly near to us, difficult as that may be for us to conceive. God's immanence as we have understood it is the heart of biblical redemption, the very name of Jesus, God with us.

God's covenant presence is primarily with his redeemed people. But in a broader sense it is with his whole creation, for the whole creation is part of the program of redemption.

> For the creation waits with eager longing for the revealing of the sons of God. For the creation was subjected to futility, not willingly, but because of him who subjected it, in hope that the creation itself will be set free from its bondage to corruption and obtain the freedom of the glory of the children of God. For we know that the whole creation has been groaning together in the pains of childbirth until now. (Rom 8:18–22)

Indeed, there is a sense in which the creation itself will be redeemed through Christ:

> He is the image of the invisible God, the firstborn of all creation. For by him all things were created, in heaven and on earth, visible and invisible, whether thrones or dominions or rulers or author- ities—all things were created through him and for him. And he is before all things, and in him all things hold together. And he is the head of the body, the church. He is the beginning, the firstborn from the dead, that in everything he might be preeminent. For in him all the fullness of God was pleased to dwell, and through him to reconcile to himself all things, whether on earth or in heaven, making peace by the blood of his cross. (Col. 1:15–20)

So we should understand God's immanence, the covenant presence of his lordship, to be everywhere in the universe, as well as being especially intense in particular locations. God is "omnipresent," present every- where (Ps. 139:7–12), not only because he made everything and governs everything by his plan (Eph. 1:11) but because the created world serves his redemptive covenant purposes.

Scripture does not require us to use the terms *transcendent* and *immanent*, and some misuses of these terms have brought theological confusion. But if we define these concepts to express God's lordship, his covenant relations to his world and to his people, they can be used to express wonderful truths of God's word: the riches of Christ, the depth of our relationship to God.

BIBLIOGRAPHY

Bavinck, Herman. *Reformed Dogmatics*. Vol. 2. Grand Rapids: Baker Academic, 2004.

Frame, John. *The Doctrine of God*. Phillipsburg, NJ: P&R Publishing, 2002. See esp. 1–115.

Van Til, Cornelius. *An Introduction to Systematic Theology*. Ed. William Edgar. Phillipsburg, NJ: P&R Publishing, 2007.

44

The Sovereignty of God

LORD, OR *SOVEREIGN*, is the word that designates God's relation to us and to everything he has made. God's sovereignty contains three significant components: his *control*, his *authority*, and his *presence*.[3] Theologians who discuss divine sovereignty usually have the first of these in mind, his *control*.[4] Indeed, the Bible teaches that God controls all things. He has an eternal plan for all of nature and history (Eph. 1:9–11). When God meets with Moses in Ex. 3 and reveals his name *Yahweh*, that name, God's lordship, reveals to Moses that God, not Pharaoh, rules over the affairs of Egypt and Israel:

Note the last four words of this promise. Because God is Lord, the sovereign, he will certainly deliver Israel from Egypt and bring his people into the promised land. Nothing can stop the Lord from fulfilling his promise.

God's control is always *efficacious*; nothing can prevent him from accomplishing his purpose. See Pss. 115:3, 135:6, Isa. 14:24–27, 43:13, 55:11, and Rev. 3:7. It is also *universal*; that is, it covers all the events of nature and history. This includes the natural world (Ps. 65:9–11; 135:6–7), human history (Acts 17:26), and individual human life (1 Sam. 2:6–7;

---

3. See especially Frame, *The Doctrine of God* (Phillipsburg, NJ: P&R Publishing, 2002), 21–115. See also my essay "Transcendence and Immanence" in the *Concise Theology* series.

4. I have discussed this lordship attribute in more detail in my essay "Divine Sovereignty and Human Freedom" in the *Concise Theology* series.

James 4:13–16). God even governs the free decisions of human beings (Prov. 16:9), including our attitudes toward others (Dan. 1:9; Ezra 6:22). More problematically, God even foreordains people's sins (Ex. 4:21; Deut. 2:30; Rom. 9:17–18). But, as sovereign Lord, he also ordains that some will come to faith and salvation (Eph. 2:4–10). So salvation is God's work from beginning to end, doing for us what we could never dream of doing for ourselves. We should always remember that God's saving grace in Christ is part of his control over creation as the Lord.

Several passages summarize the doctrine of the efficacy and universality of God's sovereign control. See Lam. 3:7, Rom. 8:28, Eph. 1:11, and Rom. 11:33.

But God's sovereign lordship is more than control. It also embodies his *authority*: what the Lord commands, his creatures must do. In the Decalogue, the covenant which Moses delivers to Israel after God sovereignly redeemed them from Egypt, God begins by identifying himself as Lord (Ex. 20:1–2) and on the basis of that identification goes on to utter his Ten Commandments. It is because God is the sovereign Lord that we must obey him. Compare Deut. 6:4–6, John 14:21, Matt. 7:21–22, and Luke 6:46. Because he is Lord, his authority is *absolute*. That means (1) we should not waver in our obedience to him (Rom. 4:16–22), (2) his lordship transcends all our other loyalties (Matt. 10:34–38), and (3) that his authority over us exists in all areas of human life, not just in the areas that we arbitrarily call religious or sacred (1 Cor. 10:31; cf. Col. 3:17, 24; 2 Cor. 10:5).

The third attribute that defines God's sovereign lordship is his covenant solidarity with his creatures, which I often abbreviate by the term *presence*. In Scripture, the covenant Lord is one who takes people to be his own (Ex. 6:7; 2 Cor. 6:16). He declares this intention often in Scripture (Gen. 17:7; Ex. 29:45; Heb. 11:16; Rev. 21:3). When God takes us to be his people, he fights our battles, blesses us, loves us, and sometimes (as a loving Father should) gives us special punishments for our sins (as Amos 3:2). He summarizes all this by saying that he is *with* us. He places his name upon us (Num. 6:27) so that he dwells with us and we with him. In the OT, he fulfills his presence with Israel in the tabernacle and the temple. In the NT, he dwells with us particularly in

Jesus, "God with us," Immanuel (Isa. 7:14; Matt. 1:23). He "tabernacles" with us (John 1:14). And after his ascension he sends the Holy Spirit to dwell in us as his temple (1 Cor. 3:16).

But God's presence is not only with his chosen human beings. For God's whole creation is also in covenant with him: he is the Lord of all creation. His presence is everywhere (or, as theologians say, he is *omnipresent*) (Ps. 139; Acts 17:28).

So even though Scripture teaches that God controls everything, we should not think of his sovereignty as an impersonal, mechanical determinism. God's sovereign lordship is deeply personal. As Lord, God not only controls everything (efficaciously, universally), but also utters commands, words of life, that graciously govern the ongoing life of his creatures. And as Lord he has made a sovereign commitment to be "with" those who are his. Indeed, God's sovereignty is a broad concept, including all that God is and all that he does. Indeed, God's sovereignty embraces his love.

BIBLIOGRAPHY

Boston, Thomas. *The Crook in the Lot: God's Sovereignty in Afflictions.* Amazon Kindle, 2018.

Coles, Elijah. *A Practical Discourse of God's Sovereignty.* https://www.monergism.com/thethreshold/sdg/elishacoles.html.

Desiring God. *The Sovereignty of God: A Topical Survey.* https://www.desiringgod.org/topics/the-sovereignty-of-god#.

Frame, John. *The Doctrine of God.* Phillipsburg, NJ: P&R Publishing, 2002.

Packer, J. I. *Evangelism and the Sovereignty of God.* Downers Grove: IVP, 2012. Available in PDF at https://www.wtsbooks.com/common/pdf_links/9780830837991-1.pdf.

Pink, A. W. *The Sovereignty of God.* https://www.monergism.com/thethreshold/sdg/pink/sov2015_p.pdf.

Poythress, Vern. *Chance and the Sovereignty of God: A God-Centered Approach to Probability and Random Events.* Wheaton: Crossway, 2014.

———. *The Lordship of Christ: Serving Our Savior All of the Time, in All of Life, with All of Our Heart.* Wheaton: Crossway, 2016.

45

Divine Sovereignty and Human Freedom

THE TERM *SOVEREIGNTY* is rarely found in recent editions of Scripture, but it represents an important biblical concept. A *sovereign* is a ruler, a king, a lord, and Scripture often refers to God as the one who rules over all. His most common proper name, *Yahweh* (see Ex. 3:14), is regularly translated *Lord* in the English Bible. And *Lord*, in turn, is found there over 7,000 times as a name of God and specifically as a name of Jesus Christ. So to discuss the *sovereignty* of God is to discuss the *lordship* of God—in effect to discuss the Godness of God, the qualities that make him to be God.

Elsewhere[5] I have discussed the major components of the biblical concept of divine sovereignty or lordship. These are God's *control, authority,* and *presence.* His control means that everything happens according to his plan and intention. Authority means that all his commands ought to be obeyed. Presence means that we encounter God's control and authority in all our experience, so that we cannot escape from his justice or from his love.

When theologians discuss "Divine Sovereignty and Human Freedom," however, they usually focus on only one of these three aspects of God's sovereignty, what I have called his *control.* I too will focus on this aspect in the remainder of this article. But we should keep in mind that God's

---

5. Especially in Frame, *The Doctrine of God* (Phillipsburg, NJ: P&R Publishing, 2002), 21–115. See also my essay "Transcendence and Immanence" in this *Concise Theology* series.

control over the world is only one aspect of his rule. When we consider only his control, we tend to forget that his rule is also gracious, gentle, intimate, covenantal, wise, good, and so on. God's sovereignty is an exercise of all his divine attributes, not just his causal power.

GOD'S SOVEREIGN CONTROL

But it is important for us to have a clear idea of God's sovereign control of the world he has made. That control is a major part of the context in which God reveals himself to Israel as Yahweh, the Lord. That revelation comes to Israel when that nation is in slavery to Egypt. When he reveals his name to Moses, he promises a powerful deliverance:

> But I know that the king of Egypt will not let you go unless compelled by a mighty hand. So I will stretch out my hand and strike Egypt with all the wonders that I will do in it; after that he will let you go. (Ex. 3:19–20)

> I will take you to be my people, and I will be your God, and you shall know that I am the LORD your God, who has brought you out from under the burdens of the Egyptians. I will bring you into the land that I swore to give to Abraham, to Isaac, and to Jacob. I will give it to you for a possession. I am the LORD. (Ex. 6:7–8)

God shows Israel that he truly is the Lord by defeating the greatest totalitarian empire of the ancient world and by giving Israel a homeland in the land promised centuries before to Abraham, Isaac, and Jacob. Nothing can defeat Israel's sovereign. He will keep his promise, displaying incredible controlling power, or he is not the Lord.

God's control is *efficacious*:

> Our God is in the heavens; he does all that he pleases. (Ps. 115:3)

> Whatever the LORD pleases, he does, in heaven and on earth, in the seas and all deeps. (Ps. 135:6)

> The LORD of hosts has sworn: "As I have planned, so shall it be, and as I have purposed, so shall it stand, that I will break the

Assyrian in my land, and on my mountains trample him under-foot; and his yoke shall depart from them, and his burden from their shoulder." This is the purpose that is purposed concerning the whole earth, and this is the hand that is stretched out over all the nations. For the LORD of hosts has purposed, and who will annul it? His hand is stretched out, and who will turn it back? (Isa. 14:24–27)

Also henceforth I am he; there is none who can deliver from my hand; I work, and who can turn it back? (Isa 43:13)

... so shall my word be that goes out from my mouth; it shall not return to me empty, but it shall accomplish that which I purpose, and shall succeed in the thing for which I sent it. (Isa. 55:11)

The words of the holy one, the true one, who has the key of David, who opens and no one will shut, who shuts and no one opens. (Rev. 3:7)

Not only is God's control efficacious, it is also *universal*. It governs every event that takes place anywhere in the universe. (1) The events of the *natural world* come from his hand (Pss. 65:9–11; 135:6–7; 147:15–18; Matt. 5:45; 6:26–30; 10:29–30; Luke 12:4–7). (2) The details of *human history* come from God's plan and his power. He determines where people of every nation will dwell (Acts 17:26). (3) God determines the events of *each individual human life* (Ex. 21:12–13; 1 Sam. 2:6–7; Pss. 37:23–24; 139:13–16; Jer. 1:5; Eph. 1:4; James 4:13–16). (4) God governs the *free decisions* we make (Prov. 16:9) including our *attitudes* toward others (Ex. 34:24; Judg. 7:22; Dan. 1:9; Ezra 6:22).

More problematically, (5) God foreordains *people's sins* (Ex. 4:4, 8, 21; 7:3, 13; 9:12; 10:1, 20, 27; Deut. 2:30; Josh. 11:18–20; 1 Sam. 2:25; 16:14; 1 Kings 22:20–23; 2 Chron. 25:20; Ps. 105:24; Isa. 6:9–10; 10:6; 63:17; Rom. 9:17–18; 11:7–8; 2 Cor. 2:15–16). But he is also (6) the God of grace, who sovereignly ordains that people will come to *faith and salvation*:

But God, being rich in mercy, because of the great love with which he loved us, even when we were dead in our trespasses, made us alive together with Christ—by grace you have been saved—and raised us up with him and seated us with him in the heavenly places in Christ Jesus, so that in the coming ages he might show the immeasurable riches of his grace in kindness toward us in Christ Jesus. For by grace you have been saved through faith. And this is not your own doing; it is the gift of God, not a result of works, so that no one may boast. For we are his workmanship, created in Christ Jesus for good works, which God prepared beforehand, that we should walk in them. (Eph. 2:4–10)

So salvation is God's work from beginning to end, doing for us what we could never dream of doing for ourselves.

If we need any further evidence of the efficacy and universality of God's sovereign control, here are passages that summarize the doctrine:

Who has spoken and it came to pass, unless the Lord has commanded it? Is it not from the mouth of the Most High that good and bad come? (Lam. 3:37)

And we know that for those who love God all things work together for good, for those who are called according to his purpose. (Rom. 8:28)

In him we have obtained an inheritance, having been predestined according to the purpose of him who works all things according to the counsel of his will. (Eph 1:11)

Oh, the depth of the riches and wisdom and knowledge of God! How unsearchable are his judgments and how inscrutable his ways! "For who has known the mind of the Lord, or who has been his counselor?" "Or who has given a gift to him that he might be repaid?" For from him and through him and to him are all things. To him be glory forever. Amen. (Rom 11:33)[6]

---

6. I have discussed this great number of Scripture passages, and many more, in the pages cited in the first footnote of this article. There I have presented analyses of these passages in their biblical contexts.

HUMAN FREEDOM

So the question posed by the title of this article is very pointed. Granted the overwhelming power of God's sovereign control, its efficacy and universality, how can human freedom have any significance at all?

The term *freedom* has been taken in various senses. In our current discussion, two of these are particularly relevant: (1) *compatibilism*,[7] which is the freedom to do what you want to do, and (2) *libertarianism*, which is the freedom to do the opposite of everything you choose to do.[8] If you have libertarian freedom, your choices are in no sense caused or constrained, either by your nature, your experience, your history, your own desires, or God.

In ordinary life, when we talk about being "free," we usually have the compatibilist sense in mind.[9] I am free when I do what I want to do. Usually, when someone asks me if I am free, say, to walk across the street, I don't have to analyze all sorts of questions about causal factors in order to answer the question. If I am able to do what I want to do, then I am free, and that's all there is to it. In the Bible, human beings normally have this kind of freedom. God told Adam not to eat of the forbidden fruit; but Adam had the power to do what he wanted. In the end, he and Eve did the wrong thing. But they did it freely. God's sovereignty didn't prevent Adam from doing what he wanted to do.

Our earlier discussion shows, however, that according to the Bible human beings do not have libertarian freedom: as we have seen, God ordains what we will choose to do, so he causes our choices. We are not free to choose the contrary of what he chooses for us to do. Scripture also teaches that the condition of our heart constrains our

---

7. It is called "compatibilism," because it is compatible with causation. Someone may force me to eat broccoli; but if that is something I want to do anyway, I do it freely in the compatibilist sense.

8. Libertarianism is sometimes called "incompatibilism," because it is inconsistent with necessity or determination. If someone forces me to eat broccoli, I am not free, in the libertarian sense, to eat it or not eat it. On a libertarian account, any kind of "forcing" removes freedom.

9. Of course, many, perhaps most, conversations about freedom are about *political* freedom, which is not our present topic of discussion.

decisions. So there are no unconstrained human decisions, decisions that are free in the libertarian sense.[10]

People sometimes think that we must have libertarian freedom, for how can we be morally responsible if God controls our choices? That is a difficult question. The ultimate answer is that moral responsibility is up to God to define. He is the moral arbiter of the universe. This is the exact question that comes up in Rom. 9:

> You will say to me then, "Why does he still find fault? For who can resist his will?" But who are you, O man, to answer back to God? Will what is molded say to its molder, "Why have you made me like this?" Has the potter no right over the clay, to make out of the same lump one vessel for honorable use and another for dishonorable use? What if God, desiring to show his wrath and to make known his power, has endured with much patience vessels of wrath prepared for destruction, in order to make known the riches of his glory for vessels of mercy, which he has prepared beforehand for glory—even us whom he has called, not from the Jews only but also from the Gentiles? (Rom 9:19–24)

This passage rules out any attempt to argue libertarian freedom as a basis of moral responsibility.

Nevertheless, we should remember that even this passage presupposes freedom in the compatibilist sense: God *prepared* the two kinds of vessels, each for their respective destiny. He made the honorable vessels so that they would appropriately receive honor, and vice versa. When a human being trusts in Christ, he does what he wants to do and therefore acts freely in the compatibilist sense. We know from that choice that God has prepared him beforehand to make that choice freely. That divine preparation is grace. The believer did not earn the right to receive that divine preparation. But he responds, as he must, by freely embracing Christ. Without that free choice of Christ, prepared beforehand by God himself, it is impossible for anyone to be saved.

---

10. In op. cit., I have assembled eighteen detailed arguments against libertarianism. I have included here only a brief summary.

BIBLIOGRAPHY

Carson, D. A. *Divine Sovereignty and Human Responsibility: Biblical Perspectives in Tension*. Eugene, OR: Wipf and Stock, 2002.

Frame, John. *The Doctrine of God*. Phillipsburg, NJ: P&R Publishing, 2002.

———. *No Other God: A Response to Open Theism*. Phillipsburg, NJ: P&R Publishing, 2001. In this book I address the open theist movement of Pinnock, Rice, Sanders, Boyd, and others. These writers accept libertarian freedom as their foundational premise and draw from it that God cannot know in advance the decisions of free agents.

Henry, Carl F. H. *God, Revelation and Authority*. 4 vols. Waco, TX: Word Books, 1976–82.

Packer, James I. *Evangelism and the Sovereignty of God*. Downers Grove: IVP Books, 2012.

Van Til, Cornelius. *An Introduction to Systematic Theology*. Nutley, NJ: Presbyterian and Reformed, 1962.

Warfield, B. B. *Biblical Doctrines*. Grand Rapids: Baker, 1981.

46

Openness Theology
and Divine Omniscience

SCRIPTURE AFFIRMS that God's knowledge of himself and of the world is exhaustive:

> Great is our Lord, and abundant in power; his understanding is beyond measure. (Ps. 147:5)

> (Peter) said to (Jesus), "Lord, you know everything; you know that I love you." Jesus said to him, "Feed my sheep." (John 21:17)

> For the word of God is living and active, sharper than any two-edged sword, piercing to the division of soul and of spirit, of joints and of marrow, and discerning the thoughts and intentions of the heart. And no creature is hidden from his sight, but all are naked and exposed to the eyes of him to whom we must give account. (Heb. 4:12)

> For whenever our heart condemns us, God is greater than our heart, and he knows everything. (1 John 3:20)

God knows all about the starry heavens (Gen. 15:5; Ps. 147:4; Isa. 40:26; Jer. 33:22) and the tiniest details of the natural world (Pss. 50:10–11; 56:8; Matt. 10:30). God's knowledge is absolute knowledge, a perfection, and so it elicits religious praise (Ps. 139:17–18; Isa. 40:28; Rom. 11:33–36).

Wicked people often think that God will not notice what they do, but they will find that God does know, and that he will certainly condemn their sin (Pss. 10:11; 11:4; 73:11; 94:7; Isa. 29:15; 40:27; 47:10; Jer. 16:17–18; Ezek. 8:12). To the righteous, however, God's knowledge is a blessing of the covenant (Ex. 2:23–25; 3:7–9; 1 Kings 18:27; 2 Chron. 16:9; Pss. 33:18–20; 34:15–16; 38:9; 145:20; Matt. 6:32). He knows what is happening to them, he hears their prayer, and he will certainly answer.

God knows everything because he is the *lord* of all. He made the heavens and the earth; he knows his own plan for its history (Eph. 1:11). He has *control* over all things (Rom. 11:36), his judgments of truth have ultimate *authority* (John 17:17), and he is *present* everywhere to observe what is happening (Ps. 139).[11] The theological term *omniscience* refers to God's exhaustive knowledge of himself and of the creation.

GOD'S KNOWLEDGE OF THE FUTURE

His omniscience includes knowledge of the past, present, and future. His knowledge of the past and present is clear from the texts cited above. Scripture is equally clear in teaching God's knowledge of the future. Note, for example, this part of the definition of prophecy in Deut. 18:21–22:

> And if you say in your heart, "How may we know the word that the LORD has not spoken?"—when a prophet speaks in the name of the LORD, if the word does not come to pass or come true, that is a word that the LORD has not spoken; the prophet has spoken it presumptuously. You need not be afraid of him.

In this passage, part of the work of the prophet (appointed by God to bring his word to the people) is to foretell the future. If he claims to foretell the future, and that prophecy fails, then the people may conclude that he is a false prophet. The assumption behind this provision is that God knows the future, and therefore any true prophet will predict the future accurately.

---

11. I have elsewhere analyzed the concept of divine lordship to include his *control* of all things, his *authority* over all things, and his *presence* throughout the universe. See Frame, *The Doctrine of God* (Phillipsburg, NJ: P&R Publishing, 2002), especially 1–117.

Knowledge of the future is not only the test of a true prophet. It is also the test of a true God. In the contest between Yahweh, Israel's lord, and the false gods of the ancient Near East, a major issue is which God knows the future. This is a frequent theme in Isa. 40–49, a passage that focuses on the sovereignty of Yahweh over against the absurd pretensions of the false gods:

> Set forth your case, says the LORD; bring your proofs, says the King of Jacob. Let them bring them, and tell us what is to happen. Tell us the former things, what they are, that we may consider them, that we may know their outcome; or declare to us the things to come. Tell us what is to come hereafter, that we may know that you are gods; do good, or do harm, that we may be dismayed and terrified. (Isa. 41:21–23)[12]

So true prophets do announce the future: not only momentous events like the coming of the Messiah (Isa. 9:6–7; 11:1–9), but also very concrete and specific events of the near future (as 1 Sam. 10:1–11). These passages indicate that God has a knowledge in advance, even of free human decisions. That is also true of prophecies that indicate the broad structure of human history. An example is God's promise to Abraham:

> Then the LORD said to Abram, "Know for certain that your offspring will be sojourners in a land that is not theirs and will be servants there, and they will be afflicted for four hundred years. But I will bring judgment on the nation that they serve, and afterward they shall come out with great possessions. As for you, you shall go to your fathers in peace; you shall be buried in a good old age. And they shall come back here in the fourth generation, for the iniquity of the Amorites is not yet complete." (Gen. 15:13–16)

This general prediction presupposes an indefinite number of more specific future facts: that Abraham will have many descendants, that they

---

12. Prediction of the future is not, of course, the only element of prophecy. And some prophecies that appear at first to be straightforward predictions actually have conditions attached, as in Jonah 3:4, 10; Jer. 18:7–9. But Deut. 18 and other passages make clear that prediction of the future is *one* element of prophecy.

will migrate to lands with unfriendly rulers, that the rulers of the nations will afflict them, that these afflictions will end after four hundred years, and so on. These events result from many free human decisions: by the rulers, by Abraham's offspring, by the Amorites, and so on. This prophecy of great redemptive-historical events is also a prediction of many free actions by many people. The biblical picture here is that God knows the future exhaustively, meticulously, in every detail.

The prophetic prediction of free human actions is found in many other passages. See Gen. 27:27–29, 39–40, 49:11, Num. 23–24, Deut. 32:1–43, 33:1–29, 1 Sam. 23:11, 1 Kings 13:1–4, and 2 Kings 8:12. God knows everything we will say or do, before we say or do them (Ps 139:4, 16). He knew the prophet Jeremiah before his conception (Jer. 1:5). That implies that he knew in advance who would marry whom in Israel, and all the various combinations of sperm and egg that would lead to the conception of this one individual. Many free human decisions led to Jeremiah's conception, and the Lord knew them all.

In the New Testament, Jesus teaches that his Father knows the day and hour of his return (Mark 13:32). But that day will not come until after other events have taken place—events that depend on free human decisions (13:1–30). Jesus also predicted that Judas would betray him (John 6:64; 13:18–19), though Judas certainly made his wicked decision freely and responsibly.

OPENNESS THEOLOGY

The view of divine omniscience summarized above has been the traditional view of orthodox Christianity, Eastern Orthodox, Roman Catholic, and Protestant. But some within the church have questioned it. Among these were Lelio (1525–62) and Fausto (1539–1604) Socinus. Robert Strimple describes their view as follows, contrasting it with Arminianism:

> Arminianism denies that God has foreordained whatsoever comes to pass but wishes nevertheless to affirm God's foreknowledge of whatever comes to pass. Against the Arminians, the Socinians insisted that logically the Calvinists were quite correct in insisting that the only real basis for believing that God *knows*

what you are going to do next is to believe that he has *foreordained* what you are going to do next. How else could God know ahead of time what your decision will be? Like the Arminians, however, the Socinians insisted that it was a contradiction of human freedom to believe in the sovereign foreordination of God. So they went "all the way" (logically) and denied not only that God had foreordained the free decisions of free agents but also that God foreknows what those decisions will be.[13]

In the later part of the twentieth century, a movement sprung up, associated with Clark Pinnock, Richard Rice, Gregory Boyd, John Sanders, and others, called by such names as "open theism," "free will theism," and "openness theology." Strimple compares their teaching to that of the Socinians:

> (The Socinian doctrine) is precisely the teaching of the "free will theism" of Pinnock, Rice, and other like-minded "new model evangelicals." They want their doctrine of God to sound very "new," very modern, by dressing it up with references to Heisenberg's uncertainty principle in physics and to the insights of process theology (although they reject process theology as a whole ...). But it is just the old Socinian heresy rejected by the church centuries ago.[14]

As Strimple suggests, openness theology sees itself primarily as a defense of human free will. There are various understandings of human freedom in theological discussion. One view, called "compatibilism," asserts that we are free whenever we can do what we want to do. To be free is to act according to what you desire. On this view, it doesn't matter whether your decision is caused or necessitated. The term "compatibilism," in fact, indicates that freedom is compatible with causes and constraints. As long as you can choose to do what you want to do, your choice is free.

13. Strimple, "What Does God Know?" in *The Coming Evangelical Crisis*, ed. John H. Armstrong (Chicago: Moody Press, 1996), 140–41.
14. Ibid.

The other meaning of freedom commonly discussed in theology is "libertarian" freedom. On a libertarian basis, your decisions are free only insofar as they are not caused or constrained by anything at all. If your choice is made necessary—by your own desire, your nature, your inclinations, someone else's power over you, or even God—your decision is not free. Libertarian freedom is sometimes called "incompatibilism," because it is incompatible with any kind of causation.

Now in ordinary life, I think our usual concept of freedom is compatibilist. As long as we can do what we want to do, we believe that we are free. It would never occur to us to think that being compelled by our own desires removes our freedom (except, perhaps, in cases where our desires are obsessive). That is also the concept of freedom taught in Calvinist theology and, I believe, in Scripture. In Scripture, we can be free even when our actions are determined by our own desires, our nature (significantly, our heart: Matt. 15:18–20; Luke 6:45), our circumstances, or by God. God's sovereign determinations are, of course, all important. According to the Bible, God controls everything that happens (Rom. 11:36; Eph. 1:11), but that fact does not detract from our freedom and responsibility. God hardened Pharaoh's heart to oppress the Israelites (Rom. 9:17–18), but that divine judgment did not take away Pharaoh's freedom and responsibility.[15]

Openness theology, however, denies that compatibilist freedom is "real" freedom. It insists that libertarian freedom, freedom from all causation, is the only freedom worthy of the name, and therefore the only possible basis of moral responsibility. Arminian theology also champions libertarian freedom. But Arminianism tries to combine libertarian freedom with a strong view of God's omniscience. In particular, Arminians, like Calvinists, believe that God knows the future exhaustively. This is the biblical view as I have presented it above.

But open theists, like the Socinians, point out that if God knows the future in all its details, then the future is certain. And if the future is certain, then there can be no libertarian freedom. All of our actions

---

15. For more discussion of these matters, see my essay, "Divine Sovereignty and Human Freedom," in this series of articles.

are constrained, if God knows them in advance. So openness theology takes a step beyond Arminianism. It not only affirms libertarian freedom as Arminianism does, but it denies that God knows in advance all the details of the future. In open theism, the (libertarian) free actions of human beings are inherently unknowable, because nothing makes them happen, not even God. So God cannot be omniscient in the traditional orthodox sense. He is ignorant of what any free agent will do in the future.

This is a startling view in a Christian context. Open theists try to relieve some of the sharpness of it by emphasizing that God, like human pundits, has the ability to project present trends in the future, so as to make a good guess as to what will happen next week, or years from now. But it is hard to imagine how such celestial punditry could explain the detailed predictions of biblical prophets, centuries before their fulfillment. And it is hard to imagine how we can fully trust a God who is ignorant of the course of our lives. A God who is ignorant of the world he has made is certainly less than the *lord* of the Bible.

BIBLIOGRAPHY

ADVOCATES OF OPEN THEISM

Basinger, David. *The Case for Freewill Theism: A Philosophical Assessment.* Downers Grove, IL: InterVarsity Press, 1996.

Boyd, Gregory. *God of the Possible.* Grand Rapids: Baker, 2000.

Cobb, John B., and Pinnock, Clark, eds. *Searching for an Adequate God: A Dialogue Between Process and Free Will Theists.* Grand Rapids: Eerdmans, 2000.

Pinnock, Clark H., Richard Rice, John Sanders, and William Hasker. *The Openness of God.* Downers Grove, IL: InterVarsity Press, 1994.

Rice, Richard. *God's Foreknowledge and Man's Free Will.* Minneapolis: Bethany House, 1985.

Sanders, John. *The God Who Risks.* Downers Grove, IL: InterVarsity Press, 1998.

CRITIQUES OF OPEN THEISM; ADVOCATES OF TRADITIONAL
DIVINE OMNISCIENCE

Frame, John. *No Other God: A Response to Open Theism.* Phillipsburg, NJ: P&R Publishing, 2001. Contains interactions with open theist writers as well as Bible exegesis.

———. *The Doctrine of God.* Phillipsburg, NJ: P&R Publishing, 2002. See esp. 21–79, 469–512.

Helm, Paul. *The Providence of God.* Leicester: InterVarsity Press, 1993.

Nicole, Roger. "A Review Article: God of the Possible?" *Reformation and Revival* 10:1 (Winter 2001): 167–94.

Piper, John, and Justin Taylor, eds. *Beyond the Bounds: Open Theism and the Undermining of Biblical Christianity.* Wheaton, IL: Crossway, 2003.

Strimple, Robert. "What Does God Know?" in Armstrong, J., ed., *The Coming Evangelical Crisis.* Chicago: Moody Press, 1996.

Ware, Bruce. *God's Lesser Glory: The Diminished God of Open Theism.* Wheaton, IL: Crossway Books, 2000.

———. *Their God is Too Small: Open Theism and the Undermining of Confidence in God.* Wheaton, IL: Crossway, 2003.

Wilson, Douglas, ed. *Bound Only Once: The Openness of God as a Failure of Imagination, Nerve, and Reason.* Moscow, ID: Canon Press, 2001.

Wright, R. K. McGregor. *No Place for Sovereignty: What's Wrong with Freewill Theism.* Downers Grove, IL: InterVarsity Press, 1996.

47

God the Creator

WHEN SCRIPTURE FIRST INTRODUCES us to God, in Gen. 1:1, it presents us, not with a definition of God, or a list of attributes, but an *act:* "In the beginning, God created the heavens and the earth." That act nevertheless tells us much about who God is and how he is different from the world he has made. Indeed, this verse presents us with the biblical worldview in a nutshell: Reality is twofold. Everything must be understood within the context of a distinction between creator and creature.

Therefore it is misleading to understand the world, as did the Greek philosophers, as "Being" in general. There are two distinct realities, and they cannot be mixed together or confused with one another. All of our knowledge about the world is qualified by this distinction. There is divine being and created being, different in their attributes, powers, actions, rights, and obligations.

The term *creation* applies both (1) to God's original act of bringing being out of nothing (*ex nihilo*) (Gen. 1:1) and (2) to God's subsequent actions bringing structure to created being, described in Gen. 1:2–2:3. These two phases are sometimes called *original* and *subsequent* creation. A good definition of *creation*, therefore, will embrace both of these. I suggest: *Creation is an act of God alone, by which, for his own glory, he brings into existence everything in the universe, things that had no existence prior to his creative word.* Some have defined creation as "the continual dependence of everything on God," but such definitions fail to anchor the concept as Scripture does in the events of Genesis 1.[16]

In what follows, I shall set forth some of the main contexts in which Scripture speaks of creation. These shall introduce additional clarifications into the concept.

LORDSHIP

I have emphasized elsewhere[17] that the chief name of God in Scripture is *Yahweh*, which English translators render as *Lord*, around 7000 times. I have argued that God's lordship includes his *control* over all things, his *authority* over all the universe, and his *presence* in every part of creation. God's work of creation underscores his lordship in all three of these respects.

Creation establishes God's ownership of all things in heaven and earth (Ex. 20:11; Neh. 9:6; Ps. 146:5; Acts 14:15; 17:24; Col. 1:16; Rev. 4:11; 10:6; 14:7). Because all things are his, there is no limitation to his controlling power.

It also establishes his *authority*, his right to tell all creatures what to do. So in Gen. 1, the very method of creation is his word: he commands and things obediently come into being. (See also Ps. 33:6, 9; John 1:3; Col. 1:15–16.) Jesus shows that he himself is the creator, as his commands still the waves (Mark 4:35–41) and bring healing (Luke 7:1–10).

Creation is also the basis of God's *presence* in all places of the universe. Contrary to some false views of transcendence, God is not far removed from any of us, for we exist by the direct touch of his creative power. Contrary to some false views of immanence, we are not God, for we are his creatures.[18] Since God has created all things out of nothing, he has touched everything in his creation directly. There is no "chain of being," no continuum between God and the world, but a

---

16. Of course, creation is indeed continually dependent on God. But I think that is best discussed under the headings of providence, preservation, and concurrence.

17. Frame, *The Doctrine of God* (Phillipsburg, NJ: P&R Publishing, 2002); *Systematic Theology* (Phillipsburg, NJ: P&R Publishing, 2013). See also my essays on "The Sovereignty of God" and "Divine Sovereignty and Human Freedom" in *Concise Theology*.

18. See my essay "Transcendence and Immanence" in *Concise Theology*.

duality of divine and created being in which God creates and governs us by his direct touch.

WORSHIP

God's creation, therefore, is a universal revelation of his lordship. Confronted by that lordship, by his control, authority, and presence, our obligatory response is worship. Often in Scripture, consideration of creation motivates worship. See Neh. 9:6, Pss. 8:3–9, 33:6–9, 95:3–7, 146:5–6, and Rev. 14:7. Paul tells the Gentiles at Lystra and Athens that the Lord has created all things, and that therefore they should not worship men or idols (Acts 14:15; 17:24–25). How absurd it is that men "worshiped and served the creature rather than the Creator, who is blessed forever! Amen" (Rom. 1:25). God has made the world for his own glory; therefore when we consider creation we should bring him praise (Rom. 11:36).

REDEMPTION

Salvation is of the Lord (Jonah 2:9). Since creation is a vivid revelation of God's lordship, we should expect significant parallels between creation and our redemption from sin. In Genesis, the story of creation anticipates God's deliverance of Israel from bondage and their establishment as his own special people, his new creation. See Ps. 89, Isa. 43:1–7, 14–15, and Jer. 33:20–25. In the New Testament, our salvation in Christ is a "new creation" (2 Cor. 5:17; Gal. 6:15; Eph. 4:24; Col. 3:10). As God originally brought the universe out of nothing, so he brings to us in Christ new life out of the death of sin. The faith of Abraham, the great model of Christian faith, was a faith in God "who gives life to the dead and calls into existence the things that do not exist" (Rom. 4:17).

DISPUTED QUESTIONS

1. *The Six Days*: Genesis 1 presents what we have called *subsequent* creation as occurring in six days, culminating in a day of divine rest. According to Ex. 20:8–11, this pattern

provides a model for the human work week and Sabbath rest. That the Sabbath is also a day of worship reinforces what I said earlier about creation as a motivation for human worship. Theologians have disputed the length of these days. Some have argued that they are "literal" or "ordinary" days; others have said that they each represent long geologic ages. Still others hold to what is called the "framework hypothesis," namely that the whole narrative is a literary device and makes no chronological claims.

2. *The Age of the Earth*: The genealogies in Genesis of Adam, Noah, Abraham, and others suggest a "young earth" view, that the world is somewhere in the vicinity of 10,000 years old. But many theologians have said that in such questions we should defer to the present scientific consensus, that the earth is something like 4.5 billion years old and the origin of *homo sapiens* (modern man) was about 200,000 years ago. This is called the "old earth" view. Some have also held mediating positions, observing places in the Genesis narratives where there may be gaps in the apparent chronology, allowing for a longer period of time than the young earth view supposes, or suggesting problems with the usual ways of measuring geologic time.

3. *Evolution*: A third area of dispute concerns whether the creatures mentioned in Gen. 1 (especially Adam and Eve) were directly created by God or whether each kind of life (including mankind) developed from previous kinds by a process similar to that described in the theory of evolution. Whatever one concludes about questions #1 and #2 above, it is very difficult to argue from Genesis that Adam and Eve are anything other than special creations: (a) According to Gen. 2:7, God made Adam from earth and brought him to life by a special inbreathing. In verses 21–22, the creation of woman (from the rib of Adam) is even more obviously a supernatural event. (b) The

frequent repetition in Gen. 1 of "according to their kinds" indicate at least that there are divinely imposed limits on what can result from reproduction. It is difficult to reconcile any such limits with the theory of evolution. (c) The theory of evolution appears to be a generalization of the principle that species change according to their inherent genetic possibilities in response to change in environments. That principle is called "microevolution," and it seems to be well-established scientifically. But whether that principle can be universally generalized to explain *all* differences in life forms, even beyond existing genetic possibilities ("macroevolution") is dubious.[19]

BIBLIOGRAPHY

Behe, Michael. *The Edge of Evolution: The Search for the Limits of Darwinism*. Free Press, 2008.

Carson, D. A. "A Theology of Creation in Twelve Points." Interview by Tony Reinke. https://www.desiringgod.org/interviews/a-theology-of-creation-in-12-points.

Emadi, Samuel. "Theological Triage and the Doctrine of Creation." https://www.thegospelcoalition.org/article/theological-triage-and-the-doctrine-of-creation/.

Frame, John. *Systematic Theology*. Phillipsburg, NJ: P&R Publishing, 2013.

Levering, Matthew. *Engaging the Doctrine of Creation: Cosmos, Creatures, and the Wise and Good Creator*. Grand Rapids: Baker Academic, 2017.

Meyer, Stephen. *Darwin's Doubt: The Explosive Origin of Animal Life and the Case for Intelligent Design*. Wheaton: Crossway, 2014.

---

19. Space precludes extensive analysis and evaluation of these positions. I have discussed them in somewhat more detail (with bibliographical references) in *Systematic Theology*, 195–203. On the historicity of Adam and Eve, see also 803–6.

Moreland, J. P. *Theistic Evolution: A Scientific, Philosophical, and Theological Critique*. Wheaton: Crossway, 2017.

Poythress, Vern. *Interpreting Eden*. Wheaton: Crossway, 2019.

Schlehr, Karisa. "What is R. C. Sproul's Position on Creation?" https://www.ligonier.org/blog/what-rc-sprouls-position-creation/.

Stump, J. B., ed. *Four Views on Creation, Evolution, and Intelligent Design*. Grand Rapids: Zondervan, 2017.

Tripp, Paul. "The Doctrine of Creation." https://www.paultripp.com/articles/posts/the-doctrine-of-creation-article.

Wilson, Jonathan R. *God's Good World: Reclaiming the Doctrine of Creation*. Grand Rapids: Baker Academic, 2013.

48

Narrative Theology

THE BIBLE includes literature of many different genres: theology, poetry, prophecy, apocalyptic, correspondence, and others. But arguably the main structure of Scripture, including within it these other genres, is best described as a *narrative*: an account of a series of important events. Scripture presents the story of God's involvement with the world, beginning with creation (Gen. 1:1), and ending with new creation, the new heavens and new earth (Rev. 21:1). In the narrative, the story of the fall of mankind (Gen. 3:1–24) presents the issue to be resolved through the rest of history. The resolution of the issue, the redemption of God's people, comes through God's Son Jesus Christ, who becomes incarnate, speaks authoritative words from God, dies on the cross for sin, rises from the dead, ascends to heaven, and will come again in God's own time. When he returns, he will bring final judgment on the wicked and final blessing on his people. The Holy Spirit of God enters the narrative often, at the creation (Gen. 1:2), in the inspiration of the prophets (Eph. 3:5), the conception of Jesus (Luke 1:35), his empowerment (Luke 4:1–2, 14), his resurrection (Rom. 8:11), and the equipping of the church (Acts 1:8) to carry out their mandate (Matt. 28:18–20), to bring the good news, the narrative, to everybody in the world.

By definition, a narrative may describe either truth or fiction. What is remarkable about the biblical narrative is that it embraces all of world history and it claims to be entirely true (2 Tim. 3:16–17).

Traditionally, most theology has sought to analyze, describe, and proclaim the biblical narrative, but it has not itself been in the form of narrative. People have sometimes complained while Scripture itself tells a wonderful "story," theology rarely tells stories. Rather, it tends to be written in academic prose. According to this criticism, it often attempts to set forth timeless and general (and therefore ahistorical) truths, in the form of a series of intellectual propositions.

So some theologians have tried to write in a way that emphasizes the historical-narrative character of the message of Scripture. This concern is plain in the writings of Irenaeus (approx. 130–202 AD), in some of the works of the Protestant Reformers (particularly their development of covenant theology), and in Jonathan Edwards's *A History of the Work of Redemption*, developed from a series of sermons preached in 1739. More recently, the concern to stress narrative developed in the "biblical theology" or "redemptive history" movement. Graeme Goldsworthy describes it thus:

> Biblical theology, as defined here, is dynamic not static. That is, it follows the movement and process of God's revelation in the Bible. It is closely related to systematic theology (the two are dependent upon one another), but there is a difference in emphasis. Biblical theology is not concerned to state the final doctrines which go to make up the content of Christian belief, but rather to describe the *process* by which revelation unfolds and moves toward the goal which is God's final revelation of his purposes in Jesus Christ. Biblical theology seeks to understand the relationships between the various eras in God's revealing activity recorded in the Bible. The systematic theologian is mainly interested in the finished article—the statement of Christian doctrine. The biblical theologian on the other hand is concerned rather with the progressive unfolding of truth. It is on the basis of biblical theology that the systematic theologian draws upon the pre-Pentecost texts of the Bible as part of the material from which *Christian* doctrine may be formulated.[1]

---

1. Goldsworthy, *Gospel & Kingdom*, The Goldsworthy Trilogy (London: Paternoster Press, 2006), 1:45–46. Evangelical proponents of biblical theology have included Geerhardus Vos,

But the more recent "narrative theology"[2] takes this interest a step further. Narrative theology is often called "postliberalism," because it not only focuses on biblical narrative, but sees this focus as a way beyond the theological divisions between orthodoxy and liberalism. Postliberals reject both the orthodox understanding of Scripture (an inerrant book that gives us a divinely authoritative account of redemptive history) and the liberal view (which became prominent in the "Enlightenment" period 1650–1800) that theology must defer to autonomous human rationality, especially as practiced in secular science and philosophy.

The postliberals argue a third alternative: that Scripture presents to us a language[3] governed by a distinctively Christian logic, which governs Christian thinking about God and Christian practices. That language is concentrated in the narrative of creation, fall, and redemption. But it is not important whether that narrative is objectively true or false. To discuss such things as "inerrancy" or "objective truth," which the orthodox affirm and the liberals deny, is to impose upon Scripture theories of truth that owe more to the Enlightenment than to the Christian story. In their view, defending the objective truth of Scripture assumes a "foundationalist" epistemology—the idea that all knowledge is based on absolutely certain premises, universally available to human reason. But biblical truth, according to postliberalism, simply takes the narrative as a model for theological speech and action, without being bound to the assumptions either of orthodoxy or of Enlightenment liberalism. Postliberals emphasize that we ought to do theology without philosophical assumptions (either ontological or epistemological), using forms of reasoning that emerge from the narrative itself.

Herman N. Ridderbos, Richard Gaffin, and Meredith Kline. Some Roman Catholic and Protestant critical scholars have also been associated with the movement, such as Raymond Brown, Joseph Fitzmyer, Walther Eichrodt, Gerhard Von Rad, and Rudolf Bultmann.

2. Postliberalism/narrative theology first became prominent at Yale University in the 1960s, with the work of Hans Frei, Brevard Childs, and George Lindbeck in the forefront. Since then, it has gained wide influence among theologians, chiefly academic theologians.

3. Compare the "language games" of Ludwig Wittgenstein, who argued that the meaning of language is its use in human practice.

The narrative theologians are right, in my view, to seek standards of truth and reasoning from the biblical narrative itself, rather than from philosophical sources that pretend religious neutrality. But in their positive account of truth, these theologians often veer sharply into relativism, as they seek to avoid foundationalist formulations. Although the phrase "objective truth" is not in the Bible, the idea is, and that idea is not negotiable. The Bible presents its narrative as truth revealed by God (e.g., John 17:17, 2 Tim. 3:16–17). To the biblical writers, it is vitally important that the events of redemptive history really and truly took place. In 1 Cor. 15:12–20, for example, Paul says that if Christ is not raised, our faith is dead and we are yet in our sins. It is important that the events of the biblical narrative really and truly happened, just as the biblical writers have stated and interpreted them.

Something should also be said about the isolation of "narrative" from "eternal truth" that one hears in postliberal writings. Narratives may treat either factual or fictional sequences of events. In the Bible, there are some fictional narratives (such as Jesus's parables). But Scripture presents the main narrative of creation, fall, redemption, and consummation, not as fiction, but as truth, indeed the most important truth we know as human beings. Narrative presents these events in a temporal sequence. But this sequence of events is a *fact*. For all eternity, that sequence will always be true. Further, the events of the narrative presuppose further truths, the truths of eternal realities. The work of Christ presupposes an eternal plan of God (Eph. 1:11). God's providence presupposes his eternal omnipotence and omniscience (Ps. 139). Theology gives an account of the narrative, but also of the eternal realities behind the narrative.

That theology not only states truth, but also serves as a criterion for all other truth, a standard of human knowledge.

So systematic theology and biblical theology are not as far apart as they are sometimes thought to be. Every systematic theologian has given an account of the history of Jesus's incarnation, his death, resurrection, ascension, and certain return. Every biblical theologian presents the work in history of the Triune God, a God with the attributes of aseity, eternity, and unchangeability. Systematic theologians typically give more attention to divine election, and biblical theologians typically give more attention to covenants, but this is a matter of emphasis. And there is no reason in principle why theologians of one type should not mention topics emphasized by the other. More generally, narrative is a subset of truth, and eternal truth is a presupposition of narrative. You cannot understand narrative without eternal truth, and vice versa. Any systematics worth its salt must present the narrative, and any account of the narrative must present it as a narrative determined by God's eternal truth.

BIBLIOGRAPHY

Postliberal narrative theology, as noted above, is generally not committed to theological orthodoxy or to biblical authority in the evangelical sense. I would therefore urge caution to those who would read the titles listed below. For further evaluation and commentary from an orthodox Reformed point of view, note the excellent short summary by Ra McLaughlin, "Narrative Theology," http://reformedanswers.org/answer.asp/file/40249, and also pp. 453–56 of my *A History of Western Philosophy and Theology* (Phillipsburg: P&R Publishing, 2015). My review of Lindbeck's *The Nature of Doctrine* can be found in my *Doctrine of the Knowledge of God* (Phillipsburg: P&R Publishers, 1987), 380–81.

Belvedere, Berny. "What Narrative Can't Say: The Limits of Narrative Theology." https://mereorthodoxy.com/what-narrative-cant-say-limits-narrative-theology/.

Childs, Brevard. *Biblical Theology in Crisis*. Philadelphia: Westminster Press, 1970.

———. *Biblical Theology of the Old Testament as Scripture*. Philadelphia: Fortress Press, 1979.

———. *Biblical Theology of the Old and New Testaments: Theological Reflection on the Christian Bible*. Philadelphia: Fortress Press, 1993.

Comstock, Gary. "Two Types of Narrative Theology." https://www.jstor.org/stable/1464681?seq=1#metadata_info_tab_contents.

Frei, Hans. *The Eclipse of Biblical Narrative: A Study in Eighteenth and Nineteenth Century Hermeneutics.* New Haven, CT: Yale University Press, 1974.

Hauerwas, Stanley, and L. Gregory Jones, eds. *Why Narrative? Readings in Narrative Theology.* Eugene, OR: Wipf and Stock, 1997.

Jacobs, Alan. "What Narrative Theology Forgot." https://www.firstthings .com/article/2003/08/what-narrative-theology-forgot.

Lindbeck, George. *The Nature of Doctrine: Religion and Theology in a Postliberal Age.* Philadelphia: Westminster Press, 1984.

49

Analytic Theology

PHILOSOPHY (which I define as the articulation and defense of a worldview) and theology (which I define as the application of God's revelation to all areas of human life) have influenced one another greatly over the centuries. Analytic theology is a fairly recent instance of this interaction.

Let us first look at its philosophical side. Western philosophy has typically sought to build up a structure of human knowledge by its use of human reason and sense experience. But the results of this quest have disappointed many. Although we may talk of "progress" in the natural sciences such as astronomy, physics, and chemistry, it seems that philosophers continue to discuss the same problems today that they discussed thousands of years ago. Why has there been so little progress in the discipline of philosophy? In the late nineteenth and early twentieth centuries, philosophers such as Bertrand Russell, G. E. Moore, and Ludwig Wittgenstein expressed the view that the problem was language. Philosophers, this group argued, had been talking past one another because they have not expressed their views clearly.

So through the twentieth century, many philosophers sought to focus very sharply on the clarification of language in philosophical discourse. This movement became known as "philosophical analysis," "language analysis," or "analytic philosophy." Some of the analytic philosophers abandoned the traditional philosophical program of system-building, arguing that philosophers have no access to facts unavailable to the sciences. Others, however, like Wittgenstein, argued that once language has been clarified we can get a true picture of what the world is like.

Analytic philosophy went through a number of phases in the twentieth century. The early writings of Russell and Wittgenstein advocated a system that Russell called "logical atomism," which tried to reduce language to its smallest essential elements, which were thought to correspond to the essential structure of the world. This was a metaphysical assertion about the nature of reality, that the world consists of elementary "atomic facts," and each of these could be represented by an "atomic sentence" in a supposedly perfect language, so that in that language, the sentences would constitute a perfect picture of the world.

But later analytic philosophers sought to abandon metaphysics altogether. "Logical positivism" argued that language could not make a meaningful assertion unless it could be verified or falsified by quasi-scientific methods. For the positivists, that implied that religious or metaphysical language was "cognitively meaningless"; it was incapable of making a true or false assertion. Only science, then, gives us access to the facts of the world, and the only job left for philosophy is clarification of the language of science. Logical positivism, however, fell out of favor when it was argued that the positivist theses themselves could not pass the verification test.

What replaced logical positivism as the predominant method of analytic philosophers was the "ordinary language philosophy" of the later Wittgenstein. In his *Philosophical Investigations*, Wittgenstein argued that the goal of philosophy was not (as in the previous analytic movements) to reconstruct language in order to make it clearer, but rather to accept ordinary language as it is and to study the jobs it does in human life. Wittgenstein called these jobs "language games." In his view, the work of philosophy was done when we have learned to restrict our language to the functions it plays in ordinary human life. But other analytic philosophers questioned whether it was not also possible to use analysis in a more positive way, to develop technical languages in areas somewhat removed from ordinary life.

Theologians and Christian philosophers interacted with all of these philosophical developments. Naturally, they saw logical positivism as a serious challenge, for if logical positivism were true, then the entire discipline of theology was largely nonsense. But many theologians sought to make affirmative use of ordinary language philosophy and other analytic movements that treated religion with some respect. These discussions were called by names such as "philosophy of religion" and "philosophical theology," but those phrases have been used for many centuries and do not catch what is distinctive about the dialogue between theology and *analytic* philosophy.

Nevertheless, there was in the later twentieth century a substantial interaction between analytic philosophy and religious philosophers and theologians. Some of the Christian thinkers associated with this development were William Alston, R. B. Braithewaite, William Christian, Thomas Flint, Paul Helm, Paul Holmer, George Mavrodes, Thomas V. Morris, Alvin Plantinga, Ian Ramsey, Eleonora Stump, and Nicholas Wolterstorff. The Society of Christian Philosophers (founded in 1978) and its journal *Faith and Philosophy* were major influences in encouraging an analytic philosophical approach to Christian doctrines.

Many of these philosophers have continued to write and teach into the twenty-first century. But "analytic theology" names a movement distinctive to the 2000s. One of its founders, Michael Rea, discussed as follows the discussions of the mid-2000s that led to the book edited by himself and Oliver Crisp, which set the movement going:

> As we discussed the matter, we thought that perhaps a volume might be called for a volume tendentiously entitled Analytic Theology, which would include a few essays making a case directed toward theologians on behalf of analytic approaches to theological topics, a few essays that offered criticism of such approaches, and a few more essays that addressed some of the historical, methodological, and epistemological issues that seemed to lurk in the background of the disciplinary divide. Broadly speaking, our primary task in the volume was to say a bit about what we take "analytic theology" to consist in, and

then to make a sort of cumulative case in favor of its being a worthwhile enterprise.[4]

The book contemplated here, *Analytic Theology: New Essays in the Philosophy of Theology*, by Oliver Crisp and Michael Rea,[5] is sometimes considered the beginning of analytic theology as a movement. Reviews were quickly published pro and con. There was a significant discussion of the book at the American Academy of Religion (2012), and the *Journal of Analytic Theology* began in 2013. Since then a great many books and articles have been published that associate themselves explicitly with the analytic approach.

There is no hard and fast distinction between this movement and earlier interactions between theology and analytic philosophy. But the earlier interactions tended to focus on issues commonly discussed in the history of philosophy, such as the existence of God, the nature of evil, and the nature of truth and goodness. Analytic theology is more distinctively theological than previous schools. It takes up doctrinal matters (in many religions, but particularly Christianity) that have previously been limited to exegetical, historical, and systematic theology. These include the Trinity, divine sovereignty, free will, the incarnation of Christ, his two natures, his resurrection, the relation of faith to justification, the nature of liturgy and the sacraments, and heaven and hell.[6] Analytic theologians have also discussed developments in the history of theology: creeds, confessions, and important thinkers like Augustine, Anselm, and Aquinas. In this literature there is emphasis on defining terms very precisely, distinguishing various uses of terms, analyzing in depth the logic of theological arguments, and discussing the developments among secular analytic philosophers relevant to theology.

---

4. Michael Rea, "Analytic Theology: Precis," *Journal of the American Academy of Religion* 81:3 (September 1, 2013), 573.

5. Oxford University Press, 2011.

6. In this emphasis on distinctly theological doctrines, analytic theology follows Alvin Plantinga's "Advice to Christian Philosophers," *Faith and Philosophy* 1:3 (1984), 253–71. In this very influential essay, Plantinga urges Christian philosophers to discuss issues arising from their own faith commitment, rather than restricting themselves to issues discussed by secular thinkers.

Analytic theology has come to dominate discussions of philosophical issues among Christians in recent years. Its aspiration to produce works of high-quality thought and cogency has been acknowledged and appreciated, as has its use of more recent logical and analytic tools. In my judgment, however, analytic theology, like previous forms of interaction between philosophy and theology, has been weak in its failure to apply theological norms to the work of philosophy itself. Many writings in the analytic theology movement, even writings by people who are unquestionably committed to Christ, sound like attempts to be religiously neutral, as if the Bible and the confessions had nothing authoritative to say to the issues at hand. Analytic theologians need to take up seriously the question of how revelation directs philosophical thought. How does Scripture direct the thinking of a philosopher? And how does biblical authority, therefore, affect the conclusions of philosophical argumentation?

BIBLIOGRAPHY

EARLIER WORKS OF ANALYTIC PHILOSOPHY

Austin, J. L. *Philosophical Papers*. Oxford: Clarendon, 1990.

Ayer, A. J. *Language, Truth, and Logic*. New York: Dover, 1952. Classic exposition of logical positivism.

Moore, G. E. *Selected Writings*. Ed. Thomas Baldwin. New York: Routledge, 1993.

Russell, Bertrand. *The Basic Writings of Bertrand Russell*. Ed. Robert E. Egner and Lester E. Dunonn. New York: Routledge, 2009.

Ryle, Gilbert. *The Concept of Mind*. Chicago: University of Chicago Press, 2000.

Urmson, J. O. *Philosophical Analysis: Its Development between the Two World Wars*. New York: Oxford University Press, 1956.

Wittgenstein, Ludwig. *Philosophical Investigations*. Translated by G. E. M. Anscombe, P. M. S. Hacker, and Joachim Schulte. Rev. 4th ed. Oxford: Blackwell, 2009.

INTERACTIONS BETWEEN ANALYTIC PHILOSOPHERS
AND THEOLOGIANS BEFORE 2000

Alston, William. *Perceiving God: The Epistemology of Religious Experience.* Ithaca, NY: Cornell University Press, 1993.

Flew, Anthony, and Alasdair McIntyre, eds. *New Essays in Philosophical Theology.* London: Macmillan, 2012.

Helm, Paul. *Belief Policies.* Cambridge: Cambridge University Press, 2007.

Mavrodes, George I. *Belief in God: A Study in the Epistemology of Religion.* New York: Random House, 1970.

Plantinga, Alvin. *God and Other Minds: A Study of the Rational Justification of Belief in God.* Ithaca, NY: Cornell University Press, 1990.

———. *Warrant.* 3 vols. New York: Oxford University Press, 1990, 1993.

Swinburne, Richard. *The Existence of God.* 2nd ed. New York: Oxford University Press, 2004.

Wolterstorff, Nicholas. *Reason within the Bounds of Religion.* 2nd ed. Grand Rapids: Eerdmans, 1988.

THE ANALYTIC THEOLOGICAL MOVEMENT

Abraham, William J. *Analytic Theology: A Bibliography.* Highland Loch Press, 2012.

Crisp, Oliver, and Michael Rea. *Analytic Theology: New Essays in the Philosophy of Theology.* London: Oxford University Press, 2011.

McCall, Thomas. *An Invitation to Analytic Christian Theology.* Downers Grove, IL: IVP Academic, 2015.

Pawl, Timothy. *In Defense of Conciliar Christology: A Philosophical Essay.* London: Oxford University Press, 2016.

Stump, Eleonore. *Atonement.* London: Oxford University Press, 2018.

PART 6

Philosophy and Apologetics

50

Apologetics

This short essay was published as "Let the Church Test Its Apologetics by Biblical Standards," in Aaron B. Hebbard, ed., 95 Theses for a New Reformation (Eugene, OR: Resource Publications, 2017), 69–70.

LET THE CHURCH TEST ITS APOLOGETICS by biblical standards. Apologetics is the attempt to present a reason for the hope that is in us (1 Pet. 3:15). But too often, since the beginning of the apologetic tradition in the second century, the church has fallen to the temptation of compromising biblical principles while defending them. We have too often sought to make the agreement between biblical and non-Christian thought seem greater than it is, so that we can not only persuade others, but be intellectually respectable as well. As examples, consider Justin Martyr's claim that Scripture's doctrine of creation is the same as Plato's, Thomas Aquinas's Aristotelian doctrine of "natural reason," Schleiermacher's attempt to base the Christian faith on feeling rather than Scripture. Too often modern apologists adopt non-Christian views of knowledge (such as empiricism, rationalism, coherentism) in the vain hope that these strategies will lead to Christian conclusions. But these epistemologies regard the authority of the human mind as absolute and final. And one cannot assume the all-sufficiency of the human mind in order to prove the all-sufficiency of the biblical God.

So, although the church's apologetic may lead some to Christ, on the whole it has not been as powerful as it ought to be. Scripture says that with God's help we can "take every thought captive to obey Christ" (2 Cor. 10:5). But it is inconsistent with that goal to start with the principle that the human mind is sufficient and does not need to be grounded in God's word. Scripture itself denies that principle and calls on God to sanctify all our thinking with the truth of his word (John 17:17). To deny that is to "suppress the truth" by our unrighteousness (Rom. 1:18).

It surprises many people, indeed many Christians, to learn that Christ's lordship extends, not only to their worship and morals, but also to their thinking, to their intellectual life. But the unsanctified mind drains the power of Christian witness. The world can see the inconsistency, and they are rarely persuaded by the arguments. This is the main reason, in my judgment, why the world has such a low regard for Christian apologetics. Many people well-educated in fields like philosophy and science dismiss Christian apologetics (and therefore the gospel) as superstitious credulity.

So if the church fails to reform its apologetic, we should expect that there will be fewer and fewer intellectually serious Christians, in an era where their influence is needed more than ever.

But if the church turns back to a biblical view of knowledge and an uncompromising apologetic built on God's supremacy in the life of the mind, we should expect great flourishing in evangelism and the growth of the body of Christ.

So, as Luther and Calvin called the church back to a more consistently biblical view of salvation, rejecting the medieval compromises, so a new reformation will call the church to a renewal of all human thinking, based on Scripture's teaching.

To bring about this intellectual reformation, we need first to pray, for only God can being about such a drastic transformation. The transformation we seek is a transformation of the heart, and only God can reach into people that deeply. But God will make use of efforts on our part, as we train ourselves and others to think according to the principles of his word. Our pulpits, Sunday schools, and seminaries should proclaim consistently that unless God is who he says he is, nothing else makes sense. Only the God of the Bible explains how the human mind can appropriate data from the world of experience and draw from that data reliable conclusions for human life. God is not so much a conclusion of human reasoning as its presupposition. It is God who validates human reason, not human reason that validates God.

51

Believing in Jesus in the First Century

I HAVE WRITTEN AN ESSAY on "Believing in God in the Twenty-First Century,"[1] and I suppose that is the question we are most interested in. How can a secular modern person come to believe in a supernatural savior, based on an ancient book? But perhaps before we formulate the answer to that question it is important to understand why people believed in him in the first century. Why was it that the number of Christians began in the first century to grow from twelve people to become the largest world religion, 2000 years into the future? The exponential growth started with the three thousand (Acts 2:41) that committed to Christ after Peter's Pentecost sermon Three thousand came to believe in Christ after Peter's sermon on the feast of Pentecost in the first century (Acts 2:41), and as the apostles continued to preach, Luke tells us in Acts 4:4 that "the number of men grew to about five thousand." The reference to "men" may suggest that there were also a number of women. And in Acts 5:14 we learn that "more and more men and women believed in the Lord and were added to (the church's) number." In the book of Acts, the huge, surprising growth of the church is a major emphasis. Evidently, contrary to what Christians today sometimes suppose, God does care about numbers.

---

1. See SSW2, 151–75.

But why? What was there about this early preaching that led so many to make a commitment to a tiny religious movement? Christian doctrine offers some important answers: (1) The Old Testament (as Christians call it) looked forward to the coming of a Messiah, and in many ways the Old Testament prophecies well-described Jesus. (2) Jesus taught "with authority" (Matt. 7:29), to an extent that was unique. (3) He performed many miracles, the greatest being his own resurrection from the dead. (4) After his ascension, he sent the Holy Spirit, who constrained the hearts of people to embrace the gospel (Acts 1:8; 6:10; 10:44; cf. John 3:5).

But granting the importance of these elements, it is still worth asking a more specific question: What processes of thought led these ancient people to conclude that Jesus was the Messiah, and to entrust their lives to this Lord, whom many despised? Their commitment to Christ was by faith; but it was not without thought. Their faith was a supernatural work of the Spirit. But the work of the Spirit did not bypass the mind, but engaged it.

For many, doubtless, the Old Testament prophecies, Jesus's miracles, and particularly his resurrection, would have been enough. But I believe that his teachings also played a role, one that has not received sufficient attention.

Jesus came on the scene as a teacher (though, of course, not ONLY a teacher). As a teacher, a rabbi, Jesus taught many things on the authority of the Old Testament. But he often put an unexpected twist into his use of the Scriptures.

While the Pharisees were gathered together, Jesus asked them, "What do you think about the Messiah? Whose son is he?"

"The son of David," they replied.

He said to them, "How is it then that David, speaking by the Spirit, calls him 'Lord'? For he says,

" 'The Lord said to my Lord:
    "Sit at my right hand
    until I put your enemies
        under your feet." '

"If then David calls him 'Lord,' how can he be his son?" No one
could say a word in reply, and from that day on no one dared to
ask him any more questions.

The Pharisees were "testing" Jesus, and he passed all their tests, to their
disappointment. But then he presented an interpretation of Ps. 110 that
they weren't expecting and to which they had no answer. Jesus's interpretation pointed in an obvious way to his own Messianic claim, and
that was something the Pharisees could not abide. I note that Jesus's
teaching should always be understood in the context of his contentious
relationship to other teachers, to those who considered themselves "official" teachers: Pharisees and Sadducees. This rivalry became more and
more intense through Jesus's ministry, and in the end the official teachers collaborated with the Roman government to kill Jesus.

But I suspect that the ordinary people had less tolerance for political murder. They knew that Jesus was, at the very least, a good man.
He had shown compassion on the sick, and upon sinners (John 8:11).
Many of them welcomed him when he entered Jerusalem on a donkey
(Matt. 21:1–11). I do not believe this was the same group of people that
shouted "Crucify him" later in the week (Matt. 27:22–23). The latter
group were partisans of the Jewish establishment. The former group
were the godly people of Jerusalem, who longed for their Messiah and
who hoped Jesus might be the One. They might have expected Jesus to
pay some penalty because of his differences with official Judaism. But
I suspect they were utterly shocked when it turned out that the officials
actually wanted to murder this good man.

Jesus placed before his hearers a clear question: What side did they
want to be on? Jesus's side, or the side of the hypocritical Jewish leaders? That division became all the more intense when Jesus was condemned to death.

I don't know how much they understood of the atonement that took
place on Calvary. I imagine that it occurred to some of them that Jesus
was dying a death that other people deserved. And they hoped against
hope that there was some way the good man Jesus could be avenged.
Jesus's death, of course, was utterly unique. But it many ways it was

similar to other deaths of good people at the hands of wicked people. Many of the people of Jerusalem wished there were some way in which Jesus's side could prevail over his enemies.

But after the resurrection everything looked different. On Pentecost, Peter proclaimed that yes, it was still possible to be on Jesus's side. And three thousand flocked to him. This good man's cause was not a lost cause; it was nothing less than God's cause in the world. The three thousand conversions were by the Spirit. But the Spirit instilled a faith that not only believed the impossible but was a passionate love of goodness.

I have drawn a picture that brings together a number of factors of those I alluded to earlier: Old Testament Messianism, Jesus's teachings, his miracles, his kindness, especially his resurrection. I am exploring whether one string that binds these doctrines together is a moral passion, a profound desire to be on the side of good and against the forces of evil. Many of us despise preaching and piety that is "moralistic," that is a mere moral passion without redemption. But we should not exclude the moral sense from the quality of faith. Redemption itself is about morality: it is God's solution to human sin. One thing that rightly draws people to faith in Christ is his goodness, in a world that hates that goodness.

That still draws people to Christ today. There is a movie about Christ made in 1979 that has been shown all over the world as an evangelistic effort of CRU (formerly known as Campus Crusade for Christ). It is known today simply as "The Jesus Film." CRU workers testify that often when the Jesus Film is shown in tribes that have not been exposed to the gospel, the first noticeable response is weeping—weeping that the good man Jesus is forced to be crucified by the villainous leaders of the Jews and Romans. Often this weeping leads viewers to take sides, to love Jesus and to be angry at his persecutors. This is an obvious human reaction, often a precursor to conversion. I would not be surprised if the same reaction did not occur also in the first century and lead to conversions then as well. Conversion is the work of the Holy Spirit; but the Spirit works through the word, and the word is about Jesus's teachings and life. So in evangelism we should not ignore the power of moral outrage.

52

Post-Truth and Chaos

ONCE IT WAS SOCIALLY ACCEPTABLE to believe that the world was flat, that the sun revolved around the earth, that storms at sea were caused by the breath of Poseidon. But eventually people stopped believing these things. Instead they came to believe that the earth was round, that the earth revolved around the sun, and that storms were caused by wind currents. Why did people change their beliefs? The earlier beliefs were in some ways more comfortable to hold. They were often based on parental teaching and cultural acceptance. But for most people the authority of parents and culture became insufficient. They started holding the new beliefs, because they thought they were true, and the older beliefs false.

That process was the motivating force in what has been called the scientific revolution. In science, we are told, people do not believe what is merely comfortable, or traditional, or cultural. They form their beliefs, rather, by formulating hypotheses and performing experiments to see if those hypotheses are true or false.

The point is not that science (i.e. the most recent scientific consensus) is infallible or that it serves as the highest authority. For we are also told that science never stands still. The consensus of scientists a hundred years ago, or even twenty years ago, may be very different from the scientific consensus today. Nor is the point that the consensus today is infallible; for wise scientists recognize that we may have

313

to give up the contemporary consensus in the light of future discoveries. The issue, then, is not science (versus religion, for example) or contemporary thought (versus that of the past). The issue is, rather, as it has always been, truth versus falsehood. We revere science because we believe that it is an unusually good guide to truth.

There are, of course, other disciplines that lead to truth, or which claim to lead to truth. Religion is one, and the different religions argue for different paths. Novels and poems usually claim to present truth of a different sort from science. And people often claim that different human faculties (reason, sensation, intuition, faith) lead us toward truth of various kinds.

But the question of truth cannot be avoided. When someone argues a scientific hypothesis (e.g., "the Higgs boson exists") or a political theory (e.g., "socialism is better than capitalism,") or a religious proposition (e.g., "Mohammed is the prophet of Allah"), the main question before us is, Is this proposition true, or false?

Now it is hard to believe, but since the beginnings of science and philosophy, many have tried to avoid that fundamental question. In ancient Greece, the Sophists, like Protagoras and Gorgias, held that there is no such thing as objective truth. In their view, there is no truth that everybody ought to acknowledge. Rather, there is only private truth: truth for you, truth for me. According to them, if James believes that the sun revolves around the sun, then that is true for him; but if Janet thinks the earth revolves around the sun, that is true for her. Janet cannot tell James that he should hold a different belief, for everyone is entitled to his or her own belief. No belief is objectively true, or truer than any other. There is no truth; there is only your truth and my truth.

This Sophist position has become common in our own day, so much that many seem to take it for granted. This is what people mean when they observe that we are living in a "post-truth society." But they seem to have no idea how destructive Sophism is, how it can turn all of our thought and discourse into chaos. If everyone has the right to his or her own truth, then there is no way that one can persuade another. If I believe that socialism is too expensive for our society, and you disagree, we can go back and forth with different arguments. But the discussion ends if I say, "Well, capitalism is true FOR ME, whatever you may think." And if everyone holds that Sophist point of view, then all argument is useless.

We have not come that far in our society, but we are approaching such an impasse. People (especially, I believe, on the "left" of the political spectrum) have reached a point where they think it is not helpful to conduct reasoned discussion with the other side. And if we are unable to resolve our disagreements by rational discussion, only one solution remains: to use force. Hence, people seek to force others to accept their point of view whether or not there are sound arguments for it. That is what lies behind attempts by student groups and university administrators to keep dissenting speakers away from their campuses. The "antifa" riots are the most frightening symptom of this policy.

For these are the two competitive ways of reaching consensus in a society: reasonable discussion and violence. Human history is a history of competition between these two methods of resolving conflict. The United States is somewhat unique among the nations, for it adopted a system of government based on reasonable discussion: elections, three branches of government, many opportunities for mutual persuasion. But today there are still many societies governed by violence, and there are many in the United States that would like our society to be governed that way too.

But that is what happens when people deny the existence of objective truth. Without objective truth, there is no goal for reasonable discussion, and the only way to resolve disagreement is through force.

Again, the conflict is not between science and religion. Religion emphasizes objective truth as much as science does. The Bible, for example, speaks over and over about the strife of truth against falsehood. It teaches that God is truth (Pss. 51:6; 119:160), that his word is truth (John 17:17), and that Jesus Christ is the truth (together with being the way and the life; John 14:6).

And the Bible teaches that this world is God's creation, so that he is the source of truth. Science, as we have seen, much as it deserves our respect, is able to offer us only a present-day consensus within a changing process. God, according to Scripture, is unchanging, and so he offers us the truth that is behind all other truth. He gives us a criterion before which all other claims to truth must submit, a truth that sweeps aside all false claims to human wisdom (1 Cor. 1:18–2:16).

Without God, our debates lack a final criterion of truth. And without a criterion of truth, there is no truth at all, even in science. Even those philosophies and scientific theories that claim to have objective truth cannot justify that claim without an unchanging, universal criterion. So God is the objective truth behind all objective truth. Without God, our discussions have no foundation, and our societies can find stability only through violence.

Today, many are saying that we must deal with questions of marriage, sexuality, and government (as examples) without regard to religion. But without biblical religion, there is no criterion of truth, and therefore no way, ultimately, of resolving our arguments without violence. Opponents of biblical religion are increasingly motivated, not to argue against Christianity, but to silence it. Today, among religions around the world, Christianity is the most persecuted. Society has come full circle, for now, as in the first four centuries, there is a huge movement to do away with Christianity, and violence seems like the only way that can be done.

But Jesus has promised to protect his church (Matt. 16:18), and his Father is working to re-establish this world as a kingdom of righteousness and peace (2 Pet. 3:13). And in that kingdom, we will get used to thinking and arguing differently, with God's word as our unchanging criterion.

53

Presuppositionalism and Perspectivalism

This article was previously published in J. Frame, Wayne Grudem, and John Hughes, eds., Redeeming the Life of the Mind: Essays in Honor of Vern Poythress *(Wheaton: Crossway, 2017), 234–50.*

IN A PREVIOUS ARTICLE I indicated how Westminster Theological Seminary, though considered "conservative" for its stand on biblical authority and the Reformed Confessions, has actually been a fount of theological creativity.[2] One of the most impressive and enduring examples of this creativity has been the apologetics of Cornelius Van Til, sometimes called "presuppositionalism." Presuppositionalism was, and is, not only an apologetic, but a Christian philosophical epistemology. It bears on human knowledge of God and of all aspects of God's creation.

Another fruit of Westminster's theological creativity is called "perspectivalism." It too bears on human knowledge, both of God and of God's creation. I may be the first Westminster professor[3] to have articulated perspectival methodology, but I confess that my own confidence in this method was greatly bolstered in the early 1970s by the partnership

---

2. Frame, "In Defense of Something Close to Biblicism," *Westminster Theological Journal* 59:2 (Fall 1997), 269–91, especially 277–80. Republished in *SSW*3, 27–65.

3. Now I teach at Reformed Theological Seminary in Orlando, FL.

of Vern Poythress, then a student, later and still a Westminster professor, whom we honor in this volume. Initially, I thought that perspectivalism was useful primarily in the work of philosophy and theology. But Poythress saw applications of it to linguistics and other sciences. And since the early 1970s perspectivalism has been a joint project between the two of us.

So my contribution to this Festschrift will be an attempt to analyze the relationship between presuppositionalism and perspectivalism. Poythress and I emphatically endorse both positions, but that raises the question of their biblical and logical connections. It is not obvious that adherents of Van Til's apologetics should also favor perspectivalism. Indeed, a superficial look at the two ideas sometimes leads critics to think the two are inconsistent. Van Til's critics typically refer to him as an absolutist, while critics of perspectivalism often refer to it as a relativistic method. But we must get beyond superficial descriptions and look more carefully at these two developments in Westminster's theology. My thesis is that when rightly understood the two ideas reinforce one another. Indeed, each makes the other inevitable.

PRESUPPOSITIONALISM

The name "presuppositionalism" was invented, not by Van Til, but by one or other of his opponents.[4] The name was applied to Gordon H. Clark as well as Van Til, and occasionally to others. Clark seems to have liked the term better than Van Til did, but Van Til deferred to others in occasionally using it to refer to himself. My discussion here deals only with Van Til's form of presuppositionalism.

Presuppositionalism in this sense begins with two observations related to the biblical doctrines of creation and fall, respectively. The doctrine of creation establishes a distinctively biblical metaphysic. In that metaphysic, or worldview, there are two distinct levels of reality, the creator and the creation. The creator is the biblical God alone,

---

4. Most likely James Oliver Buswell, whose apologetics can be roughly described as empiricist. For the debate between Van Til and Buswell, see Van Til, *The Defense of the Faith*, 4th ed. (Phillipsburg: P&R, 2008), ed. by K. Scott Oliphint, 240–64, 321.

described as in Scripture: one God in three persons, "a Spirit, infinite, eternal, and unchangeable, in his being, wisdom, power, holiness, justice, goodness, and truth."[5] He created the universe at the beginning of time, out of nothing, by the word of his power. This creative act proceeded from God's eternal plan, so that God's knowledge of the creation is exhaustive. The universe is dependent on God for everything, including its continued existence. And it depends on God for its meaning. It is what God says it is, and its ongoing history is under God's direction.

God made human beings as part of the creation, but a part of the creation that uniquely bears his image (Gen. 1:26–27). He gave to the first couple a commission, to "be fruitful and multiply and fill the earth and subdue it and have dominion over the fish of the sea and over the birds of the heavens and over every living thing that moves on the earth" (Gen. 1:28). This commission presupposes that Adam and Eve were capable of knowing and understanding something of the world they were to explore. But to know rightly requires obedience to God. Mixed among the privileges of this commission was a prohibition: "But of the tree of the knowledge of good and evil you shall not eat, for in the day that you eat of it you shall surely die" (Gen. 2:16).

Since God has established the meaning of everything in creation, human thought is first of all a reflection on this pre-established meaning. It recognizes the authority of God to say what everything is and what role everything is to play in the God-ordained history. Human thought is secondary interpretation—a reinterpretation of God's original interpretation. The tree of the knowledge of good and evil, like everything else in the creation, is what God says it is. All human interpretations must take God's interpretation as settled.

This is another way of saying that human interpretations of creation must *presuppose* God's original interpretation of it, insofar as he has shared it with us. He has shared it through *revelation*, as in the words he spoke to Adam and Eve in Gen. 1–2. Human knowledge must presuppose God's original knowledge of the world he has made.

---

5. WSC, 4.

So essentially presuppositionalism is a view of knowledge that acknowledges and utilizes the truth of God's revelation to us. Presuppositionalism is the epistemology of Eden. It is the way we would all think and reason if we were not fallen. It follows necessarily from the doctrine of creation.

But we should also consider the doctrine of the fall. Scripture teaches that Adam and Eve did not obey God's prohibition of eating the forbidden fruit. At that point, our first parents did not think according to their original presuppositional epistemology. Satan tempted them by questioning God's revelation (Gen. 3:1–4). What followed was a different kind of reasoning:

> So when the woman saw that the tree was good for food, and that it was a delight to the eyes, and that the tree was to be desired to make one wise, she took of its fruit and ate, and she also gave some to her husband who was with her, and he ate. (Gen. 3:6)

As Eve reflects on the choice before her, she expresses no reverence for what God commanded, but merely accepts Satan's view that either God commanded nothing or God's word was false. She assumes that her own tastebuds, eyes, and mind are sufficient to make her decision. This is what Van Til called *autonomous* thinking—thinking that rejects God's authority and imagines that the human mind is the ultimate criterion of truth and falsehood. Autonomous thought is the opposite of presuppositionalism, an epistemology that opposes God's lordship.

Apart from God's saving grace, autonomous thinking became the rule among human beings, so that, not only Eve's original disobedience, but all the other sins of human history, arose out of autonomous thought. In the Bible, God rebukes this kind of thought over and over again. Typically, he describes this thinking by the word "foolishness" (e.g., Pss. 14:1; 39:8; 74:22; 92:6; Prov. 1:7; 8:5) and its opposite as "wisdom" (Deut. 34:9; 1 Kings 3:28; 4:29–34). The fear of the Lord is the beginning of knowledge (Prov. 1:7) and of wisdom (Ps. 111:10), so those who do not fear God are foolish.

The apostle Paul makes much of the distinction between wisdom and foolishness, as in 1 Cor. 1:18–3:23, and in Rom. 1:18–32 he attributes foolishness to the "suppression" of the truth. What is the remedy for a sinful suppression of the truth? Only the redemption of Christ, which enables us again to serve God with our minds.

So there are two roots of presuppositionalism: (1) because we are creatures, we should serve God with our minds as well as with all our other created faculties; (2) because we are sinners, we need his salvation to receive new hearts, and therefore the mind of Christ (1 Cor. 2:16). These are two reasons why it is necessary for us to think presuppositionally.

Since Van Til taught apologetics, presuppositionalism became known as an "apologetic method," though its applications extended beyond apologetics to cover every kind of human thinking. Presuppositional apologetics addresses the question: How can we think presuppositionally in an evangelistic conversation with a non-Christian, given that the non-Christian is not willing to accept Christian presuppositions? The method answers that evangelism is no exception to the rule, that we must always presuppose God's revelation. Evangelism, like all Christian speech, must be *true* in what it says, and that means true according to God's standards. Truthful reasoning requires us, even in a conversation with a non-Christian (indeed, *especially* there—1 Pet. 3:15), to honor Christ as Lord.

The most common objection to appealing to presuppositions in conversation with non-Christians is this: the procedure is circular. That is to say, the presuppositionalist, supposedly, is presupposing what he ought to be proving, namely the truth of God's revelation. But presuppositionalists have a ready reply: In arguments over an ultimate standard of knowledge, *everyone* appeals to his own presuppositions in trying to prove them. For example, a rationalist[6] has no choice but to prove the primacy of human reason by appealing to human reason. An empiricist[7] necessarily appeals to his senses to prove the primacy of his senses.[8] Otherwise, both rationalists and empiricists are incon-

---

6. Rationalists believe that all knowledge is grounded in the deliverances of the human mind, our logic, science, mathematics, etc.

7. Empiricists believe that all knowledge is grounded in the deliverances of the senses, what we see, hear, etc.

8. Empiricists rarely if ever attempt this, because the project is so implausible. Most thinkers agree that sensation does not in itself warrant absolutes.

sistent, for they would be appealing to something other than their final criterion to prove the final criterion. If their final criterion is subject to the authority of anything other than itself, then it is not ultimate or final.

That everyone has his own presuppositions would seem to bring an end to the argument. It would seem that the Christian would make his final case by saying "The Bible says this," and the non-Christian would conclude his argument by saying "Reason says this," or "Science says this," or "The Qur'an says this," bringing an end to the dialogue. But in fact there is more to be said, even after both parties identify their presuppositions. When Van Til argues with philosophical rationalists, for example, he points out that human reason cannot function without presupposing the biblical God. If human reason alone is the ultimate criterion of truth, then it cannot gain knowledge. From logic and reason alone, no conclusions follow. Logical arguments require premises that cannot be deduced from logic alone. And they require us to presuppose that our minds are made in such a way as to gain knowledge from the empirical world.[9]

Still, we should avoid the mistaken impression that presuppositional apologetics requires us constantly to talk about presuppositions to the exclusion of other subjects. Critics sometimes say that presuppositional apologetics rejects appeal to evidence, for example, but Van Til always insisted that evidences were an important testimony to the truth of Scripture. He only wished to remind us that appealing to evidence is never neutral, never something we may do without presuppositions. Evidences are what they are because God has made them such. The empty tomb, for example, is evidence for Jesus's resurrection because God brought it about and communicated it to witnesses that he appointed to speak truth.[10] If one tries to evaluate this evidence using a non-biblical epistemology, such as the skepticism of David Hume,[11]

---

9. Evolution does not provide a sufficient explanation for the remarkable correlation between mind and universe. Evolution, if it exists, programs the mind for survival, not for discovering truth as such.

10. Note that Paul argues for the resurrection in 1 Cor. 15:1–2, 11–12 by pointing out that the resurrection was part of the apostolic preaching of the gospel.

11. Hume argued that there *cannot* be, in principle, testimony sufficient to authenticate a supernatural event. For in our experience (Hume was an empiricist) natural explanations are

then he will not find this evidence persuasive. More on this issue at a later point in the paper.

PERSPECTIVALISM

I. BROAD MEANING

Now perspectivalism is also an implication of the biblical revelation. As the doctrine of creation requires a presuppositional epistemology, so it also requires a perspectival understanding of human knowledge. Perspectivalism has both a broad meaning and a narrow meaning. The broad meaning (like presuppositionalism) derives from the doctrine of creation.

Both presuppositionalism and perspectivalism teach that God's knowledge is very different from ours, because he is the creator and we are creatures. God's knowledge is exhaustive. He knows all things, by knowing himself, knowing his eternal plan, and knowing what he has done to carry out that plan. He knows every human being exhaustively as well (Ps. 139). But our knowledge is limited; we cannot know everything God knows (Ps. 139:6; Isa. 55:8–9; Rom. 11:33).

Another way of putting this point is to say that our knowledge is always from a limited *perspective*. A perspective is a *way* of knowing, a *means by which* we know something. It is the *place from which* we regard the world. God's perspective is infinite. He not only knows everything that is true, but he knows everything from every perspective. He not only knows what is outside my office window, but he knows how it looks to me, from my perspective. So God's perspective includes mine. He knows how everything looks to me, and how everything looks to you. He knows how my office looks to a fly on the wall. Indeed, even if there is no fly on my wall, God knows what it would look like to such a fly, *if there were* a fly on my wall.[12] So God is not only omniscient; he is also omniperspectival.

---

always more likely than supernatural ones.

12. As many theologians have said, God knows the truth of hypotheticals as well as categoricals.

As we saw earlier, God has made us able to know what we know. So, specifically, he has given us perspectives by which we gain knowledge. Most obviously, our own bodies are perspectives of knowledge. Everything I know, I know from the position my body occupies in the world. I know how the world looks through my own eyes, but not immediately through someone else's eyes. To know what the world looks like to another person, I must find out indirectly, particularly by asking the other person to describe his own perspective.

As I move my body around, my perspective enlarges. Looking at a tree from north, south, east, and west magnifies my knowledge of the tree, for I am including in my perspective more and more information. And as I gain testimony from others, I add their knowledge to mine. In effect, in such a case, I am adding their perspective to my own, though sometimes I have to make allowances for the other person's limitations or dishonesty. Books and electronic communications enrich my perspective too, by adding to it perspectives from other people.

But ultimately, enlargements in my perspective come from God. In that sense and in others, all human knowledge comes through divine revelation. And to gain knowledge from divine revelation is to some extent to share in God's own perspective. Our knowledge aligns with God's perspective whenever it is true. This alignment exists in all the different locations where God reveals himself, such as nature, prophecy, and Scripture. When a human being rightly understands, say, John 3:16, and believes it, he is seeing reality from God's perspective.

Like presuppositionalism, then, perspectivalism rests on God's revelation. Indeed, these are two different ways of saying the same thing. Both understand that human beings are creatures, so that their true knowledge requires divine revelation. Presuppositionalism says that this revelation must be the starting point or criterion of our reasoning. Perspectivalism says that in learning truth we must share God's own starting point, "thinking God's thoughts after him."

Presuppositionalism addresses the *cause* that produces human knowledge and the *authority* that warrants it. Perspectivalism speaks of the *presence* of God as we share his perspective: knowledge as union with God.[13]

So perspectivalism does not succumb to the criticism that it is (unlike presuppositionalism) a relativist position. It is indeed a means of recognizing relative aspects of knowledge: the world from my perspective looks somewhat different from the world from my friend's perspective, or the perspective of the fly on the wall. So as has often been noted, the world looks different to a poor man than it looks to a rich man, or to a sad person than to a happy person. But these differences of perspective do not imply, as with relativism, that objective knowledge is impossible. Rather, (1) typically they illumine different and complementary elements of the objective truth. The sad person and the happy person both understand elements of the real world as God sees it. And (2) God's perspective is available to us. It is fully objective.[14]

2. NARROW MEANING

But Poythress and I have explored further the divine perspective in its unity and complexity. Since God is one God in three persons, his perspective is singular (the one perspective that governs all others) but also threefold, including the distinct perspectives of the Father, the Son, and the Holy Spirit.

The church affirms that the three persons are equal in divinity, equal in glory, equally deserving of worship. They share, therefore, the supreme divine perspective that rules all other perspectives. God's perspective rules all others, because he is himself, by very nature, *lord* over everything other than him. So his perspective is the supreme criterion over the perspectives of creatures.

But the church also affirms that the three persons are distinct from one another. They are not mere "modes" or appearances of one divine person. Rather, they are three real persons, engaging together in a divine community of love. So each performs distinct actions. The Father sent

---

13. *Cause, authority,* and *presence* is a triad of a very important kind, which I will explore later in this paper.

14. Or, in another sense, fully subjective, because it is identical with the content of God's own mind.

his Son into the world to redeem sinners (Matt. 15:24; 21:37; Mark 9:37; John 3:16, 34; 4:34; 5:23–30). The Son was crucified for us (Rom. 8:32; Eph. 5:2). The Spirit was sent to empower the church (John 14:16–17; 15:26; 16:13; 20:22; Acts 1:5). These tasks are not interchangeable. Each willingly performs his allotted role.[15]

As God is both singular and differentiated, so his lordship is both singular and differentiated. In the Bible, Father, Son, and Spirit are all sometimes designated by the divine name *Yahweh*, which English translators render as *Lord*. God's lordship is singular because it is the lordship of the one true God. But it is differentiated as well. The Father's lordship is seen particularly in that he originates the divine plan which all the universe obeys. Even the Son willingly subjects himself to the Father's plan (John 5:36; 12:49–50). And the Spirit does not bear witness to himself, but to the Son, as the Father has given him authority to speak (John 16:12–15). We may summarize this biblical teaching by speaking of the Father's lordship as *supreme authority*.

The Son's lordship is supreme as he carries out the Father's will. He carries it out perfectly, so that our salvation is certain. As such, I summarize his lordship as *control* or *power*. This is not to say that he lacks authority. He shares the authority of his Father, for he perfectly conveys the Father's will, and his Father attests what he says:

> I can do nothing on my own. As I hear, I judge, and my judgment is just, because I seek not my own will but the will of him who sent me. If I alone bear witness about myself, my testimony is not true. There is another who bears witness about me, and I know that the testimony that he bears about me is true. (John 5:30–32)

But Jesus does more than speak; he translates the Father's words into actions:

> So Jesus said to them, "Truly, truly, I say to you, the Son can do nothing of his own accord, but only what he sees the Father doing. For whatever the Father does, that the Son does likewise.

---

15. The origin of these allotments, and their relation to the eternal generation of the Son and the eternal procession of the Spirit, will have to be discussed elsewhere.

For the Father loves the Son and shows him all that he himself is doing. And greater works than these will he show him, so that you may marvel. For as the Father raises the dead and gives them life, so also the Son gives life to whom he will. The Father judges no one, but has given all judgment to the Son, that all may honor the Son, just as they honor the Father. Whoever does not honor the Son does not honor the Father who sent him." (John 5:19–23)

So the Son is one with the Father in works and words. Jesus carries out the plan of the Father, so that all might equally honor both the Father and the Son. What the Father's *authority* has planned, Jesus's *power* has accomplished.

The work of the Spirit is to take these words and works and apply them to the hearts of people. Such is the teaching of those passages I quoted above, where Jesus promises that he and the Father will send the Spirit upon the church. So as the Father's work focuses on his *authority* and the Son's on his *power*, so the Spirit's focuses on his *presence*, in and with his people. This does not mean that Father and Son are not present with God's people. Rather, the Father and Son are *in* the Spirit, and the Spirit in them, so that the Spirit's presence carries with it the presence of the Father and the Son.

So as I have indicated elsewhere, then, the *lordship* of God can be expressed as his authority, control, and presence in the world he has made.[16]

Here we note a continuing connection between presuppositionalism and perspectivalism. Both of these analytic tools focus our attention on the lordship of God. Presuppositionalism says that in all areas of life, including the intellectual, God is lord. Human thinking is a moral issue: it is either belief or unbelief. For believers, it is an aspect of discipleship. We must worship our God in the intellectual sphere as in all the others. Acknowledging the authority of God's word in the intellectual sphere is what it means to think according to God's revealed presuppositions. Apologetic conversations with nonbelievers are not occasions for setting

---

16. Frame, *DG*, 21–119; *ST*, 14–52.

aside the lordship of Christ; rather, occasions to "honor Christ the Lord as holy" (1 Pet. 3:15).

Perspectivalism explains further the nature of Christ's lordship, calling us to see all of life through his perspective, his power, authority, and presence. But there is no substantial difference between "seeing all things in the perspective of Christ's lordship" and "thinking according to the presuppositions of divine revelation." So presuppositionalism and perspectivalism coincide as descriptions of how believers should think, understand, seek knowledge, and reason.

So it is wrong to criticize perspectivalism as relativism, or to criticize presuppositionalism as an illegitimate dogmatism. Bringing these together reminds us that yes, we should respect the legitimate diversity among perspectives, but yes, these perspectives are perspectives on something objective, which is the eternal truth of our Triune God.

THE THREE PERSPECTIVES OF HUMAN KNOWLEDGE

Perspectivalism in the narrower sense, as we have seen, emerges from the biblical doctrine of the Trinity. It is useful to view the world alternately from the perspectives of the Father (authority), the Son (power or control), and the Spirit (presence). Ultimately the three vantage points coincide, because they are perspectives on the omniperspectival knowledge of God himself. But they are also distinct, because they are genuinely different vantage points or angles from which we may view our experience.

1. The Normative Perspective

I distinguish the *normative*, the *situational*, and the *existential* perspectives. The normative perspective derives from the *authority* of God the Father. As I said earlier, God did not make our minds to think autonomously. The mind, like every other aspect of human life, is subject to rules originating outside itself. Most thinkers understand that logic, at least, is a norm for thought. But human logic is an image of divine logic. And beyond logic, God sets many rules for human thinking and knowing. In general, the comprehensive rule for human thought is his *revelation* to us. God reveals himself in the entire creation (Ps. 19:1) including ourselves (Gen. 1:27–28), but especially in Scripture, which he has designated as sufficient for all of life:

> All Scripture is breathed out by God and profitable for teaching, for reproof, for correction, and for training in righteousness, that the man of God may be complete, equipped for every good work. (2 Tim. 3:16–17)

If we think according to God's word, we will always arrive at the truth, no matter what subject matter we are inquiring about. So the normative perspective does not yield only a portion of human knowledge. It yields all of it. Thinking according to God's rules is all that we need to do. So the normative perspective is a way of viewing God and everything in the creation. To gain truth, all we need to do is think according to the rules.

2. The Situational Perspective

But although the normative perspective is comprehensive and complete, it is not the only perspective. There is also a situational perspective, which derives from the *power* of God the Son:

> For by him all things were created, in heaven and on earth, visible and invisible, whether thrones or dominions or rulers or authorities—all things were created through him and for him. And he is before all things, and in him all things hold together. (Col 1:16–17, ESV)

The Son has a special role in the creation of the world (John 1:3; Heb. 1:10–12) and in the ongoing processes of nature and history. When we study the *facts* of the world around us, we are studying the creative and providential work of God the Son. Of course, the Father is also active in creation and providence, so we are talking here about two perspectives, rather than exclusive domains. To study the facts is to study the world from the situational perspective. In the end there is no difference between studying the facts of creation and studying the laws of thought. Both perspectives include everything we would want to know. To understand the facts and to think according to God's rules, these are the same thing.

3. The Existential Perspective

We encounter a third perspective when we consider the work of the
Holy Spirit. The apostle Paul says,

> [The blessings given to believers] God has revealed to us
> through the Spirit. For the Spirit searches everything, even the
> depths of God. For who knows a person's thoughts except the
> spirit of that person, which is in him? So also no one compre-
> hends the thoughts of God except the Spirit of God. Now we
> have received not the spirit of the world, but the Spirit who is
> from God, that we might understand the things freely given us
> by God. (1 Cor. 2:10–12)

The Spirit goes deep into the hearts of people and into the heart of God
as well. He communes with us, not only by communicating rules and
facts, but by communicating the very presence of God in our experience.
To gain knowledge of the world around us we must know and understand the divine presence everywhere. For God does not enlighten us
merely by teaching us rules and facts; he teaches us by revealing his
own self in our midst. What I call the existential perspective focuses on
that divine presence. It also focuses on our own subjective experience,
for the Spirit enters our very hearts and souls in order to help us see
God's truth as it really is.

Even this very deep kind of revelation is nothing different from
the normative and the situational. Ultimately the three coincide. If we
understand perfectly God's norms for knowledge and follow them to
their conclusions, they will include the deepest subjective dimensions of
our thinking hearts. And if we understand perfectly the facts that God
has created, we will understand ourselves as one of those facts. So the
normative and the situational include the existential.

And the existential includes both of them. When we understand the
workings of our inner mind, we will understand that this mind must
think according to God's rules and God's facts. So it is wrong to despise
the "subjective" as theologians often do. All knowledge is subjective in
that it occurs in the mind. So our subjective experience, rightly understood, is a gateway to all the knowledge available to us.

PERSPECTIVALISM AND
APOLOGETIC METHOD

The union of perspectivalism and presuppositionalism clarifies some continuing questions about apologetic method.

I. THE PLACE OF EVIDENCE

I mentioned earlier in this paper the continuing controversy about the role of evidence in apologetics. Some have suggested that if we believe that all apologetic argument is governed by presuppositions, there is no place in apologetics for the use of evidences. But to appeal to evidence is nothing more than appealing to the situational perspective. For example, in 1 Cor. 15, Paul deals with some in the church who did not believe in the resurrection of Jesus. To them he appealed to evidence: Jesus's appearances after his death to Peter (v. 5), to the twelve (v. 5), to five hundred brethren at once (v. 6), to James (v. 7), to all the apostles (v. 7), and, "as to one untimely born," to Paul himself (v. 8). Here Paul recites facts that were generally known in the community, facts that he hoped would persuade again those who wavered in their faith.

But this appeal to fact does not at all compromise Paul's usual presuppositionalism. He does not appeal to the facts as if they were "brute" facts. A brute fact (as apologists understand the expression) is a fact without interpretation, or a fact available for autonomous human analysis. A brute fact, supposedly, is a fact that can be rightly understood without biblical presuppositions. But there are no brute facts in these senses, and Paul does not appeal to them.

Paul's appeal to testimony is consistent with a biblical form of reasoning. The eighteenth-century philosopher David Hume said there was no testimony strong enough to establish a supernatural event. To Hume, when something strange took place, it was always more likely that there was a natural explanation than that there was a supernatural one. So Hume systematically disbelieved all testimony intended to validate miraculous events. But Paul did not operate with an epistemology like Hume's. Rather, he believed in the biblical worldview, in which all nature and history proceeds according to God's plan. In that worldview, God's revelation is the ultimate interpretation of human experience. God often reveals himself, and his interpretations, through chosen representatives who testify as to what God has done. So human testimony to supernatural events is a normal part of human knowledge.

Paul himself offers such testimony. Not only does he testify to the appearance of Jesus to him personally, but he presents his whole case on his own authority as a divinely appointed church planter. In 1 Cor. 15, the underlying reason why the Corinthians are to accept the testimonies of the risen Christ is the fact that the resurrection of Jesus is part of the preaching by which Paul planted the church. He says,

> Now I would remind you, brothers, of the gospel I preached
> to you, which you received, in which you stand, and by which
> you are being saved, if you hold fast to the word I preached to
> you—unless you believed in vain. (1 Cor. 15:1–2; cf. vv. 3, 11, 12)

Paul says the Corinthians should believe the testimonies of those who saw the risen Jesus. And they should believe these testimonies because they are part of Paul's preaching: they are part of the word of God. And the word of God is the believer's presupposition.

So we appeal to facts because they are warranted by our presupposition. And (perspectivally speaking) we believe the presupposition because it is factual and because it presents the facts in their true light.

2. THE PLACE OF EXPERIENCE

The "argument from experience" has been part of apologetics for many years. William James, William Alston, and others have explored the claims of people to have experienced God directly and have sought to evaluate these claims. But many apologists of different schools of thought, presuppositional and otherwise, have criticized the argument from experience as subjective and vague.

Of course, it often happens that people present their subjective experience to validate their faith or even their doctrinal contentions, without any kind of cogent argument. "Fideism" is a name given to an apologetic that relies on mere feeling, without evidence or argument.

But there is a sense in which it is legitimate to appeal to one's own subjectivity in an apologetic argument. Indeed, there is a sense in which subjective evidence is the only evidence there is. For knowledge itself is a subjective event. It takes place inside us, in our minds, in our heads. When an argument appeals to presuppositions, it is to presuppositions that we have acknowledged in our heart. When an argument appeals to facts, it is to facts that we have acknowledged subjectively.

That is to say that presuppositions, facts, and subjective experience represent the three perspectives I described earlier. Presuppositions represent the normative perspective, facts the situational, and subjective experience the existential. And these three perspectives coincide as ways to look at the world and understand it. As I have indicated, to know the normative perspective completely is to know everything. Same for the situational and the existential. For each of these perspectives includes the other two.

Our "subjective experience" represents the existential perspective. Rightly understood, that existential perspective is a perspective on all knowledge. As we analyze the data within our minds, we come to see that these data cannot be understood apart from biblical norms (normative perspective) and the facts of God's creation (situational perspective). Fideism ignores these necessary relationships. So when someone claims he can warrant faith by his mere subjective feelings, without norms or evidence, he has failed, not only to understand the norms and evidence; he has failed to understand rightly his own subjectivity. If he had understood his own subjectivity rightly, he would have seen that he cannot understand his experience without the right norms and facts. Our subjectivity is a *perspective* on knowledge, not a standalone source of knowledge that conflicts with presuppositions and facts.

SUMMARY

I have argued in this paper (1) that presuppositionalism requires perspectivalism, for it requires us to see our own thinking as subject to God's. His thought is infinite and omniperspectival, while ours is finite and necessarily limited to our own perspectives. (2) Presuppositionalism requires perspectivalism, because it sets forth God's thought as the authoritative norm for ours and therefore as our normative perspective. (3) Perspectivalism clarifies presuppositionalism, for it shows how human thinking involves an understanding of facts and human subjectivity, as well as divine norms. (4) Perspectivalism shows the true role of evidence and subjective experience in presuppositional apologetics.

54

Ten Problems with Presuppositionalism

*Some years ago, an internet writer challenged me to address some
problems he had formulated. Here they are, with my responses. I have
elaborated those responses since the initial exchange.*

*1. Presuppositionalism denies the biblical assumption of the public nature of
the truth of the gospel.*

There are, of course, different kinds of presuppositionalists. I cannot
speak for all of them. I myself am closest to Van Til and Bahnsen. I
don't believe that either of them said anything in conflict with the public
nature of the truth of the gospel. It is clear that Scripture refers to public
events—the history of Israel, the events of Jesus's earthly ministry, his
cross and resurrection, the apostolic expansion of the church. Many of
these events were miraculous, and Scripture (as in 1 Cor. 15) stresses
the public nature of the events and the testimony about them. Van
Til always insisted that factual evidences were an important aspect of
apologetics. But of course he also insisted that these evidences be presented in the context of a biblical epistemology, not as a conclusion of
autonomous thinking.

Van Til emphasized also Paul's teaching of Acts 14:17 and Rom.
1:18–21 that the existence of God is clearly, inescapably, revealed in the
created world. This is an *emphasis* of presuppositional apologetics, not

a mere concession. So for the presuppositionalist, the truth of God and of Christ is highly public. But as Rom. 1:18 says, even this public truth is "suppressed" by unbelievers. We can deal with that suppression only with the gospel of God's saving grace, that is, by interpreting this truth by God's revealed presuppositions.

2. Presuppositionalism alters the task of evangelism from presenting the apostolic case for Jesus as Lord to the task of persuading people to accept the general tenets of Christian belief.

I know of no presuppositionalist who fails to present Jesus as a historical figure who taught, worked miracles, and rose from the dead. Nor do I understand the contrast you draw between "the apostolic case" and the "general tenets of Christian belief." We can agree that the gospel focuses on what Jesus said and did, and particularly his death and resurrection. But in the present age, nobody should question the fact that we must also set forth the biblical worldview: creator/creature, revelation, etc. Many people don't understand the gospel story, because they come at the facts with an unbiblical epistemology. Paul says that Jesus's resurrection is validated by 500 people who witnessed the resurrection together. A powerful piece of evidence, surely. But when you tell people that today, some will reply, "Well, David Hume taught us that there is NO believable testimony about a supernatural event; because it is always more probable that an event has a natural explanation than a supernatural explanation." At this point, the Christian must say something about Hume, or general epistemology. We must make sure that the evidence for Jesus must be understood on a biblical epistemology, not a Humean or deconstructionist one.

3. Presuppositionalism adopts a coherence rather than correspondence account of truth which is assumed in Scripture and by our God-given, common sense.

Scripture and common sense do not accept a "correspondence account of truth" as opposed to a coherence or pragmatic theory. Scripture and common sense don't endorse theories; rather they provide part of the basis for theories. The correspondence theory is one attempt to formulate the way we know things, but it is philosophically controversial. In my *DKG* I argue that correspondence, coherence, and pragmatics, in their best form, are not incompatible with one another, and, indeed, reduce to one another. We cannot tell what our ideas "correspond" to unless we have a system of ideas that deals with various things including the concept of correspondence itself. But certainly the correspondence theory is right in saying that our ideas must align with the facts of the world.

4. Presuppositionalism is a relatively new, twentieth-century doctrine, philosophical in nature and unknown to the apostles and prophets through whom God gave us the Scriptures.

The apostles and prophets were not philosophers, so they did not develop philosophical theories of knowledge. But of course later theological reflection legitimately tries to analyze and apply the implications of what the apostles and prophets taught. So theologians talk about the "Trinity," though you will not find that term in the Bible. The question is whether the idea of the Trinity is consistent with what the Bible teaches and whether it helps us in understanding the Father, Son, and Spirit. Same with epistemological theories. The Bible doesn't mention presuppositions (nor does it mention coherence or correspondence—see #3 above), let alone presuppositionalism, but many of us have made the case that presuppositionalism is helpful in formulating what is implicit in the biblical doctrine, e.g., of revelation.

5. Presuppositionalism, as a doctrinal mixture of philosophy and Christian Reformed theology, violates a cardinal principle which is perhaps most distinctive to that theology, namely, sola Scriptura *(or Scripture alone as the basis for our faith and practice).*

Presuppositionalism seeks to show precisely why and how we must base our teaching on Scripture alone. You may prefer "correspondence" or "evidentialism" or "classical apologetics." But those systems are no less philosophical than presuppositionalism, and they are no less controversial. All of them go beyond Scripture in the *language* they use. All of them seek to defend *sola Scriptura*. What presuppositionalism says about *sola Scriptura* is that we should develop our doctrines in a way that renounces autonomy and recognizes only Scripture as the foundation of human thinking.

6. *Presuppositionalism boldly recasts what the Bible says is fundamentally a problem of sin as a problem of knowing.*

No. Sin affects every area of human life, including knowing. The fall affected the *thought* of Adam and Eve, not just their actions. Evil actions, indeed, flowed from evil thoughts. So Paul says that sinful man "represses the truth in unrighteousness" (Rom. 1). The gospel reorients both our thoughts and our actions to serve Jesus as Lord.

7. *Presuppositionalism claims that apart from regeneration in Christ and the Scriptures people cannot know or convey truth truly or objectively.*

Romans 1 tells us that non-believers know God clearly from the things he has made. So in fact they CAN know truth truly and objectively without being regenerated. So Jesus commends the teaching of the Pharisees, telling us to believe what they say, but not to do what they do. The problem is not so much with their knowledge as with what they do with it. Paul says that these nonbelievers "suppress the truth in unrighteousness." So that actually their thinking is a mess. Sometimes the truth they know bubbles up, and they admit it while seeking to minimize its force; other times they deny what they know deep in their hearts. Only regeneration in Christ and the Scriptures can restrain this suppression of the truth.

8. *Presuppositionalism weakens by implication the church's public stance for truth.*

On the "public stance," see my answer to question one. Since the events of salvation were public events, the apostles proclaimed them in public. We should do the same today, and no presuppositionalist denies this.

9. *Presuppositionalism indirectly confirms the relativism of our age by affirming that truth is relative to Christian presuppositions.*

Not true. Presuppositionalism emphasizes strongly that the gospel is objective. It is that truth that all people must acknowledge. Now of course, when someone comes to the gospel with ungodly presuppositions, he can make it look bad. In that situation (as in the case of Hume, question two above) we insist that the objective truth must be understood by the objectively true biblical epistemology. God has revealed in history who Jesus is and what he has done. He has also revealed (objectively) how we should think about it. It is not very helpful to say that truth is "relative to Christian presuppositions," though with sufficient analysis that statement can be affirmed. Better to say that truth is objectively fixed in the mind of God, and that we must believe it as God has revealed it to us.

10. Presuppositionalism burdens uneducated (and even educated) persons in the church both here in America and throughout the world with obscure problems about knowledge or truth that they are in no position to understand or evaluate.

Presuppositionalism is no less philosophical or technical than any other epistemology. It raises no problems that rationalism, empiricism, correspondence, coherence, and pragmatism don't also raise. It just answers those questions differently. It does not require uneducated people to study philosophy. It only points out that anyone who wants to be a disciple of Jesus must apply his lordship to all areas of his life. If you are a telephone lineman, you should do that to the glory of God. If you are a homemaker, the same. If you are a philosopher, then you should seek to do that to God's glory. But there is no reason why everyone must be a philosopher, any more than that everyone should be a homemaker. But whatever your calling, you must carry it out to the glory of God (1 Cor. 10:31). And if you do, you will be thinking presuppositionally even if you don't know what presuppositionalism is.

55

Cornelius Van Til

This is a biographical entry written for inclusion in Wiley-Blackwell's
Dictionary of Christian Apologists and Their Critics (*forthcoming*).

VAN TIL was born in 1895 in Grootegast, the Netherlands. His parents were dairy farmers. At the age of ten, Cornelius moved with his family to Highland, Indiana. He was the first in his family to receive a formal higher education. The Van Tils were members of the Christian Reformed Church, which maintained Dutch Calvinist traditions in theology and worship. Specifically, they honored the work of Abraham Kuyper (1837–1920), who led the Dutch Christians of his day in many fields: he wrote theology and philosophy, founded a university, founded a newspaper, engaged in politics, becoming prime minister of the Netherlands from 1901 to 1905, and led many to form a new denomination which opposed the liberalism of the existing Reformed church. More narrowly focused on theology was Kuyper's friend Herman Bavinck (1854–1921), whose four-volume *Reformed Dogmatics* became the greatest theological influence among conservative Calvinists, both in the Netherlands and in the US.

Kuyper is famous for saying, in his inaugural address as a professor, "Oh, no single piece of our mental world is to be hermetically sealed off from the rest, and there is not a square inch in the whole domain of our human existence over which Christ, who is Sovereign over *all*, does not cry: 'Mine!' "[17] This view determined the emphasis of Kuyper's followers, that all human endeavors, not just worship and theology, should be brought captive to Christ. So there developed in the Netherlands Christian schools and universities, Christian newspapers, Christian political parties, etc., in addition to churches. Of course, competing with these were parallel institutions representing other religious and philosophical viewpoints. Kuyper's vision was that all of these institutions would receive equal government support, while being free to advocate and apply their own worldviews.

So in the US the Christian Reformed Church sponsored a full complement of Christian schools from elementary through high school, and then Calvin College and Calvin Theological Seminary. Van Til's education followed this course until after his first year of seminary. He then determined to leave Calvin Seminary to attend Princeton Theological Seminary. Princeton in those days was firmly committed, as was Calvin, to the historic Reformed faith. But Calvin's history was Dutch and Kuyperian, while Princeton's was Scottish and American. Famous Princeton professors included Charles and A. A. Hodge and B. B. Warfield (arguably the greatest theological scholar America had produced). These were deceased by the time Van Til arrived at Princeton. But J. Gresham Machen taught New Testament there, who became a famous defender of orthodox Christianity and was to have a large influence on Van Til. Van Til was also a good friend and student of Geerhardus Vos, who established at Princeton the discipline of biblical theology. Like Van Til, Vos had entered Princeton from a Dutch Calvinist background.

Princeton appreciated Kuyper's work. The school had brought Kuyper to give its Stone Lectures in 1898.[18] But in philosophy and apologetics, the fields Van Til was most interested in, Princeton's approach

---

17. Kuyper, *Sphere Sovereignty*, 488, cited in James D. Bratt, ed., *Abraham Kuyper: A Centennial Reader* (Grand Rapids, MI: Eerdmans, 1998).

18. These lectures were published as *Calvinism: Six Lectures Delivered in the Theological Seminary at Princeton* (New York: Fleming H. Revell, 1899). They serve as an excellent, concise introduction to Kuyper's thought.

was different from that of Kuyper and Bavinck. To the Dutch thinkers, the great danger in these fields was the temptation to think autonomously, to reason outside the boundaries of Scripture. But the Princetonians were primarily interested in fighting the danger of anti-intellectualism. The Hodges and Warfield emphasized that Christianity was capable of rational defense, and that because of the doctrine of general revelation even unbelievers could become aware of its truth. Disciples of Kuyper and Bavinck worried that the "rational defense" of the Princetonians would encourage autonomous rationalism. In this controversy, Van Til sided with the Dutch. But he came to believe that rejecting autonomy did not preclude rational defense; indeed, he thought, the only truly rational way of defending Christianity was to renounce autonomy and to begin with divine revelation as the ultimate presupposition of human knowledge. For human reason itself requires a foundation in God and therefore in Scripture.

Van Til was a philosopher as well as a theologian, which led him to formulate a theological foundation for reason itself. Shortly after his seminary work, he earned a Ph. D. from Princeton University (an institution separate from Princeton Seminary). There he studied philosophy, advised by Prof. A. A. Bowman. His main field of study was philosophical idealism. Modern idealism is associated particularly with G. W. F. Hegel (1770–1831); but Van Til focused on later English idealists such as T. H. Green, F. H. Bradley, and Bernard Bosanquet. These thinkers emphasized that human knowledge is not an accumulation of "brute facts," but begins with "presuppositions." Our presuppositions determine the perspectives through which we interpret the facts of experience. Van Til rejected the pantheist and/or secularist presuppositions usually assumed in the idealist philosophical community. But he made it his life project to explore the importance of *Christian* presuppositions for human thought.

After the completion of his academic work in 1927, Van Til spent one year as pastor of the Christian Reformed Church in Spring Lake, MI, a work which he deeply enjoyed. He took a leave of absence from the pastorate to teach apologetics at Princeton Seminary during the academic year 1928–29. At the end of that year, the seminary offered him the chair of apologetics (in effect, a full professorship). Van Til declined that offer and returned to Spring Lake. He strongly desired to remain in the pastorate, and in addition he did not wish to cooperate with the reorganization of Princeton Seminary which had been mandated that spring by the General Assembly of the Presbyterian Church in the USA. The reorganization was intended to purge the seminary's historic stand for orthodox Calvinism and make the school more representative of "all the points of view found in the church." To be included were the points of view of the thirteen hundred ministers who in 1924 had signed the notorious Auburn Affirmation, which declared the doctrines of biblical inspiration, the virgin birth of Christ, his substitutionary atonement, his bodily resurrection, and his literal second coming to be humanly formulated theories, to which candidates for ministry would no longer be required to subscribe.

However, there were those in the Presbyterian Church in the USA. who sought to fight against the unbelief growing throughout the denomination and the church at large. The most notable of these was J. Gresham Machen, Van Til's friend and Professor of New Testament at Princeton Seminary. Van Til admired Machen's scholarship, his ability to articulate the truth, and his stand for orthodox doctrine. Most everything Van Til taught and wrote reflects Machen's theme that orthodox doctrine is indispensable to a Christian profession. The great doctrines of the faith are not human inventions, but the teachings of God himself to us in his word. Indeed, Van Til went one step beyond Machen, seeking to show that orthodox Christianity is, in one sense, a necessary presupposition for any rational speech and conduct.

Machen and some other professors left Princeton in the wake of the reorganization, and eventually Van Til joined them to form Westminster Seminary in Philadelphia, a seminary dedicated to Reformed orthodoxy and independent of any denomination. In 1936, Machen and several other orthodox men were suspended from the ministry of the Presbyterian Church U. S. A. He and 130 other ministers founded a new denomination, originally called the Presbyterian Church of America, but later forced to change its name under legal threat. They became the Orthodox Presbyterian Church. In sympathy, Van Til transferred his membership from the Christian Reformed Church to that body, where he remained until his death in 1987.

Through his career, Van Til influenced many at Westminster and elsewhere to adopt a "presuppositional" method in apologetics. That movement influenced many thinkers, but did not come to dominate the apologetics of the evangelical and Reformed churches. So Van Til spent much of his time attempting to refute rival apologetic methods, particularly what he called the traditional method influenced by Thomas Aquinas and Joseph Butler.

The heart of Van Til's philosophy and apologetics is this epistemological claim: human knowledge in any field presupposes the revelation of God. For this claim, he cites two reasons: (1) Since God created all things and man in his image, nothing can be rightly understood apart from God. (2) The sin into which human beings fell corrupts their thinking as well as all their other activity. Unless one is regenerated by the Holy Spirit, he will "suppress the truth" (Rom. 1:18). Regeneration, the new birth, installs in the human mind a new disposition, a new presupposition that enables a person to stop this suppression and to think rightly. These claims are based on Scripture and Reformed theology, particularly the doctrines of divine sovereignty and total depravity.

So for Van Til, apologetics is never a neutral discipline, in which we lay aside our presuppositions and try to reason with non-Christians on common ground. For Van Til, there is no common ground. Echoing Kuyper's famous "square inch" manifesto, Van Til argues that nothing at all can be intelligibly understood unless we presuppose the revelation of God in Scripture. Of course, many *try* to understand the world apart from God's revelation. Van Til's apologetics seeks to show that such a task is impossible.

Van Til was, of course, referring primarily to knowledge of ultimate meaning. He acknowledged that by common grace non-Christians were able to accept simple truths like "the sky is blue." But they utterly fail, he said, to understand the larger issues of eternal importance. And those matters of eternal importance often affect their immediate knowledge of practical matters like government and technology.

Van Til used many tactics to prove his thesis. Some have complained that there is no place in Van Til's system for the consideration of evidences, since for Van Til the presupposition of revelation is the foundation of evidence and therefore in a sense prior to evidence. But Van Til spoke positively about the importance of evidence. He believed that an examination of evidence unquestionably points to the truth of God's revelation for the very reason that it cannot be understood apart from the truth of that revelation. Similarly, Van Til sought, as Christian apologists have always done, to reveal logical inconsistencies in non-Christian positions and arguments. So Van Til's thought is like the traditional apologetics in that it examines evidences and logical consistency. But it examines these data in a fresh and unusual way. Van Til does not argue straightforwardly that evidence or logical consistency proves the truth of Christianity, as does the "traditional apologetic." Rather, he seeks to show that the very concepts of evidence and logic are unintelligible if the biblical God does not exist.

In an apologetic debate, Van Til tries to show that without God, human reasoning is nothing more than a chance occurrence. But if human reasoning is based on chance, and if reasoning itself is a chance event, we have no basis for thinking that it enables us to understand reality. He gives examples of this intellectual frustration in the history of philosophy.[19] In each case of non-Christian philosophy, Van Til shows a "rationalist-irrationalist dialectic." The philosopher, rejecting God's revelation, seeks to reason autonomously, that is, as a rationalist. He presupposes, then, that his reasoning is the only way to truth, that it is thoroughly competent and self-sufficient. But inevitably he discovers mysteries that his autonomous reason cannot account for. So he retreats to a second presupposition, the presupposition that the world itself is irrational, governed in the end by chance.

---

19. Many apologists write for unsophisticated readers. Van Til sometimes addresses these too, as in his pamphlet, "Why I Believe in God" (now available at https://reformed .org/apologetics/index.html?mainframe=/apologetics/why_I_believe_cvt.html). But most of Van Til's argumentation is addressed to professional philosophers, on the assumption that if an apologist can refute thinkers most famous for their intellectual achievements, he will simultaneously refute the lesser thinkers whose work is derived from the philosophers.

This dilemma creates many problems for the non-Christian thinker: (1) Rationalism and irrationalism are inconsistent. The world cannot be both accessible to autonomous reason and governed by pure chance. (2) The non-Christian has no rational basis for affirming his rationalism; so his rationalism is based on irrationalism. (3) He adopts his irrationalism because of his rationalism, that is, because he thinks his autonomous rationalism gives him a license to deny the rationality of the universe. So his irrationalism is based on rationalism. So the principles of rationalism and irrationalism are inconsistent with one another; yet each requires the other to warrant itself. Both rationalism and irrationalism are necessary presuppositions of thinking that excludes an absolute-personal God; but these two presuppositions defeat one another.

Some non-Christian philosophers seek to be pure rationalists, others pure irrationalists. Parmenides is a textbook rationalist; but his rationalism proves a universe vastly different from the universe we experience, a university without change, diversity, origination, or corruption. So Parmenides concedes that our practical life must be based on a non-rational worldview. Protagoras is a textbook irrationalist, arguing that there is no universal truth; but his only basis for saying this is his autonomous rationality. So both Parmenides and Protagoras are both rationalists and irrationalists, caught in a contradiction that robs their thought of intelligibility.

Van Til points out that some thinkers, aware of the problems noted above, tried to be rationalists in one part of their worldview, irrationalists in another. Plato, for example, thought that the world of our experience is irrational, and could be understood only through a world of "forms" that is perfectly rational. The forms, he thought, were the source of the world of experience and its ultimate explanation. But, Van Til points out, the forms are incapable of explaining the irrationalities of experience, since they are supposed to be perfectly rational. In the end, the irrationalities of experience are the result of pure chance, and the rationality of the forms cannot connect with our experience.

Van Til summed up non-Christian philosophy by saying that it attempts to impose a rational scheme on an irrational world, an impossible task, resulting in an unintelligible worldview. He was also critical of the traditional apologetics for compromising with non-Christian philosophies in similar ways. And he brought the same critique against some professedly Christian theology: the liberalism against which Machen fought; the neo-orthodoxy of Barth and Brunner; the attempts of Roman Catholic thinkers (and, more recently, of Protestant thinkers as well) to accommodate the Scriptures to the Aristotelian philosophy of Thomas Aquinas.

Van Til encountered many criticisms of his presuppositional apologetics. The most common was the claim that Van Til's argument is viciously circular: that is, it presupposes what it purports to prove, namely the reality of God and the truth of his revelation. Van Til replied that although circular argument is usually a bad thing, it is unavoidable when one seeks to argue for an ultimate ground of reasoning. Non-Christian worldviews, he said, are circular in the same way that the Christian worldview is. For example, when a non-Christian rationalist argues in defense of his rationalism, he will inevitably offer a rational argument, appealing to reason in defense of reason. Since reason is his highest principle, he has no other choice. Similarly, an idealist must appeal to the idealist worldview in supporting idealism. And the same is true of religious worldviews: a Muslim must appeal in the end to his highest authority, the Koran.

But, for Van Til, this does not mean that Christian and non-Christian worldviews have identical weaknesses. For non-Christian worldviews, he says, fall prey to the rationalist-irrationalist dialectic and therefore cannot even be stated coherently.

On this fundamental point, I believe that Van Til's apologetics is unassailable. The main weakness of his work, in my judgment, was his tendency to interpret other writers, especially rival Christian apologists, in the worst possible way, without much attempt to be sympathetic. In person, Van Til was exceedingly gracious and kind; but his writings were often unnecessarily shrill. I believe that with a bit more empathy, Van Til might have seen that his Christian opponents in fact presupposed the same things he presupposed—the reality of God and the truth of Scripture—though they compromised that presupposition with their rhetoric about reasoning on common ground with unbelievers. Van Til saw a great divide, an antithesis, between his presuppositionalism and the traditional apologetics. Scripture, on the contrary, places the antithesis between belief and unbelief.

Van Til's apologetic is especially relevant to the challenges faced by Christian thinkers today. It is very plain that both rationalism and irrationalism can be found in present day unbelief. Many modern thinkers, such as the "new atheists," Dawkins, Dennett, Hitchens, et al., believe that autonomous science alone is the way to truth, and that religious convictions should be radically excluded. Van Til would identify this movement as "rationalism," and would point out that these atheists have no non-circular way of defending unbelieving science as the one way to truth. Same with those who adopt autonomous irrationalism, particularly postmodernists like Lyotard, Derrida, and Foucault: they can defend their irrationalism only by presupposing the validity of their autonomous powers of reason.[20] And then there are also modern thinkers who, like Plato, seek to delineate what parts of the universe are accessible to reason and which ones are not. Examples would include Immanuel Kant and his followers. But their thought fails as Plato's did, since it is unable to cogently define this distinction without adopting a self-refuting affirmation of human intellectual autonomy. As in Van Til's day, so today, rationalism presupposes irrationalism and vice versa.

Van Til is today considered the founder of "presuppositionalist"[21] apologetics, but there are others who have been called by that name. One is Gordon H. Clark (1902–1985). Clark and Van Til were friends and mutual supporters during the 1930s, but a rift developed between them in the next decade. Van Til and some of his followers complained against the ordination of Clark to the ministry of the Orthodox

---

20. Postmodernists typically accept rational accounts for the experiences of daily life, but they renounce "grand narratives" or metaphysical accounts that claim to include all of reality. But their own epistemology, both its negations and its affirmations, is itself a grand narrative, claiming to deal with all philosophical and epistemological questions.

21. "Presuppositionalist" was not Van Til's chosen term to describe his work; it originated among his critics. But he did sometimes apply it to himself.

Presbyterian Church, on the ground that Clark failed to honor the creator/creature distinction in the areas of language and logic. Clark believed that God's mind contained the same concepts, propositions, and words as are contained in human thinking at its best. Otherwise, he argued, we are doomed to skepticism. He said that unless there is an identity of content between divine and human minds, human knowledge is impossible, for if we have knowledge at all it must be identical with the knowledge of God's own mind. Van Til considered this view rationalistic and insisted that there can be no identity between anything in God's mind and anything in man's.

I believe that in this controversy Van Til and Clark talked past one another. Despite his emphasis on divine-human discontinuity, Van Til did believe that God and man have common factual beliefs. Similarly, Clark, despite his emphasis on continuity, believed that God and man think according to different "modes." In these concessions, as I see it, both Van Til and Clark granted the essence of the other's position. Unfortunately, the atmosphere of controversy, especially church politics, drove the two men to a place where both interpreted one another in the most negative possible way and almost obsessively refused to see any truth in the other's position. Though both men have gone to glory (and therefore have been reconciled) each has many disciples who maintain the debate in its original terms, without any further analysis, neither side making any concessions whatever.

Clark did accept the label "presuppositionalist" more readily than Van Til did. But Van Til insisted that the whole revelation of God was the necessary presupposition of human knowledge. Clark, trying to avoid the apparent circularity of this position (see above), appealed to human logic (identical, as he saw it, with God's logic) as the infallible way to truth. His argument was that only the Christian worldview is, in the final analysis, logically consistent; and non-Christian alternatives are always inconsistent in one way or another. To Van Til, Clark failed to recognize (1) that human logical systems have erred and that therefore none is equivalent to the logic of God's mind, and (2) that on a Christian worldview, logical reasoning is not the only path to truth;

rather all of God's revelation correlates with all our created human faculties to draw us toward God.

Edward John Carnell (1919–1967), a student of Van Til, was also called a "presuppositionalist." Carnell reproduced much of Van Til's emphasis on how human thought must presuppose God's revelation in order to obtain truth. But for Carnell, we adopt this presupposition by entertaining it first as a hypothesis, then seeking to verify that hypothesis through sense experience, logic, and inner subjectivity, that is, by what Carnell called "systematic consistency." He denied Van Til's claim that these verification faculties themselves needed to presuppose God's revelation.

Francis Schaeffer (1912–1984) was also a student of Van Til. An evangelist rather than an academic, he nevertheless sought to deal with serious epistemological issues. Like Carnell, he taught that God's revelation must be the fundamental presupposition of human thought, but (also like Carnell) he focused on evidences and logic more than Van Til did, with a particular emphasis on aesthetics.

Other students of Van Til maintained his ideas in a purer form. One was Greg Bahnsen (1948–1995). Bahnsen offered no substantial criticisms of Van Til, but applied Van Til's ideas to various issues and thinkers in a philosophically sophisticated way. And he sought to train younger apologists to take presuppositional apologetics "to the streets." Scott Oliphint, one of Van Til's current successors as Professor of Apologetics at Westminster Theological Seminary, also emphasizes the need to maintain Van Til's original ideas and emphases. William Edgar, another Professor of Apologetics at Westminster, maintains Van Til's emphases, combining them with a rich understanding of aesthetics and modern culture. Edgar is greatly influenced by Schaeffer, but believes that Van Til was closer to the truth when he and Schaeffer disagreed. James Anderson, Professor of Philosophy at Reformed Theological Seminary in Charlotte, NC, makes creative use of Van Til's ideas in his own work and manages the website "Van Til Info."[22] My own writings (see below) accept Van Til's main con-

---

22. http://www.vantil.info/. This site maintains a large collection of titles of books and articles that interact with Van Til's thought.

tentions and seek to apply them to contemporary issues, but they also criticize Van Til in some details, as I have above.

Van Til's work continues to be very important, for it seeks not only to be logical, accurate, and persuasive, but also, above all, to be Christian. Apologetics has often been an attempt by Christians to achieve a reputation for academic respectability. But this attempt has regularly led to apologetic and evangelistic failure. Van Til, though he held impeccable academic credentials and developed impressive logical and exegetical arguments, refused the goal of meeting the standards of the academic establishment. He sought above all to be true to the teachings of the word of God. If his critics seek to refute his position, they will have to argue with him on the basis of Scripture far more than they have done.

BIBLIOGRAPHY

PRIMARY SOURCES

Van Til, Cornelius. *Christian Apologetics*. Ed. William Edgar. Phillipsburg, NJ: P&R Publishers, 2003.

———. *The Defense of the Faith*. Ed. K. Scott Oliphint. Phillipsburg, NJ: P&R Publishers, 2008.

———. *An Introduction to Systematic Theology*. Ed. William Edgar. Phillipsburg, NJ: P&R Publishers, 2007.

———. *The New Modernism*. Phillipsburg, NJ: P&R Publishers, 1973.

———. *Christianity and Barthianism*. Phillipsburg, NJ: P&R Publishers, 2004.

———. *Christian-Theistic Evidences*. Ed. K. Scott Oliphint. Phillipsburg, NJ: P&R Publishers, 2016.

———. *Cornelius Van Til Audio Library*. Labels Army, 1997; now available from Logos Bible Software.

———. E. D. Bristley, and E. R. Geehan. *The Works of Cornelius Van Til*. 39 vols. Labels Army Co., available from Logos Bible Software.

SECONDARY SOURCES

Bahnsen, Greg. *Van Til's Apologetics*. Phillipsburg, NJ: P&R Publishers, 1998.

Frame, John M. *Cornelius Van Til: An Analysis of His Thought.* Phillipsburg, NJ: P&R Publishers, 1995.

——. *A History of Western Philosophy and Theology.* Phillipsburg, NJ: P&R Publishers, 2015.

——. *The Doctrine of the Knowledge of God.* Phillipsburg, NJ: P&R Publishers, 1987.

FURTHER READING

I'm not sure how to distinguish "Further Reading" from "Bibliography." But if someone wants to continue and deepen his study of Van Til, I would suggest the following course:

Bahnsen, Greg. *Van Til's Apologetics.* Phillipsburg, NJ: P&R Publishers, 1998.

Frame, John M. *Cornelius Van Til: An Analysis of His Thought.* Phillipsburg, NJ: P&R Publishers, 1995.

Cowan, Steven, ed. *Five Views of Apologetics.* Grand Rapids: Zondervan, 2000.

Bristley, Eric D. *A Guide to the Writings of Cornelius Van Til.* Spokane, WA: Olive Tree Communications, 1995.

Frame, John M. *Apologetics: A Justification of Christian Belief.* Ed. Joseph Torres. Phillipsburg: P&R Publications, 2015.

——. *Christianity Considered: A Guide for Skeptics and Seekers.* Bellingham, WA: Lexham Press, 2018.

56

Transcendental Argument

A friend asked me to define the precise point at which I disagreed with Greg Bahnsen about Van Til's "Transcendental Argument." Before his last trip to the hospital, where he died, Greg wrote me, affirming our friendship. However, he ended the letter, "But I still disagree with you about the transcendental argument." Quintessential Bahnsen. I replied to my friend as follows:

AS FOR TRANSCENDENTAL ARGUMENT (which Van Til more typically called "presuppositional argument"), my most thorough discussion of that is in my *Apologetics*, the second edition (2015), chapter four (67ff). That's a fairly technical discussion, and I really cannot handle that sort of thing any more. But when you boil it all down, my main concern about that was the same as in *Evangelical Reunion*. I thought that CVT (Bahnsen and Collett followed him) was introducing a new, unnecessary division into the church. I am always suspicious of division in the church, both between and within denominations. CVT had introduced a division among Calvinists between Van Tillian and non–Van Tillian Calvinists. I thought that of course there were some differences between Van Tillians and non–Van Tillians, but that difference should not have been turned into a war. A few points important to me:

1. All Christians are presuppositionalists, in that we all treat the Scriptures as the highest authority, and we judge every other authority by the Bible.

2. All Christians are "evidentialists" in that we believe in general revelation.

3. All apologists believe in transcendental argument, believing that Scripture establishes the presuppositions of intelligibility.

4. All apologists try to DEMONSTRATE that #3 is true, by showing how this or that presupposes God.

5. "X presupposes God" is logically equivalent to "X implies God and non-X implies God."

6. So presuppositional-transcendental argument is equivalent to the "implication" of traditional apologetics.

7. So the difference between Van Tillian and traditional apologists is that the former take more seriously the presuppositional side of this equivalence, and the latter take more seriously the importance of #4.

8. Between these two EMPHASES, there is room for mutual exhortation back and forth. But the difference between them does not warrant breaking into two warring factions, nor the ugly insults exchanged back and forth.

57

My Last Word on the Van Til Controversy

Taken from a Facebook thread by someone who thinks Van Til is guilty of circular argument, therefore that we should adopt a "classical" (i.e., Thomistic) apologetic method. He also thinks I am a "fideist," i.e., somebody who thinks you should not argue rationally for the Christian faith, but rather just believe, without any reason at all.

THE FOLLOWING is my last word on the subject. (1) "Circular" is confusing. The only point important to presuppositionalists is that any worldview must make its final appeal to a principle consistent with itself. (2) All theistic arguments must presuppose epistemologies consistent with theism. (3) I don't use the term "classical" for an apologetic which rests on Aristotelian philosophy. (4) I don't think I'm a fideist, because I believe there are valid and sound reasons for faith.

58

Foreword to *Thinking through Creation*, by Chris Watkin

READERS who approach this book with a background in Reformed and presuppositional thought will find much that is familiar here. Watkin ably argues the proposition that Scripture presents not only a way of salvation but a distinctive worldview—a philosophy in which God is creator-Lord and the world is his creature-servant. Only this biblical worldview presents the supreme being as simultaneously absolute and personal. This God is transcendent, not in the sense that he is limited to a realm beyond ours and cannot be known, but in the sense that he is fully able to exert supreme power within the world he has made. And therefore he is also immanent, not as a mere spiritual haze within experience, but as a personal being who creates relationships with human beings and directs nature and history toward his personal goals. If God were an impersonal force, then the meaning of the universe would reduce to power. But because he is personal, even tri-personal, the deepest truth of the universe is to be found in personal relationships—indeed, in love.

Watkin also expounds the implications of the doctrine of the Trinity, the original loving relationship. Like Van Til, he finds the Trinity to be the root of all one-and-many relationships in the universe.

But Watkin carries this discussion further than have his predecessors. In chapter two, Watkin shows the importance of God creating by his *word*, so that formlessness and emptiness are filled by form and content, resulting in a world that is "unnecessarily diverse and abundant." That "unnecessary" abundance shows that the world is not only an object of science, wonderful as that is, but also a place of beauty and art than inspires the great aesthetic gifts of mankind. The world's diversity is a diversity of ways in which the very richness of God's own nature, his *goodness*, is displayed in the world. The materialists and rationalists of philosophy have tried to reduce the world to something much less than this, but because it is God's creation it will not be reduced.

Chapter three focuses on God's creation of mankind in his image and explores that biblical concept in great depth. Watkin explores substantial, formal, and relational interpretations of the divine image and the "complementarity" of male and female. He discusses also the creation mandate and the concept of work, work limited by Sabbath rest. Along the way he answers important questions: What does it mean to "fill" the earth and "subdue" it? To what extent can we imitate God's creative work without trying to usurp his prerogatives? To what extent should we seek to preserve the natural environment, and to what extent use it for our own purposes? What about the rights of other human beings to participate in the bounties of the creation?

I was moved and delighted at the depth of Watkin's analysis, and the richness of insight that God has taught him through the study of the Bible's creation account. He is a good writer and illustrates his points very well. You will note for example his diagrams illustrating "diagonalization." Scripture, he says, rejects many common dichotomies between concepts in secular thought. For example, philosophers have placed before us the choice between morality governed by an impersonal structure, and morality governed by an unstructured personal entity. But Scripture says that morality is governed by a personal being who has his own structured morality. There is a "diagonal" relationship between personality and structure, meaning that we do not need to choose between the two of them. Watkin is a surprise: a well-trained philosopher who is also a clear and helpful writer.

I hope that through the publication of this volume his work will become much better known in America and that he will become a major player in our discussions of Christian philosophy. *Thinking through Creation* is an edifying book. It glorifies God.

59

Interview with Dave Moore on
History of Western Philosophy and Theology

Dave Moore interviewed me in connection with the publication of my HWPT. The interview was first published at http://www.patheos.com /blogs/jesuscreed/2017/12/09/interviewing-john-frame/. Dave's work can be found at www.mooreengaging.com and www.twocities.org.

Moore: You have covered some of this terrain in other books. What was the impetus that made you want to cover the entire sweep of Western philosophy and theology?

Frame: Dave, thanks for inviting me to your interview. I wrote the book, because I had for many years lectured on the history of philosophy and theology, and by 2012 or so I thought the material was ready for publication. My main purpose was to have a good textbook for my students: one that was both comprehensive and unambiguously Christian.

Moore: Sadly, too many Christians place little premium on the study of theology. An even greater number find no real value in the study of philosophy. How would you seek to persuade these folks to consider the importance of studying both theology and philosophy?

Frame: I don't think there is much difference, conceptually, between philosophy and theology. Both may be defined as the exposition and defense of a worldview. We use the word "theology" when there is some kind of god involved. "Philosophy" often pretends to be operating by reason alone, without reference to religious revelation; but of course reason can never operate alone. It always operates with premises derived from outside reason itself. There is, of course, a difference in emphasis. Theologies, typically (though not always) focus on their revelation, philosophies focus on what can be learned from reason. But those are differences in emphasis, not principle.

As history has developed, "philosophy" and "theology" have developed different traditions: What we call philosophy is usually, but not necessarily, non-Christian. What we call theology usually emphasizes the study of the Bible and Christian tradition. It is often authentically Christian, but not necessarily so.

I think we need to study both, because they cannot be sharply separated, and because they have determined different intellectual and cultural traditions. Christians need to study philosophy because they need to be more aware of the primary principles underlying recent culture and thought. Our Lord calls us to spread the gospel, and we need to be ready to answer questions from the unbelieving world (1 Pet. 3:15). Then, everyone needs to study theology, for in theology, rightly understood, can be found God's provision for our eternal salvation, including the salvation of human thought.

Moore: Does believing in the Christian God give any kind of advantage in better understanding philosophy?

Frame: Yes, because God in Scripture tells us what is going on in philosophy (Col. 2:8; Rom. 1:18–21). Believing in God also helps us to see why all thought requires a foundation, a sure presupposition. Philosophers presuppose such foundations, or seek to find one.

Moore: Who are the living philosophers working out of the Christian tradition that you respect the most?

Frame: Vern Poythress (Westminster Seminary, Philadelphia), James Anderson (Reformed Theological Seminary, Charlotte), Doug Groothuis (Denver Seminary), Esther Meek (Geneva College), Scott Oliphint (Westminster), Bill Edgar (Westminster), Bill Davis (Covenant College).

Moore: Though you cover pretty much everyone, I was curious why the Canadian philosopher, Charles Taylor, was not mentioned.

Frame: Well, I was not persuaded that Taylor had an importance equal to the thinkers that I did cover. That was to some extent a subjective decision. To be honest, I did not know Taylor's work as thoroughly as I knew the work of some other thinkers. Maybe my nationality has something to do with that. Perhaps if I were rewriting the book I would make a different decision.

Moore: Søren Kierkegaard has made somewhat of a comeback in evangelical circles. Do you think this is a positive change?

Frame: Kierkegaard does not fit well into any classification. He himself emphasized his individuality to the point of uniqueness. There are many things in him that can benefit evangelicals. For one thing he had a positive view of subjectivity, which is an antidote to the adulation of academic intellectualism common in our circles. But he was fairly confused about the importance of having a clear object of faith. That confusion emboldened neo-orthodox theology (Barth, Brunner) and secular existentialism. So whether Kierkegaard can benefit modern evangelicalism depends on which strain of K's thought evangelicals choose to emphasize.

Moore: What are a few things that you hope readers will gain from your book?

Frame: (1) All thinking, both Christian and non-Christian, is based on presuppositions that can be defended only by something like faith, not by "reason alone." (2) Human thought, just like human worship and ethics, is under God's standards (1 Cor. 10:31), and it fails when it refuses to accept those standards. (3) Rom. 1 shows the futility of thought that is not submitted to God's revelation. It is not seeking after truth, but repressing the truth (v. 18). (4) So the history of thought, whether philosophical or theological, is not in itself a reliable guide. Everything in history must be judged by the word of God in Scripture. (5) Christian thought fails when it compromises its commitments in order to gain acceptance by non-Christians, to become intellectually respectable. (6) Christian philosophy and theology, when consistently scriptural, can resolve many (not all) of the questions that trouble the history of thought, and can stand legitimate rational scrutiny by fair-minded observers.

60

Introduction to My Logos Courses

This was originally a blog post.

OVER THE LAST FIFTY YEARS I have taught theology and have written books on systematic theology and philosophy. Now Logos has given me the opportunity to do some short videos on my favorite themes and to distribute them to Logos users. Some of these emphases you may not find anywhere else. For example:

1. Scripture has much to say, not only about how to be saved from sin, but about how to know anything in God's world.

2. The fall in Gen. 3 affected not only our moral character, but also our ability to know reality as it truly is.

3. Since the fall was comprehensive, corrupting human life in all its dimensions, so redemption is also comprehensive. Christ gives his people new ways of understanding and acting in all areas of life.

4. The history of philosophy displays not only the progress of human thinking, but also the dynamics of the fall and redemption in the intellectual world.

5. In the history of philosophy, some thinkers are rationalists (claiming they can know reality without God's revelation); others are irrationalists (claiming that there is no objective truth).

6. Both rationalism and irrationalism are manifestations of our fallen rebellion; both fail to provide a basis for knowledge; both cancel one another out; but each requires the other to maintain a semblance of intelligibility.

7. The word of God in Scripture provides the only sufficient basis for human knowledge, and therefore for human decisions.

8. God's revelation integrates the natural world, human language, and human subjectivity, providing us with a rich understanding of God's creation, a gift from the one who created it.

I hope that you will take advantage of the opportunity to profit from my courses.

61

Introduction to *History of Western Philosophy and Theology* (Korean translation)

MY WIFE'S MOTHER was born in Pyongyang, Korea. Her father, William Hunt, and her brother, Bruce Hunt, were American missionaries. Since then, my wife and I have had many close friends from Korea. I had a number of Korean classmates in my student years at Westminster Seminary (Philadelphia), and I taught many Korean students when I was a professor there and later at Westminster Seminary California and at Reformed Theological Seminary (Orlando, FL). Many of our best friends have been from Korea.

So I am delighted to see my book translated into the Korean language. I pray that it will be a blessing to the church and will encourage the proclamation of the gospel. Korean churches are now "sending churches": they send missionaries all over the world, and I am delighted that my book can be a part of their training.

It is good for Korean students to learn about the history of Western theology and philosophy, though they are not themselves Westerners. "Western philosophy and theology" describes the intellectual atmosphere in which the church began after Jesus ascended to heaven, when the apostles and their successors carried on the Great Commission of Christ to bring the gospel to the whole world.

But I hope that readers of my book will not use my book only to accumulate facts. Rather, I pray that it will encourage them to think through the philosophical and theological problems afresh, to communicate the everlasting gospel to people of our own time, in all nations. I pray that the book will help the Korean churches to avoid making mistakes that the Western churches have made, chiefly the mistake of trying to achieve academic responsibility, even at the expense of faithfulness to the message of Scripture.

And I hope that some reader will be encouraged to write a history of philosophy and theology as it has taken place in Korean culture, a history of Korean philosophy and theology. So my book should not remain just as it is, but should encourage further thought and writing. And it should encourage praise to God, who always shows, in all of church history, that the gates of hell do not prevail against the church for which Jesus shed his blood.

62

Doubt, Skepticism, and Faith

DOUBT is a major problem for Christian believers, but we are very reluctant to admit it. We are reluctant, of course, to admit many spiritual problems, like anger, anxiety, and envy. But doubt may be the hardest to admit, because doubt seems to be the opposite of faith itself. The Heidelberg Catechism, Q 21, says that faith is "an assured confidence." How can there be any doubt in an assured confidence? And salvation itself is "by faith" (Eph. 2:8). If doubt is a lack of faith, how can a doubter be saved at all?

The Bible itself presents doubt largely negatively. It is a spiritual impediment, an obstacle to doing God's work (Matt. 14:31; 21:21; 28:17; Acts 10:20; 11:12; Rom. 14:23; 1 Tim. 2:8; Jas. 1:6). In Matt. 14:31 and Rom. 14:23, it is the opposite of faith and therefore a sin. Of course, this sin, like other sins, may remain with us through our earthly life. But we should not be complacent about it. Just as the ideal for the Christian life is perfect holiness, the ideal for the Christian mind is absolute certainty about God's revelation.

We should not conclude that doubt is always sinful. Matt. 14:31 and Rom. 14:23 (and indeed the others I have listed) speak of doubt in the face of clear special revelation. To doubt what God has clearly spoken to us is wrong. But in other situations, it is not wrong to doubt. In many cases, in fact, it is wrong for us to claim knowledge, much less certainty. Indeed, often the best course is to admit our ignorance (Deut. 29:29; Rom.

11:33–36). Paul is not wrong to express uncertainty about the number of people he baptized (1 Cor. 1:16). Indeed, James tells us, we are always ignorant of the future to some extent and we ought not to pretend we know more about it than we do (James 4:13–16). Job's friends were wrong to think that they knew the reasons for his torment, and Job himself had to be humbled as God reminded him of his ignorance (Job 38–42).

So although Scripture presents doubt negatively, as a sin, as a spiritual impediment, it is not a sin that invalidates a Christian profession of faith. It is inconsistent with faith, as all sin is. But like other sins, it may remain with us for many years. A believer will struggle against it, but may not gain total victory over it until he or she enters into glory.

But how are we to struggle against the doubts that beset us? First, we should be honest before God about our doubts. In Mark 9:24, a man wanted Jesus to heal his son, but when Jesus told him the importance of believing, the man admitted to Jesus, "I believe; help my unbelief!" Jesus honored the man's honesty and healed his son. Often writers of the psalms express questions to God, questions that indicate some level of doubt about God's promises. In Ps. 73, for example, Asaph questions the justice of God's dealings with the wicked:

> But as for me, my feet had almost stumbled, my steps had nearly slipped. For I was envious of the arrogant when I saw the prosperity of the wicked. (Ps. 73:2–3)

Later in the psalm, Asaph is reassured; but there is also Ps. 88, in which there is no explicit reassurance. It is right for us to express our doubts to God and ask him to restore our faith. For ultimately, only he can deal with them. The final solution for doubt is God's supernatural work in our heart, enabling us to understand his ways and enabling us to praise him even when we do not understand.

But secondly, it is possible even in this life to gain some victory over our doubts. I have said that absolute certainty is the appropriate (if ideal) response to God's special revelation. How can that be, given our finitude and fallibility? How is that possible when we consider the skepticism that pervades secular thought? How is it humanly possible to know anything with certainty?

First, it is impossible to exclude absolute certainty in all cases. Any argument purporting to show that there is no such certainty must admit that it is itself uncertain. Further, any such argument must presuppose that argument itself is a means of finding truth. If someone uses an argument to test the certainty of propositions, he is claiming certainty at least for that argument. And he is claiming that by such an argument he can test the legitimacy of claims to certainty. But such a test of certainty, a would-be criterion of certainty, must itself be certain. And an argument that would test absolute certainty must itself be absolutely certain.

So skepticism, the view that we can know nothing with assurance, necessarily fails, for the skeptic is never skeptical about his skepticism. And if he claims assurance about his skepticism, he is no longer a skeptic.

In a biblical view of knowledge, God's word is the ultimate criterion of certainty. What God says *must* be true, for, as the letter to the Hebrews says, it is impossible for God to lie (Heb. 6:18; compare Titus 1:2; 1 John 2:27). His word is truth (John 17:17; compare Pss. 33:4; 119:160). So God's word is the criterion by which we can measure all other sources of knowledge.

When God promised Abraham a multitude of descendants and an inheritance in the land of Canaan, many things might have caused him to doubt. He reached the age of one hundred without having any children, and his wife Sarah was far beyond the normal age of childbearing. And though he sojourned in the land of Canaan, he didn't own title to any land there at all. But Paul says of him that "no unbelief made him waver concerning the promise of God, but he grew strong in his faith as he gave glory to God, fully convinced that God was able to do what he had promised" (Rom. 4:20–21). God's word, for Abraham, took precedence over all other evidence in forming Abraham's belief. So important is this principle that Paul defines justifying faith in terms of it: "That is why [Abraham's] faith was counted to him for righteousness" (v. 22).

Thus Abraham stands in contrast to Eve who, in Gen. 3:6, allowed the evidence of her eyes to take precedence over the command of God. Abraham is one of the heroes of the faith who, according to Heb. 11, "died in faith, not having received the things promised, but having seen them and greeted them from afar ..." (v. 13). They had God's promise, and that was enough to motivate them to endure terrible sufferings and deprivations through their earthly lives.

I would conclude that it is the responsibility of the Christian to regard God's word as absolutely certain, and to make that word the criterion of all other sources of knowledge. Our certainty of the truth of God comes ultimately, not through rational demonstration or empirical verification, useful as these may often be, but from the authority of God's own word.

God's word does testify to itself, often, by means of human testimony and historical evidence: the "proofs" of Acts 1:3, the centurion's witness in Luke 23:47, the many witnesses to the resurrection of Jesus in 1 Cor. 15:1–11. But we should never forget that these evidences come to us with God's own authority. In 1 Cor. 15, Paul asks the church to believe the evidence because it is part of the authoritative apostolic preaching: "so we preach and so you believed" (v. 11; compare vv. 1–3). Today, we learn about the "proofs" of the gospel from the Bible, God's authoritative word.

But how does that word give us psychological certainty? Even good arguments often leave us with psychological doubts. Christians sometimes make great intellectual and emotional exertions, trying to force themselves to believe the Bible. But we cannot make ourselves believe. Certainty comes upon us, as I said earlier, by an act of God, through the testimony of his Spirit (1 Cor. 2:4, 9–16; 1 Thess. 1:5; 2 Thess. 2:14). The Spirit's witness often accompanies a human process of reasoning. Scripture never rebukes people who honestly seek to think through the questions of faith. But unless our reason is empowered by the Spirit, it will not give full assurance.

So certainty comes ultimately through God's word and Spirit. The Lord calls us to build our life and thought on the certainties of his word, that we "will not walk in darkness, but have the light of life" (John 8:12). The process of building, furthermore, is not only academic, but ethical and spiritual. It is those who are willing to do God's will that know the truth of Jesus's words (John 7:17), and those that love their neighbors who are able to know as they ought to know (1 Cor. 8:1–3).

Secular philosophy rejects absolute certainty because absolute certainty is essentially supernatural, and because the secularist is unwilling to accept a supernatural foundation for knowledge. But the Christian regards God's word, illumined by the Spirit, as his ultimate criterion of truth and falsity, right and wrong, and therefore as the standard of certainty. Insofar as we consistently hold the Bible as our standard of certainty, we may and must regard it as itself absolutely certain. In this life we will do this imperfectly. All sin comes from our failure to trust God's word as our absolute standard. But we should rejoice that in God's word we have a firm basis for assurance of his truth. By the grace of Jesus Christ, we have a wonderful treasure, one that saves the soul from sin and the mind from skepticism.

BIBLIOGRAPHY

Frame, John M. *Christianity Considered*. Bellingham, WA: Lexham Press, 2018.

———. *The Doctrine of the Knowledge of God*. Phillipsburg, NJ: P&R Publishers, 1987.

———. *The Doctrine of the Word of God*. Phillipsburg, NJ: P&R Publishers, 2010.

———. *Nature's Case for God*. Bellingham, WA: Lexham Press, 2018.

Poythress, Vern. *Knowing and the Trinity: How Perspectives in Human Knowledge Imitate the Trinity*. Phillipsburg, NJ: P&R Publishers, 2018.

Van Til, Cornelius. *A Christian Theory of Knowledge*. Philadelphia: Presbyterian and Reformed Publishing Co., 1961.

———. *A Survey of Christian Epistemology*. Phillipsburg, NJ: P&R Publishers, 1980.

63

Mystery

RECENTLY I was asked to review how my apologetics has changed since my retirement and my eightieth birthday, to tell in effect "Why I Am Still a Christian."[1] Our reasons for faith do sometimes change through life, though I think not drastically. Every Christian's faith is ultimately based on the same thing—the gospel brought to us by Jesus recorded in God's authoritative Scripture.[2] But as we study the Bible and compare it with God's revelation in nature and history,[3] different things become more prominent at different times. As I have gotten older, I continue to hold to the beliefs I expressed in many published writings on apologetics,[4] but some arguments and evidences have played a smaller and smaller role in my thinking and others a greater and greater one.

My essay on my current thinking on apologetics concluded with a little paragraph on "mystery," and I've been asked to expand on that here. Although I have had a fifty-year career expounding reasons for faith, I have always had a deep sense of the "incomprehensibility of

---

1. For the whole essay I wrote, see "How Has John Frame's Apologetic Changed over Time?" https://frame-poythress.org/how-has-john-frames-apologetic-changed-over-time/.

2. In this sense, every Christian is a "presuppositionalist."

3. Since we all do this and should do it, every Christian is also an "evidentialist."

4. Especially *Apologetics to the Glory of God* (Phillipsburg, NJ: P&R Publishers, 1994); *Cornelius Van Til* (same publisher, 1995); *Apologetics: A Justification for Belief* (same publisher, 2015); and *Five Views of Apologetics* (Grand Rapids: Zondervan, 2000).

God." That is to say, no matter how clear our concepts and cogent our arguments, God is in the end a transcendent being, one who is above and beyond us, one whom we cannot master either by our physical strength or by our mental skills. His immanence is important too, his coming into history to reveal himself to us and redeem us in Christ. But, even in his most intimate nearness, he remains God. And as God, his knowledge, even of the things most familiar to us, is vastly different from our own. He and I both know the sago palm in my front yard, but he knows far more about it than I could ever grasp. More than that, he knows it as its creator, as the one who made the whole universe and foreordained its history (Eph. 1:11), as the one who planned from the beginning the process by which that sago palm would grow up in my front yard. Further, his knowledge is *normative* knowledge,[5] a knowledge that governs how all his creatures should think about everything. Because God is the supreme King, he has the right to tell me and show me how I should think about that sago palm.

So, although God reveals to us much truth, his knowledge of that truth is vastly different from ours. He knows as the creator; we know as creatures. His knowledge of my sago palm is a creator-knowledge; mine a creature-knowledge. God knows *everything* about my sago; I know whatever he chooses to let me know. When I learn something new about my sago, I am learning it from God, according to his standards.

But these thoughts entail that I do not know anything quite as God knows it. There is certainly a strong similarity, a strong analogy, between God's knowledge and mine, because I am seeking to know according to his revelation. He has ordained it that way. He has determined that such knowledge is adequate for me. But I do not now have his creator-knowledge. I don't know anything, even my sago palm, as the creator of that thing. I don't know anything as the final standard of truth concerning that object. My knowledge is not identical to God's, because I am not God.

---

5. The word "normative" will resonate to some of my readers who have thought about my "three perspectives," the normative, situational, and existential. See Frame, *Theology in Three Dimensions* (Phillipsburg, NJ: P&R Publishers, 2017).

All of that implies that there is a deep dimension of mystery in the universe. God tells Isaiah that the evil man should "forsake his thoughts," because

My thoughts are not your thoughts,
　　neither are your ways my ways, declares the Lord.
As the heavens are higher than the earth,
　　so are my ways higher than your ways
　　and my thoughts than your thoughts. (Isa. 55:8–9, NIV)

So, no matter how much we know, there will always be something beyond us. We cannot know God as God knows himself. Nor can we know anything in creation as God knows it. We cannot even know ourselves precisely as God knows us. Our knowledge is adequate to serve God as he intends us to. Our ignorance is never an excuse for disobedience. But our knowledge is never a divine knowledge, a knowledge of sago palms arising from our creation of sago palms, a knowledge of ourselves as the ultimate criteria of truth about sago palms.

In my study of the history of thought,[6] I have seen many sophisticated thinkers struggle with God's mystery. The ancient Greek philosophers tried to achieve an ultimate, exhaustive knowledge of things through human reason alone, without the assistance of divine revelation. But the best they could do was to conceive of a "pure being" from which somehow emanated lower beings. They knew that they could not achieve their goal without something transcendent. But they could not understand how a pure being could contain enough impurity to make it emanate impure beings. More recent thinkers have tried a different approach, anticipated by the Greek atomists. They have tried to come up with a comprehensive rational explanation of the world by chopping the world up into smaller and smaller pieces: molecules, atoms, subatomic particles, perhaps "superstrings." But the tiniest particles they claim to exist cannot be the ultimate explanation of everything, for they cannot be understood except by reference to the larger things.

---

6. See Frame, *A History of Western Philosophy and Theology* (Phillipsburg, NJ: P&R, 2015); *We Are All Philosophers* (Bellingham, WA: Lexham Press, 2019).

"Atom" is meaningless except as a component of something larger. Even more so, "superstrings."

Today some thinkers believe that the world is largely made of "dark matter" and "dark energy." But these, by definition, are realities that we don't know, for they are dark. This is to say that for all our sophisticated philosophical and scientific schemes, the most fundamental reality of the world is unknown to us, perhaps unknowable.

The same is true of theology. We "see but a poor reflection in a mirror" (1 Cor. 13:12, NIV). In theology, we seek to take Scripture, God's revelation of himself, and apply it to our lives in the world. At best, this is "wisdom" (Prov. 1:7). Wisdom is a practical knowledge God gives us to help us accomplish the work he assigns to us. But we need to get over the idea that theology takes all the mystery out of the world. As I get older, I am less and less impressed by thinkers, including theologians, who think they have everything figured out. Theologians readily confess God's incomprehensibility as a doctrinal point, but often they go on from there to write as if they had that ultimate and final knowledge that belongs to God himself, as if they had something more than mere practical wisdom. In conservative theology, writers tend to confess mystery, but then go on to meticulously explain such things as the order of God's decrees and the inner activities of the Trinitarian persons without any clear biblical basis. Liberal writers say that conservative theologians claim too much knowledge of the mysterious God, but then they go on to explain in great detail what government programs God demands of us to help the needy, again, without biblical basis. At age 80, I look at both types of theology with both sadness and amusement. God is not here to motivate our rationalistic quest. God is Lord of heaven and earth. He comes to drive us to repent of sin and embrace Jesus Christ as Lord and Savior.

PART 7

———

Ethics and Politics

64

The First Commandment:
Living for a Person

"You shall have no other gods before ME." Deut 5:7. [This sermon is about ME—paradoxically enough, using the term in the third person rather than the first.]

ONE OF YOU ASKED ME to preach in the Ten Commandments series, and I thought, well, that should not be so difficult, since I've written a big book (DCL) that's half about the Ten. I thought I'd make a grab for the first commandment, before somebody asks me to preach on something more obscure. And after all, the first commandment is about God's lordship, isn't it? "You shall have no other gods before ME," and ME is the Lord, right. And I've written a bunch of books on the lordship of God; so it looked like an easy assignment.

But when I started working on it, it began to look hard. Where do I start? With covenants? Verbal revelation? The lordship attributes? The three perspectives? Epistemological presuppositions?

I decided to develop this sermon in a different way. It's a kind of existential perspective approach, if you're into that lingo. But it's a way of getting to the essence of the first commandment, as long as you understand that the essence of something can be viewed from different perspectives. What I want to focus on is that ME, that prominent ME, which constitutes really the whole content of the first commandment. The commandment is entirely about a person—a great, big, mysterious person—who stands athwart every thought and decision of our lives. And he tells us here, that HE is what our lives are all about.

In the book of Exodus, HE begins to emerge out of the fog of history. Israel lives in Egypt, with some stories about their ancestors. Pharaoh turns against them. The faithful ones, like the midwives of Ex. 2, *fear* the God of their fathers and obey him heroically. But things get worse and worse, and at the end of Ex. 2 they are crying out to this God to deliver them from their terrible slavery. I don't think the people, even the faithful people, knew much *about* this God. They evidently knew something of God's dealings with Abraham, Isaac, Jacob, and Joseph, but that was 400 years before—430 years according to Ex. 12:40. Four hundred years ago from our time, 1616, both William Shakespeare and Miguel de Cervantes passed away. The same year, Nicholas Copernicus's *De Revolutionibus* was placed on the Index of Forbidden Books by the Roman Catholic Church. A few years earlier, in 1611, the King James Bible was published. The founding of Jamestown, VA, was in 1607, and the founding of Plymouth Colony in 1620. I mention those events to give you a feeling for 400 years—what it must have been like to base your hopes on events 400 years earlier. Most of us educated people have a feeling for the early seventeenth century, but not much knowledge of the precise events that animated people in those days, and some hesitation about sharing the worldviews and aspirations of people who lived back then.

Into this setting enters Moses, who was to be the great leader of Israel. Moses evidently did not at first ask God what role he should play in delivering Israel, for he chose the wrong role, incurred the anger of both the Israelites and the Egyptians, and ended up in exile in Midian. But one day he was tending sheep and he encountered an astonishing sight: a bush that burned, but was not consumed. Yet more amazing, perhaps, a voice came out of the fire and *addressed* Moses: take off your sandals, for the place on which you stand is holy ground. The Voice identified himself as the God of Moses's father (identified as Amram in Ex. 12:20), the God of Abraham, the God of Isaac, and the God of

Jacob. Three figures from ancient history, and one figure who brought the ancient faith of the patriarchs down to the present.

God seems to think this should be enough identification. I know their sufferings; I have heard their cries; and I'm ready to fulfill my promise to Abraham, to bring them out of here to a good land up north. Now you, Moses: you go down there and lead them out. Moses probably remembers that solving Israel's troubles is something he tried to do before, and that is no easy feat (Ex. 2:11–15). Imagine telling the Israelites, I'll do better this time, because our traditional God will be with us to bring us through. They will say, the God from 400 years ago? How do YOU know our traditional God? Tell us his *name*.

Moses might have answered this question by saying something like, "the God of my father, and the God of your fathers." But God himself has a different suggestion. He brings in a mysterious, new idea. I AM THAT I AM, was the name, I AM in the short form, and YAHWEH in the shortest form. This name was not used commonly in the older period, and it pushes Israel ahead to a new era. The verb I AM can refer to the present or the future, but most likely not the past. The God of our fathers, in other words, is not *merely* the God of our fathers. He is our God as well; the God of Amram, the God of me, and the God of my *children* and *grandchildren*.

Moses still worries that Israel won't believe him. So God gives Moses some things he can do, that they can see: the staff that turns into a snake and back again, the hand that becomes leprous when it comes out of Moses's cloak, the ability to turn water into blood, and a press secretary/surrogate, his eloquent brother Aaron. And Yahweh summarizes for Moses the ten plagues that he will bring upon Egypt for their hardness of heart, down to the death of the firstborn son.

All of that would seem to give Moses, and the Israelites, a foundation for theological reflection. Yahweh is the God who acts, the God who can do all these miracles. Moses and Aaron are his spokesmen, his friends, and you can trust them to represent what he wants. But on the way back from Egypt, the plot turns mysterious again. God met Moses in an inn and, the text says, "sought to put him to death." All of a sudden, God is Moses's enemy. It reminds us of God wrestling with

Jacob back in Genesis. The controversy turns out to be about circumcision, which hasn't come up yet in this particular story. Moses is supposed to threaten Pharaoh that God will kill the Egyptians' firstborn sons. But how can he do that when he, himself raised as an Egyptian, has neglected to circumcise his own son to identify him with Israel? If Pharaoh's son must die, so must Moses's, and Moses himself. Moses's Midianite wife Zipporah alone understands what is happening, performs the circumcision herself, and redeems her husband and son. But what kind of God is this, who promises a miraculous deliverance one moment and then with no warning becomes our enemy?

But Yahweh becomes Moses's friend again. He does deliver Israel from Egypt, as he has said, prevailing with his mighty hand over all the forces of nature, over the Egyptian magicians, and the Egyptian gods. And he fulfills one more promise: after he delivers Israel, Israel will meet him at Mt. Sinai, the mountain of the burning bush.

At the mountain, God declares that Israel is his special people: his treasured possession among all peoples a kingdom of priests and a holy nation. But the Sinai meeting is no friendly conference. God scares them to death, as he scared Moses at the bush and at the inn. They must wash their garments and not touch the mountain, lest they die; for like the burning bush it is a holy place. There are thunders and lightnings, a thick cloud, and what is called in the ESV "a very loud trumpet blast" (not the shofar, but something else). The priests must be consecrated, and must not come up to the Lord, "lest he break out against them" (Ex. 19:24). This sounds like Yahweh's visit to Moses on the road back to Egypt: God as a mysterious enemy, a hostile force. At the second giving of the law, in Deuteronomy 4:33, Moses asks, "Did any people ever hear the voice of a god speaking out of the midst of the fire, as you have heard, and still live?" God is a great friend, but also a frightening presence, who will not be trifled with. He saves, he delivers—but in a way that leaves no doubt about his holiness, his transcendence, his omnipotence, his ferocity. Good, but not tame, in the famous words of C. S. Lewis.

This is the "ME" of the first commandment, you shall have no other gods before ME. The Decalogue has much to say about worship, speech, the Sabbath, our parents, and so on, but in the end it's all about that person who designates himself as "ME." So the ethics of the Decalogue is intensely personalistic. It has many elements, but it is first of all an attachment and loyalty to a person. And lest we think we can reduce this ethic to a finite group of ethical principles, God over and over again directs us to his mystery: the one who loves us above all the nations, but who maintains his inclination to "break out against us." He loves us and calls us to love him—the first commandment is a version of the love commandment—but not without awe and wonder, not without a kind of fear.

The first commandment, indeed the whole Decalogue, tells us to be on the side of this ME, this wonderful, loving, terrifying being. When modern people say, "Oh, my God wouldn't send people to hell," we are to say "the true God does." And if the unbeliever says, "But that's inconsistent with his love," we reply, "I don't know how his love and wrath fit together. But he has said that they do, and I am on his side." You may prefer to try harder that I just did to explain the mystery, and that's OK. But eventually you too will run up against the mystery, the wonder. And if you are a believer you will be on the side of that wonder. You'll be on the side of the mysterious ME, against all the rivals for his throne, against all the rival thoughts of gods and men. You shall have no other gods before ME.

Somebody may say, "You need to accept certain lifestyles that the Bible condemns." You ask why? They say, "So you won't be guilty of discrimination." You say, "I must discriminate where my God discriminates, because I am on his side."

Now, fast forward a thousand years or so, past another 400-year gap in divine revelation. God's people still exists, and many among them still try to keep the first commandment. But many of their leaders lead them astray, and God "breaks out upon them," sending them into exile. Those who return attend to the prophecies of the mysterious Messiah, the Servant of the Lord who is to rule the earth in the name of God, but who seems to be very hard to locate. But eventually he comes. As God named Israel his chosen people, so God baptizes Jesus, through John, as his Son, in whom he is well pleased. Then, again like Israel, the Messiah Jesus spends time in the wilderness, tempted by the devil.

Unlike Israel, he passes every test. Then he comes to Galilee and sees two brothers, Simon and Andrew, casting their nets into the sea. He says to them, "Follow me, and I will make you 'fishers of men' " (Matt. 4:19). And Matthew says, "immediately they left their nets and followed him."

What was going on here? We are tempted to suppose a back story: perhaps Simon and Andrew knew Jesus from a previous time. Maybe they grew up with him in places like Nazareth and Capernaum. Maybe they had heard stories about his baptism by John and the Father's voice from above and the Spirit's descent like a dove … maybe they had even been there. Maybe they had heard of Jesus's teaching or miracles. But it's hard to see that any of these past contacts would have been sufficient to motivate the profound and immediate change of lifestyle described here. Simon and Andrew might in addition have heard some of the contemporary Messianic theology and the mysterious declaration by John that Jesus was the Lamb of God who would take away the sin of the world. But the Gospels are clear that they really didn't have a proper understanding of this until after Jesus's resurrection.

Luke tells us more than Matthew does about the call of Simon and Andrew. There was a miracle involved, a miraculous catch of fish. Jesus told them to put out their nets farther into the deep, and they caught enough fish that their nets were breaking and the boat started to sink. You might think that the disciples (which according to Luke included also James and John) might have said to one another, "Wow, this man is pretty powerful; we'd better follow him." I'm not saying that argument didn't enter into their thinking. But there is something more:

> But when Simon Peter saw it, he fell down at Jesus's knees, saying, "Depart from me, for I am a sinful man, O Lord." For he and all who were with him were astonished at the catch of fish that they had taken. (Luke 5:8–9)

This response goes way beyond thanksgiving (Thanks, Lord, for all the fish) or even astonishment. This is the language of worship. Imagine: Jesus does a mighty work and Peter says depart from me, for I am a sinful man. Peter should want this benefactor to stay around, but he says, "Depart from me." Somehow, Peter has seen beyond the veil. Jesus is not just a skilled expert in successful fishing. Not just a benefactor; he is God, who (as Moses learned earlier) cannot abide being near sin. Peter has violated the holy ground of Yahweh. The incongruity between sin and such holiness is intolerable.

Simon and Andrew may have carried the back story in the back of their minds, but the back story mainly served to heighten the sense of mystery about this man. But it was the man they followed, the incredibly holy man who exposed all their sin, their unfitness to be near him, not the back story. There was something about him as a person that constituted an efficacious call, so that IMMEDIATELY they left their nets and followed him. Theological liberals like Albert Schweitzer (who made much of this story) liked to emphasize that the original disciples followed a person, not a theology. And although I'm as much a defender of theology as Schweitzer was a critic of it, there is truth in this representation. Yes, it is Jesus that we follow, not a theology. But to deny the theology of Jesus's death for our sins and resurrection is certainly to deny him.

But just as Yahweh called Israel first—in the first commandment—to be on his side, against all his would-be detractors in the world under Satan, so Jesus calls us first of all to confess him as Lord, to be on his side, and therefore to stand against all the other so-called lords and gods of this world. Many have noticed that, unlike many religious teachers, Jesus puts himself in the foreground. In John 14:6, he says, "I am the way, the truth, and the life; no one comes to the Father but through me." In Mark 8:34, he says, "If anyone would come after me, let him deny himself and take up his cross and follow me." That ME is the ME of the first commandment.

So Paul tells us, "If you confess with your mouth that Jesus is Lord and shall believe in your heart that God has raised him from the dead, you will be saved." New Testament ethics is just as personal as Old Testament ethics—more so, because we now have a much greater knowledge of the ME that excludes all other gods.

All the Ten Commandments converge on Jesus. The reason we don't bow to carved images is that Jesus is the one image of God who deserves worship. We avoid taking God's name in vain, because Jesus is his name and that name is precious to us. We keep the Sabbath, because Jesus tells us to come to him and he will give us rest. We honor our parents, because Jesus unites all fatherhoods in himself. We do not murder, because Jesus is the Lord of life. We don't commit adultery, because Jesus is our holy husband. We don't steal, because in Jesus are all the treasures. We don't bear false witness, because Jesus is the Lord of truth. And we don't covet, because Jesus rules all the inward thoughts of the heart as well as the outward actions.

So the first commandment, the commandment behind all the other commandments, is to follow Jesus, to stand with him in all the decisions of life and against all his detractors. Of course we cannot do this in our own strength. In keeping this commandment and in keeping the others wrapped up in it, we stand in his strength, in the power of his cross. He has given his life for us and taken away the death grip of sin. And he has risen from the dead to give us a new life. In his resurrection power, we will prevail, and because of that power we can be strong and bold.

That means calling sinners to repent and believe in Christ. And that includes powerful sinners, influential sinners.

As Moses and Aaron stood in the courts of Pharaoh, telling him to make way for the true king who wished to escort his people out of the Egyptian misery, so we are called to stand before the mighty, and call on them, in the name of Jesus, to set free those who are powerless and without a voice. There is a place to mention hell, as well, for our God is still capable of "breaking out against" those who despise his Son.

How is that possible? If you mention God in public, you get dismissed as a religious fanatic. And if you mention Jesus, well, if the news media cover your remarks at all, that name will be redacted out, lest it cause offense to other religions and to secularists. Those media never seem to wonder whether redacting the name of Jesus will cause offense to Christians. Part of the trouble is that it rarely does. They should wonder whether redacting Jesus will cause offense to his Father. We need to remind the media and everyone else that we stand, not only for the US Constitution, not only for the moral principles underlying it, not merely for theistic ethics, but for Jesus, and we don't like to see people dishonor him who loved us so much that he gave his life.

It is not that we have a religion that is greater than politics. It is rather that we have a person, a lord, who is Lord of lords and King of kings, and that he will not be denied his rights over any square inch of territory in his creation. We need to be known as people who follow him, the great ME of the Decalogue. Not as people who have a mere alternative political philosophy, or an alternative religion, or a position to the right or left of the consensus, but as followers of Jesus.

That doesn't necessarily mean talking about Jesus all the time, though most of us should be talking about him more often. Sometimes when we use the name of Jesus for emphasis or effect, his name becomes a mere sound, a trademark of an odd movement. We can present Jesus more meaningfully than that and more forcefully, as the Bible itself does, and the great writers like Augustine, Pascal, and C. S. Lewis. That way, we can better grab the attention of our listeners, and the centrality of Jesus in our message takes intelligible shape.

But even today there will be much about presenting Jesus that is mysterious, even ineffable. When modern secular people encounter Jesus, they often don't understand *how* it happens. There is rarely a single apologetic argument, even a transcendental argument, that nails down their commitment. Often it's someone's friendship, or unexpected love, that brings Jesus to them as Jesus brought himself to people in the Gospels. And when a conversion is authentic, it is a conversion to that person—to put no other gods before ME, to follow him through the course of life.

Earlier I quoted Matthew's account of Jesus calling Simon and Andrew to be his disciples. We need to tell people that yes, Jesus can provide all the food we need. But as we receive that food, if we understand who is providing it, we will be drawn into the mystery of Jesus the God-man, who amazingly draws near to sinful people. He is the one who calls us to follow him through life, in all our thoughts, decisions, and actions, despite the claims of all the other gods of our world. He calls us to have no other gods before ME.

65

Foreword to Mike Milton,
Foundations of a Moral Government

A FEW YEARS AGO I was looking forward to working with Mike Milton in my capacity as a theology professor and his capacity as Chancellor and CEO of Reformed Theological Seminary. I appreciated his ministry and his vision for theological education. But God's strange providence intervened. Mike was hit with a serious illness that led to his resignation from the seminary. I prayed that God would enable him to continue his theological leadership in some form, but I did not know him well enough to guess what form that work would take.

Well, even then I should have known better than I did that Mike was hugely gifted in many areas. As the Vita at the end of this volume indicates, he has spent 32 years in military service, first as a linguist, then as a chaplain. He has been a pastor and has done significant work in historical scholarship. Now I have learned that he has specialized in the study of Samuel Rutherford (1600–1661), the great Scottish theologian who influenced the work of the Westminster Assembly and indeed the whole subsequent course of Reformed theology.

Rutherford's greatest writing was *Lex, Rex*, which should perhaps be translated "the Law is King," or "the King is under the Law." That is, in any case, the main thesis of this momentous work. As such, it became subsequently a major influence on political thought, not only among Presbyterians, but on the philosophical developments that led

393

to the founding documents of the United States of America. The work of John Locke is arguably indebted to Rutherford, as is the work of Edmund Burke and that of the Rev. John Witherspoon, pastor and president of Princeton University, who signed the American Declaration of Independence. Therefore Rutherford, the fountainhead of this development, is important to all our current discussion about the liberty of the citizen and the powers of government.

Rutherford was mainly concerned with opposing the "divine right of kings" as that doctrine was presented in his time. On that doctrine, the authority of kings was given directly by God, without any collaboration by the citizens he rules. That doctrine was already contrary to the British tradition embodied in the Magna Carta. But some continued to defend it as a distinctly theistic and biblical doctrine of governance. Rutherford, with a deeper understanding of Scripture than his opponents, opposed this notion. A truly biblical doctrine of government is not merely the assertion that God is the source of rule. Rather, we must look carefully at *how* God confers authority on governments, according to the Bible. Rutherford insisted that in Scripture God installs kings (even kings like David whom he personally warrants by anointing) by the actions of people. Though David was anointed as a young man, he did not actually begin to rule Judah (and later Israel) until the elders of God's people concurred in his selection.

So although Rutherford emphasizes the authority of God over the state, he is known as the champion of the popular mandate and the rights of citizens over against the ruler. In his view, one can and should advocate a distinctively biblical political system without the divine right of kings and with strong checks and balances against the abuses of authority.

These are two emphases that must be heard today. First, we need to hear God's word, in the area of politics as much as in everything else. The idea that politics is a secular discipline and should be divorced from religion is a grave mistake. Without God, our politics becomes autonomous, subject to every wild fantasy of undisciplined human minds. In the present American political dialogue, the new socialism is the extreme of this development, proposals to spend trillions upon trillions of money we do not have on enormous increases in the size and authority of government, an idolatry of the state that even the defenders of the divine right of kings could not have imagined.

Second, we need to hear Rutherford's call for the liberty of citizens. The founders of the American system listened carefully to Rutherford's advice that there be checks and balances on all the branches of government, that no branch should ever claim absolute (divine) authority, and that none should ever transgress the rights of the people, rights given not by the authority of the state but by God himself. Recognizing the authority of God means recognizing the legitimate authority of the state, but also the liberty of the people from the state in their inalienable rights.

Rutherford's book is, like all books of its time, written in language that is difficult for modern people to understand. We owe many thanks to Mike Milton for careful work analyzing and paraphrasing Rutherford for modern readers. He has used well his gifts as a linguist, a pastor, and a theological scholar. As we endure this historical period of radically divisive political debate, it is hard to imagine a better gift to the American people than this restoration of Rutherford's important work.

66

Review of *We Cannot Be Silent*
by R. Albert Mohler, Jr.

This review was first published in Themelios, available at
http://themelios.thegospelcoalition.org/review/we-cannot-be-silent
-speaking-truth-to-a-culture-redefining-sex-marriage.

AS THE TITLE INDICATES, this book is a call to arms for Christians. The target is same-sex marriage and, more broadly, the sexual revolution of recent years. It is excellent as a polemic, because it is not only a polemic. Its call to arms is based on a carefully developed history of the sexual revolution and a sharp logical analysis of the issues.

It addresses my own bewilderment at the speed at which the same-sex movement has progressed: Mohler points out that in 2004 eleven states had referendums banning same sex marriage. In 2008, most thought homosexuality itself was immoral, and Prop 8 in California, an anti-gay marriage law, passed overwhelmingly. But by 2014 polls showed that the American public overwhelmingly supported same-sex marriage, and in the 2016 election candidates routinely attacked those who believe in traditional marriage as bigots. So in twelve years there was a vast change of opinion in the American electorate. How could this have happened so fast, regarding an issue that had been considered closed for thousands of years?

Mohler sheds light on this astonishing change by his longer-term historical survey. In his view, the modern sexual revolution began with the growing acceptance of contraception in the early twentieth century, which separated sex from procreation. Then came no-fault divorce in the 1960s which, in Mohler's view, brought drastic and tragic changes to family structure. Eventually cohabitation came to replace marriage entirely in some circles. And advanced reproductive technologies like in-vitro fertilization, detached childbearing even from sex itself.

Accompanying these historical developments was a new view of marriage, from traditional "conjugal" marriage (a covenant cemented by public vows, establishing kinship relations) to "revisionist" views (contractual, defined by a loving emotional bond).

And as views of marriage changed, so did views of homosexuality. Mohler defends the traditional Bible exegesis behind the view that Scripture condemns all homosexual unions, not only those that are oppressive. In that connection, he expounds the biblical view of sex in a broad context, from Gen. 2, to Paul's doctrine that marriage images the relation of Christ and the church, to the eschatological marriage supper of the Lamb.

But Mohler shows also the militant opposition to this theology that is part of the "gay agenda." Since the Stonewall riots of 1969, there was a deliberate movement by gay activists to destroy common criticisms of homosexuality. (1) Homosexuality is not "crazy." The activists successfully petitioned the psychoanalytic community to reverse its judgment that homosexuality was a mental illness. (2) It is not "sinful." Gay activists led the fight in liberal denominations to reinterpret or discard biblical prohibitions. (3) It is not "criminal." Although there were legal prohibitions of homosexuality as late as 2003, that same year the Supreme Court pronounced that such laws violated the Constitution. Justice Scalia said that this decision would lead to same sex marriage, and indeed it did. (4) It is not "subversive": literature, films, and TV sought to portray gays as normal, unthreatening people (though some gays protested that this new stereotype inhibited their freedom). These goals of the gay community were astonishingly successful, but only because the defenses of traditional marriage had already been weakened.

The logical and historical conclusion of this development, Mohler says, is the transgender revolution. This is not just a movement to give help to those with gender dysphoria, but a demand upon society to regard gender entirely as a social construct, unconnected to biological sex. The transgender movement goes beyond the homosexual movement as such: now the question is not "who may I go to bed WITH," but "who shall I go to bed AS." Taking a male or female role in sex, or some other role, is entirely up to the autonomous individual.

Hence the willingness of liberals to force the whole society to abandon its one-sex bathroom policy in the interest of the very small minority in the country who are gender dysphoric. To many of us, this policy seems to be a wildly disproportionate response to the problem of a very few. But to the LGBT activists, this is an important part of the revolution that must be imposed on society by force, not inhibited in the slightest by considerations of religious liberty.

So the issue is no longer about sex alone. It is an issue of worldview. Is the world created by God, an objective reality to which we ought to conform, or is it a world we ourselves have formed, malleable to whatever we may choose to be? Here we see the truly radical implications of the sexual revolution. And the totalitarian impulses of the LGBT movement will not tolerate dissent. Their goal is to force conformity of behavior, but also of mind, of language, of philosophy, and of theology. Arguments for first amendment liberties seem to be lost on the LGBT movement.

At this point, Mohler reprimands the silence of the evangelical community. The sexual revolution would overturn the entire biblical worldview, and many evangelicals have gone AWOL in this crucial fight.

My general view of this book is very positive. I learned a great deal from the historical analysis, and Mohler has persuaded me of the sharpness of the conflict between LGBT activists and the gospel of Christ. Sometimes in the book Mohler's critique goes farther than I think is biblically warranted. I do not agree with Mohler's view, for instance, that Scripture condemns all birth control, including "artificial" birth control. Mohler may be right, of course, that the loosening of the churches' opposition to contraception since 1900 allowed people to rethink their convictions about marriage. As a historical assertion, that is arguable. But Mohler makes this point normative, not just descriptive.

I also take a somewhat different position from him on new reproductive techniques such as artificial insemination and in-vitro fertilization. There are moral dangers here, but I think it is possible to practice these techniques without breaking biblical law. (I would not make such a case for surrogate motherhood or for artificial insemination by donor.) (For my arguments about these, see my *DCL*, chapter 40.) Again, it is possible that these developments have left some people open to the further loosening of the concept of marriage advocated by the LGBT community. That, I think, is unfortunate. But we should not be led by the great error of the LGBT movement to adopt views of reproduction that are more conservative than those of the Bible itself.

These "conservative" views are typically defended by natural law arguments rather than by biblical exegesis. Mohler commends natural law reasoning (59ff), but he also commends *sola Scriptura*, the sufficiency of Scripture. But traditionally the former characterizes Roman Catholic thinking, the latter Protestant. There is some methodological overlap, of course, between the two communities. But there are, to say the least, tensions within any attempt to combine these two methods of ethical reasoning, and Mohler doesn't help us to reconcile them. For my suggestions on these issues, see 239ff of the book cited earlier.

For all of this, the rebuke we receive in the title of Mohler's book rightly commands us to action. I hope that the Christian community will hearken to it. As Christian citizens, we must bring God's word into the present deplorable situation, lest we be prevented from speaking it at all.

67

When We Have No Recourse

This essay was published in Charlie Rodriguez, ed., Statism II *(Tanglewood Publishing, 2016).*

SCRIPTURE tells us to respect those who rule over us, both in the church (Heb. 13:17) and in the state (Rom. 13:1–7; 1 Pet. 2:13–17). Rulers over the state during the NT period were, more often than not, non-Christian, but Paul and Peter teach that we owe obedience, honor, and deference, even to those rulers who do not share our faith. God gives us these rulers "to punish them who do evil and to praise those who do good" (1 Pet. 2: 14). Paul adds,

> For rulers are not a terror to good conduct, but to bad. Would you have no fear of the one who is in authority? Then do what is good, and you will receive his approval, for he is God's servant for your good. But if you do wrong, be afraid, for he does not bear the sword in vain. For he is the servant of God, an avenger who carries out God's wrath on the wrongdoer. Therefore one must be in subjection, not only to avoid God's wrath but also for the sake of conscience. (Rom 13:3–5)

So God has provided civil rulers as a service to us. They maintain a smoothly functioning society, discouraging crimes and providing justice for our good.

For that reason, Scripture is generally opposed to civil disobedience and revolution. After Peter affirms respect to civil rulers, he
mentions analogous relationships (masters and slaves, husbands and
wives) that are often painful because the ruler is cruel and oppressive. Even in these cases, Peter does not counsel rebellion, but he
tells us to be like Christ in accepting suffering. It is a good thing, he
says, when "one endures sorrows while suffering unjustly" (1 Pet. 2:
29). We should infer, then, that we should tolerate a certain amount
of unjust suffering even from civil rulers, rather than resisting and
rebelling against them.

But there are limits to such toleration. In Acts 4:18, the priests
charged Peter and John "not to speak or teach at all in the name of
Jesus." But they replied,

> Whether it is right in the sight of God to listen to you rather
> than to God, you must judge, for we cannot but speak of what
> we have seen and heard. (Acts 4:19)

The disciples therefore disobeyed the priestly orders, and the priests
had them arrested again. The narrative continues:

> And when they had brought them, they set them before the coun-
> cil. And the high priest questioned them, saying, "We strictly
> charged you not to teach in this name, yet here you have filled
> Jerusalem with your teaching, and you intend to bring this man's
> blood upon us." But Peter and the apostles answered, "We must
> obey God rather than men ..." (Acts 5:27–29)

The priests were among the rulers of the Jewish people, and they had
soldiers at their disposal (Acts 5:26). Normally, Peter and John would
have accepted their obligation to obey the commands of the priests;
but in this case they declined. The priests had no right to silence the
gospel of Jesus Christ.

Is this the only exception to our obligation to obey rulers? I think not.
Later in the book of Acts, Paul was arrested again under the authority of
Felix, the Roman governor of Caesarea. Felix was unconvinced by the
evidence against Paul, but he kept Paul in prison, and after two years

he was succeeded as governor by Porcius Festus (Acts 24:27). Shortly afterward, Paul was tried before Festus. He pled his innocence:

> But Paul said, "I am standing before Caesar's tribunal, where I ought to be tried. To the Jews I have done no wrong, as you yourself know very well. If then I am a wrongdoer and have committed anything for which I deserve to die, I do not seek to escape death. But if there is nothing to their charges against me, no one can give me up to them. I appeal to Caesar." Then Festus, when he had conferred with his council, answered, "To Caesar you have appealed; to Caesar you shall go." (Act 25:10–12)

Here we see Paul's subordination to civil magistrates and civil law, just as he recommends this to Christians in Rom. 13. He is willing to obey the law, even if the law prescribes death for him. But he is not willing to accept false charges against him. And he is willing to use provisions of the law to defend himself. As a Roman citizen, he has the right to appeal to the emperor himself, and he does.

Just as in modern nation-states, "obeying the law" can be a complicated business. For there are many administrators of the law, from Caesar, down to the Roman governors, down to the puppet kings (like Herod Agrippa, Acts 25:13–27), centurions, and soldiers. Any of these may order a person to do something, and their words are in effect law, at least for the moment. But of course all of these lawgivers are human beings, fallible, and sometimes wicked. These human lawgivers often make mistakes, and sometimes they willfully distort the legal process. To remedy such misuses of the law, most legal systems allow means of appeal to higher authorities. But to appeal to higher authority is to question, temporarily at least, the lower authority.

Does this mean that the highest civil authority, Caesar, is above the law, or that the law is whatever Caesar says it is? In most cases, no. The emperor or king is himself subject to other authorities, such as a legislature like the Roman Senate, or a system of courts. So we speak of "checks and balances." The society functions best when these authorities all operate within the boundaries of the law, resisting encroachments by other authorities.

When Paul tells Christians to be subject to authorities, he refers to that whole system of laws and appeals. It is that system that rewards good and punishes evil, even when an individual administrator fails or refuses to carry out his responsibility.

But what happens when the highest ruler, the emperor or king, becomes lawless? This is the definition of tyranny. In an otherwise well-ordered state, however, there is a remedy for that: what Calvin and the Reformed tradition have called the "lesser magistrates." In a well-ordered state, the emperor or king may not do anything he likes. He is, like everyone else in the society, under law, the same law that everyone else must observe. The legislature, the courts, and the other administrators of the law have the right to call the emperor or king to account. If he breaks the law, he must bear its punishment. In an extreme case, the law may provide that he be removed from office.

Of course, all this is more easily said than done. Emperors, kings, and presidents often do not respond gladly to those who attempt to enforce a nation's laws against them. Frequently, the misbehavior of the highest magistrate leads to a "constitutional crisis." And often the written statutes of the law do not tell the society what to do in a constitutional crisis. Even the most well-ordered society can be broken down by the efforts of sinful rulers.

And so we should consider the "worst-case scenario," a system like that of Nazi Germany in which the state, instead of being a terror to bad conduct (Rom. 13:3) becomes a terror to the good. In such a terror state, all mechanisms of appeal break down, and an evil ruler enforces his arbitrary ability to arrest or kill anyone who gets in his way.

Such a state, in my judgment, is not a "governing authority" "instituted by God" in terms of Rom. 13:1. But even in this sort of situation we ought to observe the respect for authority that we have seen in Rom. 13 and 1 Pet. 2. We should never be anarchists, people who reject all authority in favor of their own autonomy. We should seek to form something better. We should gather together in a group that has the goal of being a functional government. That embryo government must seek justice. That group may, and should, become a fighting force; for that is one of the important functions of government, to defend its society by force if necessary.

The terror state will not acknowledge the legitimacy of our embryo government. They, and uncommitted people in the society, may well characterize it as a rebellion or a revolutionary movement. They may invoke against it the passages we cited earlier, from Rom. 13 and 1 Pet. 2. Ultimately, God will judge.

In the Vietnam war, there was often confusion as to who was the "legitimate government" in a territory. In a village, the Saigon government might establish rule during the day, while the Viet Cong would rule at night. Christians were faced with the question of which of these, or a third, was a legitimate government in terms of Rom. 13. Sometimes the question did not have an obvious answer. But Christians were forced to pray for wisdom to gain God's answer, and then to act accordingly.

So there are times when God authorizes Christians to be part of what some would characterize as a rebellion or revolution against a state. We should not enter lightly into such a movement. It can be a matter of life and death. And we should approach such a decision with a keen sense of our own sin, our need of God's grace in Christ, and prayer for the wisdom of God's Holy Spirit.

68

Why I Signed the Nashville Statement

The Nashville Statement, dealing with marriage, can be found at
https://cbmw.org/nashville-statement/.

I SIGNED THE NASHVILLE STATEMENT, because it is a true statement of biblical teaching on a set of topics of great importance today.

According to Scripture, marriage is the fundamental building block
of society, and it symbolizes the covenantal union between ourselves
and our creator. God established it before our fall into sin, in Gen.
2:22–24, so it is an essential part of our life on earth. And the Genesis
account of marriage immediately follows and presupposes God's miraculous division of Adam into two sexes (vv. 10–23). When Scripture uses
marriage as a symbol of our relationship to God, as in Eph. 5:22–33,
sexual differentiation is again at the forefront. Husbands have one set
of roles, wives another. Our relation to Christ is that of his bride, not
his bridegroom.

Today, many question this biblical concept of marriage. Indeed,
many consider it bigoted to hold such a view. Many think that it is
harmful, that it disparages and condemns others. Indeed, it does present
a position that seems wrong to many. But if our society were to embrace
this position, together with the worldview it presupposes, the results
would be joyful and delightful. So it would be wrong for Christians to

withhold these blessings from others in our society by failing to proclaim them. And it is wrong for anyone to ignore, deny, or distort this wonderful truth.

It would have been better if this message had been set forth by the church, rather than by a group of individual Christians. The church is the people of God, and it should be unmistakably setting forth all of God's truth. But the failure of the church does not excuse individual Christians from their task of proclaiming the good news. That the Nashville group set forth this statement was an excellent thing, one that all Christians should be cheering.

Of course, there is much more to the gospel than the biblical view of marriage. The gospel, the good news, is that God sent forth his only Son to live our life, die for sinners, and rise again, receiving from his Father all authority in heaven and on earth. But the biblical vision of marriage is part of the gospel worldview, the gospel promise. The gospel is not only a promise of heaven; it is a promise of blessed life here and now. And part of that blessed life is a renewal of earthly marriage as the anticipation of heavenly marriage.

69

Review of Douglas Groothuis's
Walking through Twilight: A Wife's Illness—A Philosopher's Lament

I posted this review to Amazon.com and to Facebook.
The book itself was published by IVP in 2017.

DOUG GROOTHUIS and I recently exchanged memoirs. Inside the cover of my *Theology of My Life* (Eugene, OR: Cascade Books, 2017) I wrote, "Doug, I thought I had written a half-decent memoir until I read yours." Mine was a kind of general autobiography, with theological observations. Doug's was focused on a single, sad aspect of Doug's recent life: the descent into dementia of his wife Becky. So it reaches depths of humanity I never tried, in my own book, to describe.

Rebecca Merrill Groothuis was a brilliant woman, the author of several books, the invaluable editor of Doug's writings. Doug readily admits that Becky was his intellectual superior. But now she is unable to eat a meal or brush her teeth without assistance. Her illness is not Alzheimer's, but the rarer primary progressive aphasia, which has many (but not all) of the same effects as Alzheimers. Like Alzheimer's, Becky's disease is not curable, and it is fatal.

Doug suffers as a Christian, and as a philosopher. His reflections in this book, therefore, are profound in many different ways. He contemplates the nature of evil—a common theological and philosophical topic—but with an intimacy made necessary by his situation. He speaks of the temptation to hate God, a temptation he boldly resists. He describes "learning to lament," moved by the Psalms and Ecclesiastes, and shows how even the profoundest of lament can be suffused with joy. He expounds some Scripture texts at length, notably Ps. 90.

The combination of tragedy and divine comfort determine a unique lifestyle. His grief has not turned him away from practical life, from his divine calling. Doug describes "Lamenting in the Classroom," "Lamenting Online," the place of humor in the midst of grief, the use of language in lament, the continuing role in his life of books of all kinds, his love for jazz, for art, and for the family dog, Sunny. Doug's love for God's world and its culture might be described as "escape," but Doug shows to what extent and in what way escape is justified to one who is afflicted. He "escapes into meaning"; that is, through all his learning and experience he seeks to understand Becky and his own grief, and to engage in the world, providing a context for his grief, both within and outside of his suffering, that will benefit others.

I love this book and value it greatly for my own edification. It is philosophy at its best, working through traditional philosophical problems in the middle of real pain. That kind of philosophy can clarify these subjects as nothing else can, testing the theories by the extreme case. Most of us have not been called to suffer in the same way as Doug and Becky. But living in a fallen world, as fallen creatures, gives each of us some grief, some reason to lament. From one perspective, the Bible is all about suffering and loss. And Doug's meditations help us draw near to God—the God of Job as well as the God of Jesus; the God of Lamentations and the God of Paul's "Rejoice in the Lord Always." The Bible's story of loss ends in grace and glory—seemingly far from us now, but summoning us from within our lament.

70

Diet, Theology, and Medicine

For many people, their main thought about me is that I am overweight. Uglier words, like "obese," have doubtless been entertained. (Most acquaintances would agree that I have not reached the point of being "morbidly obese.") One negative reviewer called me a "roly-poly theologian."

In the present time, writers are often very conscious about characterizing people with afflictions. If someone lacks a leg, you speak about his affliction very gently and gingerly; you don't speak of him as a "cripple," and even "disabled" is not politically correct. You may call him "differently abled," but even that language may be criticized for making too much of his condition, drawing unnecessary attention to it. Same for conditions that a person is arguably responsible for, at least partially: e.g., alcoholism and addiction. Same for other medical conditions.

Overweight is the only condition you may joke about, and about which you can without qualification blame the person who has the condition. Alas, I do think there is some injustice about how fat people are treated in our society, but I will not here seek gentler treatment for them or for myself. Rather, I will meditate here a bit on how I should think of myself. Is being overweight a sin? Stupidity? Laziness? An affliction, or even an illness? An attack of Satan?

It is relevant to note that I like food a lot—in most all varieties and quantities. I feel the opposite way about exercise. I have always been hopeless as an athlete, though in younger days I used to enjoy swimming and walking. Today, moderate exercise only makes me tired, and it never takes weight off. I think that the only diet I could follow to rid me of my 100 or so excess pounds would be a diet with NO red meat, NO carbs, NO sweets, and I look at such a diet with extreme distaste. Further, I would have to follow such a diet for the rest of my life, and I cannot abide the thought of such torture. It's not that I don't enjoy diet meals. My wife makes them deliciously, and I love them. But I love other things too. My problem with diets is not what I may eat, but what I may not eat. My dear wife thinks that if I "eat healthy," eventually my taste buds will "change," and I will not enjoy high-calorie food. I've tried that many times in my life, and my taste buds have never changed, even by a small degree.

I have been on every kind of diet there is, and every kind of diet supplement, pill, and powder. Some of these have worked for a while. But eventually they all lead to plateaus and frustration. None of them will keep me thin for the rest of my life.

Does my theology speak to these issues? I once wrote an essay on "Triperspectival Dieting,"[1] drawing on my threefold scheme for treating theological questions. Applied to diet, the "normative perspective" has to do with what Scripture requires of me, the "situational perspective" with what does the most good and the least harm, and the "existential perspective" with what will bring me the best inner satisfaction.

The normative perspective has not helped me much, because Scripture doesn't say much about what we may eat, except in specialized contexts like Gen. 3 and 1 Cor. 11. It does say that we should not treat the belly as God (Phil. 3:19). It also says that we should eat and drink to God's glory (1 Cor. 10:31). These are serious teachings, but I haven't been convicted of having violated them. First Corinthians 6:19 says that the body is a temple of the Holy Spirit, and that certainly warrants care for our health. The immediate context of that verse is sexual morality, however, a topic somewhat removed from the question of diet.

1. Frame, SSW2, 368–70.

But I must take seriously the issue of health, which takes me into the situational perspective. The consensus today is that you ought to "eat healthy" and exercise in order to be maximally healthy. But I am not entirely persuaded: (1) Medical consensus constantly changes. What was "healthy" last year is no longer considered healthy today. What was considered healthy 100 years ago is often repudiated today, and we wonder what will be considered healthy 100 years from now, if the Lord tarries. (2) How healthy do you need to be? I am 79; my father died at 73, my mother at 85. I am in good health today, and I don't believe that my eating habits have led to any negative physical complications. Of course, eventually I will die, probably in the next few years. But does it really make sense to undergo terrible misery (the misery of dieting and exercising) in order to grab another month or year of life? I have had a good life, have made some contributions to my chosen field, have provided well for my family. Can anyone expect or demand more of me? Can a healthier lifestyle be reasonably considered as an application of any normative biblical obligation?

So the existential perspective has become my regular approach to these matters. In eating, my main interest is inner satisfaction. In most circumstances, it means that I will eat what I want. In others, I will gain more inner satisfaction by trying to make my wife and others happy.

My appearance is another issue that is certainly relevant. Fat people are not considered attractive in our society. But it is not clear how much I am obligated to fit people's images of what I should look like. I would like to look better—at least to my wife, maybe to a few others. But in general I believe that our society is too preoccupied by appearances. And there's the following point that I rarely mention: my ungainly looks have limited demands on me for public appearances. People usually don't ask me to preach or teach outside my campus. I am not asked to do public relations work. I am not invited to meet with donors. People are happier with me if I hide away and write, doing a minimum of other things. That hiding has not hurt me. I am an introvert, and I do not function well at parties, conventions, convocations, conferences, and so on. My enjoyment comes when I can be myself or when I can spend time with family and/or close friends. It is in those contexts that I best carry on my calling. My overweightness has thus been an advantage in many of the areas of my life, and it has enabled me better to serve God.

I will probably try again, to please my wife, to eat more respectably. But I can only go so far with this. And I am not convinced as of now that "healthy" dieting is a requirement of Scripture or that neglecting it is a sin.

UPDATE, August 2020: I have lost sixty pounds in COVID isolation.

71

The Priority of Medicine

IN MY YOUTH, I rarely saw doctors. I got medical examinations required by schools and to prepare for foreign trips. I saw doctors when I really felt sick, or when I was injured. Through those years I believe that I developed a good appreciation of medical science and of the quality of care given by medical professionals. I sometimes describe my relationship to medicine in those days as "old school."

Today, however, people seem to be demanding of me a different approach to medicine, which I refer to as "new school." Partly, I think, this is due to my advanced age, which is thought to entail new medical requirements. But to an extent, it seems that people of whatever age are expected to put a much higher priority on medicine. One way to characterize this new approach is with the word "prevention." We are told that it is not enough to treat diseases and injuries as they come; it is necessary to turn regularly to doctors to *prevent* any such problems from taking place. This approach, of course, requires us to put a much higher priority on medicine, to take much more time and care with medical issues.

The demands of health insurance (whether private insurance or governmental arrangements like Medicare or Obamacare) are one factor promoting the new school approach. Patients (we are all patients now!) are expected to see their doctors once a year for "wellness" exams. People with special needs are expected to make additional preventive visits, such as women receiving mammograms. The wellness exam is essentially a "fishing expedition." The physician looks as hard as he can to find something wrong with you. When he does (and there is almost always *something* wrong) he refers you for tests, examinations by specialists, prescriptions, diagnostic and curative procedures, hospital stays, and the like, so that medicine takes up more and more of our time and attention. Although physicians often talk about how the body has the capacity to heal itself, they almost never give it the opportunity to do so. They see their job as one of taking action—interfering with natural processes so as to deal with the symptoms they have discovered.

I'm a bit of a rebel against new school medicine. I describe myself (even to doctors) as "old school," defining that as above. I respect medical science and have often been deeply grateful for it. I would not hesitate to see a doctor if I felt really sick or had received a bad injury. But I tend to avoid "routine exams," "wellness visits," and so on, though that is hard to do given the demands of insurance companies and the doctors' view of their own responsibility. Part of my attitude arises from my concept of my calling. I believe I am called to attend to my family and my theological work, even at some possible (theoretical?) cost to my health.

Another part of my attitude arises from a certain skepticism about the contemporary claims of medicine. Some of this skepticism came from my interaction with Franklin Edward Payne, himself a physician, who wrote *Biblical/Medical Ethics*.[1] In this book, Payne calls his own profession to task, claiming that doctors too often make claims for medicine that are too grandiose, and which influence people to give medicine too high a priority in their lives. Payne is a Christian, and much of his critique is based on the biblical teaching that we need to give more emphasis to the kingdom of God (Matt. 6:33) and less to the perfecting of our physical life on earth.

Medicine is constantly changing. What was good medicine ten years ago has been subject to much correction since. And we shudder to think

---

1. Milford, MI: Mott Media, 1985. See also his article, "Medical Ethics: Building on John Frame and His Work," in John J. Hughes, ed., *Speaking the Truth in Love: The Theology of John Frame* (Phillipsburg, NJ: P&R Publishing, 2009), 802–29.

of how medical conditions were treated 100 years ago. If the Lord tarries, we wonder what people in the year 2119 will think of 2019 medicine. Medicine in 2019, or any other time, is not suitable to govern all aspects of our lives. It is not suitable to perform divine functions. God alone is able to govern my total well-being, both in the spiritual sphere and in the physical sphere.

Today I see my cardiologist twice a year and have blood tests twice a year for his convenience. I see my sleep apnea doctor once a year, because Medicare tells me I must, even though those visits rarely illumine my condition. Those visits sometimes lead to sleep tests, which usually require one night with virtually no sleep and no benefit except for some boxes to be checked on forms. I see the dentist three or four times a year, because he tells me I have periodontal disease, a "silent killer." I also have silent killers like high blood pressure and cholesterol, now treated with prescription drugs. My heart disease is also without symptoms: I've never had a stroke or a heart attack. Might it be that my examinations for these diseases are to some extent part of defensive medicine—to avoid lawsuits—not to make me healthier?

In addition to all these, I'm supposed to go to a "primary care physician," to receive a level of care as an umbrella over all these other conditions. Medicare requires me to have one. I had one once who would not renew prescriptions unless I had an office visit with him. I would call on Wednesday and ask him to renew my prescription which had run out. He would say no; I would have to have an examination before the end of the week, very short notice, inconvenient as that usually was for me and for him. So I would go in on Friday. His secretary would ask why I was there. I would tell her, to get my prescription refilled. I would go in, but the doctor's staff still failed to know why I was visiting. They would make me wait, then poke me and ask me questions. It always seemed like a waste of time. I still have the name of a doctor whom I designate as my primary care physician; but I manage in many ways to avoid seeing him. I wish that Dr. Ed Payne could be my primary care physician.

To repeat myself, I have had great experiences with some doctors, and I appreciate the profession greatly. Physicians make huge sacrifices of time, money, and heartache to be trained and to attend to their patients. They have accumulated huge stores of knowledge and most of them have also attained much wisdom. I ask only that they look harder at the big picture—the place of medicine among biblical priorities, and the right of patients to make more of their own decisions.

72

Being on Jesus's Side

From my journal.

TUES., DEC. 29, 2020: I wrote a student yesterday, who asked me how the church could identify those who are true Christians. Baptism and church membership are often misleading. Creedal affirmations are important, but we cannot forget that the Pharisees were largely orthodox. Fruits of the spirit are often difficult to identify. What about people who make major mistakes in doctrine, sometimes because they've been misled? What about people who reject orthodox Christianity because it's been misleadingly presented to them, or because the people presenting it are beset by inconsistencies of life and doctrine?

I told him something I'd been thinking a lot about lately: being a Christian is being on Jesus's side.

In the OT, God called people (as through Joshua [24:15ff]), to "choose this day whom you will serve." It was like a political decision. In Jesus's earthly ministry, he always forced people to choose between the false piety of the Jewish leaders, the cruel power of the Romans, and his own kingdom which was "not of this world." Jesus healed people, taught them to love God and one another, and to hate evil. In his atoning work, the powers of the world under Satan gained an apparent victory. But his resurrection defeated them.

In Acts 2, Peter again made the challenge to choose this day. Jesus was aligned against Herod, Pilate, the Jews, and the Gentiles. The people could choose to follow that good man who called them to love God and one another, who was unjustly put to death, or to follow his murderers, who followed the world's religion of power and hate. Three thousand chose Jesus.

There was not an elaborate catechetical period. The people knew, and Peter made it clearer, what the issues were. Those on Jesus's side were known as Christians. The others returned to their old ways. Of course, God's sovereign choice was behind it all.

So when I want to know whether someone is a Christian, I ask them whether they are on Jesus's side. If the Chinese communists, say, were to come to your door and ask your allegiance, if you are a Christian, you will testify of Jesus. Your testimony may be weak and inaccurate. You may have even been raised in some other faith. You may have been taught very badly. But when the choice is stark, between this good man Jesus and the people who put them to death, you are a Christian if you stand on Jesus's side.

Personal Reflections

Personal Reflections

73

1 Thessalonians 1 and Church Planting: Charge at Ross Meyer's Ordination

Ross was being ordained as a missionary to a Muslim section of London.

[1] Paul, Silvanus, and Timothy, To the church of the Thessalonians in God the Father and the Lord Jesus Christ: Grace to you and peace. [2] We give thanks to God always for all of you, constantly mentioning you in our prayers, [3] remembering before our God and Father your work of faith and labor of love and steadfastness of hope in our Lord Jesus Christ. [4] For we know, brothers loved by God, that he has chosen you, [5] because our gospel came to you not only in word, but also in power and in the Holy Spirit and with full conviction. You know what kind of men we proved to be among you for your sake. [6] And you became imitators of us and of the Lord, for you received the word in much affliction, with the joy of the Holy Spirit, [7] so that you became an example to all the believers in Macedonia and in Achaia. [8] For not only has the word of the Lord sounded forth from you in Macedonia and Achaia, but your faith in God has gone forth everywhere, so that we need not say anything. [9] For they themselves report concerning us the kind of reception we had among you, and how you turned to God from idols to serve the living and true God, [10] and

Part 8 | Personal Reflections

to wait for his Son from heaven, whom he raised from the dead, Jesus who delivers us from the wrath to come. (1 Thess. 1:1–10)

Ross, you are entering a ministry as a church planter, so I would like to charge you with a biblical picture of what kind of church you should seek to plant. First Thessalonians 1 gives us such a picture. The church Paul and Timothy planted (according to Acts 17) was not a perfect church. The believers had some misunderstandings about the last days (don't we all?) and about the place of work in the Christian life. But the overall picture, which we see in chapter one, is very nearly ideal. I pray, Ross, that this description will fit the churches in England that God will enable you to plant.

Paul sums up this picture with the triad of faith, hope, and love, which we see elsewhere in the NT, especially in 1 Cor. 13. Paul remembers, he says, "your work of faith and labor of love and steadfastness of hope in our Lord Jesus Christ" (v. 3). Let's start with the love. It begins with God's love to them (v. 4), evidence of their election. That is remarkable. From their behavior, Paul discerns that God not only loves them, but has elected them—that is, that he has loved them before the foundation of the world. Since God loved them in Christ before the foundation of the world, they welcomed Paul and Timothy (v. 9). They loved, because God had first loved them.

This divine love led them to follow Paul and Timothy, both in their beliefs and in their behavior. This is what Paul calls their "work of faith." When Paul preached the gospel in their town, God's love moved them to believe it, even though they had been worshiping idols (v. 9).

They received Paul's words, but those words were not just words. They had a power, God's own power, to transform the people, and much of that power came because of the apostles' *lives*. The Thessalonians knew "what kind of men we proved to be among you for your sake" (v. 5). "And," he goes on, "you became imitators of us, and of the Lord." I pray, Ross and Aislinn, that you will live lives of such integrity that through God's grace people will want to be like you.

This is all the more remarkable, because this church was founded in a time of persecution. Paul says, "you received the word in much affliction, with the joy of the Holy Spirit" (v. 6). Interesting couplet there: affliction and joy. The affliction didn't hinder their faith. They went on believing in Jesus, no matter what the unbelieving authorities did to them. But they didn't just grit their teeth and resolve, stoically, to accept persecution; rather, their faith actually made them joyful. Whatever the persecutors do, they thought, Jesus is King, and Jesus will prevail. In a time where culture and political forces oppose the gospel as they did then, I pray, Ross, that your gospel, like Paul's, will generate, not only steadfastness, but also joy.

Notice the progression: the people imitated Paul, his words, and his life. And as Paul's words settled in them, they too became examples—not just to others in Thessalonica, but, says Paul, their faith became known everywhere: Macedonia, Achaia, everywhere (v. 8). Their faith became famous. So Paul didn't need to boast about his achievements there; the famous spiritual growth of the church alone was enough to vindicate Paul's ministry among them. Ross, I pray that you too will benefit from this kind of advertising, so that people will want you to export your ministry into many other places.

I've talked briefly about the Thessalonians' labor of love, and their work of faith. Now their steadfastness of hope. When the Thessalonians "turned from idols to serve the living and true God," part of that was "to wait for his Son from Heaven, whom he raised from the dead, Jesus, who delivers us from the wrath to come" (vv. 9–10). Again, as we learn later in Paul's letter, they were some misunderstandings in the church about Jesus's return and its implications for their daily lives: they needed to know that Jesus's return didn't imply that they should stop working. Work was a good thing, and it still is.

But even amid those misunderstandings, the promise of the return of Christ was precious to them, and that is a good thing. If you hold a sign in London that says Jesus is coming, fashionable Britons will greet you with sophisticated, smug unbelief. Modern man can believe in a god who stays in heaven and never touches time or space, who resolves never to do anything that offends philosophers or scientists. But when you suggest that God is going to come visibly and do what none of the fashionable people think is possible, then you will endure seemingly universal scorn. But it may be just the thing to grab their attention. They need to know that the Christian faith is not a religious vocabulary for expressing a secular vision. They need to consider that it may be nothing less than the word of a living and true God.

For all their misunderstandings—the amazing thing is that this was a very young church—the Thessalonians understood this. And the knowledge of Jesus and his coming energized them to stand firm, to be courageous, and to spread the gospel to peoples all around them. I pray, Ross, that you will plant churches like this, and that these will make a great difference—in Britain, in East Asia, and throughout the world.

74

Blurbs

FOR MANY YEARS I have been asked to write endorsements for the books of other authors, and other authors have been asked to write endorsements for mine. But recently, as I have entered retirement, these requests have come in even more thick and fast. I'm hoping that the next generation of writers and publishers will develop a different model.

What mainly motivates the avalanche of blurbs is the need of publishers to market their products. These days, it seems, nothing ever gets published unless there are at least two or three well-known authors who are willing to put their commendations on its cover or its inside.

These endorsements—or blurbs—do seem to be of some help to book purchasers. But like everything in this fallen world, blurbs are problematic.

Since blurbs are usually only a sentence or two (sometimes more), it seems that writing them should be an easy task. But to say that ignores the obvious fact that the blurb writer must actually read the book before he writes his two-sentence endorsement. And if he is to write with integrity, he must read carefully, making evaluations as to content and style. That is not so easy.

I confess that I am a slow reader (though I can skim very fast— often a temptation in such tasks). Forty pages an hour is about all I can manage with good comprehension. Even at that pace, I need to take breaks in order to maintain attention. And I need to re-read sections, perhaps even to read the whole book twice, in order to have a clear and cogent opinion. For a 300-page book, that may take two full work-days, or even a week of work on the book when I am trying to complete other work at the same time.

That's a matter of integrity. When I read a book for endorsement, I believe that I owe that book as much care as a book for which I might write a 20-page review. I could probably fool the public pretty well, endorsing books on the basis of a skim. (I joke sometimes about my "intensive skim" which, to be honest, I have sometimes had to apply to these assignments.) But that is a confession of sin. I should not do that, and I should not agree to a schedule that forces me to do that.

James I. Packer is well known as a leading theologian and a prolific writer of blurbs. A student once asked him, "Dr. Packer, do you actually read all the books you endorse?" Packer replied with terrifying indignation that the question was insolent and insulting. Of course he reads the books he recommends! To do otherwise would be to sin against the living God! I want to be like Packer, as he is like Jesus. And I do not want only to read the books I endorse; I believe that I owe it to the author, the readers, and God, to read them thoroughly, to give them more than a "skim." But I confess that I have sometimes made commitments that I could not carry out with this kind of integrity.

When I take up a normal writing project, I am able to plan the time it takes. I determine my own deadline, and the various steps needed to complete the project in that amount of time. That is important to me. Under time pressure, I do not write well. But usually when I get a request for an endorsement, that request does not express the slightest respect for my schedule.

After a publisher has accepted a manuscript, he will typically sit on it for months, rarely giving out any information as to when he expects to publish it. The manuscript remains in a queue, until other manuscripts are dealt with. Then the publisher sets up a schedule. Typically, that schedule forces everybody (the author, the editor, the copyreader, the typesetter, the blurb-writer) to operate at breakneck speed to accommodate the publisher's deadlines.

So it hasn't been uncommon for me to receive someone's manuscript and be asked for an endorsement in two weeks, or even in two days. Often that forces me to drastically remake my schedule, generally at the expense of my own writing projects. That kind of treatment tempts the endorser to shoddy work.

And incidentally, the economics of publishing dictate that I may not be paid for these hours or weeks of work, which I consider to be as hard as anything else I do.

Very occasionally, I "just say no." I can do that, if the book is far removed from my field of study. But I rarely get books like that. Often the request comes laden with all sorts of reasons why I cannot refuse: the author was a former student of mine; he has labored for years on the mission field; he is trying desperately to meet his family budget. Or often: he has given an endorsement to one of *my* books, so I really have an obligation to endorse his in return.

So to some extent the book endorsement business becomes a matter of authors scratching one another's backs. It is very difficult to refuse an endorsement to an old friend, or to someone who likes your ideas, or to a member of your own theological party. And it is relatively easy to refuse an endorsement to someone who is not your friend, or who belongs to an opposing faction. One may, of course, start by saying "I do not vouch for every statement in this volume," but one rarely does this, if he wants his blurb to be accepted. But however that may be, the endorsement business exacerbates the theological and political factionalism that divides the Christian world.

I retired in May of 2017. Retirement is increasingly meaningless; I will certainly continue to study and write in my field. But some change will be necessary. I would like to announce that after June 1, 2017, I will not write any more blurbs, but I really cannot make that announcement. One should never say "never." Dr. Packer has endorsed books into his 90s, and if God gives me that many years, I expect that I will feel the obligation to do the same. But I do expect to be saying "no" more often than I did before June of 2017.

I understand publishers' need to market their products and to motivate buyers. I don't know what system will improve on the present one. But I do pray that God will lead publishers and authors to a better system—one that will meet the genuine needs of publishers without compromising the schedules and the integrity of endorsers.

75

Interview with *Theology for Life* Magazine

T4L: Thank you very much for agreeing to do this interview with *Theology for Life* magazine, Dr. Frame. Can you tell us a bit about your life, marriage, ministry, and your current ministry projects?

John Frame: I was born in Pittsburgh in 1939, received Jesus as my Savior and Lord around the age of 12. I got my A. B. at Princeton University, studied theology at Westminster Seminary, earned two Masters' Degrees at Yale University. I married Mary Grace in 1984, served as stepdad to Debbie, Doreen, and Skip, and as biodad to Justin and Johnny. I taught theology at Westminster Seminary in Philadelphia, Westminster in California, and Reformed Theological Seminary in Orlando.

T4L: Can you briefly outline the work of Christ as King?

Dr. Frame: As God, Jesus shares the rule of the Father and the Holy Spirit over all things. As man, he receives the authority over all things that the Father has given him (Matt. 28:18).

T4L: Can you help us understand Christ as Prophet, please?

Dr. Frame: As God, Jesus IS the Word of God, the word that all the prophets spoke (John 1:1–14). As man, Jesus speaks all the truth the

Father has given him to speak. So he is the greatest of the prophets. He came to fulfill all the law and the prophets (Matt. 5:17).

T4L: Can you please briefly outline Christ as Priest, please?

Dr. Frame: As God, Jesus is the one God who alone can be mediator between God and man (1 Tim. 2:5). As man, he laid down his life as a sacrifice for sinners, dying the death they deserved (Matt. 20:28).

T4L: Can you please help us understand what triperspectivalism is and how this concept came to be so important to you and why you've written so much on it over the years?

Dr. Frame: Often when Scripture distinguishes parts or aspects of a doctrine, it does not separate them, but shows how they are inseparably united to one another. In the case of the three offices of Christ, Jesus could not have been king unless he had been prophet (uttering God's word of supreme power) and priest (who can mediate God's power to the created universe). He could not have been the supreme prophet unless his word had kingly power and the supreme priestly ability to reach our hearts. Nor could he have been the greatest priest unless he had the kingly power to break through man's sin and the truth that is a perfect reflection of the Father's intentions.

T4L: Why does triperspectivalism matter for the Christian and those in Christian ministry?

Dr. Frame: It begins in the mysterious doctrine of the Trinity. In every phase of our experience and in all of our salvation, God acts as Father, Son, and Holy Spirit. There is a simplicity to it: he saves us completely from our sins and all their consequences. But in that simplicity there is a wonderful richness, for we have fellowship with God in every way. In him we have a strong Father, a loving Son, and a Holy Spirit who dwells with us and in us. We have a relationship with God in all his fulness. So in every moment he governs us as King, speaks to us as Prophet, and nurtures us as Priest.

T4L: Thank you for taking time out of your busy schedule to do this interview, Dr. Frame!

Dr. Frame: You're welcome!

76

Thoughts on My Friendship
with Steve Hays

Steve was a close friend of mine. He passed away early in 2020. One of his colleagues at his blog, Triablogue, asked me to write some reflections.

I THINK I MET STEVE in the early 90s. When you teach theology, people come out of the blue and ask you questions. And that's what happened, in a way, with Steve. Typically, such correspondents want to ask about predestination or the millennium— the conventional topics of the day. But Steve's question was very different.

He asked something like, "Can Reformed Christians believe in 'occasionalism,' following Malebranche?"[1] When people try to understand causality, they think in terms of David Hume, and determinism, and freedom. Malebranche was a philosophical predecessor to David Hume. Steve had been reading a history of philosophy, and Malebranche was kind of like a theistic Humean, except that he lived prior to Hume. His occasionalism held that God is the only causal agent, and that creatures provide the "occasion" for divine action.

Steve's question threw me for a loop. I had never considered this question. I tried to persuade Steve that God did create the world with

---

1. See, for example, the article on Malebranche at https://plato.stanford.edu.

a real causal structure. That God causes things in such a way that the world does produce genuine causes. But his question was very unlike the questions I received from others. Typically, when people write to a professor of theology, they ask about predestination, or the millennium. Sometimes they will ask someone like me in the field of apologetics about presuppositionalism. But Malebranchian occasionalism? This was the first and only time.

According to my very fallible memory, after our brief correspondence, Steve joined us at WSCal as a student. He took some classes for about a year, and then he went back north.

Maybe a year later, I got a note from a former student and WSCal alumnus in the Northwest. He had become a pastor.

He wrote to me, "Is it possible that there's such a thing as a theological prodigy?" He wrote about this fellow he knew, and, given the details and the locations, I knew it had to be Steve Hays.

Steve came back to WSCal in the late 1990s, and he took most of my classes. We became good friends.

On one occasion, my wife had Steve to dinner, and he seemed to trail me around the house, asking question after question, and writing my answers in a notebook.

Unfortunately, that was the time when things became sticky for me at WSCal. What had been a wonderful, congenial, and collegial faculty in the eighties had become faction-ridden, and it seemed that everybody was at each other's throats. Steve was an encouragement to me, but he didn't take sides in the controversies. Looking back on the experience, Steve later described himself as neither confessional enough, nor Klinean enough, for the culture there. "I'd prefer to stay closer to the Scriptures," he said. Me too.

In 1999 I got my family together and moved to Orlando, Florida. Teaching at Reformed Theological Seminary was the greatest 17 years of my life.

Around that same time, Steve and his mother decided to move east, to Charleston, SC. Steve was close to his parents, and his father had died in 1999, a month before Steve's fortieth birthday. RTS also had a campus in Charlotte, NC, and Steve became associated there.

Together we became involved in producing a distance education program. I taught a number of courses, in theology, philosophy, ethics, and apologetics. Steve worked as my teaching assistant, as well as working on his own project.

Unfortunately, Steve became disassociated with RTS. I think he was in an online discussion that became a little too heated. I'm not sure what it was, but something happened, and he began blogging at Triablogue.

I've followed Steve over the years. In fact, Triablogue is the only blog that I've read consistently. When I went to my office each morning and turned on the computer, Triablogue was part of my regular routine.

Over the years, Steve has been helpful to me in a number of ways, such as in discussions with some of the neo-Thomists in recent years. For a while, it looked as if the whole Reformed world was about to go neo-Thomist. Paul Helm, Richard Muller, and many other Reformed thinkers joined the movement.

I recognized, and still do, that there are many good things in the work of Thomas Aquinas. But Thomas mixed up his good biblical theology with a lot of pagan philosophy from Plato, and especially Aristotle. I am a student of Cornelius Van Til, and like Van Til I have always been critical of Thomas's compromises with Greek philosophy.

I wrote some brief essays such as "Two Models of Divine Transcendence: Pure Being vs. Divine Lordship"[2] to indicate my view of things.

I realize that Thomas was trying to reconcile some Christian theologies with ideas from some of the great philosophies. It would be unthinkable for a Christian thinker living in his time not to do that. But "pure being" is not in the Bible. The biblical God is not Aristotle's "prime mover," although some try very hard to make that identification. God is YHWH, who makes covenant with Abraham, Isaac, and Jacob.

Over the course of those years, Steve became a very sophisticated philosopher. I've been at some of the leading seminaries and universities in the country, and I was amazed at how much philosophical reading Steve did. He was aware of philosophical conversations that I'd never heard of.

---

2. Reprinted earlier in this volume.

He had personal correspondence with many philosophers, as well as theologians, and he learned quickly how these professional thinkers discussed issues. Steve avoided stereotyped lists of talking points (alas, the common content of evangelical theology) and instead developed careful, cogent chains of argument, nuanced and qualified.

He tended to develop his arguments as I also do, with numbered lists of points. He'd develop one point, then another, indicating that he wanted to focus on this issue, rather than that. Whatever it was that Steve wrote, you always could tell that he knew what he was talking about.

I was interested that in our numbered-list approach, and in our way of approaching problems, Steve and I were very similar. I think he learned from me, but the reverse was also true.

In sum, I regarded Steve as a kindred spirit. He wasn't always on my side, but he was a godly man, devoted to his family, seeking to think God's thoughts after him.

He wasn't afraid to step outside of boundaries. So while he was always thoroughly Reformed in his thinking, he didn't use buzz words. He didn't always make conventional arguments. He wasn't afraid to delve into unpopular topics.

Consider the issue of cessationism, the question of whether the gifts of tongues and miracles ceased at the end of the apostolic age. In my judgment, the central question in this controversy is the sufficiency of Scripture. The question is not whether tongues or miracles occur, but whether they occur in such a way as to compromise the finality of the written word. Yes, natural revelation is helpful, and we learn that from Romans 1. We also know that God has spoken to people through dreams and visions. But Scripture is a sufficient source for doctrine.

In order to guard the sufficiency of Scripture, some Reformed thinkers have argued that at the death of the last apostle, God absolutely stopped speaking to human beings. To many Reformed thinkers, the Charismatic tradition is entirely anathema.

My position was that yes, the canon of inspired Scripture is closed. That is to say, Scripture alone is God's "covenant document" (Kline) to rule his church. But Scripture never says that God's revelation will stop with the death of the last apostle. God communicates any way he chooses.

Natural revelation, for example, continues. We may legitimately make various distinctions within the concept of revelation, but in ordinary life we need not only to hear Scripture, but also to work in a godly way to APPLY Scripture to other forms of experience in which God makes himself known. So there is a bit of looseness here that we cannot avoid, a looseness hard for many Reformed thinkers to tolerate.

Steve, though a highly principled Calvinist, was willing to embrace that looseness. He did not feel bound by Reformed tradition to avoid anything that sounded Charismatic. Indeed, he maintained an independence from tradition that seemed to me to express *sola Scriptura* in the best possible sense.

Other Triabloggers write about paranormal phenomena, such as the Enfield poltergeist. Steve welcomed such writing on the part of his colleagues, though he did not himself work in such areas. He evidently saw in these discussions the attempt to acknowledge the greatness of God's power in the present day. He has often told me that "naturalism" is the greatest enemy that we face. God can work in unusual ways. In this way and others, Steve showed himself to be very flexible, within the bounds of orthodoxy.

So over the years, even after our collaboration at RTS was over, Steve and I continued to be good friends. We were also part of a group that began at Westminster back in the 1990s. Philip Marshall, Greg Welty, later James Anderson, and I all stayed in touch, and every once in a while Steve would write to the whole group about philosophical and theological ideas that he was in touch with. We'd all get together by email and go over the issues.

I thought the world of Steve, and I will miss him very much. I look forward to resuming our conversations in glory (with so many more resources at our disposal!). Until then, I will still be reading Triablogue, where Steve's influence lives on, where a number of godly thinkers remain to take up his torch.

Permissions

"Apologetics" was previously published as "Let the Church Test Its Apologetics by Biblical Standards," in Aaron B. Hebbard, ed., *95 Theses for a New Reformation* (Eugene, OR: Resource Publications, 2017), 69–70. Used here by permission.

Essays from The Gospel Coalition's *Concise Theology* are reprinted here under a CreativeCommons Attribution ShareAlike license. They can be found online here: https://www.thegospelcoalition.org/essays.

"Foreword to Scripture and the People of God" was previously published in *Scripture and the People of God*, ed. John DelHoussaye (Wheaton, IL: Crossway, 2018). Used here by permission.

"Foreword to Thinking through Creation, by Chris Watkin" originally appeared in Chris Watkin, *Thinking through Creation: Genesis 1 and 2 as Tools of Cultural Critique* (Phillipsburg, NJ: P&R Publishing, 2017). Used by permission.

"Is Scripture's Self-Attestation Sufficient?" was previously published in *Scripture and the People of God*, ed. John DelHoussaye (Wheaton, IL: Crossway, 2018). Used here by permission.

"Preface to *Redeeming the Life of the Mind*" was previously published in John Frame, Wayne Grudem, and John Hughes, eds., *Redeeming the Life of the Mind: Essays in Honor of Vern Poythress* (Wheaton, IL: Crossway, 2017), 234–50. Used here by permission.

"Presuppositionalism and Perspectivalism" was previously published in J. Frame, Wayne Grudem, and John Hughes, eds., *Redeeming the Life of the Mind: Essays in Honor of Vern Poythress* (Wheaton, IL: Crossway, 2017), 234–50.

"Review of Anthony Thiselton's *Systematic Theology*" was previously published in *Westminster Theological Journal* 78:1 (Spring 2016): 196–99. Used here by permission.

"Scripture as a Divine Book" was previously published as "Let the Church Read Scripture as the Very Word of God," in Aaron B. Hebbard, *95 Theses for a New Reformation* (Eugene, OR: Resource Publications/ Wipf and Stock), 11–12. Used here by permission.

Index of Subjects & Authors

A

Aaron 164, 385, 390

Abraham 97, 157–60, 163, 166, 270, 279–80, 287–88, 373, 384–85, 437

Adam 71, 109–10, 161, 163, 250, 254, 273, 288–89, 319–20, 338, 407

Adams, Jay 41–42, 50

Alexandrian tradition 236

All That Is in God 88, 99, 101, 119, 127

Allah 314

Analytic Theology: New Essays in the Philosophy of Theology 297, 299–302

ancient Near East 279

angels 250, 252

apostles 161–62, 185, 208, 211–12, 216, 219–20, 244, 252, 309, 331, 337–38, 369, 402, 424

Aquinas, Thomas 75–77, 81–88, 95–100, 102, 107, 114–16, 122–23, 131, 133, 300, 305, 345, 348, 437

Aramaic 239

Aristotle 12, 37, 77, 82–88, 94–100, 122–23, 125, 129, 133, 437

Arminianism 10, 63–64, 79, 187–89, 280–83

aseity 81, 95–97, 102, 104–5, 294

Athanasius 220

atomism 298, 379

Auburn Affirmation 344

Augustine 66, 87, 300, 391

Authorized: the Use and Misuse of the King James Bible 241

authorship 144, 220

autonomous thought 320

B

Bahnsen, Greg 42, 51, 335, 351–53, 355

Barth, Karl 20, 59, 64, 129, 134, 183–84, 348, 352, 365

Bartholomew 183–84

Bavinck, Herman 16, 20, 104, 106, 197, 201, 214, 225, 229, 233, 258, 263, 341, 343

Berkouwer, G. C. 129

Biblical/Medical Ethics 416

bondage 188, 243, 262, 303

C

Calvary 311

Calvin, John 82, 84, 87, 133, 157, 306, 404

Calvinism 10, 20, 45, 79, 187–89, 214, 280–82, 341–44, 439

canon 43, 88, 15, 219–21, 438

the centurion 374, 403

Childs, Brevard 293, 295

Christ

as King 431

as Priest 432

as Prophet 431

church 3, 6, 7, 12–13, 25–27, 44, 48, 63,
    68, 88, 214, 280, 291, 316, 325–27,
    339, 398, 408, 419
  Anabaptist 152
  Christian Reformed 138, 341–43, 345
  confessions 45, 47, 88, 99, 129, 142–43,
    146
  Corinthian 244, 331–32, 374
  division in 355
  doctrine 15, 42, 130, 157, 338
  early 43, 53, 133, 146, 170, 221, 244, 335
  errors 140, 305–6
  evangelical 66
  fathers 66, 92, 258
  fellowship 185
  government 70–71, 143, 153, 220, 401
  history 23, 50, 55, 60–61, 102, 154, 228,
    236
  Korean 369–370
  medieval 84
  partisanship 67
  Pentecostal 244
  planting 332, 423–26
  Presbyterian 344
  Roman Catholic 62, 81–82, 204, 384
  Scripture in 87, 220, 224, 245, 252, 438
  teachers in 57, 95, 113, 232, 240
  theologians 58, 200
  Thessalonian 423–25
  tradition 195–96
Christianity Considered 12, 201, 353, 375
compatibilism 188, 273, 281–82
communism 186
"cone of certainty" 171
conscience 67, 86 203–5, 401
Copernicus 384
correlativism 103, 105
cosmos 195, 289
Covenant College 155–56, 289
Crisp, Oliver 299–300, 302
Crossroad Bible Institute 138
CRU (Campus Crusade for Christ) 312

D

David, King 109, 151, 157, 243, 271,
    310–11, 394
dementia 409
demons/demonic 32, 168
denominations 5, 58, 66–67, 137–38, 185,
    244, 355, 398
Didache 26–27
diet 411–14
Divine sovereignty 108, 265, 269, 282,
    286, 300, 345
Docetism 106
Doctrine of God 93, 98, 105, 108, 125, 251,
    258, 263, 265, 269, 278, 281, 286
Doctrine of the Knowledge of God 167, 178,
    260, 295
The Doctrine of the Word of God 155, 167,
    197, 201, 209, 212, 214, 217, 221,
    225, 229, 233, 238, 241, 245, 251
Dooyeweerd, Herman 51, 82–83, 102
Dolezal, James 75–76, 83–84, 88, 99,
    101–17, 119, 127–130
Duby, Stephen 134
duty 232

E

Edwards, Jonathan 55, 205, 292
Egypt 174, 196, 243, 253, 260, 265–66,
    270, 384–86, 390
empiricism 305, 339
Enlightenment 58, 102, 293
epistemology 50, 105, 142, 148, 167, 235,
    293, 317, 320–23, 331, 335–36,
    339, 349
eternal plan 23–24, 46, 79, 146, 189, 224,
    265, 294, 319, 323
ethics 53, 366, 437
  and epistemology 167
  biblical 4, 56, 389
evangelical feminism 44–46, 62
evangelical fundamentalism 59, 66, 156
Evangelical Reunion 57, 67, 355
Evangelical Theological Society 45, 47,

evidentialist/ism 337, 356, 377
ex nihilo 285
exile 384, 387

F

Faith
  and doubt 371–72
  and justification 300
  and salvation 266, 271–72
  alone 139, 191
  biblical 122
  Christian 17, 98, 138, 150, 213, 216, 231,
      287, 305, 331, 357, 372–74, 377,
      426
  defense of 42, 365
  doctrines of 107, 122–23, 140, 344
  hope and love 424
  in God 156, 287, 423
  in Scripture 146, 156, 232, 337, 370
  personal 137, 181–82
  Reformed 16, 86, 342
  work of 424–25
faithfulness of Christ 86, 156
faithfulness to Christ 15, 133, 174, 384
fall, the 182, 195, 203, 214, 291, 320, 338,
    367
Father (God). *See* God, Father
fear of the Lord 320
feminism 7, 44–45, 62–63
Fideism 332–33
Fiennes, Joseph 183
final judgment 200, 291
firstborn 262, 385–86
first cause 87, 94, 96–97, 122–24
first century 11, 93, 309, 312
First Commandment 145, 383–91
foolishness 165, 181, 184, 186, 320–21
The Force Awakens 181
Forms, world of 91, 121, 132
free will 64, 187–88, 281, 300
freedom 31, 67, 71–72, 188–89, 269,
    273–75, 281–83, 398, 435

G

Gerstner, John 61, 191
Gnosticism 132
God
  as author (of Scripture) 43, 142–45,
      154, 228,
  as creator 10, 99, 106, 109–10, 112, 127,
      130, 285–89, 318, 323, 359, 378,
      407
  as I AM 92–93, 251, 260–61, 270, 385
  as immutable 101, 110, 129, 133
  as personal 37, 84–87, 93, 97–98,
      124–25, 129–31, 149, 161, 176,
      196, 249, 251–52, 254, 267, 347,
      359–60, 394
  as sovereign 99–100, 130, 133, 178, 232,
      265–67, 269–75, 279, 282, 300,
      342, 345, 420
  authority of 14, 24, 44, 46, 71, 213–14,
      251–54, 260–62, 266, 269, 286,
      319–320, 326–29, 374, 394–95
  essence of 109–10, 113, 128, 130, 133–34,
      350, 383
  Father 23–24, 30, 37, 45–47, 70, 86–87,
      98, 114–16, 125, 160, 196, 252,
      254, 266, 280, 316, 325–29, 337,
      388–90, 408, 423, 431–32
  goodness of 11, 84, 312, 319, 360
  is truth 315
  mystery of 93, 108, 115, 258–59, 379,
      387, 391
  presence of 52, 133, 147, 196, 232, 251,
      253–54, 259, 261–62, 265–67,
      269, 286–87, 325, 327–28, 330
  promises of 28–29, 85–86, 99, 129, 140,
      158, 160, 196, 213, 224, 241, 261,
      265, 270, 279, 372–73, 385–86
  Triune 130, 134, 294, 328
  transcendence of 10, 67, 71, 79, 89, 92,
      98, 257–61, 286, 386
gospel 11, 16, 25–33, 42, 53, 69, 76–77, 79,
      87, 106, 113, 131–34, 140, 165, 171,
      181–82, 189, 216, 224, 239–42,

252, 335–39, 364, 369–74, 377, 399, 402, 408, 424–26
Great Commission 25–28, 32, 68–69, 71, 239–40, 369
Great Commission training center 26, 29–30, 32
Greek philosophy 9, 82, 84, 90, 93, 96–97, 119, 123, 129, 132, 437
grief 410
Groothuis, Doug 365, 409
Grudem, Wayne 20, 41–48, 51, 54, 103, 141, 225, 229, 233, 241, 245, 317

H
Hagar 158, 237
heaven(s) 54, 115, 152, 178, 184, 187, 236, 257, 270, 277–78, 285, 291, 319, 379
Hebbard, Aaron B. 139, 305, 441–42
Hebrew 124, 228, 239
Heidegger, Martin 235
Heidelberg Catechism 86, 371
Helm, Paul 76, 83, 107, 284, 299, 302, 437
Heraclitus 91
hermeneutics 6, 35, 52, 54, 235
heresy 104, 116, 281
Higgs boson 314
History of Western Philosophy and Theology 81, 85, 119, 295, 353, 363, 369, 379
holiness 67, 71, 84, 147, 207, 319, 371, 386, 389
history
  church 23, 27, 39, 50, 60, 102, 139, 154, 157, 196, 200, 204, 228, 236
  God's actions in 10–11, 24, 77, 80, 99, 112–13, 124, 187–89, 203, 259, 359, 377–78
  human 112, 130, 184, 194, 199, 271, 279, 315, 320
  interpretation of 56, 61
  of canon 220

of doctrine 35, 42, 59, 61, 84, 88, 102
of Israel 182, 208, 335
of theology 36, 49, 89, 300, 342, 364
redemptive 46–47, 134, 146, 195, 253, 292, 294
human knowledge 124, 151, 235, 294, 297, 317, 319, 323–24, 328–29, 332, 343, 345, 350, 368
Hume, David 167, 322, 331, 336, 339, 435

I
idolatry 104, 116, 199–200, 395
illumination 143, 152, 221
inerrancy 42, 47, 61, 64–66, 141, 143, 293
inner court 207, 259
interpretation
  God's 319, 331–32
  of God 360
  of Jesus's work 12, 185
  of Scripture 20, 65, 125, 133, 235–38, 311
  of tongues 26, 244
  of women's roles in the church 13
Irenaeus 220, 292
Isaac 97, 158, 270, 384, 437, 239
Islam 31, 55, 85, 186
Israel/Israelites 71, 93, 144, 173–74, 207, 219, 223, 228, 232, 243, 251, 253, 261, 265–66, 270, 280, 287, 384–89, 394

J
Jesus
  as creator 286
  as God 87, 140, 216, 269, 432
  as God's son 139, 170–71, 291, 310, 327
  as Messiah 243, 310–11, 387
  as Lamb of God 125, 175, 388
  as prophet 243
  as savior 86, 149, 161, 164, 196, 221, 272
  as Word of God 162, 224, 249–50, 310, 389–90, 431
  birth of 99, 250, 254, 291, 294

death of 11, 28, 174, 181–84, 311–12, 389
gospel of 25–30, 336, 377, 402
healings of 11, 286, 372, 419
humanity of 107
kingdom of 137
presence of 27, 133, 185–86, 262, 267
resurrection of 170–71, 184, 200, 244,
        322, 331–32, 336, 374, 388
return of 425–26
teachings of 11, 72, 167, 170, 173, 208,
        211, 215, 221, 280, 294, 310–12,
        326, 374, 388
John the Baptist 243
joy 30, 132, 140, 176, 183–85, 343, 407,
        410, 423, 425
Judah
  house of 174
  land of 394
Judas 280
justification, doctrine of 25, 61, 84, 86,
        110, 125, 147, 167, 191, 300
Justin Martyr 27, 92, 133, 305

K

Kierkegaard, Søren 59, 365
Kline, Meredith 16, 41–42, 209, 221, 225,
        293, 438
Koran 348
Korea 369–70
Kuyper, Abraham 6, 69, 102, 214, 255,
        341–45

L

Let God Be True 156
Lewis, C. S. 386, 391
liberalism 58, 63, 293, 348
  academic 20
  Protestant 255
  Reformed 341
libertarianism 188, 273–74
linguistics 52, 55, 318
Lord's Supper 181
logical positivism 298–99, 301

Logos 367
Lot 158
Luke (apostle) 170, 208, 220, 309, 388
Luther 8, 45, 62, 82, 84, 86–87, 98, 133,
        157, 306

M

Magna Carta 394
Malebranchian occasionalism 435–36
manuscript 428–29
marriage 46–47, 316, 407–8
  same-sex 397–400
metaphysics 103, 105, 108–9, 112, 167,
        298
  of Scripture 108, 124
Mohammed 314
Mohler Jr., R. Albert 397–400
Moses 71, 92–93, 144, 157, 161, 212, 243,
        251, 253, 265–66, 270, 384–86,
        389–90
Murray, John 41–43, 50, 141
mutualism 103, 105
Mt Sinai 144, 160, 162, 386
mystery 12, 31, 93, 108–10, 113, 115, 122,
        130, 220, 258–59, 377–80, 387,
        389, 391

N

narrative
  as a literary device 288
  gender 37
  grand narrative 349
  historical 129,
  lordship 125
  Risen 183
  of Scripture 10, 24, 36, 108, 124–25,
        184, 402
Nashville Statement 407–8
natural reason 95–96, 305
natural world 82, 200, 252, 265, 271, 277,
        368
Nature's Case for God 201, 205, 375
Neoplatonism 93, 122

neutral/neutrality 56, 65–66, 294, 301, 322, 345
New Covenant 71, 174
new heavens and new earth 54, 115, 237, 291
New Testament 12, 27, 30, 43, 174, 220, 280, 287, 389
Nicene Creed 87, 134
No Other God 105, 156, 275, 284

O

obedience 38, 168–70, 176, 213, 231, 266, 319, 379, 401–2
Old Testament 16, 12, 43, 175, 310, 312, 389

P

Packer, James I. 60, 103, 155–56, 267, 275, 428–29
pantheism 12, 55, 128–29, 261, 343
parables 30, 133, 294
Parmenides 90–97, 120–25, 128–29, 132, 347
Paul (the apostle) 26–33, 67–69, 119–20, 244, 287, 321–22, 331–32, 398, 402–4, 423–25
Pentecost, Day of 239, 309, 312
perspectivalism 43, 55, 317–18, 323–29, 331–34
personalism 98, 119, 127, 129–30, 133–34
Pharaoh 265, 282, 284, 386, 390
Pharisees 228–29, 310–11, 338, 419
Philosophical Investigations 298, 301
philosophy
  analytical 297–302
  Greek 9, 82, 84, 90, 93, 96–97, 119, 123, 129, 132, 437
  Medieval 81,
Plantinga, Alvin 103, 299–300, 302
Plato 12, 82, 91–97, 121–22, 125, 132, 305, 347, 349, 435
Plotinus 12, 93, 95, 122, 132
poems/poetry 291, 314

Poseidon 313
Post-truth society 313–14
Poythress, Vern 42–45, 49–53, 57, 101, 197, 217, 238, 241, 267, 290, 317–18, 325, 365, 375, 377, 441–42
pragmatism 61, 336–37
predestination 187–89, 435–36
presence (of God) 52, 133, 147, 196, 232, 251, 253–54, 259, 261–62, 265–69, 286–87, 325, 327–30, 386
Prestige, G. L. 113
presuppositionalism 50, 55, 105, 317–34, 335–39, 349, 436
Prime Mover 37, 77, 83, 85–88, 94–96, 100, 122, 129, 437
Princeton Seminary 49, 343–44
profession of faith 372
prophecy
  contemporary 44, 54, 324
  in the Bible 43, 195–97, 211–12, 243–45, 278, 280, 291
prophets 161–63, 166, 196, 208, 211–12, 243–245, 253–54, 278–80, 337, 431–33
Protagoras 121, 314, 347
providence 99, 112, 195, 286, 294, 329, 393
Pseudo-Dionysius 93
punishments 132, 266, 404
"pure being" 12, 89–92, 96–100

Q

Qur'an 148, 322
  see also Koran

R

rationalism 58, 305, 339, 343, 347–49, 368
Rea, Michael 299–300, 302
reconciliation 113, 181, 214
redemption 99–100, 106, 112, 130, 150, 181–82, 196, 214, 262, 287, 291, 293–94, 312, 321, 361

history of 24, 46–47, 134, 146–47, 195
Reformation 57–58, 62, 70, 82, 84, 98,
    133, 146, 156–57, 255
controversy 152
New 8, 139–40, 306
Reformation theology 196
Reformed Dogmatics 54, 197, 201, 214,
    225, 229, 233, 263, 341
Reformed orthodoxy 41–42, 49–50, 344
Reformed Theological Seminary 51, 53,
    101, 317, 351, 365, 369, 393, 431,
    436
regeneration 204, 338, 345
revelation
general 153–54, 199, 203, 228, 231, 252,
    343, 356
special 195–97, 207, 231, 244, 252, 254,
    371–72
Revelation and Inspiration 197, 209, 212,
    255
righteousness 147, 164, 169, 174, 373
breastplate of 31
kingdom of 316
training in 70, 76, 144, 163, 251, 329
Risen 183–85
Roman ethos 183
Rome 183, 185–86
Russell, Bertrand 297–98, 301
Rutherford, Samuel 393–95

S

Sabbath rest 288, 360
sacraments 86, 98, 133, 300
Sadducees 311
salvation 10–11, 45, 86–87, 95, 140–43,
    146–47, 150–51, 163, 165, 175,
    189, 227–28, 239, 250, 261, 266,
    271–72, 287, 306, 326, 359, 364,
    432
by faith 86, 371
events of 338
Greek philosophy of 132–34
gospel of 117, 216, 224

helmet of 31
in Jesus 11, 30, 76, 98, 139, 165, 321
in the Westminster Confession 70
medieval understanding 98
Reformation doctrine of 131
Salvation Belongs to the Lord 201, 209,
    212, 214
Sarah 157–58, 237, 373
Schleiermacher, Friedrich 59, 305
scholasticism 104, 114, 116, 131
and biblical personalism 119, 123
for evangelicals 127
post-Reformation 76
Thomist 101–3, 133
Scripture
authority of 58, 61, 139–41, 143–44, 214
doctrine of 140, 142, 145, 235, 305
inerrancy of 47, 61, 64–66, 141, 143,
    293
infallibility of 143
self-attestation of 141–43, 154
study of 7, 30, 36, 44, 53, 88, 116, 173,
    232, 237, 360, 364, 377
sufficiency of 43–44, 70, 144, 227–29,
    305, 400, 438
theology of 6, 93
truthfulness of 212, 215–16
servant of the Lord 387
sex/sexuality 6, 63, 316, 397–99, 407, 412
Shepherd, Norman 191
sin
conviction of 147, 294
of doubt 371–72, 375
of humanity 38, 149, 152, 162, 165,
    169–72, 181, 184, 203, 266, 271,
    278, 312, 320, 338, 345, 388, 407,
    432
of Sodom 158
personal 6, 11, 28, 86, 98, 106, 367, 405
punishment for 112, 131–34, 188, 266,
    291
repentance from 189, 380

salvation from 112, 125, 171, 174–75, 182, 196, 250, 253–54, 261, 287, 311, 321, 326, 367, 389

sinful mind 172–73, 176

sinners 32, 84, 86, 98, 124, 133, 151, 169, 178, 199–200, 203, 252–53, 311, 390, 408, 432

skepticism 258, 322, 350, 371–75, 416

slavery 196, 253, 260, 270, 384

Socinians 280–82

Sodom 158–59

sola fide 86

sola Scriptura 43, 57–60, 62–63, 67, 70, 72, 84, 98, 104, 116, 119, 123, 144–45, 154, 157, 196, 337, 400, 439

suffering 27–29, 99, 131–32, 374, 385, 402, 410

supernatural 11, 166, 221, 239–40, 244, 288, 309–10, 322–23, 331–32, 336, 372

T

tabernacle 207, 219, 223, 266–67

temple 106, 207, 219, 223, 259, 266–67, 412

Ten Commandments 144, 156, 207–8, 211, 223, 266, 383, 389

ten plagues 385

theism
classical 77, 107
open 64, 101, 111, 156, 179, 281, 283–84

theistic mutualism 103, 105

theology
academic 20, 27, 36, 76, 101
Anabaptist 152
analytic 297–301
biblical 50, 52–53, 292, 294, 342, 437
Christian 24, 36, 68, 93, 122–23, 128, 199, 348, 364–66
Christian Reformed 337, 341
classical 12, 87
conservative 380

definition 3–4, 5, 16, 88, 155, 364
disagreement in 9
evangelical 42, 59, 63, 438
existential 20, 58
historical 15, 60, 88, 104, 116, 119
liberal 49–50, 58–59, 63–66
narrative 59, 291–96, 291–95
natural 63, 81–82, 200
of Calvin 49, 133, 181–82, 341
of Scripture 6, 50, 87, 108, 142
openness theology 277–83
process 59, 64, 281
Protestant 84, 123
Reformed 43, 49, 57, 76, 119, 345, 393–94
scholastic 108, 110, 123
Roman Catholic 58, 84
Trinitarian 23–24
situational 19–20
systematic 16, 35–39, 42, 51, 59, 61, 104, 116, 292–94, 300, 367
trendiness in 6–7
Western 369–70

Theology for Life 431–33

theophany/theophanies 106, 195–97

Thielicke, Helmut 6

Thinking through Creation

Thomism 79, 81–88, 101, 111, 133–34, 357, 437

Timothy 28, 423–24

tongues, gift of 54, 239, 244–45, 438

translation 44–45, 52–53, 95, 236, 239–41, 369

Trinity

V

Van Til, Cornelius 20, 36, 42, 50–51, 55, 63, 76–77, 81–83, 102–5, 119–20, 131, 317–22, 335, 341–53, 355–57, 437

Vietnam 405

vessel(s) 274

W

Watkin, Chris 359–60
Ward, Mark 241
Warfield, B. B. 42, 197, 209, 212, 255, 275,
        342–43
Western philosophy 120, 297, 363, 369
Westminster Confession of Faith 49, 70,
        133, 142, 146, 154, 213, 227
Westminster Shorter Catechism 84, 151
Westminster Theological Seminary 41,
        49, 81, 317, 351
What All Christians Believe 137–38
wisdom 121, 154, 160, 320, 380
        common 131, 380

divine, 33, 84, 165, 168–68, 224, 258,
        272, 319, 405
human 32–33, 58, 71, 184, 224, 228,
        316, 418
Wittgenstein, Ludwig 293, 297–98, 301
Word of God. *See* Scripture
worldview 24, 53, 55–56, 85, 91–92,
        124–25, 128, 133, 184, 236, 285,
        297, 318, 331, 336, 342, 347–48,
        357, 359, 364, 399, 407–8

Y

Yahweh 93, 265, 269, 270, 279, 276, 326,
        385–86, 389
Yale University 50–51, 59–60, 81, 102,
        293, 431

Index of Scripture

OLD TESTAMENT

Genesis

1 .... 67, 300, 301–3
1–2 .... 42, 333
1:1 .... 123, 285, 291
1:2 291
1:2–2:3 285
1:24 47
1:26–27 .... 252, 254, 319
1:27–28 329
1:28 .... 152, 319
2 398
2:7 .... 250, 288
2:10–23 407
2:16 319
2:22–24 407
3 .... 38, 367, 412
3:1–4 320
3:1–24 291
3:6 .... 320, 373
3:8 250
3:17–19 214
4:1–16 53
6:5 204
11:1–9 241
12 157
12:3 241
12:7 208
13:18 208
15:5 277

15:13–16 279
17:7 266
18:23–33 159
18:25 159
21:22 261
26:28 261
27:27–29 280
27:39–40 280
28:15 261
28:18 208
28:20 261
31:3 261
31:5 261
35:14 208
39:3–4 261
49:11 280

Exodus

2 384
2:11–15 385
2:23–25 278
3 .... 259, 265, 278
3:7–9 278
3:11–12 261
3:14 .... 92, 93, 98, 133, 283
3:14–16 251
3:19–20 270
4:4 271

4:8 271
4:21 .... 266, 271
6:7 .... 261, 266
6:7–8 270
7:3 271
7:5 196
7:13 285
9:12 271
10:1 271
10:20 271
10:27 271
12:20 384
12:40 384
14:18 196
16:6–10 197
19–24 160
19:24 386
20:1–2 266
20:1–3 260
20:8–11 387
20:11 386
20:19 .... 197, 245
21:12–13 271
24:12 208
29:45 266
31:18 .... 144, 145, 208
34:1 208
34:24 271
34:27–28 208

453

Leviticus

1:3–8 164
19:1–4 260

Numbers

6:27 266
23–24 280

Deuteronomy

2:30 .... 266, 271
4:1–8 214
4:2 .... 57, 70
4:7 261
4:7–8 251
4:13 .... 223, 224
4:20 261
4:33 386
4:39 257
5:7 383
5:24–26 160
5:27 161
6:1–9 214
6:4–6 266
6:7–9 173
6:24–25 214
7:6 261
7:11 214
8:3 224
8:11 214
12:32 70
14:7 261
18 .... 279n2
18:15-19 161
18:18–19 .... 197, 212, 245
18:18–22 254
18:21–22 278
18:22 216
26:18 261
29:29 .... 170, 371
30:11–14 .... 232, 233, 251
31:24–29 221
32:1–43 280
32:46–47 208

33:1–29 280
34:9 320

Joshua

1:7 70
1:7–8 208
1:8 140
11:18–20 271
23:6 214
24:15 419

Judges

7:22 271

1 Samuel

2:6–7 .... 265, 271
2:25 271
10:1–11 279
16:14 271
23:11 280

2 Samuel

7:24 261

1 Kings

3:28 320
4:29–34 320
8:27 .... 104, 259
13:1–4 280
18:27 278
22:20–23 271

2 Kings

8:12 280

1 Chronicles

1:1–7 163

2 Chronicles

16:9 278
25:20 271

Ezra

6:22 .... 266, 271

Nehemiah

9:6 .... 286, 287

Job

38–42 .... 170, 372

Psalms

2 .... 31, 184, 274
4:2 163
6:3 163
8:1 257
8:3–9 387
10:11 278
11:4 278
13:1–2 163
14:1 320
18:30 216
19:1 .... 153, 200, 328
19:7–11 214
19:9 216
23:1–6 164
33:4 373
33:6 286
33:6–9 287
33:9 286
33:18–20 278
34:15–16 278
35:17 163
37:23–24 271
38:9 278
39:8 320
40:7 160,
47 260
50:10–11 277
51:6 315
56:8 277
57:5 257
62:3 163
65:9–11 .... 265, 271
73 372
73:2–3 372
73:11 278
74:22 320

88 372
89 387
90 410
92:6 320
93:1 260
94:7 278
95:3–7 287
96:10–13 260
97:1 260
97:9 257
99:1 260
104:1–35 200
105:24 271
110 311
111:10 320
113:5 257
115:3 .... 265, 270
119 224
119:11 174
119:142 216
119:160 .... 315, 373
135 196
135:6 .... 265, 270
135:6–7 .... 265, 271
136 196
139 .... 76, 109, 128, 267,
          278, 294, 323
139:4 280
139:6 323
139:7–12 262
139:13–16 271
139:16 280
139:17 129
139:17–18 277
145:20 278
146:5 286
146:5–6 287
147:4 277

147:5 277
147:15–18 271

Proverbs

1:7 .... 224, 320, 380
3:3 174
3:5–6 .... 165, 168
8:5 320
16:9 .... 266, 271
30:5 216
30:6 70

Ecclesiastes

5:2 257

Isaiah

6:9–10 271
7:14 .... 257, 261, 267
8:8 257
9:6–7 279
10:6 271
11:1–9 279
14:24–27 .... 265, 271
29:13 70
29:13–14 .... 58, 229
29:15 278
40–49 279
40:26 277
40:27 278
40:28 277
41:21–23 279
43:1–7 387
43:13 .... 265, 271
43:14–15 287
47:10 278
51:7 174
55:8–9 .... 178, 323, 379
55:11 .... 265, 271

63:17 271
66:1 259

Jeremiah

1:4–12 .... 197, 212, 245
1:5 .... 271, 280
16:17–18 278
18:7–9 .... 279n12
22:16 169
23:29 251
25:4 149
31:31–34 174
33:20–25 287
33:22 277

Lamentations

3:7 266
3:37 272

Ezekiel

8:12 278

Daniel

1:9 .... 266, 271

Hosea

6:6 169

Amos

3:2 266

Jonah

2:9 387
3:4 .... 279n12
3:10 .... 279n12

Malachi

3:6 99

NEW TESTAMENT

Matthew

1:23 .... 257, 261, 267

4:4 .... 172, 224
4:19 388
5:17 432

5:17–19 208
5:45 232
6:26–30 271

6:32 278
6:33 416
7:21–22 266
7:29 310
10:19–20 212
10:29–30 271
10:30 277
10:34–38 266
11:15 149
12:6 259
14:31 ....170, 371
15:8–9 ....58, 70
15:18–20 282
15:24 326
16:18 316
17:1–8 254
20:28 432
21:1–11 311
21:21 371
21:37 326
22:37 170
24:35 212
27:22–23 326
28:17 371
28:18 431
28:18–20 ....68, 241, 391

Mark

4:35–41 286 ....
4:41 254
7:8 229
8:34 389
8:38 212
9:24 372
9:37 326
13:1–30 280
13:32 280

Luke

1:4 170
1:20 212
1:35 291
4:1–2 291

4:14 291
5:4 152
5:8–9 388
6:45 .... 173, 282
6:46 266
7:1–10 386
12:4–7 271
14:28 153
23:47 374
24:27 ....182, 237

John

1:1 ....140, 161, 249
1:1–14 ....212, 251,
253n2, 431
1:3 ....286, 329
1:14 ....76, 250, 252
2:11 196
2:19–22 259
3:3 149
3:5 .... 11, 310
3:16 ...... 164, 252, 324, 326
3:34 ....162, 254, 326
4:34 326
5:19–23 326–27
5:23–30 326
5:24 ....162, 212
5:30–32 326
5:36 326
5:45–47 ....208, 212
6:63 ....162, 212
6:64 280
6:68 ....162, 212
7:17 ....167, 374
8:11 311
8:12 374
8:26 216
8:31 162
8:34–36 188
10:27 221
10:34–36 208
10:35 ....216, 221
12:48 ....162, 251

12:49–50 326
13:18–19 280
14:6 ....315, 489
14:9 197
14:15 225
14:16–17 326
14:21 ....225, 266
14:26 212
15:10 225
15:26 326
15:26–27 212
16:12–15 326
16:13 .... 212, 326
17 ....67, 249
17:3 ....170, 250
17:17 ..... 217, 278, 294, 306,
315, 373
18:37 162
20:22 326
21:17 277

Acts

1:3 374
1:5 326
1:8 ....391, 310
1:11 259
2 ....239, 420
2:5–12 241
2:17 197
2:41 309
4:4 309
4:13 27
4:18 402
4:19 402
5:14 309
5:26 402
5:27–29 402
6:10 310
8:21–39 237
10:20 371
10:44 310
11:12 371
11:27–28 245

14:15.....................286, 287
14:15–17......................200
14:17.............................335
15:12.............................196
17....................................424
17:22–34.......................200
17:23–28.......................104
17:24.............................286
17:24–25.......................387
17:26.............. 253, 265, 271
17:28.............................267
20:27.............................150
21:9–14..........................245
23:1................................204
24:14..............................208
24:27.............................403
25:10–12........................403
25:13–27........................403

Romans

1.....................172, 366, 438
1–11:32..........................259
1:18..........120, 123, 149, 172,
              250, 252, 306,
              336, 345
1:18–20.........................250
1:18–21...168, 231, 233, 259,
              335, 364
1:18–22..........................258
1:18–32..........119, 200, 320
1:19–21..........................153
1:20.......................119, 261
1:25......................149, 287
1:28................................149
2:1–5.............................204
2:14–15..........................204
3:1–4.............................156
3:4.................................156
3:10–12...........................204
3:23................................151
4:16–22.........................266
4:17................................387
4:19–21...........................158

4:20–21...........................373
4:22................................373
6:16–20..........................188
8:11.................................291
8:18–22..................214, 262
8:28.............. 79, 266, 272
8:32................................326
9......................................274
9:17–18..........266, 271, 282
9:19–24..........................274
10:5–10................. 232, 233
11:7–8.............................271
11:8................................149
11:33.............266, 272, 323
11:33–34.........................170
11:33–36..........258–59, 277,
                      371–72
11:35–36.........................104
11:36..............278, 282, 287
12:1–2............................169
12:2...............................204
12:6...............................245
12:7...............................237
13.................403, 404, 405
13:1................................404
13:1–7.............................401
13:3...............................404
13:3–5............................401
14..5
14:17...............................56
14:23.....................170, 371
15:4.......................208, 221

1 Corinthians

1–2...................................184,
1–3..........................67, 154
1:16.................................372
1:18–2:16........................316
1:18–3:23........................320
1:19.................................224
1:19–20...........................225
2:4..................................374
2:6–13.............................225

2:9–16............................374
2:10–12...........................330
2:16.................................321
3:16.................................267
6:19.................................412
8:1..................................168
8:1–3..............................374
9:22..........................:67, 69
10:31......165, 214, 228, 229,
          266, 339, 366, 412
11................................13, 412
11:3..................................44
11:4–5.............................245
11:26................................182
12:10...............................245
12:28–29....... 233, 237, 245
13....................................424
13:3................................424
13:4................................424
13:9................................424
13:12..............................380
14.............................13, 69
14:1–40...........................245
14:26................................26
14:37................................162
14:37–38........ 208, 212, 252
15............................ 335, 374
15:1–2.............. 322n10, 332
15:1–3.............................374
15:1–11............................374
15:3................................332
15:5.................................331
15:6.................................331
15:7.................................331
15:8.................................331
15:11.......................332, 388
15:11–12.........................336
15:12................................332
15:12–20........................294

2 Corinthians

1:12............................... 204
2:15–16.......................... 271

3:2 175,
4:6 204
5:17 .... 173, 287
5:19 113
6:16 266
6:18 261
10:5 ....69n21, 266, 306

Galatians

4:21–31 237
6:6 233
6:15 287

Ephesians

1 146
1:4 271
1:9–11 265
1:11 ....79, 187, 266, 272,
           278, 282, 294,
           308, 378
2 10
2:4–10 ....266, 272
2:8 371
2:10 173
3:5 291
4:11 233
4:24 287
5:2 326
5:8 169
5:22–33 .... 47, 407
5:23 44
5:33 ....166, 180
6:10–20 31

Philippians

1:9 169
3:19 412

Colossians

1:15 343
1:15–16 286
1:15–20 262
1:16 286

1:19–20 214
2:8 364
3:10 287
3:17 .... 70, 266
3:23 70
3:24 266
4:16 .... 208, 212

1 Thessalonians

1 443–46
1:1–10 423–24
1:3 424
1:4 424
1:5 ....172, 221, 241, 374,
                424
1:6 425
1:8 425
1:9 424
1:9–10 425

2 Thessalonians

2:2 229

2:14 374
2:15 197
3:14–15 .... 208, 212

1 Timothy

1:10 237
1:15 124
2 13,
2:5 432
2:8 371
4:1–2 204
4:13 .... 233, 237
4:16 237
5:1 ....7, 116
6:2–3 237

2 Timothy

1:12 170
1:13 237
1:14 221

2:1 30
2:1–2 25-33
2:1–7 27
2:2 ....28, 237
2:5 28
2:7 ....28, 29
2:15–17 208
2:16–17 71
3:15 221
3:15–17 .. 140, 163, 212, 214,
        217, 252, 254
3:16 ....211, 212, 237
3:16–17 ....70, 144, 145,
      163, 229, 251, 291,
         294, 329
4:3 237

Titus

1:2 373
1:9 237
1:13 237
1:15 204
2:1–2 237
3:3 188

Hebrews

1:10–12 329
4:12 .... 147, 150, 251, 277
5:11–14 169
5:14 204
6:18 373
8–10 174
8:13 174
10:5–10 160
11 373
11:13 373
11:16 266
11:19 158
13:17 401

James

1:6 371
1:8 38

3:1.......................................3
3:13–18 169
4:11–12 208
4:13–16...........266, 271, 372

1 Peter

2 ....404, 405
2:13–17............................401
2:14 401
2:29 402
3:15........305, 321, 328, 364
3:16 204

2 Peter
1:16–21............................208
1:19–21 ....212, 217, 254
2:1....................................245
2:19 188
3:13.................................. 316

1 John
1:1–3 197
2:27 387
3:4....................................38
3:20 277

Revelation
1:21–27 214
3:7 ....265, 271
4:11 286
7:9 241
10:6 386
14:7 286
20 171
21:1 291
21:3 266
21:7...................................261
22:18–19 70

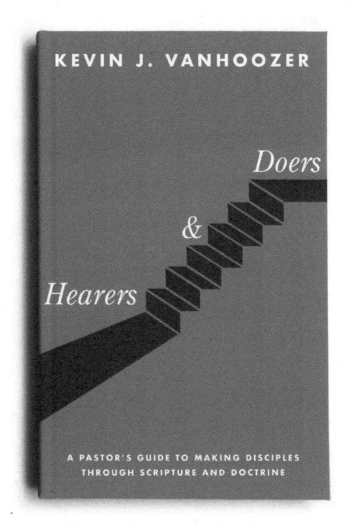